The Making of a Justice

Also by Justice John Paul Stevens

Five Chiefs: A Supreme Court Memoir

Six Amendments: How and Why
We Should Change the Constitution

THE MAKING
OF A
JUSTICE

Reflections on My First 94 Years

Justice John Paul Stevens

Little, Brown and Company

New York Boston London

Hachette Book Group supports the right to free expression and the value of copyright. The purpose of copyright is to encourage writers and artists to produce the creative works that enrich our culture.

The scanning, uploading, and distribution of this book without permission is a theft of the author's intellectual property. If you would like permission to use material from the book (other than for review purposes), please contact permissions@hbgusa.com. Thank you for your support of the author's rights.

Little, Brown and Company
Hachette Book Group
1290 Avenue of the Americas, New York, NY 10104
littlebrown.com

First Edition: May 2019

Little, Brown and Company is a division of Hachette Book Group, Inc. The Little, Brown name and logo are trademarks of Hachette Book Group, Inc.

The publisher is not responsible for websites (or their content) that are not owned by the publisher.

The Hachette Speakers Bureau provides a wide range of authors for speaking events. To find out more, go to hachettespeakersbureau.com or call (866) 376-6591.

ISBN 978-0-316-48964-5
LCCN 2018962439

10 9 8 7 6 5 4 3 2 1

LSC-C

Printed in the United States of America

Maryan Stevens — my beautiful wife and dietician

Contents

CONTENTS

CONTENTS

The Making of a Justice

My First Ninety-Four Years

I N A RECENT interview with a *New York Times* reporter, I mentioned Marcel Proust's *Remembrance of Things Past* as one of the books that I had always intended to read but had not. After reading that interview, my good friend Ken Manaster presented me with a copy of Proust's masterpiece at a surprise party that my wife, Maryan, orchestrated for my ninety-fourth birthday. Frankly, I found it less interesting than another book given to me on the same occasion. *Empire of the Summer Moon* is a fascinating story about Quanah Parker, the son of a Comanche chief and a white woman, and his experience as a leader of that tribe. Quanah was a fierce warrior, an astute politician, and ultimately a luncheon guest of Teddy Roosevelt. In contrast to the action-packed story about the Comanches, Proust's book reminded me of Jerry Seinfeld's attempt in *Seinfeld* to negotiate a contract to do a television series about "nothing" — *Remembrance of Things Past* is a beautifully written account about nothing. It does, however, have a title I would like to plagiarize. For I plan to write an account of some of my remembrances of a past that included both mundane and unusual experiences that my nine grandchildren and thirteen great-grandchildren may one day enjoy reading.

1

My Ancestors

I

T WAS NOT until after her death ten days before her ninety-eighth birthday that I learned that my mother had been almost three years older than my father. She was a beautiful woman who always wore her blond hair in a nineteenth-century bouffant style. She was also — like her mother — a devout Christian Scientist who regularly read Mary Baker Eddy's texts explaining the importance of "mind over matter." Because she did not believe that physical diseases really existed, she did not accept medical advice or remedies; instead, she relied on frequent uses of enemas as an all-purpose response to childhood ailments. Her religious faith explains why the broken nose that I suffered during a high school soccer game was never repaired.

My mother and father were both proud of their ancestors. She grew up in Michigan City, Indiana; her best friend was the daughter of the warden of the nearby Indiana State Prison. I believe my grandfather used prison inmates to provide labor for the glove factory that he managed. That belief is not based on any actual knowledge, because he was employed in an office job in San Francisco when I first came to know him many years later. My mother's family included Lewis Cass, the unsuccessful Democratic candidate for president in 1848; and George Street, the

English architect who designed the Royal Courts of Justice on the Strand in London and is buried in the nave of Westminster Abbey.

My father prepared a handwritten genealogy, which states that the name "Stevens" is of Scotch origin and was originally "Fitz-Stephens." The genealogy states that Henry, "the immediate progenitor of the family, was born in the county of Cornwall, in the southwest corner of England about 1520. He was knighted by King Henry VIII." He had three sons and a daughter who "married an Asquith." Why her marriage into the Asquith family was a sufficiently important event to be mentioned by my father has always been a mystery to me.

Henry's son John had six sons. His youngest, Nicholas, had an outstanding career as a brigadier general in Oliver Cromwell's army. In 1659, after the death of Cromwell and the defeat of his son Richard by royalist forces, Nicholas came to America. I presume that he was one of the Puritans who were motivated by their fear of religious persecution and their interest in following the dictates of their own consciences in matters of faith. Nicholas and his family settled in Stonington, Connecticut.

Four generations later, members of his family moved, first to Dutchess County, New York, and later to Barrett, Vermont, where one of the daughters, in a family of ten children, married Colonel Ethan Allen. After two more generations, Socrates Stevens, the youngest son in an eleven-member family, married Amanda and moved to Colchester, Illinois. Socrates and Amanda were my father's grandparents.

While I was unsuccessfully trying to find a record of Amanda's maiden name, I was surprised to receive a letter from Colchester signed "Dev" that contained persuasive evidence that the Stevens family was well regarded by leading members of the town's community in the 1880s. Dev is an executive of the local brick company that recently acquired a parcel of real estate on which an old church is located. Her letter enclosed a colored photograph of a stained glass window in the church that had been built in the 1880s. The inscription on the window bore the names of Socrates and Amanda Stevens, presumably reflecting a favorable local reputation of my father's grandparents. Their five sons were then successful merchants in Colchester, and soon thereafter they all moved to Chicago, where they all prospered.

My grandfather James William Stevens ("J.W.") became extremely wealthy while my father was still a child. I am told that J.W. made shrewd investments in real estate, that the Illinois Life Insurance Company, which he organized, was highly profitable, and that he financed successful business ventures in Chicago, including the Charles A. Stevens Department Store, operated by one of his brothers. In 1909, he acquired what was then Chicago's newest and finest hotel. Constructed at a cost of $3.5 million, the twenty-three-story La Salle Hotel was located on the northwest corner of La Salle and Madison Streets. Notable guests at the hotel included Presidents William Howard Taft and Calvin Coolidge, as well as "Buffalo Bill" Cody, who presented my father with an autographed picture (see photo insert).

My father received a bachelor's degree from the University of Chicago in 1904 and a law degree from Northwestern Law School in 1907, a few weeks after he married my mother. She had attended both Vassar College and the University of Chicago and was teaching English in Michigan City during their courtship. My father never practiced law but became the general manager of the La Salle Hotel when it opened and later also managed the Stevens Hotel in Chicago, which was constructed in 1926 and was at the time the largest hotel in the world.

During the early years of Father's management of the Stevens Hotel, he and other hotel men in the city thought it important to persuade industry groups to hold their conventions in Chicago. Chicago's reputation as a crime-ridden city was an obstacle they had to overcome. After they received a commitment from an important trade association, Father and the manager of another hotel decided to do what they could to minimize the risk of criminal activity during the convention. They paid a visit to Al Capone, explained how Chicago's hotel business might be affected if any conventioneers were robbed, and asked for his help. According to my father's account, Capone said he understood and in fact there was not a single holdup in Chicago during the week of the convention.

2

Grammar School

As was true before the birth of each of my three older brothers — Ernest Street ("Ernie") in 1909, Richard James ("Jim") in 1915, and William Kenneth ("Bill") in 1917 — when my mother was expecting me, she wanted to name the new member of the family "Elizabeth Jane." By the time of my arrival my parents had exhausted the list of family members to provide an acceptable name for another son and therefore, for reasons that neither of them ever explained to me, they named me "John Paul."

Shortly after my birth on April 20, 1920, in a residence on Blackstone Avenue south of Fifty-Eighth Street in Chicago, our family moved about three blocks to 1314 East Fifty-Eighth Street — a three-story brick house next to the alley between Kimbark and Kenwood Avenues. The University of Chicago High School and its elementary school were, and still are, located in separate buildings in the block across the street to the south. I graduated from those two schools in 1932 and 1937, and then attended college at the University of Chicago, which was also within easy walking distance from our home.

When I finished kindergarten, the school doctor gave all the students in the class a physical exam and then administered an oral test to determine whether the pupil belonged in the "A" or "B" section of the first grade. Although I was probably the smallest child in the class, I passed the physical exam with flying colors but flunked the mental test. I did not know the answer to the question of why stoves are not made of silver. My mother challenged the doctor's ruling, arguing that the question was unfair and provided no relevant evidence of a kindergarten student's mental ability. Her challenge was rejected, and I ended up in Class 1B. My father must have been disappointed in me, because I recall his frequent quotation of Julius Caesar's advice that he would rather be "first in a little Iberian village than second in Rome." In any event that advice may have provided the motivation that enabled me to make it into Class 2A the next year.

My teacher in Class 2A was Thelma Polkinghorn. In 1977 I received a wonderful letter from her describing my arrival at class the morning after the opening banquet at the Stevens Hotel in 1927. Guests at the banquet dined on sets of china that my father had designed for the occasion and received gifts of either bronze ashtrays or bronze bookends. The dinner plates contained five profiles of my mother and this verse composed by my father:

> *Her silhouette in profile*
> *Is pleasing to the eyes —*
> *But her own dear self in person*
> *Makes home my Paradise.*

The gifts were replicas of the two statues located in fountains in the entrance hall of the hotel. The ashtray featured my brother Jim riding a dolphin in his birthday suit, and the bookends featured my brother Bill and me (also au naturel) with a large fish. I think the figures were sculpted by Frederick Hibbard, a well-respected artist who I believe had also created the statue of my oldest brother, Ernie, in the Blue Fountain Room of the La Salle Hotel, where we enjoyed many family dinners.

Amelia Earhart, the famous aviator, was the principal speaker at the banquet. After her talk, my father introduced me to her. All that I can remember about meeting her was her suggestion that I was out pretty late on a school night. Despite her concern, I know that I was not only on time for school the next morning but, according to Miss Polkinghorn's letter, as usual, the first student to arrive. She said that she remembered the occasion because I presented her with a set of the bookends.

A few weeks later, when Charles Lindbergh was making a triumphal tour of the United States after miraculously completing his thirty-three-hour solo flight from New York to Paris in a single-engine plane, he was a guest at the Stevens Hotel during his visit to Chicago. I was allowed to accompany my father when he went to Lindbergh's suite to welcome him; the suite was cluttered with piles of gifts that had been sent to him by a host of admirers. I remember him as a tall, friendly man who made a point of being nice to a child and who explained that he did not know what to do with all his gifts. I joyously accepted when he asked me if I would like to have the caged dove on the table. My memory of that occasion remained vivid long after our loss of the bird that we named "Lindy."

My father played a central role in other memories of happy years in grammar school. He took my brothers and me to the opening game of the 1929 World Series between the Chicago Cubs and the Philadelphia Athletics. It was my first visit to Wrigley Field. I had listened to Hal Totten's broadcast of most of the Cubs' home games — and to Pat Flanagan's ticker-tape account of most of their away games — during the season and knew the batting average of every player in the Cubs' lineup. We were seated directly behind home plate, where I expected my heroes — Hack Wilson (who had hit fifty-four home runs during the regular season) in center field, Riggs Stephenson (a .300-plus hitter) in left, the base-stealing Kiki Cuyler in right, Charlie Grimm on first base, and Gabby Hartnett behind the plate — to demolish the Athletics. Contrary to expectation, instead of having either Lefty Grove or George Earnshaw — the A's two leading pitchers — start the opening game, the wily Connie Mack gave the assignment to a has-been with a sidearm delivery named Howard Ehmke. Ehmke fanned one Cub after another; his thirteen strikeouts set a series record. The contrast between my anticipation of an overwhelming

Cub victory after a slugfest and the actual outcome of a pitching duel could not have been more dramatic. Watching the A's beat the Cubs 3–1 was an unforgettable tragedy.

During my years in grammar school, our home provided the location for the afternoon recreation of many of my classmates. Because the traffic on Fifty-Eighth Street was then almost nonexistent, we located the goal in our kick-the-can games in the center of the street that also provided the arena for fiercely contested stick hockey games. During cold weather, groups of my friends were attracted to the house to enjoy sliding down the banister from the second to the first floor, playing hide-and-seek and blindman's buff throughout the house, and a fairly rough game we called "miniature football" (because we had to remain on our hands and knees on every down) in the large attic on the third floor. The location and size of our house probably explain why my brothers and I had so many friends.

We spent our summer vacations in Lakeside, Michigan, which was about a two-hour drive from Chicago. Our large stucco house was on a bluff overlooking Lake Michigan to the west. Our property occupied a rectangular area with about seventy-five yards of lake frontage and a gravel road about a quarter of a mile long that connected the bluff to the public road. We had our own concrete tennis court and a large garden, where my mother grew both vegetables and flowers. Different sets of my mother's relatives were regular guests. Perhaps the most frequent visitor was her sister Julie and Julie's daughter, Nancy, who lived in Berkeley, California. My brother Bill's affection for Nancy probably explains his decision to attend the University of California, while the rest of us attended the University of Chicago. My mother's parents spent several summers with us. Her father taught me to swim and to play two-handed card games, both lifelong hobbies of mine.

My father routinely spent the first several days of the week in Chicago working at the hotel, but he came to Lakeside for the weekends, sometimes arriving as early as Thursday afternoon. When we received word of his probable arrival time, Jim, Bill, and I would usually walk down the gravel road to the front gate of our property to welcome him. His presence always made life more enjoyable. He often brought canisters containing several reels of films that he invited our neighbors to watch in our living room on Saturday evenings. On the Fourth of July, he supervised a fireworks display on the beach that attracted a fairly large audience. I have especially fond memories of sitting with him in the screened portion of the "pump house" on our beach watching lightning streak across the sky during thunderstorms. One weekend he arrived in a single-engine floatplane that landed in the water in front of our beach. The pilot flew back to Chicago while Father waded ashore in business clothes.

Father enjoyed both tennis and golf. Sometimes when he was playing doubles with friends, he would pay me a penny for each ball that I retrieved. He taught me how to play both of those games. On the golf course he explained the importance of strict adherence to the rules. Any cheating was sure to be noticed by other golfers, who would likely infer that anyone who cheated at golf might violate other rules as well. I have thought of him over and over again when young lawyers have asked me for advice about practicing law, and I have responded by telling them that a lawyer's most valuable asset is his or her reputation for integrity. Bending the rules may provide a benefit to a client, but that benefit is always outweighed by the inevitable injury to the lawyer's good name.

Almost every weekend, Father would take the entire family to see a movie either in Sawyer, Bridgman, Saint Joe, or Benton Harbor, Michigan, or sometimes in Michigan City, Indiana. He had an infectious sense of humor. I think W. C. Fields was his favorite, but I can also remember him laughing uncontrollably in movies starring Charlie Chaplin, Buster Keaton, Harold Lloyd, Stan Laurel, and Oliver Hardy. Mae West was his favorite movie actress, while he was also a fan of Will Rogers, Eddie Cantor, and Fanny Brice on the stage. I was able to see those stars perform in New York, thanks to my mother's summer travels.

In late August each year she took some of her children with her on a trip to Boston to attend events sponsored by the "mother church" of Mary Baker Eddy. With our chauffeur, Orson Washburne, at the wheel, we drove from Lakeside to Detroit, where we put our car on a ship (either the "City of Detroit" or the "City of Buffalo") and made an overnight voyage on Lake Erie. After docking in Buffalo, we visited Niagara Falls and drove to Watkins Glen and ultimately on to Boston. On one or more of those trips, Father surprised us by arriving in Boston a day or two later, having shipped his car on the train that brought him to the East Coast. From Boston he drove the family to New York City to see the sights and attend a play or two on Broadway. What happened to Orson and the other car, I simply do not remember. I do, however, remember seeing Eddie Cantor in the play *Whoopee* as well as performances by Fanny Brice and Will Rogers. I also remember a family dinner at what I believe was a new hotel that was featuring a show that included an act by an artist who painted a cartoon of a face on the front of a nude female model. The large eyes in the cartoon were particularly memorable. I don't believe there were any grammar school students at any other table.

We engaged in other travel that I only dimly remember. Several spring vacations were spent in Biloxi, Mississippi, where I fished for crabs using a piece of meat on a long string as bait. On one trip to Washington, D.C., I saw Vice President Charles Curtis preside during a session of the Senate. On our drive back to Chicago, we had an accident in which Mother broke her arm. She refused to accept medical care, but I have no memory of her healing process. On another trip we visited Havana, Cuba; rather than Morro Castle, my principal memory of that trip was the distressing number of beggars in public areas.

Sundays were always enjoyable days at home. They would frequently begin when Father was shaving and dramatically reciting his version of "Casey at the Bat" — instead of referring to the score as "four to two" as the author of the poem did, he made it "two to four," and instead of referring to Flynn and Casey as "hoodoo" and "cake," he said "the former was a no-good and the latter was a fake." Or he might favor us with a rendition of Rudyard Kipling's "If," which famously begins, "If you can keep your head when all about you are losing theirs," and ends with "You'll be a Man, my son!" Mother, for her part, used couplets as teaching tools.

Instructions about the proper way to drink soup at the dinner table included: "Like a ship put out to sea, I push my spoon away from me." And she conveyed a more important message when she recited (as she often did), "Lips that touch wine will never touch mine." My brother Jim would often favor us with Lewis Carroll's wonderful lines:

> 'Twas brillig, and the slithy toves
> Did gyre and gimble in the wabe:
> All mimsy were the borogroves,
> And the mome raths outgrabe.

The first poem that I recall committing to memory was Longfellow's "Village Blacksmith."

Jim, Bill, and I would don our Sunday best and walk three blocks together to the Christian Science Church, where each of us attended a Sunday school class of about a half dozen students. Thereafter, our oldest brother, Ernie, and his bride, Dorothy (and sometimes other guests as well), would join us for the Sunday dinner. They were happy occasions.

3

FDR and Babe Ruth

FATHER WAS A loyal Republican. He had a framed letter signed by Warren G. Harding hanging on the wall of his bedroom; the letter thanked him for voluntary service to the federal government. During the Depression, he frequently announced to the family, "Business is looking up!" He would then explain, "It is flat on its back." Despite his politics, he took Bill and me with him to hear President Roosevelt's acceptance speech on the last day of the Democratic Party's convention in 1932 at the Chicago Stadium. The speech is memorable for many reasons, including the fact that, in his closing sentence, FDR first used the term "new deal" to describe his campaign promises. Although I have no recollection of the text of the speech, I do recall that he was accompanied by his son, who assisted his moving to the podium in a way that prevented the audience from noticing that he had a serious physical disability.

Later that same year, FDR returned to Chicago, where he threw out the first pitch of the third game in the World Series between the Cubs and the Yankees. Father took me to that game and we sat about twenty rows behind the third-base dugout. I have no recollection of FDR's presence in the crowd, but I do recall verbal exchanges between Guy Bush and Babe Ruth during the early innings of the game. Bush was one of the Cubs' starting pitchers, but he was not on the mound that day.

Presumably he and the Babe were debating the fairness of the Cub players' decision to award only a half share of their World Series bonus to Mark Koenig, a former Yankee who had been traded to the Cubs late in the season. When Ruth came to bat in the fifth inning, apparently responding to a shouted comment by Bush, he pointed his bat at the center-field scoreboard. On the next pitch he hit his "called shot" over the center-field scoreboard.

A few years ago, during a question-and-answer session at a judicial conference in Columbus, Ohio, I described my recollection of that event. After that session, a young bankruptcy judge introduced himself and advised me that his grandfather had also attended that game and had been seated in the left-field bleachers, where he had been successful in recovering the ball that Ruth had hit on that occasion. He did not want to embarrass me in front of the audience by pointing out that my memory of the direction of Ruth's called shot was inaccurate. Because my attendance at that game has long been my most important claim to fame, and because the judge's account would be difficult to dispute, when I returned to Washington after the conference, I asked my law clerk Merritt McAlister to do the necessary research to determine the direction of Ruth's hit.

This was unquestionably the easiest research assignment any of my clerks ever received; for the answer to the question is revealed by a copy of the box score that hangs on a wall in my office. The box score was given to me in 1947 by my friend Jim Marsh, an avid baseball fan who was then serving as the law clerk for Justice Robert Jackson and who later had a distinguished career as a Philadelphia lawyer. It shows that Ruth hit two home runs in that game. The ball that the bankruptcy judge's grandfather retrieved from the left field bleachers must have been hit in the second inning; the "called shot" was hit in the fifth. Since the card also identifies Charlie Root as the Cubs' starting pitcher, it is consistent with my recollection that Guy Bush was the Cub engaged in the unfriendly colloquy with Ruth.

4

The Armed Robbery

WHEN THE STEVENS Hotel opened in 1927, the economy was booming, but the stock market crash in 1929 had a disastrous impact on the hotel business in Chicago as well as the rest of the economy. In the ensuing months, in order to pay the interest on its debts, the hotel borrowed over a million dollars from the Illinois Life Insurance Company, which was controlled by my grandfather James W. Stevens ("J.W."), my father's older brother, Raymond W. Stevens ("R.W."), and my father, Ernest J. Stevens ("E.J."). As matters developed, the economy did not recover, and neither the Insurance Company's loan, nor an additional $522,000 that J.W. advanced from his own funds, saved the hotel from insolvency. Although the loan did not violate any law regulating the insurance business, the state's attorney for Cook County viewed the decision to make the loan as a criminal act and at the end of January 1933 obtained an indictment charging J.W., R.W., and my father with embezzlement of over $1 million. J.W. then suffered a stroke and R.W. committed suicide, leaving my father as the only defendant to stand trial. Sensational coverage of the charges in Chicago newspapers apparently convinced several men who later robbed us that Father had concealed $1 million in cash in tomato cans in the basement of our home.

A few days after the indictment, Orson Washburne, our chauffeur, was kidnapped when he was walking back to his home after locking Mother's car in our garage. At gunpoint he was ordered into the backseat of a sedan and forced to crouch on the floor so that he would not be visible to any potential witnesses. For over an hour his abductors drove around, interrogating him about the precise location of the horde of cash that was supposedly hidden in our home. Orson knew nothing about any cash, but apparently described the location of our two telephones, one in the library on the first floor and the other in my father's second-floor bedroom. Following Orson's description of his terrifying ordeal in the back of the sedan, Father hired an armed private detective to spend every night in our home, beginning around 8 p.m.

After an early dinner on February 11, 1933 — two days before Father's forty-ninth birthday — Mother, Bill, and I were sitting in the library listening to Father as he read aloud from one of Dickens's novels; our older brother Jim was studying in the University of Chicago law library; our cook, Hanna, and the maid, Sarah, were in the kitchen doing the dishes. I think it was Sarah who responded when the doorbell rang. Four armed men then burst into the front hall; one announced that they had a warrant to search the house; a second dashed into the library and cut the telephone line; a third ran upstairs to cut the second phone line; and the fourth ran into the kitchen to prevent anyone from leaving through the back door. The largest of the four was wearing a Chicago police officer's uniform; the other three wore suits and ties and might well have been plainclothes officers. The one who looked a little like Groucho Marx was carrying a submachine gun.

With the premises secured, the robbers ordered all of us to go upstairs into the front bedroom, where the uniformed "officer" stood guard while his three companions spent at least thirty minutes searching the basement and the rest of the house. During that period, we were interrupted on three occasions. Father was first ordered into the basement to help them find the tomato cans full of cash — a completely unproductive search. Second, I was required to go into my bedroom to unlock the safe because I was the only person who knew its combination. When I did so, the gunman stood over me and told me to hand over the twenty-dollar bills that he saw and asked me what the red book in the back of the safe was. I pulled it out, explained that it was just my diary, and was allowed to replace it without opening it. He never learned that it contained three 1897 ten-dollar gold pieces that my grandfather had given to me as Christmas presents; those coins are now pendants on necklaces that my daughters still wear. The third interruption occurred when my brother Jim arrived home from the library; the man guarding the door asked him who he was, and Jim replied with the same question. A shouting match ensued, with Father adding his voice to the confusion. Ultimately Jim was persuaded to join us in the second-floor bedroom. He was convinced at the time — and remained convinced when I asked him his opinion shortly before he died — that the robbers were in fact members of the Chicago Police Department.

Shortly thereafter everyone in the house was directed to go downstairs into the front hall and line up in the entrance to the large parlor. The man who seemed to be in charge then brandished the machine gun and threatened to "mow everybody down" unless one of us revealed the location of the cash. My father pleaded with him, repeatedly stating that there were no tomato cans or bundles of cash anywhere in the house and urging him to kill him rather than anyone else. During that frightening confrontation, the doorbell rang.

When one of the robbers answered the door, our neighbor Mr. Gorrell, who had come to pay my father a visit and to express confidence in his innocence of the criminal charges, entered with a look of astonishment on his face. Father immediately identified the intruders as police officers who had come to search the premises and stated that they were just leaving. They then did decide to leave, but not before reminding us that a report to the police would be followed by reprisals against Bill and me. Shortly after they left, the recently hired private detective arrived.

What happened next earned my brother Jim a family nickname as "the marksman." He dashed upstairs, found Father's .32-gauge rifle in his closet, pointed it at the floor, and pulled the trigger "to see if it was loaded," as he later explained. In the meantime, Mr. Gorrell had gone into the parlor and was standing about two feet away from a large oil painting on the wall. Jim's shot rang out, and the bullet went through the living room ceiling and severed the wire hanging the painting, which then crashed to the floor. Despite threatening comments and behavior by the armed intruders, Mr. Gorrell came the closest to being a victim of a real tragedy when Jim's shot so narrowly missed him. Jim earned his nickname because his bullet did no damage to the painting or the wall.

Concerned about the threat of reprisals, Mother took Bill and me to Fairhope, Alabama, for the next couple of weeks. Although she enrolled us in the local grammar school, we attended it for only a day or two because both of us had already been taught the subject matter that the classes were studying. So our stay in Alabama turned into a short vacation. I do not recall any special fear for our safety during the ensuing months in that year.

5

The World's Fair

CHICAGO HAS BEEN the host city of two remarkably successful world's fairs. Congress authorized and named the first as the "Columbian Exhibition" to celebrate the four-hundredth anniversary of Columbus's discovery of America, but since it was a year behind schedule in opening, it is better known as the "1893 World's Fair." It attracted over 20 million visitors and had an important impact on Chicago, and specifically on the area where I grew up. I frequently visited the coal mine and other exhibits in the Museum of Science and Industry, which is still open to the public, and my friends and I regularly played baseball and football in Jackson Park or on the Midway. Although then and now the Midway is a mile-long open grassy area, during the fair it was the amusement area where attractions such as "Little Egypt" performed. The second fair was named the "Century of Progress" because it opened in 1933, one hundred years after Chicago was incorporated as a city. Its kinship to the first Chicago fair was dramatized by having the lights turned on by a charge of electricity that supposedly originated on the star Arcturus forty years earlier. The 1933 fair was such a success that it opened for a second season in 1934.

In 1933 and 1934 the American economy was still in the depth of the Great Depression, and my father's connection with the Stevens Hotel was a thing of the past. Nevertheless, he obtained the restaurant concession in the English Village at the fair, and I assume that he helped my oldest brother, Ernie, to obtain the restaurant concession in the Spanish Village. Both concessions were a success. Ernie had the bright idea of specializing in the sale of spaghetti dinners that cost only fifty cents and allowed the customers as many helpings as they wanted. The connection between his "All you can eat for 50 cents" signs and Spain may have been pretty tenuous, but it made him a fortune. I think his proximity to Sally Rand's fan dancing may have helped his business.

Among the attractions that made the English Village popular was the replica of London's Globe Theatre, where two Shakespeare plays were performed every day. The establishments that my father operated included the "Red Lion Inn," a first-rate restaurant where, in homage to Queen Elizabeth I, he hired only red-haired waitresses, and the "Dog and Duck," a pub where my brother Jim was the bartender. I held my first job as a strolling salesman of Banbury tarts — triangular raisin sandwiches that were supposedly typical of Merrie Olde England. I don't remember any favorable comments on that delicacy, but I do remember that a tray full of them was a heavy load. The principal benefit of the job was my entitlement to a free pass to the fairgrounds and to Globe Theatre performances.

Two incidents that occurred during the fair contribute to my positive appraisal of that chapter of my life. From time to time, thoughts about the threats made by the leader of the four robbers in our home made me reluctant to go out alone. For that reason, I remember the evening when I made the decision to go to a movie by myself at the Chicago Theater on State Street. The incident-free solo train rides between the Fairgrounds and the Loop and watching the movie without any companions put an end to my lingering fears.

And it was during the fair that my father received word that the Illinois Supreme Court had unanimously reversed his conviction and written an opinion stating that the record of his trial did not contain even a "scintilla" of evidence of criminal intent. By that time an Iowa company had acquired the assets of the Illinois Life Insurance Company and assumed responsibility for its liabilities to policyholders. The assumption that the directors' attempted rescue of the Stevens Hotel had produced a disaster for the customers of the insurance company — presumably the prosecution's motivations — turned out to be baseless. The only people harmed by the unwise loan were members of the Stevens family.

In recent years, my firsthand knowledge of the criminal justice system's fallibility has reinforced my conviction that the death penalty should be abolished.

6

Delavan, Wisconsin

M Y FATHER'S AND my brother Ernie's post-fair business activities diverged dramatically. Ernie took his earnings and moved to Fort Myers, Florida, where he lived for the rest of his active business career. He became an investment counselor who touted that he "had assets over" a large sum of money because his office was on the second floor of a bank building. He provided financial advice to the City of Naples when it was incorporated and wisely purchased a large tract of vacant land for a price measured in pennies per acre that he later sold for dollars per acre.

My father assumed that his outstanding success operating the Red Lion Inn during the fair could be replicated in the Chicago Loop. I remember attending the family dinner celebrating the opening of his new restaurant, with the same name, the same menu, and the same red-haired waitresses as the one at the fair. It was an unforgettable occasion because the room was empty (except for the staff) when we arrived and still empty when we finished our dinner. Thereafter, he abandoned the restaurant business and accepted a job as the manager of a hotel on Chicago's South Side.

A few years later, he and an old friend named Harley Darlington jointly leased a resort known as the Highlands, in Wisconsin on the shore of Lake Delavan. The resort included a nine-hole golf course, two tennis courts, a pier extending into the lake, and several cottages, as well as a two-story hotel building. Harley was the resident manager and my dad was basically a silent partner who visited the premises on an occasional basis. I don't know whether or not his investment produced a profit, but it did provide me with a job during two summers. My second year, working as a bellhop for fifteen dollars a month plus tips, was more rewarding but less interesting than the first.

The first year, my close friend Robert W. ("Doc") Jampolis (who later became a surgeon at the Mayo Clinic in Minnesota and developed the Palo Alto Clinic in California) and I worked in the laundry and on the golf course on alternate days. On the days when I ran the mangle and hung sheets, towels, and napkins out to dry, Doc mowed the greens with a hand mower and the fairways with a larger mower pulled by a tractor that should have been an exhibit in an antique show. We started work at seven in the morning and usually finished around three-thirty or four in the afternoon. On the days when Doc worked in the laundry, I took over on the golf course, and vice versa. In addition to receiving free room and board and having access to the lake, the golf course, and the tennis courts after work (subject to the prior rights of hotel guests), I think we were paid thirty dollars a month.

Early one morning, when Doc was at the wheel, the tractor came to a halt about thirty yards directly in front of the first tee. It remained there for well over a week while Oliver, the hotel mechanic, tried one remedy after another to get it back in motion. The tractor and its attached mower became a stationary hazard that many golfers could not avoid. Even those who succeeded in hitting their drives over or around it found themselves pacing back and forth in the tall grass in what seemed an endless search for their balls. Our shared memory of stooped golfers wandering about in circles in the unmowed fairway on the first hole produced many a hearty laugh for years.

Oliver's skills as a mechanic were about equal to his talent as the coach of the Texaco Oilers, a baseball team sponsored by a gas station that played occasional night games in the town of Delavan. One evening he allowed me to substitute for the second baseman, and I succeeded in sliding safely into second base. Oliver concluded that my slide was adequate evidence of my qualification to play second base for the rest of the season. I turned out to be a pretty lousy infielder, but I did earn the right to wear a Texaco Oilers jersey.

That summer I had comparable athletic success on the tennis court. Somehow I befriended the drummer in the band at the nearby Delavan Gardens dance hall and played tennis with him from time to time. We were evenly matched and convinced each other that we were qualified to do well as a doubles team in the Wisconsin state tournament. Negotiations with our respective employers enabled us to take enough time off to drive over to Milwaukee for the event. We were eliminated in the first round.

My spotty athletic achievements in Delavan were on par with my high school sporting career. At U-High we did not have a football team because the son of the athletic director had received a fatal injury during a football game a few years before I enrolled. We played soccer instead. Being the only guy who could kick with his left foot, I played left wing in the line. Our home games were played on a field across the Midway from the school. Although we thoroughly enjoyed the competition, I am not sure that we ever won. Watching soccer as a spectator today vividly reminds me of how much running the game requires.

Our accomplishments in basketball were similar. There were two sets of teams in the South Suburban League — "lightweights," who had to be less than 135 pounds, and "heavyweights." I played forward and was the captain of the lightweight team; we had many close games, but I'm not sure we won any. (I have often been tempted to brag that I played high school basketball in the same league with Lou Boudreau, the accomplished professional baseball player and manager, without mentioning that I was just a lightweight while he was a heavyweight.)

I also played on our high school tennis team and remember an interview in the school paper in which our coach made the comment that I had "the worst serve in captivity." Even so, we did win our share of tennis events, and I played well enough to make the "B" team at the University of Chicago, where I won, not the maroon "C" jacket that was awarded to first-string athletes like my friend Doc Jampolis, who was the quarterback on Chicago's last football team, but a gray wool sweater with a large maroon Old English "C" on it. I was proud of that sweater.

After my brief stint as a second baseman on the Texaco Oilers, my next participation in competitive baseball did not occur again until 1979. That year the Supreme Court police force fielded one of the teams in a league that required at least two female members on each team. When she was in high school, my daughter Sue was a better athlete than most of her male classmates and also better than the female officers eligible for the Supreme Court team. I agreed to make Sue available for one of the two female positions on our police force team if they would let me play second base for a few innings in each game. She made a much more positive contribution to the team than I did, but I don't remember fumbling any ground balls.

7

The University of Chicago

WHEN I ATTENDED the University of Chicago the term "BMOC" referred to a big man on campus. Most, but not all, BMOCs were members of fraternities. For example, my classmate Chuck Percy, who later became the CEO of the Bell & Howell Company and an outstanding United States senator, was a member of Alpha Delta Phi. Chuck would later have a profound impact on my career. His status as a BMOC was supported by at least four facts: (1) he was extremely popular; (2) he was captain of an excellent water polo team; (3) he was president of Owl and Serpent, the senior men's honor society; and (4) perhaps of most importance, he was selected to be the escort for Paulette Goddard when she visited the campus to promote her new movie. There were those who thought his selection unfortunate because he was known to be a Christian Scientist whose faith would require him to decline any opportunity to engage in intimate conduct that might arise out of their meeting. They in fact did form a platonic friendship that lasted for many years.

During my freshman year, Bill McNeill, one of my brother's high school classmates, was the editor of the *Chicago Daily Maroon*. Bill, who lived to be ninety-eight, would go on to have a distinguished career as a historian, writer, and professor at the University of Chicago, where he chaired the history department. But for reasons that I do not remember, the *Daily Maroon*'s editorial policy under Bill's leadership was not popular with most of the BMOCs; hence they decided to subject Bill to a traditional form of campus punishment by throwing him into the "Botany Pond" — an unfair punishment in my view.

Although I had not previously had any experience or interest in journalism, I decided to join the staff of the paper with the thought that I might be able to help it improve. Three years later I became the chairman of its board of control. Ernest Leiser, who later became an executive with CBS, wrote most of our editorials, but I also did a fair amount of writing.

My most memorable contribution was a review of Laurence Olivier's performance of the leading role in one of Shakespeare's plays. I had not enjoyed the play and thought that he had overacted his part. That, in substance, is what I recall saying in my review. As I now think about the fact that as a college student I had the temerity to express that opinion of the quality of a great actor's performance, I am a little embarrassed. The reason I remember that review is that it provoked a favorable comment by Norman McLean, the teacher who had inspired my decision to major in English. He said something like, "Before reading your review, I didn't think you could write." He taught me that I should have confidence in my own judgment. He also taught me that it is far more important to be honest than to be right. Or, to quote Polonius's advice to his son, Laertes:

> *This above all: to thine own self be true,*
> *And it must follow, as the night the day,*
> *Thou canst not then be false to any man.*

In writing, as well as in judging, intellectual honesty is indispensable.

During my years in college, Robert Hutchins, who had become president of the university at age twenty-nine, and Mortimer Adler, who cotaught the "Great Books" class, were regarded as the leading intellectual giants not only on campus but throughout academia. Yet they opposed each other on the merits of the most important issue facing the country — whether to provide material support to Britain during the war with Adolf Hitler that was then raging. Adler argued that when your house is on fire, you must take prompt action to put the fire out. Hutchins responded that it was not our house but the house next door that was on fire; he was an isolationist. Their debates taught me an unforgettable lesson. Even the most intelligent and well-informed and well-intentioned people can disagree about the merits of a serious public issue.

Disagreement about such issues — no matter how firm — need not be accompanied by disrespect. In later years, the fact that I repeatedly disagreed with Bill Rehnquist or Nino Scalia did not lead to a lack of respect for them or their views or preclude the continuation of our personal friendships.

During the Christmas break in 1939, when I was a junior in college, my parents, one of my brothers, and I drove from Chicago to Florida to visit my oldest brother, Ernie. On our way we stopped for the night in Atlanta, where *Gone with the Wind,* which had just been released that week, was playing. I have a vivid memory of the audience's reaction to the portrayal of what for them was a tragic episode in their defeat in the War of Northern Aggression. The reaction of the theater audience convinced me that their appraisal of the actual events portrayed in the movie might be distorted by the depth of their emotions.

Margaret Mitchell's understandable bias in favor of the defeated participants in the Civil War undoubtedly also colored her understanding of events that provided the background for her story. Given the extraordinary popularity of her book, it in turn influenced the thinking of millions of readers less familiar with the history of the period than she. For example, she had no kind words for Rufus Bullock, the Republican governor of Georgia during the first four years of Reconstruction, whom she describes as incompetent and corrupt. In fact, he was acquitted by two separate juries of all of the charges that Margaret Mitchell described in her book and later became one of Atlanta's leading citizens. Moreover, John B. Gordon, Bullock's unsuccessful Democratic opposing candidate in 1868 — who is described by Margaret Mitchell as "one of Georgia's best loved and most honored citizens" — has been identified as the leader of the Ku Klux Klan in Georgia during the years after the Civil War.

My reflections about the tense atmosphere in the theater where *Gone with the Wind* was playing in 1939 have convinced me that there were serious omissions in both my high school and college educations. In neither school did I have a course in American history. Moreover, although I majored in English literature in college, I did not take any courses in English history. A reader's appreciation of the quality of much great writing is necessarily incomplete if not accompanied by an understanding of the issues being debated in those writings.

8

Joining the Navy

SHORTLY BEFORE I graduated from college in June 1941, Dean Leon Smith asked me to come to his office to talk about my future. He mentioned my academic record — I had been elected to Phi Beta Kappa and chosen as the student head marshal of my class — and suggested that I might be qualified for cryptographic work in the navy. If I was interested, he said that he would arrange to have me enrolled in a secret correspondence course conducted by the navy. I was indeed interested and accepted his proposal. In due course I signed an oath of secrecy and received my first lesson in the mail. Apart from my meeting with Dean Smith, I had no direct contact with any navy personnel, but I did receive written descriptions of different types of codes and ciphers and a series of increasingly difficult assignments. Early in December I received a letter advising me that I had successfully completed the course, that I was eligible for a commission as an ensign, and that I should report to the Great Lakes Naval Station for a physical exam on the following Saturday. (For years I never publicly mentioned either the correspondence course or the nature of my work in the navy, but Congress eventually passed a statute terminating my duty of silence.) I passed the physical even though I almost fainted as I watched the corpsman take a blood sample from my arm. I have since had blood drawn on literally hundreds of occasions and always looked away to avoid the risk of fainting.

The following day I attended the football game between the Chicago Bears and the Chicago Cardinals in Comiskey Park. During intermission between halves, a rumor that we were at war with Japan spread through the crowd. As Mr. Know-It-All, I remember advising my companions that the rumor must be false because Congress was not in session on Sunday and therefore could not have declared war. It was not until our exit from the park that we saw the headlines describing the Japanese attack on Pearl Harbor.

The following morning President Roosevelt delivered the famous speech describing December 7, 1941, as a "date that will live in infamy" and asking Congress for a declaration of war against the empire of Japan. That speech, together with the nature of the surprise attack itself, had the effect of producing a public reaction that was more unifying than anything the United States has experienced before or since. I still vividly remember the atmosphere that permeated the country during the war. I have no memory of anyone publicly questioning the merits of our position throughout the war.

Almost three months elapsed before I was ordered to report for duty at the Navy Department in the Munitions Building on Constitution Avenue in Washington, D.C. Stuart Schulberg, the younger brother of Budd Schulberg, author of the 1941 novel *What Makes Sammy Run,* who had become a friend when we both served on the staff of the *Daily Maroon,* had a job as a reporter for a Washington paper and had agreed to let me share his room in a boardinghouse on Massachusetts Avenue less than a block from DuPont Circle in exchange for my agreement to pay half the rent. My share came to fifteen dollars a month. I paid that exorbitant rent until the first week in June, when I married my first wife, Betty Sheeren, and we moved into an apartment at 4121 W Street in Northwest D.C. While I had walked to work before my marriage, thereafter I rode the bus until early in December, when I was transferred to Pearl Harbor.

My first two chores as an officer in the navy assigned to "Op-20-G" —
the communications intelligence section of the service — required skills
unrelated to my training. Encrypted messages that were exchanged
between one communications intelligence unit and another — between
station "Hypo" at Pearl Harbor and station "Negat" in Washington, for
example — were classified "ultra" rather than merely "secret," "confiden-
tial," or "restricted." The originator of such a message typed the plain text
into a cypher machine that created five-letter blocks of scrambled letters.
The addressee, using a comparable machine, typed out the scrambled text
to convert it back into plain language. When I arrived in Washington,
the navy allowed only commissioned officers to decrypt "ultra" messages.
Though I had become a pretty good typist while working at the *Maroon,*
neither I nor any of the other commissioned officers doing that work
could type as well as most of the enlisted men. The navy eventually permitted qualified typists to decrypt "ultra" messages.

To protect the secrecy of the work performed in Op-20-G, waste
paper was deposited in "burn bags" that were later incinerated in Washington. An armed commissioned officer was required to supervise the
transportation and incineration of all burn bags. After a brief practice
session with a revolver, I performed that assignment. During my practice
I learned that a .45-caliber handgun has such a strong kick that only an
expert is likely to hit anything near his target. Thankfully, I never had to
use the weapon. I eventually progressed beyond typing and burn bag
assignments and was transferred from the communications section of
Op-20-G ("GC") and began work in the traffic analysis section ("GT").

Before and during the early stages of the war, Japanese radio traffic
was intercepted by our operators at Cavite in the Philippines, at Wahiawa
on Oahu, and on Bainbridge Island in the state of Washington. The radio
men on duty at those stations were either members of the "On the Roof
Gang" or had been trained by them. The members of the original gang
earned that title by spending months on the roof of the navy building on
Constitution Avenue in Washington, D.C., where they listened to the
radio traffic sent or received by the Japanese embassy. The Japanese

equivalent of our alphabet contained fifty-one kana, each of which had its own symbol of dots and dashes. Although I never learned the Japanese language, I soon became familiar with its kana and the likelihood that an operator might incorrectly confuse, for example, the four-dot symbol for the kana "NU" for the three-dot symbol for "RA," just as a sloppy transmission of the letter "H" in the Morse code might be read as an "S."

The job of a traffic analyst is to obtain intelligence from an examination of the external characteristics of enemy communications. Very few of those communications were in plain language. Diplomatic messages were sent in a "purple" code that we learned to read by studying the messages copied by the radio operators in the On the Roof gang. Most Japanese naval messages were sent in the "JN-25" code; the originator of such a message would first use a code book to find the five-digit number assigned to each word in the message and then use a book of "additives" to locate the sequence of five-digit numbers to be added to the code words to produce the sequence of five-digit numbers that formed the text that was broadcast on the radio. An American cryptographer deciphering a JN-25 message had to know the meaning of coded words, the sequence of additives, and the place in the additive book where a specific message began. In combat situations, the Japanese often used a simple three-kana code known as "JN-4." Usually the choice of JN-4 rather than JN-25 indicated that there was something urgent about the message.

Obtaining intelligence from intercepted enemy communications required the coordination of several skills. Subsection "GM" — the "machine" section — printed and sorted the hundreds (and sometimes thousands) of messages intercepted every day and performed research tasks assigned by the officers in subsection "GY" who were skilled in cryptanalysis — the art of converting enciphered messages into plain language. The "language officers" in subsection "GZ" translated Japanese text into English. The "DF" subsection analyzed the bearings received by "direction finder" equipment located at the various stations intercepting enemy radio traffic. When stations at different locations intercepted the same message, the intersection of lines drawn from the receiving stations to the transmitter would identify its location.

Ordinary letters sent in the mail are marked by the name and address of both the sender and the intended recipient. During the war, the Japanese used "call signs" to identify the senders and the recipients of radio transmissions. Recovering the meaning of the Japanese call signs was an essential part of the work of our traffic analysts. Stations transmitting high volumes of traffic from fixed locations, such as Tokyo or the naval base at Truk in the Caroline Islands, could be easily identified by direction finders. Similarly, brief messages of a standard length sent out at regular intervals could often be recognized as weather reports. Other "idents" were often obtained from the text of translated messages, or by association with other previously identified call signs.

In late May 1942, the cryptographers, language officers, and traffic analysts in the Fleet Radio Unit at Pearl Harbor (FRUPAC) had learned enough about Japanese naval communications to predict that a major assault on one of our Pacific outposts designated as "AZ" was about to occur. They suspected, but were not certain, that AZ was Midway Island. Knowing that the Japanese were monitoring our naval communications, they arranged for an exchange of plain-language messages commenting on a supposed accident that had produced a serious water shortage on Midway Island; those messages produced a comment in the enemy's communications that confirmed our suspicions. As a result of that ruse, combined with the earlier intelligence obtained from decrypted JN-25 messages, Admiral Chester Nimitz's forces were prepared for the Japanese attack on June 6 and ultimately prevailed in what many experts have concluded was the decisive battle in our war with Japan.

As a traffic analysis trainee in Washington, I had no role in that historic triumph. I do, however, recall the strong reaction of several senior officers in Op-20-G. That reaction, rather than a celebration of a great victory, was one of fury against the *Chicago Tribune.* On the front page of its Sunday edition, it had published three stories about our victory at Midway, one of which was captioned, "Navy Had Word of Jap Plan to

Strike at Sea." In that story, the *Tribune* stated that the strength of the enemy force was well known to American naval sources several days before the battle began, described those forces in the same detail that they had been described in intercepted Japanese messages, and noted that the Americans had known in advance that the Japanese would make a feigned attack on Kiska the day before its actual attack on Midway. An adequately informed enemy agent would unquestionably have learned from that story that we had broken the JN-25 code.

The Japanese had changed that code on June 1, before the story was published, but some of the top brass in the navy and some high officials in the Executive Branch of the government received the impression that the change was a response to the *Tribune* story. A grand jury was convened to consider indicting the *Tribune* and the reporter who had written the story. After several weeks of investigation, no indictment was returned, presumably because public disclosure of the whole story would have done more harm than good. With the advantage of hindsight and postwar conversations with knowledgeable Japanese naval officers, we now know not only that the change in the JN-25 code was entirely unrelated to the *Tribune* story but also that the Japanese never read or were even informed about the story. Apparently the author, Stanley Johnson, had seen a copy of a secret message sent by Admiral Nimitz to various naval units at sea that included a detailed description of the Japanese force that was headed for Midway. Details in Johnson's description of the enemy force quite obviously had been copied from the admiral's dispatch. Moreover, it was those details in the admiral's dispatch that enabled a reader to conclude that we had broken the Japanese code.

The incident demonstrates the importance of providing adequate protection against the risk of disclosure of important secrets. During the war, Lewis Powell, later a good friend when we were colleagues on the Supreme Court, was responsible for providing our pilots and other fighting men with intelligence that had been obtained from decrypted German messages. Because of the ever-present risk that those men might become prisoners of war, Lewis never revealed the true source of such intelligence; instead, he provided them with various fictions that could be repeated to an enemy interrogator. There may have been no parallel procedure that would have enabled Admiral Nimitz to share with other officers at sea the information provided by our intelligence before the Battle of Midway without any risk of disclosing its source. In hindsight, however, it seems clear that the virtually verbatim repetition of the contents of intercepted messages enhanced the likelihood of disclosure that enabled the *Tribune* reporter to write his potentially damaging story.

9

Naval Service on Oahu

XCEPT FOR A handful of naval officers, all of the passengers on the
USS *Henderson* who made the week-long voyage from San Francisco to Pearl Harbor were army personnel. Our trip is memorable for
two reasons. First, virtually everyone on board became violently seasick
about an hour or two after we left port. My unpleasant memory of sharing crowded quarters with other equally seasick passengers is offset by my
present awareness of the fact that I have never been either airsick or seasick at any time thereafter. Second, all of the dozen or so naval officers
who were passengers occupied the same crowded, windowless cabin. My
bunk was only inches below the ceiling of the cabin. We took turns serving as lookouts for submarines at night. When I was awakened to take my
turn, I would promptly sit up, giving my head a solid bump. That was not
the sort of injury that earns one a Purple Heart, but its repetition attested
to my lack of savvy about military hazards.

When I arrived in Pearl Harbor, FRUPAC was located in an
unmarked area in the basement of a building near the headquarters of the
Fourteenth Naval District. I was first assigned space in a house a short
distance from the end of one of the runways at Hickam Field, and shortly
thereafter I moved into the BOQ (bachelor officers' quarters) located
near the main gate of the navy yard. As a married officer I was

compensated more generously than my roommate, Bob Turner, because I received an allowance to pay for my wife's housing in the States; as a bachelor Bob received no equivalent. Another injustice persisted throughout our years of service. Although he had also been recruited for service in communications intelligence because of his outstanding academic record in college, his initial duty in Washington had been as an enlisted man. He arrived both in Washington and at Pearl shortly before I did, but I received my commission as an ensign almost a year before he did. Since promotions were the product of seniority rather than talent, I remained his senior throughout the war even though we had virtually the same responsibility at all times. The injustice persisted even after the war when we both remained in the naval reserve after starting to practice law in Chicago. During the Korean conflict, after receiving informal notice that we were both about to be recalled to duty, only officers below the rank of lieutenant commander actually received such orders. Since he then had only two stripes while I had two and a half, he spent several months in Korea while I continued to practice law in Chicago. As he later served as general counsel of Kaiser Industries, his extra time in service clearly did not cause him irreparable harm.

A few weeks after my arrival at Pearl, the name of the combat intelligence unit was changed from "FRUPAC" to "JICPOA" (Joint Intelligence Communications Pacific Ocean Area) and its location was moved from the navy yard to Makalapa, near Admiral Nimitz's headquarters. Although my contribution to the war effort while stationed in Washington primarily involved the identification of new or previously unrecognized call signs, and secondarily the construction of "garble tables" that would enable us to determine whether the call signs that our operators recorded on intercepted messages were correct, during my thirty months of continuous duty at Pearl Harbor I had more important responsibilities. I became one of the watch officers responsible for reviewing all of the enemy radio traffic intercepted during a twenty-four-hour period and writing a summary of that traffic to be delivered to Admiral Edward Layton, the Chief Intelligence Officer of the Pacific Fleet, at the end of that twenty-four-hour period. I have been told that the report was the first thing he examined each morning. For most of my time at Pearl, on every third or fourth day I was on duty for twenty-four-hour periods that began on one day at 0800 and ended at that time on the next morning; I usually took a nap of about two or three hours early in the evening. Following that nap, I enjoyed some of the worst black coffee ever brewed.

At the beginning of each watch, I had a brief conversation with my predecessor about whatever was happening. On one occasion, I remember startling advice to be on the outlook for traffic involving the call sign for one of Japan's new battleships — I think it was the *Musashi* — because its sign had been one of the addressees in messages addressed to a location on Truk, a major Japanese naval base. If that battle wagon was en route to Truk, something important and unusual was certainly afoot. The concern, however, turned out to be a false alarm because I soon received another copy of the same message that had alarmed my predecessor and learned that the call sign for the *Musashi* was actually an unintentionally garbled version of the call sign for an administrative officer on Truk. In my later career as a judge, I have recalled that incident over and over again when confronted with the question whether a legislature actually intended a statute to have the meaning that its plain language seemed to convey. Legislatures, like radio operators, occasionally make mistakes. To ascertain the correct meaning of an ambiguous statute, it is often essential for judges to review earlier drafts and other legislative history before concluding that they know what the enacting legislators intended.

In April 1943, the cryptanalysts in section GY and the translators in GZ were able to read substantial amounts of Japanese traffic in the then current version of JN-25. On April 14, they read a message that included the details of a planned trip by Admiral Yamamoto, the commander of the Japanese navy, from Base Force No. 8 at Rabaul to an airfield on the island of Bougainville. The message contained the time and the route of the planned flight. President Roosevelt was informed of the contents of the message and directed senior officers in the navy to intercept the

Japanese flight and to "get" Yamamoto—the man who had been the architect of the attack on Pearl Harbor.

The operation was difficult and dangerous. It required American pilots to fly an indirect route of over six hundred miles both to avoid detection and to intercept the Japanese flight, which consisted of two large aircraft and six escorting fighters. Nevertheless, a squadron including sixteen American fighters made contact with the Japanese, and either Rex Barber or Thomas Lamphier fired shots that killed the admiral and forced his plane to crash into the jungle. I was the watch officer on duty at the traffic analysis desk and recall reading a copy of a message addressed to senior officers in our navy stating something like "Got one eagle and two sparrows."

Although the incident could be viewed as avenging the Pearl Harbor attack and therefore one of the most newsworthy events in the war, the American public was not informed of Admiral Yamamoto's death until almost a month later when the Japanese held a memorial service in Tokyo honoring him. It was, of course, a unique military operation because its primary motive was to punish the architect of the infamous attack on Pearl Harbor. I remember being somewhat troubled by the punitive motivation for the operation, but I also recognized that it had achieved a significant strategic benefit by terminating the most competent officer in the Japanese navy.

I have no recollection of any change in Japanese communications procedures suggesting they had inferred that we had decoded the message containing the details of the admiral's flight, but sometime later the Japanese began to encode their call signs. When the encoded call signs first appeared, Stanley Moe, an exceptionally talented enlisted man who regularly monitored and deciphered weather reports, was on duty with me. We spent the next forty-eight to seventy-two hours in a continuous joint effort to break the code.

Stanley immediately identified the call sign for the most prolific enemy weather station—it was in northern Japan, probably Ominato. We soon noticed that the first kana in that sign also appeared as the first kana in other familiar call signs that shared the same first kana as the weather station. By working with signs that were easily recognizable, we were able to determine that nothing more complicated than a simple substitution code was involved. At the end of that first twenty-four hours, however, a different set of signs began to appear — indicating that we should expect to be confronted with a new problem every day. The problem turned out to be quite simple, because the same sequences of kana that we had identified during the first day reappeared on the second day. To use an English example, if A through Z in regular alphabetical order were substituted for N through M (also in regular order) on day one, but for Y through X on day two, the change could be the product of a change in the relative positions of two strips of letters, each containing the entire alphabet, placed next to each other.

We had enough traffic containing well-known call signs to reconstruct the entire sequences of kana on each of the two strips — one for the kana in the original call signs, and the other for the kana in the encoded versions that were then sent out over the radio. I think it took us a little over forty-eight hours of continuous work to solve the entire system. We were not as prompt as we should have been in sharing the results of our labors with our colleagues in Washington. For I still remember receiving an urgent message advising us of their discovery that during the first day a particular kana was the encoded version of another kana in an intercepted message. The new system required more paperwork for us (as, of course, it did for the Japanese communicators as well) but otherwise did not impair our traffic analysis.

Immediately after our move to the large-frame building in Makalapa, navy buses provided me with transportation to work. From the bus stop I walked about one hundred yards up a hill past Admiral Nimitz's headquarters to JICPOA. As I sauntered by a red flag waving in the breeze, a senior officer shouted some stern and unfriendly comments informing me that my life was in danger because the admiral was engaged in target practice. My truthful response that I did not understand the significance of the red flag prompted what promised to be a severe reprimand until the admiral generously came to my defense. That was my only direct contact with a leader I greatly admired.

Charles ("Sandy") Sims was a language officer who had spent years in Japan and was particularly fluent in the language. He lived in a rented apartment on Waikiki beach and commuted to work in a 1933 Terraplane — a car made by the Hudson Motor Car Company between 1932 and 1938. As the war in the Pacific became more active, he was assigned to the staff of the commanding officer of a seagoing task force where he would be able to translate any oral communications between enemy pilots that the fleet operator might be able to intercept. When at sea, he of course had no use for his car and therefore offered to sell me a half interest in it. He proposed that in exchange for one hundred dollars and my commitments to keep the car in running condition and to allow him to use it whenever he was not at sea, I could have the car and an appropriate share of his gas coupons. (Gas was rationed in Hawaii just as it was throughout the United States during the war.) Even though it was obvious that the ten-year-old car was not in the best condition and my mechanical skills had not improved since the tractor breakdown in Delavan a few years earlier, I accepted his proposal. I then made a separate agreement with another friend, Walt Hopkins, a former forest ranger who was as strong as an ox and knew everything there is to know about cars. In exchange for one-half of my half interest, he paid me fifty dollars and agreed to assume my maintenance obligations.

That was probably the best deal I ever made. Sandy was on sea duty almost continuously thereafter, and Walt and I became exceptionally good friends, almost always using the car in joint activities, such as repeated trips to Makapu Beach, where we enjoyed the best body surfing available anywhere in the world. (After the war, I returned to Makapu twice: in 1980 I was a guest lecturer at the University of Hawaii Law School, and needed the help of Liz Harrison, the dean's wife, to avoid either drowning or being carried out to sea on a powerful rip current; and in 1990 when I attended a bar association meeting and the U.S. marshal wisely arranged to have a former navy Seal supervise my surfing.)

The Oahu Country Club generously allowed naval officers free use of its excellent golf course. Thanks to the car and the fact that a fellow officer, Bob Seaks, who had the highest grade-point average in the history of the Duke Law School, had a set of clubs that he was willing to share with his companions in a foursome, we played the course several times. At the conclusion of one of our rounds, we were pleasantly surprised to find Bob Hope on the practice tee entertaining a group of admirers. He was at his best when performing for servicemen and when talking about golf.

Although the blackout kept us on the naval base after dark, the car also made it possible to enjoy an occasional early dinner at P. Y. Chong's restaurant. As I recall the menu, it offered a choice of either a three-dollar steak or a four-dollar steak. Both were excellent. Many years later when I was attending a conference in Hawaii playing golf with clubs borrowed from the chief justice of the State Supreme Court, he mentioned the fact that his mother had been a waitress at P. Y. Chong's. He confirmed my recollection of the high quality of the beef.

On one of Sandy's brief periods of shore duty, he brought one of his fellow officers to JICPOA to show him the facility and introduce him to his shore-based colleagues. That was the first time I met Byron White. It was after our meeting that, during the May 1945 kamikaze attack on the aircraft carrier *Bunker Hill,* Byron saved the lives of sailors buried under debris that no one else was strong enough to move. I remember our meeting because Byron was already a national hero for reasons that had nothing to do with the war. He was an All-American running back when he played for the University of Colorado and the leading ground gainer in the NFL as a pro. He was also an extremely nice guy. His characteristic greeting when being introduced for the first time was to precede a crushing handshake with a statement of his name. Years later when he first met one of the few federal judges who was even older than I am, their exchange of greetings was truly poetic: the response to his "Byron White" was "Myron Bright."

Another naval officer, who was better known as a civilian and whom I met during my tour of duty in Hawaii, was Oswald Jacoby, an expert card player whose name is attached to conventions familiar to countless duplicate bridge players. One evening Commander Tom Huckins invited the two of us to join him and his wife for dinner and a friendly bridge game in their home. Ozzie particularly impressed Mrs. Huckins when — three or four tricks before the end of the play of each hand — he was able to tell her what cards she still held. I was wise enough never to play poker with Ozzie, but on more than one occasion I was a spectator at games in the BOQ when he played; I particularly remember how frequently he tossed in his hand without making any competitive bid. He also enjoyed Ping-Pong, which he played ambidextrously, sometimes changing the hand holding his racket during a point. Although I was a rank amateur at bridge, I was the better Ping-Pong player — indeed, although I played frequently during my stint on Oahu, I think my years of competition with my older brother Jim in the spacious attic of our home in Chicago had prepared me for a tour of duty in which I was undefeated at the Ping-Pong table.

After about two years on Oahu, I was allowed a few days of "Island Leave." Bob Seaks, Walt Hopkins, and I were able to hitch rides on army planes that took us to the islands of Hawaii, Maui, and Kauai. We borrowed army jeeps for sightseeing on each of those islands. Our night in Kealakekua, on the "Big Island" of Hawaii, was memorable because the entire population appeared to be Japanese-Americans. We did not see a single native Hawaiian in what, based on the popular song "My Little Grass Shack in Kealakekua, Hawaii" (1933), we had assumed would be a traditional native village.

On Maui we drove to the parking area near the Kilauea volcano. We walked to a spot where we had an excellent view of the crater. The view was memorable, but less so than our decision not to investigate the area identified by a sign pointing to an uphill path containing the words "silver" and "swords." Not until after we had returned to Oahu and Walt satisfied his curiosity by a visit to the Honolulu public library did we learn that silverswords are beautiful flowers that grow only on that volcano and, more importantly, although they very rarely bloom, they probably were in full bloom when we decided to terminate our sightseeing that afternoon. Over the years that incident has been a frequent reminder of the importance of deliberation before refusing to take advantage of once-in-a-lifetime opportunities.

On Kauai the most impressive sight was the Waimea Canyon — the second largest canyon in the United States — where it rains most of the time. Indeed, I think it is known as one of the wettest places in the world. Not many people inhabited Kauai in 1945, but its extraordinary beauty convinced us that it would soon become a major tourist attraction.

Not long after our inter-island leave, American forces achieved a string of successes in occupying Japanese-held islands in the western Pacific. The island-to-island advances came only after bitterly fought battles in which we suffered heavy casualties. In preparation for an ultimate invasion of Japan itself, in 1945 we established communications intelligence facilities on Guam. Several of my closest friends at Pearl — including Bob Turner and Bob Seaks — helped set up the new facilities while I remained on Oahu; then, after about thirty months, I received orders to return to Washington and was granted thirty days of leave en route.

During the portion of that leave that Betty and I spent with my parents in Lakeside, Michigan, an army plane dropped an atomic bomb on Hiroshima and a few days later another on Nagasaki, leading the Japanese to surrender. Tragic as those events were for the residents of those two cities, I was then convinced (and have remained convinced ever since) that that method of bringing the war to its inevitable end saved many, many more lives — of American soldiers as well as Japanese soldiers and civilians — than the number of victims of those two bombings. An invasion of Japan would have caused hundreds of thousands, if not millions, of casualties.

When I finally reported for duty at the naval communications facility on Nebraska Avenue in Washington, I found a well-staffed cadre of personnel with nothing to do because there were no longer any enemy wireless communications to analyze. I remember a conversation with one of my senior officers as we stood outside a room filled with dozens of idle enlisted personnel, in which he asked me, "What are we going to do with all these people?" I thought my response was obvious: "Send them home." But he replied, "No, we can't do that." I assumed that a senior naval officer could not consider any change that would reduce the number of enlisted personnel under his command. Nevertheless, he was fully cooperative with my efforts to get out of the navy in time to start law school in October 1945.

Eligibility for discharge was governed by the length of one's service on active duty, with extra points being awarded for service outside the continental United States. My service in Hawaii gave me the same credit as if those months had been spent in active combat. As a result, I was released from active duty sometime in September. Three principal factors motivated my decision to go to law school: my wife's wartime job, the G.I. Bill of Rights, and a letter that my brother Jim had written to me shortly before I left Hawaii.

Betty was blessed with a fine mind and exceedingly graceful coordination. Riveters working on spars for large aircraft wings at the Pullman-Standard plant in South Chicago were compensated on the basis of their production, and she was one of the most efficient riveters in the plant. Since she lived with her parents, she was able to save her earnings. Those savings covered our living expenses during law school, and the G.I. Bill covered my tuition.

The letter from Jim described the intangible rewards that he had received as a lawyer providing meaningful assistance to people who need help. It was much the same message that John Adams conveyed when he wrote the following to Jonathan Sewall in 1759: "Now to what higher object, to what greater character, can any mortal aspire than to be possessed of all this knowledge, well digested and ready at command, to assist the feeble and friendless, to discountenance the haughty and lawless, to procure redress to wrongs, the advancement of right, to assert and maintain liberty and virtue, to discourage and abolish tyranny and vice?"[1]

---

1. See *The Works of John Adams, Second President of the United States,* ed. Bolles and Houghton (Boston: Charles C. Little & James Brown, 1850), 79–80.

10

Law School

BECAUSE I INTENDED to practice law in Chicago, I thought it would be wise to obtain my legal education at either the University of Chicago or Northwestern. I chose Northwestern partly because my father had made the same choice when John Henry Wigmore was the dean and partly because I had already spent so many years as a student in schools affiliated with the University of Chicago that I thought a new environment would be healthy. At that time, both schools, like most of the leading law schools in the country, gave students the opportunity to graduate after only two calendar years of study; each year included a third "semester" of study instead of a vacation during the summer months.

There were only about sixty students — all men — in the class that enrolled in the fall of 1945. All of us fit comfortably in Booth Hall, a tiered classroom in which we all looked down at our professor. Leon Green, the dean, taught the torts course, and Harold Havighurst, who was to become dean after Leon retired, taught us contracts. In both courses we used casebooks prepared by our teachers. Instead of organizing the subject by studying cases involving one rule after another, the books included separate chapters for cases involving different types of fact patterns. Chapter 2 of the torts casebook was titled "Threats, Insults, Blows, Attacks, Fights, Restraints, Nervous Shocks," and the contracts casebook contained four parts: "Services," "Gratuities," "Loans," and "Contracts for the Sale of Goods." Their approach stressed the importance of a thorough understanding of the facts that had given rise to disputes and identifying the decision-maker — usually either the judge or the jury, but often either a federal or a state judge, or a corporate executive rather than the directors or the shareholders — who should resolve the issues in the case. Dean Green frequently contrasted the approach adopted at Yale, where he had previously taught, and Northwestern to the rule-oriented approach followed at Harvard and Michigan. I have sometimes thought that the emphasis on facts and procedure instead of generally applicable substantive rules provided us with a vertical rather than a horizontal legal education.

It is perhaps of note that the Constitution principally identifies the decision-makers — the legislature, the executive, and the judiciary — rather than the rules that govern our behavior, with a few exceptions (for example, ex post facto laws are taboo). It tells us who shall make new rules and how to do so.

The torts class was also unique because Dean Green required the student discussing a case to stand while stating the case and answering his questions. In his view it was important for lawyers to be able to think on their feet. He had written extensively and critically about the doctrine of proximate cause, which he believed did more to confuse than to help judges analyze cases. In his opinion it made more sense to begin the analysis of a tort case by defining the duty that the defendant owed to the plaintiff rather than the remoteness or the proximity of the causal connection between the defendant's conduct and the plaintiff's injury. The dean was also a strict disciplinarian; when he learned that my friends Art Seder, Dick Cooper, Bud Wilson, and I played a few hands of bridge while eating our lunch in the basement, he concluded that card games and studying law did not belong in the same building and put an end to our games.

Unlike at most leading law schools today, in the entire Northwestern faculty when I was a student there were only about a dozen teachers, including two or three practicing lawyers who taught on a part-time basis. I was favorably impressed by each of them.

Nathaniel Nathanson, who taught constitutional law, was a few days late arriving back in Chicago after completing his wartime job with the Office of Price Administration. The students named his class "Nate's Mystery Hour" because his discussions raised so many questions that he let the students try to answer for themselves. I think we spent several weeks discussing Chief Justice Marshall's opinion in *Marbury* v. *Madison*. We had no trouble understanding the proposition that the Supreme Court has the power to decide that an Act of Congress is unconstitutional, but I am not sure we understood why Congress lacked the power to authorize the Court to grant a writ of mandamus ordering the Secretary of State to deliver Marbury's commission as a judge. What I best remember about Nat's teaching is his repeated admonition to "beware of glittering generalities." That advice, which he may well have learned from clerking for Justice Louis Brandeis, is consistent with the basic principle of judicial restraint that Brandeis described in his separate opinion in *Ashwander* v. *TVA*[1]: The Court should avoid deciding cases on constitutional grounds whenever possible, and when it is necessary to reach a constitutional issue, the Court should decide no more than is necessary to dispose of the case. Nat and his former boss would both have disagreed with the unnecessarily broad holding in *Citizens United* v. *FEC,*[2] a decision I return to in later chapters.

Our discussion of Chief Justice William Howard Taft's famous opinion in *Myers* v. *United States*[3] was memorable for several reasons. In that case, by a six-to-three vote, the Court held that a statute prohibiting the president from discharging postmasters without cause was unconstitutional. The author of the opinion was the only former president of the United States to sit on the Court. The dissenters were Justices Holmes, Brandeis, and McReynolds, each of whom wrote a separate opinion.

---

1. 297 U.S. 288, 347 (1936).
2. 558 U.S. 310 (2010).
3. 272 U.S. 52 (1926).

Relying heavily on a detailed discussion of history — including the Senate's acquittal of President Andrew Johnson after the Civil War — Taft reasoned that the statute impermissibly limited the power of the executive granted by Article II of the Constitution. In their dissents, both Holmes and Brandeis argued that the congressional power to create a post office included the lesser power to protect postmasters from discharge without cause. Just a few years later, in a challenge to President Roosevelt's attempted removal of a member of the Federal Trade Commission, the Court unanimously upheld the statutory provision that protected the commissioner from discharge without cause. *Myers* stands out in my memory because Nat insisted that we understand the competing arguments instead of casually assuming that the case had been wrongly decided because both Brandeis and Holmes had dissented and because the Court later unanimously held that President Roosevelt lacked the power to remove a member of the Federal Trade Commission without cause.

Homer Carey, who taught the courses in real property and future interests, sometimes spent class time giving us advice about practical aspects of the practice of law. On one of those occasions he commented on the importance of adopting some unique practice that would enhance the likelihood that potential clients would recognize and remember your name — his specific suggestion was to use green ink when signing letters or pleadings. The green ink idea did not appeal to me, but his suggestion made me realize that "John Stevens" was not much more unique than "John Smith" and prompted me to add my middle name to my signature. I don't know whether my new practice of including my middle name ever got me any law business, but it did prompt fairly frequent questions about whether I had been named after naval hero John Paul Jones. My truthful answer to those queries was that I had no idea why my parents picked either of my given names.

Two lessons that I learned in Jim Rahl's course on antitrust law merit special comment. First, sometimes the text of a federal statute cannot be read literally. Section One of the Sherman Act proscribes "every" contract in restraint of trade. As Justice Brandeis cogently explained in *Chicago Board of Trade* v. *United States,*[4] every enforceable contract restrains trade; indeed, that is the very purpose of an enforceable contract. Accordingly, the statute must be read as prohibiting only unreasonable restraints of trade. Second, the so-called rule of reason that the Court adopted to avoid the problem created by a literal reading of the statutory text also has a narrower scope than the name of the rule suggests. It does not protect any rule that a judge might consider reasonable, but only those rules that do not have an adverse effect on competition in a free market.

Brunson MacChesney, who taught the course in agency, did not finish his wartime work in Washington until after courses began. After only a few days of teaching, he arrived in class wearing the large, elaborately ribboned medal awarded by the French government to recipients of the Legion of Honor. Instead of immediately explaining his unusually distracting attire, it was only at the end of the class that he told us that French custom, or perhaps some provision of French law, included a requirement that every recipient of the medal wear it in public the day after it was awarded. The veterans in the class might have been more favorably impressed if he had provided us with that explanation immediately. Sometimes the timing of an explanation may be more important than its content.

Fred Inbau, who taught evidence and criminal law, had written extensively about the admissibility of confessions. One of his writings was cited by Chief Justice Warren in *Miranda* v. *Arizona.*[5] He was well liked by his students who often called him "Fearless Fred" or "Hanging Fred" because they thought of him (somewhat unfairly) as favoring unduly strict enforcement of the criminal law. I have no memory of any discussion of either the wisdom or the constitutionality of the death penalty in any of his classes.

Walter Schaefer, who had gained widespread respect for his work with

4. 246 U.S. 231 (1918).
5. 384 U.S. 436 (1966).

Albert E. Jenner in modernizing the Illinois rules of Civil Procedure, taught us that subject. He later was closely associated with Adlai Stevenson when he was the Governor of Illinois and when he was twice defeated by General Eisenhower in presidential elections. Wally also became a highly respected justice of the Illinois Supreme Court.

During our senior year, Art Seder and I served as coeditors-in-chief of what was then named the *Illinois Law Review*. Our editions included several pieces discussing the then recent Taft-Hartley Amendments to the National Labor Relations Act, and a comment that I wrote about price-fixing in the movie industry. My work on that comment — which principally discussed Judge Learned Hand's opinion in *United States* v. *Paramount Pictures* — played an important role in developing my special interest in antitrust law.

In the summer of 1947, Art and I had a meeting in our law review office with the two members of the faculty whom I have not yet mentioned. Willard Wirtz, who later served as secretary of labor under Presidents John F. Kennedy and Lyndon Johnson, had begun his teaching career at the University of Iowa Law School when Wiley Rutledge was the dean; he and Rutledge remained close friends after Rutledge became a federal judge. Willard Pedrick, who taught classes in both torts and federal taxation, had been a law clerk for Fred Vinson when he was a judge on the Court of Appeals for the District of Columbia. At our meeting, they informed us that Congress had enacted a statute authorizing Supreme Court justices to hire additional clerks for the terms beginning that October and thereafter. They were relatively certain that Vinson and Rutledge would hire applicants whom they recommended. The job with Rutledge would be for the October 1947 term, and the job with the chief justice would be for two years beginning in October 1948. The professors told us that they planned to recommend us for the two jobs, but wanted us to decide which job each of us would apply for. We both preferred the Rutledge option because we were interested in entering practice as promptly as possible. Because the professors considered us equally well qualified, we confronted a potential deadlock. Accordingly, we flipped a coin. I won and Justice Rutledge did hire me without an interview. I was permitted to depart for Washington without taking the final exam in the course on federal taxation and without attending the graduation exercises. Art taught in the law school for a year before beginning his clerkship with the chief justice.

11

Law Clerk for Wiley Rutledge

WHEN JUSTICE LOUIS Brandeis retired from the Supreme Court in 1939, the two lawyers most seriously considered to replace him were Wiley B. Rutledge, the dean of the University of Iowa Law School, and William O. Douglas, the chairman of the Securities and Exchange Commission. FDR chose Douglas, and Rutledge agreed to accept a nomination to the United States Court of Appeals for the D.C. Circuit, where he served for the next five years. Possibly because of his service on that court, Rutledge was happy to have his clerks address him as "Judge." He was well liked and well respected by all of his colleagues. Though he wrote several important opinions, his most famous was his unquestionably correct dissent from the decision affirming the death sentence imposed on the Japanese General Isoroku Yamamoto for failing to prevent troops under his command from committing atrocities against civilians in the Philippines in the closing months of World War II.

Rutledge was one of four justices who had hired two clerks — the others were Felix Frankfurter, Stanley Reed, and Harold Burton. Chief Justice Fred Vinson had three clerks, and Hugo Black, Bill Douglas, Robert Jackson, and Frank Murphy each had only one. I had the exceptionally good fortune of having Stanley Temko as my co-clerk.

As the most outstanding graduate of Columbia Law School in 1943,

Stan had been hired by Chief Justice Harlan Fiske Stone, a former dean of that school, to serve as his law clerk after Stan's overseas service in the army. After Stone died in April 1946, Rutledge chose Stan as his clerk for the October 1947 term. Three qualities made Stan an exemplary co-clerk. He had an uncanny ability to express the essence of a complicated dispute in a few well-chosen words, he had an incomparable sense of humor, and he was an all-around nice guy. During the two or three days before Rutledge returned to Washington from his summer vacation in Ogunquit, Maine, Stan explained his understanding of what Rutledge expected from his law clerks.

Our first, and most time-consuming, task was to write "cert memos" — memoranda summarizing the issues in the printed petitions for certiorari filed by litigants who had paid the filing fee required by the Court's rules; each petition requested the Court to review the merits of a decision made either by a federal court of appeals or by the highest court of a state. The justice felt that our memoranda would be more useful if its author concluded with a recommendation either to grant or deny review. Making that recommendation was sometimes much more difficult than drafting the memo. The volume of cert petitions fluctuated, but I think each of us wrote about twenty memos each week. Most of them were only a page or two in length, but an occasional complicated case might require several pages.

Our second task, unique to the Rutledge Chambers, was to prepare similar memos in in forma pauperis cases — those filed by litigants unable to pay the filing fee. The papers in those cases were often handwritten and difficult to understand. The principal reason that the chief justice had three clerks was that they examined all of those petitions and prepared an original and eight carbon copies of memos in each. Virtually all of those memos recommended denying the petition without even calling for a response from the opposing party, either because the petition had no merit or because the petitioner had not exhausted all of his available state remedies. Because Rutledge was the eighth most senior justice, his copy of those memos was almost illegible; moreover, he thought the chief's clerks were not entirely reliable judges of the potential merit of such cases. So he required Stan and me to divide up the in forma petitions, make a fresh examination of each, and write a supplementary memo for him when appropriate.

In one of those cases, despite the chief's clerk's routine recommendation to deny the petition outright, the Court called for a response from the opposing party at our request and, to our surprise, the Illinois attorney general confessed error. The petitioner, a young man who did not speak English, had pleaded guilty to murder. Instead of providing him with a lawyer, the state had used a police officer as an interpreter. The Court entered a brief order summarily reversing the state court.[1] Rutledge wrote a separate opinion highly critical of Illinois post-conviction procedures. The state Supreme Court had identified three different methods of challenging the constitutionality of a criminal conviction — writ of error, habeas corpus, and coram nobis — and the Illinois attorney general was usually able to convince federal judges that a petitioner's attempt to obtain federal review of his conviction should be denied because he had invoked the wrong state remedy. In his separate opinion, Rutledge pointed out that well over half of the post-conviction petitions filed in the United States Supreme Court during each of the preceding three years had come from Illinois. His characterization of the Illinois procedures as a "merry-go-round made up of blind alleys" — unless the state confessed error — was no doubt responsible for the Illinois General Assembly's enactment of a simplified Illinois Post Conviction Remedy Act a few months later.

The third task was to assist the justice in his preparation for oral argument in important cases. Rutledge always read the parties' briefs and welcomed any thoughts we might have and occasionally asked us to research a particular point, but he generally did not ask for (or need) any pre-argument help from his clerks. There were, however, a few cases in which the records were voluminous and the issues were unusually complicated

---

1. See *Marino* v. *Ragen*, 332 U.S. 561 (1947) (per curiam).

and in which he asked us to prepare thorough pre-argument bench memos. I prepared such memos in two antitrust cases — the *Paramount Pictures* case that had been the subject of my law review comment and *FTC* v. *The Cement Institute,* involving the legality of the so-called basing point system of determining the delivered price of cement.

The fourth area where we sometimes helped the justice was in the preparation of his opinions, both when writing for the Court and when writing separately. Because he wrote out the first draft on a yellow legal pad that was then typed by his secretary, Edna Lindgreen, Stan and I were seldom asked to play a significant role in the drafting process. On occasion, Rutledge's draft would contain a footnote reading "JPS get cites." On one such occasion, after I had produced only one hoary citation that arguably supported the broad rule of law described in the text, the opinion was modified to refer to the "better rule" rather than the "well-settled rule."

He did allow each of us to prepare the first draft of one Court opinion. Stan wrote the first draft of the Court's opinion in *Aero Mayflower Transit Co.* v. *Board of Railroad Commissioner of Montana,*[2] a case involving the constitutionality of a state tax, and I wrote the first draft in *Mandeville Island Farms, Inc.* v. *American Crystal Sugar Co.*[3] My case raised the question whether an agreement among sugar refiners in California to fix the price that they paid for sugar beets grown in California violated the Sherman Act. My draft answering what I thought was an easy question was only three or four pages long. I had assumed that all educated lawyers realized that the Court's 1895 opinion in *United States* v. *E. C. Knight Co.*[4] had been overruled by more recent cases upholding federal regulation of local activity that merely affected interstate commerce. The justice, however, used several pages to explain what I thought was a perfectly obvious proposition, namely, that the *E. C. Knight* case was a relic of the past. It was many years later — after I had become a member of the Court — that I realized that Rutledge's thorough opinion was far wiser

2. 332 U.S. 495 (1947).
3. 334 U.S. 219 (1948).
4. 156 U.S. 1.

than mine. For in his concurring opinion in a case decided in 1995, *United States* v. *Lopez,* Justice Clarence Thomas expressed the opinion that *E. C. Knight* had been correctly decided.

The first assignment the justice assigned to Stan and me after he arrived in the office in September was to make a careful check of the status of the title to his home in the Spring Valley neighborhood of Washington, D.C. He knew that a restrictive covenant associated with his title purported to prevent him from conveying the property to any non-Caucasians, but hoped that Stan and I would be able to supply him with a basis for concluding that the covenant was invalid as a matter of property law. Our time in the recorder's office taught us something about title records, but produced no solution to Rutledge's problem. As a consequence, he found it necessary to recuse himself from hearing the argument and participating in the Court's decisions in two cases involving the enforceability of racially restrictive covenants, *Shelley* v. *Kraemer,* which arose in Missouri, and *Hurd* v. *Hodge,* which arose in the District of Columbia. Justices Reed and Jackson were also recused, so only six justices were available to hear what we all recognized were two important cases that might, on the basis of precedent, have been decided either way.

During pre-argument discussions among law clerks, I learned that they were unanimous, not only in their views about how those two cases should be decided, but also about how the Court should answer the question whether racially segregated public schools were unconstitutional. We looked forward to hearing Thurgood Marshall argue one of the restrictive covenant cases as well as others later in the term. He was a respectful, effective advocate, not cowed in the slightest by the vigorous questioning from Justice Frankfurter. He prevailed, and the law took a giant step in the right direction when the Court unanimously ruled in petitioners' favor in both cases. In *Shelley,* the Court held that judicial enforcement of the restrictive covenants was state action that violated the Equal Protection Clause of the Fourteenth Amendment. Providing the same answer in the *Hurd* case required some judicial creativity because the Fourteenth Amendment's limitation on state power does not apply to the District of Columbia. To avoid what would have been an intolerable result — restrictive covenants enforceable in the district but not in the states — Chief Justice Vinson's opinion construed the Due Process Clause of the Fifth Amendment, which does apply to the District of Columbia, as implicitly containing an equal protection component akin to the Fourteenth Amendment's Equal Protection Clause. That interpretation of the Fifth Amendment has been respected ever since, despite its lack of support in the text of the Constitution itself.

Another case argued by Thurgood Marshall, *Sipuel v. Board of Regents of University of Oklahoma*,[5] had an interesting and unexpected sequel. Ada Sipuel was a qualified applicant for admission to the University of Oklahoma Law School who had been denied admission because of her race. She brought suit in state court to compel the school to admit her. Without questioning her qualifications, the state courts denied her relief. On January 7 and 8, 1948, Thurgood presented his oral argument on her behalf in the Supreme Court. He was so persuasive that, less than a week later, the Court issued a one-page unanimous opinion granting his client relief. Many years later I played golf on a regular basis with Gene Pruett, who had been a member of Ada Sipuel's law school class at Oklahoma. He remembered her well, and reported that she was not only a good student but popular with her classmates as well. Apparently the bias that distorted the judgment of the school administrators was not shared by the student body.

Tom Clark was the Attorney General of the United States during the Court's 1947 term. I remembered that our law school professor Brunson MacChesney had commented on more than one occasion about how much he admired Tom's ability as a lawyer. Tom displayed that ability when he presented the oral argument on behalf of the government in the Paramount Pictures antitrust case. Paramount was one of three movie antitrust cases decided that term — all won by the government. Tom was also the named defendant in *Ahrens v. Clark*,[6] a habeas corpus proceed-

---

5. 332 U.S. 631 (1948) (per curiam).
6. 335 U.S. 188 (1948).

ing brought by a group of German prisoners on Ellis Island challenging their postwar deportation. The Court held that only the federal court in the Southern District of New York, where the prisoners were being held, had jurisdiction of the case. My boss felt very strongly that the majority decided the case incorrectly and placed an unwise limit on the power of federal judges to issue the "great writ." In an opinion written twenty-five years later by Justice William Brennan, the Court overruled the *Ahrens* case. It was the Rutledge dissent and the later Brennan majority opinion that provided the principal support for the 2004 decision in *Rasul* v. *Bush,* which held that federal courts may review the constitutionality of the detention of alleged terrorists at Guantánamo Bay.

With the exception of Justice Frankfurter's, the law clerks seldom had an opportunity to engage in informal conversations with any justice other than their own boss. Frankfurter, however, frequently treated the clerks in other chambers like former students when he met them in the halls and welcomed the opportunity to discuss legal issues with them, occasionally revealing his profound disagreement with Justices Black and Douglas. Without actually witnessing any private debates among other justices, we all sensed some personal hostility within the Court. Justice Jackson had just finished his yearlong leave to serve as the special prosecutor for the Nuremberg tribunal. I recall Justice Rutledge making comments critical of the entire war-crimes project and suggesting that Jackson's role caused him to change his own views about creating crimes after the wrongful conduct had taken place. Jackson had been critical of Black's participation in a case argued by a former partner and was believed to have been disappointed that he was not named chief justice after Stone's death. And Justice Douglas, though occasionally mentioned as a possible presidential candidate, was regarded by the law clerks as an aloof and unfriendly justice. I remember one occasion when Stan Temko was the last clerk to join us in the cafeteria for lunch; as he sat down he remarked, "Who says Justice Douglas is unfriendly? I just rode down in the elevator with him; he looked me right in the eye and said, 'Hrumpf.'" There was a consensus, however, that Douglas was probably the most efficient author of opinions;

he wrote his own drafts and relied on his law clerk only for checking the record to confirm the accuracy of his discussion of the facts.

We understood that Justice Black frequently dictated his opinions. One day I was surprised to have him invite me to play tennis with him on the court in his backyard. We played two sets of singles. I won the first set without a great deal of difficulty, but I was embarrassed to find that he was in better physical condition than I was. He won the second set and, fortunately, did not insist on playing a third. His quiet demeanor concealed a surprisingly strong competitive character.

Two cases in which Rutledge dissented illustrate how much the law has changed since my year as a law clerk. In *Bute* v. *Illinois*,[7] the five-justice majority held that the failure to provide counsel to a defendant convicted of a felony did not violate the Due Process Clause. And in his opinion for a six-justice majority in *Goesaert* v. *Cleary*,[8] Frankfurter concluded that a Michigan statute, which prohibited a woman from receiving a license to bartend unless she was the wife or daughter of the male tavern owner, did not violate the Equal Protection Clause. Those majority decisions are no longer good law.

With two exceptions, the job of the law clerk is pretty much the same today as it was in 1947. It is still the best job available to recent law school graduates, both because of the interesting work and because of the uniformly high quality of the Court's personnel. But the increased number of clerks — from one or two to four per justice — has slightly diluted the quality of the relationships among clerks and between clerks and their bosses. And there is a world of difference between the monetary rewards then and now. Whereas my salary when I was first employed as a lawyer in the private sector was lower than my pay as a clerk, today the private sector pays as much as three times or more and offers several hundred thousand dollars as a signing bonus to lure Supreme Court law clerks.

***

7. 333 U.S. 640 (1948).
8. 335 U.S. 464 (1948).

12

The Poppenhusen Firm

W HEN I RETURNED to Chicago in the late summer of 1948, I first confronted the bar examination and then found employment with what was then a large firm — Poppenhusen, Johnston, Thompson, Raymond and Mayer — of twenty-four lawyers. I was one of a group of four newly hired associates who increased the size of the firm to twenty-eight. Three factors influenced my choice. The Poppenhusen firm was one of the few leading firms in Chicago that employed Jewish lawyers, I was favorably impressed by the other young men that they were hiring, and the firm was highly recommended by my former professor, Walter V. Schaefer. The managing partner in the firm was Floyd Thompson — who was known as "the Judge," presumably because he had been the chief justice of the Illinois Supreme Court when he was just twenty-nine years old. Two of the younger partners were Albert E. ("Bert") Jenner and Samuel Block; although both of them died many years ago, the firm is now known as "Jenner and Block." It is now much larger than it was in 1948. Indeed, its Washington office, where my son-in-law Kevin Mullen recently practiced, and where my former law clerk David DeBruin is now a partner, is larger than the entire firm was in 1948.

The four of us who were first employed in 1948 shared Mr.

Poppenhusen's spacious office because he was no longer actively practicing law. Two of the four — Bob Fuchs and Ed Rothschild — were Harvard Law School graduates, and Norman J. ("Jack") Barry had graduated at the top of his class from Notre Dame Law School. I admired and liked all three but was particularly impressed with Ed and Jack, both of whom had served in combat in World War II. Ed had played varsity basketball at Harvard College, was an officer in the infantry in Europe, and had grades at the law school allegedly comparable to those earned by Justice Brandeis. Jack was the commanding officer of a naval vessel that landed troops on the beach during the Normandy invasion and had been an end on Notre Dame's undefeated football team in 1941. The competitive spirit that made him a star athlete characterized his later career as a superb trial lawyer. Over the years Jack and Ed were to become my closest friends.

Passing the bar exam made us eligible to become lawyers, but, for us to become members of the Illinois bar, we had to travel to Springfield to participate in an oath-taking ceremony. The round-trip required us to miss a day of work, and at the end of the pay period we found that we had not been paid for that day. Moreover, our first Christmas bonus checks — instead of the expected minimum of one month's salary — were for only twenty-five or fifty dollars. While acknowledging that the measly bonuses did not violate any express commitment, I voiced my disappointment. In response, the firm increased the bonuses for all the associates. Though I suppose the response should have satisfied us, the two incidents influenced our later decision to form our own firm. Nevertheless we all gained from what we learned at Poppenhusen.

Jack received valuable experience assisting the judge in important litigation. He was especially impressed by the judge's courageous decision in his defense of Preston Tucker, the promoter of a failed enterprise to market a new automobile named the "Tucker Torpedo." At the close of the government's case, the judge apparently decided that his client's testimony might do more harm than good and that he could convince the jury that the prosecution had not proved its case beyond a reasonable doubt. He therefore rested without putting in any evidence. His judgment was vindicated when the jury returned a not guilty verdict.

Ed worked primarily with Fred Mayer and Bert Jenner on corporate and tax matters. Fred's principal client was the Continental Grain Company, and Bert represented Henry Crown and the Material Service Company, which transacted a great deal of business with the city of Chicago.

I was especially fortunate to have the opportunity to assist Edward R. Johnston in antitrust and other major litigation. Johnston had earned nationwide recognition as an antitrust litigator for his successful defense of a trade association and its members charged with fixing the price of lumber in the national market. When I went to work for him, he was preparing for trial as the lawyer for the Phillips Petroleum Company, one of the defendants in *United States* v. *National City Lines,* a criminal antitrust case. National City Lines, the principal defendant, owned a number of metropolitan transit companies that had previously operated electric street car lines. In addition to Phillips, the defendants included other suppliers: two bus manufacturers (General Motors and Mack), another oil company, and a tire manufacturer. The indictment charged that the suppliers' agreements to provide financing for the conversion from electric street car to motor-bus transit operations in exchange for exclusive supply contracts were both a conspiracy in restraint of trade that violated Section 1 of the Sherman Act and an agreement to monopolize commerce in violation of Section 2.

Shortly before the date the trial was scheduled to begin, I attended a strategy conference that included lawyers for all of the defendants and some of their clients' executives. I remember one of those executives suggesting that we request a week or two delay in the start of the trial for a reason that would have involved a misrepresentation to the trial judge. While John Chadwell, the lawyer for National City Lines, acknowledged that the brief delay would benefit the defendants, he immediately rejected the proposal, explaining that he would have other cases to try before the judge and could not afford to risk offending him. It was a trivial issue, but I have never forgotten how John did not entertain the thought of unethical behavior for even a second.

In jury selection, the government seemed to object to any potential juror with a business background and welcomed all female members of the venire, whereas the defendants sought a business-oriented panel. In the end the jury was composed entirely of housewives. After their deliberations, the jury found all the defendants guilty on one of the counts and not guilty on the other, even though that result was irrational. The case was an early example for me that the law does not require consistent jury verdicts.

My impression that the evidence did not seem to support a criminal conviction was supported by the trial judge's decision to impose fines of just one dollar on each of the defendants. The loss of the case was nevertheless important to the defendants because of the possibility that they might later be sued by competitors for treble damages. And, as a matter of federal law, the jury's finding provided prima facie proof that they had engaged in illegal conduct. I did most of the work preparing the defendants' unsuccessful appellate brief.

I also assisted Johnston in the defense of other antitrust cases, including representing Paramount Pictures and its affiliated operator of movie theaters in Chicago in cases filed by independent exhibitors; the Wisconsin Cheese Exchange in its successful defense of a charge that its method of reporting transactions constituted price-fixing; and the Coca-Cola Company and the Coca-Cola Bottling Company of Chicago in an action brought by the local bottler for Dr Pepper. In all those cases, Johnston's preparation primarily involved gaining a sufficient understanding of the facts to enable him to explain the issues to the jury or judge.

Johnston was an extremely persuasive advocate. Although bald — except for a few traces of hair behind his ears — and overweight, he was a healthy, good-looking man. He had a deep bass voice, was exceptionally articulate, and inspired the listener's confidence because he spoke with so much conviction. He also had a sense of humor. Usually before getting on the elevator to pay a visit to Nick the barber (whose shop was directly below our offices), he would remark that he was going down to give Nick a tip. As a boss he compared favorably with Wiley Rutledge, for whom I had the greatest possible admiration and affection.

We worked together on one scholastic endeavor. The Supreme Court's unanimous decision in *American Tobacco Co.* v. *United States*[1] generated debate over whether the mere size of a successful business enterprise might be sufficient to establish a violation of Section 2 of the Sherman Act. In his opinion for the Court, Justice Burton had relied heavily on Learned Hand's opinion finding Alcoa guilty of violating Section 2, and some scholars interpreted Hand's opinion as supporting the view that mere size was unlawful. Johnston had agreed to participate in a debate at the Northwestern Law School with Dean Gene Rostow of Yale Law School about that issue. He asked me to prepare a draft of his remarks and ultimately used my draft in his presentation. Characteristically, when he received an honorarium for his presentation, he endorsed the check to me. The draft was published in the *Illinois Law Review* under the title, "Monopoly or Monopolization, a Reply to Professor Rostow."

In 1951, the American Bar Association formed a new section on antitrust law. Johnston accepted the association's invitation to become the first chairman of that section. Not long thereafter he was asked by Chauncey Reed, the Republican congressman from West Chicago, Illinois, to suggest the name of a lawyer to serve as associate counsel to the Subcommittee on the Study of Monopoly Power of the House Committee on the Judiciary. Apparently some members of the bar were concerned that the subcommittee might propose legislation that would limit the size of prosperous business entities. They lacked confidence in the judgment of Brooklyn's congressman, Emmanuel Celler, who was chairman of both the Judiciary Committee and the subcommittee that was popularly known as "the Celler Committee." The new associate counsel received the same pay as the general counsel and was expected to provide

---

1. 328 U.S. 781 (1946).

the minority members of the subcommittee with legal advice during any adversary situations that might develop. The general counsel for the subcommittee had been Edward Levi, a former lawyer in the Justice Department's Antitrust Division, who was also then viewed by some as a potential threat to the status quo. Based on Johnston's recommendation, Reed offered the job to me. I accepted, and we became good friends. (Later, when the Republicans took control of Congress in 1952, he invited me to serve as chief counsel of the Committee on the Judiciary. Having just begun my practice in a new three-person law firm, I did not accept that offer.)

13

The "Celler Committee"

AFTER I ARRIVED in Washington in April 1951 to start work in my new job, I spent a few days getting acquainted with members of the subcommittee and its staff. With a few exceptions, I found that the members of the two parties respected one another and cooperated on most of their endeavors. An exception was my meeting with a Texas congressman who forcefully advised me that I would be able to understand his views on an issue as the exact opposite of those expressed by Estes Kefauver, the senator from Tennessee, whom he described as "Senator Cow Fever." I also found that the staff was more cooperative than I had expected, particularly the chief clerk of the Judiciary Committee, an extremely intelligent woman named Bess Dick, who seemed to be the principal adviser to Chairman Celler. They all had nothing but praise for Edward Levi, who later earned a national reputation as a scholar at the University of Chicago and as the attorney general under President Ford.

Among the members of the eleven-person subcommittee were congressmen who would later become important leaders: Ken Keating of New York became a senator, Edward McCullough played an important role in the enactment of the Civil Rights Act of 1957, and Peter Rodino was the chairman of the committee during the Nixon impeachment proceedings. I remember Congressman Bryson of South Carolina remarking before an impending election that it was time to go home "and renew his promises." Chauncey Reed was one of a handful of Republicans who had retained his seat during the years when FDR helped elect an overwhelmingly Democratic Congress.

Under Levi's leadership, the subcommittee had conducted investigations of a few industries — cement, steel, and newsprint — and written reports about each but to the best of my knowledge had not proposed any new antitrust legislation. The new general counsel of the subcommittee who joined us shortly after I arrived was E. Ernest Goldstein. He was an excellent lawyer but had no special expertise in antitrust work. Although we both anticipated an adversarial relationship, we found ourselves cooperating far more often than disagreeing. The subcommittee was then completing hearings on the impact of the mobilization process on a competitive economy and considering a few amendments to the antitrust laws.

Bills that were not enacted included a proposal to make treble damages for antitrust violations discretionary rather than mandatory and an amendment to the Robinson-Patman Act. That statute generally prohibits price discrimination but allows a seller to defend a discriminatory low price if made in good faith to meet the equally low price of a competitor. The proposed amendment would have limited the scope of the defense to cases in which the price being met was a lawful price. During a hearing on that proposal, I was surprised at how little Congressman Wright Patman appeared to know about the statute bearing his name.

Another bill under consideration would have provided a uniform federal statute of limitations for private antitrust actions. At that time the timeliness of the federal claim was determined by state law, meaning that the law varied from state to state and that it was often unclear which state's law applied. Such actions are often brought by private parties in the wake of a successful government prosecution. Thus, after the government prevailed in litigation against movie producers, distributors, and affiliated exhibitors, several individual theater owners filed cases alleging that they had been injured by the same parties and the same practices that had been condemned in the government cases. The Clayton Act, which authorizes those private actions, provides that the plaintiff may rely on a judgment in favor of the United States as prima facie evidence of the violation proved in that case. The bill establishing the federal limitations period included a provision suspending application of the statute during the pendency of government litigation involving the same violation as the one that allegedly injured the plaintiff. I remember discussing with a member of the subcommittee the question whether at the end of the government case the entire four-year limitations period would apply or just the portion of that period that remained when the government action commenced. His reply — "we should let the judges answer that one" — supported my belief that legislators regard judges as partners in the lawmaking process. Sometimes it is wiser to defer deciding how best to answer a question of statutory interpretation until after post-enactment experience has shed relevant light on the issue.

The most publicized work of the subcommittee was its investigation of organized baseball. In 1922, Justice Oliver Wendell Holmes had written an opinion concluding that organized baseball was a local sport rather than a business engaged in interstate commerce. That opinion is the source of the so-called baseball antitrust exemption, which does not apply to other professional sports or other forms of entertainment. The central purpose of the hearings was to determine the status of that exemption.

The investigation gave me the opportunity to interview and examine in public hearings several well-known sports figures such as Ty Cobb, "Pee Wee" Reese, "Happy" Chandler (the former commissioner of Major League Baseball), and George Trautman (the executive in charge of the minor leagues). When I interviewed Branch Rickey, instead of learning details about his hiring of Jackie Robinson, I was surprised to learn that he thought that the most effective way to develop a winning team was, as he put it, "to keep 'em hungry" — don't overpay your players.

The hearings went on for several months and produced a truly massive record. Chairman Celler often paid a visit to the staff the first thing in the morning while the hearings were in process. His evaluation of the previous day's hearing seemed to depend on the amount of coverage that it had engendered in the press, rather than the significance of any particular evidentiary development. Those conversations have often reminded me that there is a vast difference between fact-finding by neutral scholars and factual investigations by legislative committees.

At that time all professional baseball players were required to sign a standard form contract containing a "reserve clause," which obligated the player to play only for one club or its assignee during his entire career. Most of the evidence related to the impact of the rules relating to the enforcement of that clause on the players — rules that probably would have violated the Sherman Act if the statute applied. The evidence covered other aspects of the game, including the development of "farm systems" — groups of minor league teams that were owned by and provided new talent for their major league owners. In his testimony, Trautman made a persuasive case for preserving the reserve clause because he believed it necessary to protect baseball clubs' farm systems — he argued that it served a valid purpose in organized baseball not required in other professional sports. Apart from that argument, however, I recall nothing in the record supporting a claim that baseball should be treated differently from any other professional sport.

The subcommittee concluded that organized baseball should not be granted a complete immunity from the antitrust laws. It noted that four bills had been introduced in Congress that would "give baseball and all other professional sports a complete and unlimited immunity from the antitrust laws. The requested exemption would extend to all professional sports enterprises and to all acts in the conduct of such enterprises.... Thus the sale of radio and television rights, the management of stadia, the purchase and sale of advertising, the concession industry, and many other business activities, as well as the aspects of baseball which are solely related to the promotion of competition on the playing field, would be immune and untouchable." Confining its attention to baseball, the subcommittee could not place its stamp of approval on every aspect of the game as then conducted. "The restrictions on transfer of baseball franchises, together with the enforcement of those restrictions, have prevented the composition of the major leagues from reflecting tremendous population shifts which have occurred in the United States since 1903."

Our hearings took place during an exceptionally exciting season. In 1951, Bobby Thompson hit his pennant-winning home run for the New York Giants in the third game of a playoff series with the Brooklyn Dodgers. The Giants then faced the New York Yankees in a "Subway Series." In an unwise attempt to obtain relevant evidence about the sport, Ernie Goldstein and I went to New York and attended the first game in the Series. To avoid any appearance of impropriety we made a point of buying our own tickets. Sitting behind third base, we saw Monte Erwin, the Giants' most valuable player in the game, successfully steal home. From there we also saw the chairman of our subcommittee seated behind home plate with a party of baseball executives.

14

The 1952 GOP Convention

I N 1952 THE Republican National Convention was held in Chicago. Chauncey Reed provided me with his ticket to attend an early session of the convention. At that time, the contest between Senator Robert A. Taft of Ohio and General Dwight D. Eisenhower to be the party's presidential candidate appeared to depend on which competing delegations from Georgia, Louisiana, and Texas would be seated. In each of those states the more progressive delegation supported Ike. The principal spokesmen for the liberals in Georgia and Louisiana were prominent lawyers who later became federal judges — Elbert Tuttle from Atlanta and John Minor Wisdom from New Orleans. As judges, they were to play a decisive role in the desegregation of public schools in the years following *Brown* v. *Board of Education* — a decision that recognized black citizens' right to equal access to public schools but was unfortunately followed by a timid command to take corrective action "with all deliberate speed."

At the time, the Republican Party was still the party of Abraham Lincoln, and the southern states were still controlled by a Democratic Party dominated by leaders who fervently believed in segregation. The contest between the rival GOP delegations was therefore of much greater historic significance than was apparent at the time. That contest was the subject of debate in a committee meeting that I attended, occupying what must have been a seat reserved for Reed in the front row on the speaker's platform. I was only a few feet away from Senator Everett Dirksen when he made a speech supporting the delegations favoring Taft. In that speech, he offended Tom Dewey, the Party's unsuccessful candidate in 1944 and 1948, who was seated in the first row of the audience. In response to Dirksen's accusation that "[y]ou led us down to defeat four years ago," Dewey rose and stalked out of the room.

The next day in a session of the full convention, Dirksen again made a similar speech. But this time, Dewey simply smiled and ignored the personal attack. Press accounts of the latter incident apparently credited Dewey's silent response as having lent support to the vote allowing the delegations favoring Eisenhower's candidacy to be seated. Neither those accounts nor the excellent description of the convention in Professor Anne Emanuel's biography of Elbert Tuttle made any reference to Dewey's quite different reaction to Dirksen's speech at the earlier session that I attended.

15

Rothschild, Stevens & Barry

I N MAY 1952, I left government service and returned to Poppenhusen. Around then, Ed Rothschild, Jack Barry, and I decided that it was time to form our own firm. We made an oral agreement to share expenses and revenues equally, to share office space with Ed's father, Isaac Rothschild, a distinguished sole practitioner who had previously served in the Illinois General Assembly, and to make capital contributions totaling $12,000 to get our new venture under way. I borrowed $4,000 from my brother Ernie to cover my share.

Our decision to form a new firm was motivated entirely by mutual respect and mutual friendships, and it produced great diversity: Jack was a Catholic from the West Side of Chicago whose father had also been a star football player at Notre Dame and had become a trial judge with the support of the Democratic machine; Ed was a Jew from a northern suburb, played varsity basketball in college, and supported Adlai Stevenson when he was elected governor of Illinois and later ran for president; and I was a Republican WASP from the South Side. And our sole employee—Gertrude Ambrose, who served as receptionist and telephone operator and took dictation from all three of us—was a member of the Baha'i Temple in Wilmette.

Sometime in May or June, we met with Judge Thompson—the managing partner of the Poppenhusen firm—to give him notice and to discuss the timing of our departure. Thinking that our early departure might create unnecessary problems for the firm, we expected him to ask us for a postponement. Instead, he told us to leave as promptly as possible; he acknowledged that Ed and Jack would soon have income-producing clients, but predicted that "Stevens would starve if he had to rely on his own ability to produce business." So we signed our lease, bought our furniture, hired Miss Ambrose, and mailed announcements that we would be open for business on July 1, 1952.

On that morning I received a phone call from Dick McLaren, who later became the assistant attorney general in charge of the Justice Department's Antitrust Division. Dick was then working with John Chadwell as counsel to the National Tea Company, the principal defendant in an antitrust action filed by the Dean Milk Company. Dean's suit, which also named all the other major dairies in Chicago as defendants, was a response to National's decision to replace Dean as its supplier of milk and other dairy products with the Hawthorn Melody Farms Dairy, a company owned by John F. Cuneo, who had previously acquired control of National and allegedly was responsible for its decision to change milk suppliers. Dick wanted to know if I would be interested in representing Hawthorn Melody, whose counsel was developing medical problems. That call was the origin of my relationship with the dairy as well as John Cuneo himself, the Cuneo Press, and the Bellanca Corporation.

All three of us received business from unexpected sources. Based on a judge's recommendation, Ed was retained by Bruce Mackey to sue Sears Roebuck for marketing a new tool and a novelty lamp that he had developed and tried to sell to them. Without compensating Bruce, Sears had marketed similar products. We filed an action on Mackey's behalf in federal court, asserting an antitrust claim as well as common law claims. When Judge Julius Hoffman dismissed the antitrust claim, our appeal raised a novel question about the appealability of his order that led to an argument in the United States Supreme Court. Ed made that argument and prevailed on the procedural point.[1] Even though the dismissal of the

---

1. *Sears, Roebuck & Co.* v. *Mackey*, 351 U.S. 427 (1956).

antitrust count was eventually upheld, we proceeded with discovery and the trial of the case.

During discovery I took the deposition of a senior officer of Sears who had been involved in negotiations with Mackey some years earlier. I remember being favorably impressed with our judicial system because it allowed an ordinary litigant to have access to relevant evidence even though it became necessary to inconvenience an important and busy executive. After several days of testimony, notwithstanding Sears's counsel's repeated statements that Sears had a firm "no-settlement policy" in comparable cases, they made us an offer that Mackey could not reasonably refuse.

Some months later, the senior partner in the law firm representing Sears asked me to come to his office to talk about a matter that he did not want to discuss on the telephone. During our visit he told me that the position of general counsel for Sears — a position that the then CEO of the company had previously occupied — either was, or soon would be, available, and wanted to know if I would accept an offer of that job. I don't know whether such an offer would actually have been made, but I do remember how easy it was to make it perfectly clear that I had no interest in leaving my partners.

In due course the litigation that prompted Dick McLaren's telephone call was settled on terms that included cash payments to the plaintiff by the major dairies and a consent decree. The decree essentially required the defendants to obey the Robinson-Patman Act. That aspect of the settlement was, however, more undesirable than anticipated because the dairies' sales practices frequently raised difficult questions under the statute's prohibition of price discrimination. Statutory violations might give rise to liability for damages, but the same conduct if prohibited by the decree could lead to contempt proceedings. For that reason, I thought the defendants would have been far wiser to increase their cash payments and eliminate the consent decree as part of their settlement. The risk of having an executive punished by the court for contempt is obviously more serious than the risk of paying damages for engaging in conduct that may violate the statute.

My work on the Dean Milk case led to other assignments in the dairy industry. The welfare and pension fund for milk wagon drivers was managed by trustees, half of whom were selected by the union and half by management; I became the lawyer representing the management trustees and learned some of the intricacies of the Employee Retirement Income Security Act of 1974, more commonly known as ERISA, which Congress enacted to provide minimum standards for private voluntary pension and health plans. And when the federal government challenged the discounts granted to their chain store customers by the Borden Company and the Bowman Dairy, L. Edward Hart Jr. — who represented Bowman and later joined our firm — hired me to work on the case, an assignment that ultimately led to my only oral argument in the Supreme Court. As I have said on many occasions, the most memorable aspect of that argument was my surprise at how close the justices are to the advocate.

Five different litigations are etched in my memory; each for a different reason. *Hearst Corporation* v. *Cuneo Press*[2] arose out of a fire at Cuneo's printing plant in Kokomo, Indiana, that destroyed tons of paper owned by Hearst and stored in the plant. Hearst sued, claiming that Cuneo's negligent employees were responsible for its loss. Our principal defense was that William Randolph Hearst, in a conversation with John Cuneo in New York City, had agreed to insure the paper against loss. I am convinced that the oral testimony of three witnesses determined the outcome rather than any of the legal arguments discussed in the appellate court opinions in the case.

The plaintiff began its case with expert testimony from a professional roofing company executive, whose description of the care that his firm took to avoid the risk of fire gave me the impression that every individual engaged in any repair work on a roof should have a graduate degree in chemical engineering. The expert was then followed by Dewey Pace, the former Cuneo employee who was on the roof when the fire started. He was wearing what was obviously a new suit that didn't quite fit him and

---

2. 291 F. 2d 724 (CA7 1961).

had recently had his hair cut by what must have been a self-taught barber. When his lawyer asked him to state his name, Dewey arose from his chair, saluted, and responded: "Dewey Pace, Sir." When asked about his training for repairing the roof, he explained that his coworkers, who had heated the tar on the ground and used a pulley to haul it up to the roof, had been told only to "get it good and hot." The contrast between the earlier testimony by the experts and the performance by the uneducated young man from the hills of Kentucky who seemed to view Hearst's lawyer as his superior officer was quite dramatic.

Our only expert witness was the former chief of the Kokomo Fire Department, who knew nothing about the incident that caused the fire, but was a decent and likeable individual. Cuneo employed him in a supervisory capacity at the time of the trial. I do not remember the details of his testimony, but it was clear that he favorably impressed the jury. I think they felt the same way about John Cuneo when he described his conversation with William Randolph Hearst.

My principal memory of the proceedings in *Bankers Life and Casualty Co. v. Bellanca Corp.*[3] is also unmentioned in the appellate court opinion affirming the trial court's judgment. I represented Bellanca, a corporation that had once been a respected manufacturer of aircraft but, after it came under the control of a man named Sydney Albert, had abandoned that business and become the vehicle through which he engaged in speculative ventures that had produced a huge tax loss for the corporation and a criminal conviction for him. One of those ventures included a contract to sell control of the Automatic Washer Company to Bankers Life and Casualty Company owned by John McArthur, a wealthy and well-known Chicago resident.

Bankers Life had refused to pay for 500,000 shares of Automatic Washer stock that Bellanca had delivered because the contract was void as a matter of federal law and because Bellanca was unable to deliver the entire amount due under the contract. Ultimately the District Court

---

3. 288 F. 2d 784 (CA7 1961).

concluded that, even though the contract could not be enforced, Bankers Life was liable for the reasonable value of the stock that it had acquired and retained. The most interesting aspect of the proceeding was when I took Mr. McArthur's pretrial deposition. He had a brother who was a well-known actor, and he gave me the impression that he was more interested in his performance as a witness than making sure that his answers were truthful. It seemed his answers were governed by his intent to state the exact opposite of the answer that he thought I wanted.

In the third litigation, *Olson Brothers, Inc.* v. *Englehart*,[4] I was a party and a witness rather than the trial lawyer. The issue in the case concerned the validity of the stock options that Otto Englehart and the other former directors of the Bellanca Corporation had voted to give themselves as compensation for their efforts to merge the corporation with a profitable business that could take advantage of Bellanca's huge tax loss. After I had testified, opposing counsel represented to the court that one of his witnesses, a man named Summers, knew that some of my testimony was false. Knowing that I had told the truth, our lawyer, Irving Morris, immediately called Summers to the witness stand. As Summers was being sworn in, he had a heart attack. I thought he died in the courtroom, but Irving tells me that his death occurred in the ambulance en route to the hospital. In either event, it was a dramatic event that may have helped convince the trial judge that our version of the events was correct.

The fourth proceedings that stand out in my memory are the discovery depositions in the massive private antitrust cases filed in the wake of the government antitrust suits against electrical equipment manufacturers in 1961. I was retained by Foster Wheeler Corporation, an engineering firm with its headquarters in Livingston, New Jersey, to represent the company in actions brought by public utilities against several manufacturers of condensers. In due course all the cases were settled, but I spent the better part of 1962 at the federal courthouse in New York City with five or six lawyers representing the defendants in those cases. The senior

---

4. 245 A. 2d 166 (Del. 1968).

among our group was Bradley Ward, a perfect gentleman and an out-standing Philadelphia lawyer, who represented Westinghouse. We all liked and respected Brad, recognizing that he had more experience than any of the rest of us. We frequently had lunch in a Chinese restaurant a short walk from the courthouse; in efforts to persuade Brad to eat with us, we repeatedly extolled the quality of their dishes. Brad finally agreed to join us. After studying the menu and hearing each of us order an exotic dish, Brad ordered a chicken sandwich on white bread.

Brad stayed in the same hotel and in a room on the same floor as the suite that he knew members of the Kennedy family regularly occupied. After spending the day at a deposition with the rest of us, he habitually returned to his hotel room, ordered a steak dinner from room service, and took a shower while the meal was being prepared. Wearing nothing but a towel, he relaxed during dinner. On one of those occasions — as he told us the next morning — after finishing his meal, he pushed his tray into the hall, his towel got caught on the doorknob, the door slammed shut, and he found himself locked out of his room stark naked. I will never forget his explanation of his concern that one of the Kennedys might get off the elevator when he pushed the button seeking emergency assistance. Fortunately, a bellboy with a master key arrived first.

The last litigation, *Twin City Sportservice, Inc.* v. *Charles O. Finley & Co.,*[5] began in 1967 and was not concluded until several years after I went on the bench. In 1967, Charlie Finley hired me to help him move the Athletics from Kansas City, where he had become unpopular, to another city without getting sued, as the Braves had been sued by Milwaukee when they moved to Atlanta. He was considering Dallas, Seattle, and Oakland. I helped him negotiate his contract with the Oakland–Alameda Coliseum and, more importantly, obtain approval from the owners of American League clubs for the move. I made the equivalent of a closing argument at a meeting of those owners in a Chicago hotel. One of my key points was that protecting the San Francisco Giants' monopoly

---

5. 676 F. 2d 1291 (CA9 1982).

position in the Bay Area from competition from an American League team in Oakland — whose home games could be scheduled when the Giants were away — would not justify a negative vote as a matter of law or business judgment. Based on my work on the Celler Committee, I thought it clear that protecting the Giants from competition in Oakland would clearly violate the antitrust laws. Charlie kindly credited my argument as having played an important role in our obtaining authorization for the move.

We were also successful in making the move without precipitating a suit by Kansas City. As soon as we arrived in Oakland, however, we were confronted with litigation brought by another plaintiff, SportService, the concession company that had performed services for the Athletics in both Kansas City and Philadelphia. The Coliseum had a concession contract with a local company covering all events in the stadium, and SportService had a long-term contract that owner Connie Mack had signed many years ago when the team was in Philadelphia and in financial difficulty. In exchange for a large loan, the A's had agreed that SportService would have the right to continue to act as the A's concessionaire, not only if the team moved elsewhere but also for all events held in the stadium to which the team moved. We challenged the enforceability of that contract and also counterclaimed that SportService was violating the antitrust laws. The case was tried before retired Justice Tom Clark, who was sitting as a district court judge. We lost on the common law issues but won on the antitrust counterclaim.

During the trial, I called the chief accounting officer of SportService to the stand and conducted what I thought was an effective cross-examination. The witness's son, a boy about eleven years old, was seated in the courtroom during that testimony. When the witness left the stand, Justice Clark told the boy to come to the front of the courtroom and told him that he had noticed how well behaved he was during his father's testimony. He added a comment to the effect that if all boys his age were as well behaved as he was, this would be a better country. That colloquy well illustrates the kind of person that Justice Clark was. He and I later became good friends.

Three additional former clients who helped us pay our bills bear mention: the Rahr Malting Company of Manitowoc, Wisconsin; Norman Niemi of Chicago; and the Wichita Eagle newspaper of Wichita, Kansas.

I defended Rahr in a private antitrust suit that was eventually settled and also when the Justice Department threatened to bring an antitrust action to prevent the company from selling its production facilities to Anheuser-Busch. It was during depositions in the former case that I first met and formed a friendship with Bob Bork, whose subsequent nomination to succeed Lewis Powell on the Supreme Court proved to be one of the most controversial nominations in Court history.

When Clarence Alt, the number two executive at Rahr, paid our fee for the preceding year, he always did so in a letter thanking us for the quality of our work. Thinking back on those letters, I am reminded that private practitioners typically have three occasions to celebrate their work: when they are first hired, when they produce a good result for their clients, and, most importantly, when they are paid.

Norman Niemi was a brilliant and engaging individual of limited formal education who operated two successful businesses. His Whizz Office Service provided temporary secretarial help to business offices and manual labor to construction companies. He was also the nationwide distributor of calculating equipment manufactured in England by the Bell Punch Company. He took me with him on a trip to London to negotiate a renewal of his distribution agreement, but our negotiations were unsuccessful and we ended up litigating the matter in Chicago. After we convinced the court that it had jurisdiction over the English company, we reached a settlement that required the defendant to pay a royalty to Norm on every machine sold in the United States during the ensuing ten-year period.

Before the case settled, I took the deposition of a Mr. Sheldon, the senior executive supervising the English company's American operations. He taught me a lesson that affected all of my future travels. When he arrived at my office on a cold winter day in Chicago, he was not wearing an overcoat. In response to my off-the-record questioning, he explained that, in his travels, virtually all of his time in big cities was spent either indoors or in heated cabs and that keeping track of an overcoat was simply not worth the effort. Shortly thereafter an expensive new woolen coat that I had recently acquired was either stolen or misplaced at a lunch at the Chicago Bar Association. Thanks to the advice that I had received from a learned adversary, I never replaced the coat or owned one at any time thereafter.

Finally, I must say a few words about my representation of the *Wichita Eagle* in 1966 when it entered into a consent decree with the United States. I was hired by Paul Kitch, a Wichita lawyer who had been a classmate of Edward Levi, who had suggested my name to Paul for the antitrust matter. After a settlement conference at the Justice Department, Paul asked Marcellus Murdock, the publisher of the *Eagle,* how he was returning to Wichita. Murdock, who was several years older, a few inches shorter, and much heavier than I, surprised me with his response. He was flying from Washington to Kansas City as a passenger on a commercial airline, but piloting himself on to Wichita in his own single-engine plane. I thought that if he was healthy enough to be a pilot, so was I.

Thereafter I began taking flying lessons at what was then the Oselka Airport near Three Oaks, Michigan, soloed at the Howell Airport south of Chicago, obtained my pilot's license, and bought a secondhand single-engine Cessna 172 for $10,500. My use of that plane — the serial number was 1688F, or "Cessna 88 foxtrot" — became an important part of my life for almost two decades.

16

Pro Bono Work

MOST GOOD LAWYERS devote a significant amount of time to public service work for which they receive no pay. Following in the footsteps of my older brother Jim, I became active in the work of the Chicago Bar Association. Jim had been a member of the Board of Managers in 1949 when Richard E. Daley was also on the board. They had both supported the change in the "whites only" policy that had characterized the Association's membership throughout its earlier history. Over the years, I served on several different committees, the most important of which was the Committee on Judicial Candidates.

That committee spent countless hours interviewing candidates for judicial office and evaluating their qualifications. Because we had an informal commitment from Mayor Daley that he would not allow the Democratic Party to support any candidate for judicial office if our committee found him "Not Qualified," our work had a positive impact on the quality of the judges in Cook County. My experience on that committee also fortified my firm conviction that popular elections are an exceptionally unwise method of choosing judges. Too many voters are influenced by factors that have no relevance to a potential judge's ability to do his or her job.

Other pro bono assignments taught me significant lessons. The first was my representation of Arthur La Frana in a state trial court after my former professor, Nathaniel Nathanson, had convinced the United States Supreme Court that the allegations in his post-conviction petition, if true, entitled him to relief. He had alleged that his confession to a murder committed in 1937 was the product of police brutality. He claimed that the police had handcuffed his wrists behind his back, tied a rope to the cuffs, and hung him over a door and beat him until he agreed to sign a confession.

At my first meeting with him in 1952 in his cell at the state prison in Joliet, he seemed comfortable talking about his case and did not hesitate to answer my questions. When I asked him about the pain caused by raising him off the ground, I had expected a response emphasizing the pressure on his wrists; instead, he described the excruciating pain in his upper arms and shoulders. That unexpected response convinced me that he was telling the truth, and gave me a special incentive to try to help him. In time we found medical records, a photograph, and witnesses corroborating his story. If I had had any doubt about Arthur's credibility, it would have been eliminated by the obvious falsity of the testimony of the police captain and two other police officers who tried to explain his injuries as having been caused by a fall during an attempted escape after being allowed to use the men's room.

Although the trial judge denied relief, the Illinois Supreme Court unanimously reversed, explaining, "A newspaper photograph taken shortly after the confession shows that his left cheek and right eye were swollen, and that there was a cut below his right eye and on his lower lip. The record of his physical examination when he was released from police custody and placed in the county jail on January 11, a week after the confession, shows that he had a black eye and abrasions on both wrists. The county physician who then examined him, and who had been examining numerous prisoners every day for twenty-two years, testified that the injuries to defendant's wrists could have been caused by hanging him over the door, and could not have been caused by the normal use of handcuffs."[1] That case taught me that there really are occasions when

---

1. *People* v. *La Frana*, 122 N. E. 2d 583 (Ill. 1954).

police officers engage in brutal conduct and that they sometimes testify falsely to conceal their wrongdoing.

Another pro bono assignment demonstrated that even the most confident expression of a legal opinion by a good lawyer may be dead wrong. One day, Judge Julius Miner, who was then a state court judge, asked me to take part in a test case to establish the constitutionality of an Illinois statute that he had drafted. The statute imposed a sixty-day "cooling off" period that required judges to postpone the granting of a divorce even if both parties wanted immediate relief. Ben Davis, who was an excellent divorce lawyer but had no experience in constitutional matters, had agreed to have one of his clients file the test case if another lawyer would take responsibility for arguing the constitutional issues. I agreed to participate in the case but only on the understanding that I would do my best to convince the state supreme court that the new statute violated the state constitution. The judge agreed, telling me that an outstanding lawyer — Bert Jenner, a partner at Poppenhusen — had assured him that the statute was constitutional. In due course a unanimous Illinois Supreme Court agreed with my contention that the statute violated the plaintiffs' right to a speedy trial under the Illinois constitution.[2]

Another pro bono assignment allowed me to participate in meetings with some of the country's best lawyers. In June 1953, the University of Michigan Law School, under the leadership of Professor S. Chesterfield Oppenheim ("Oppie"), conducted a three-day symposium on the status of the antitrust laws. I was one of the participants in that conference, which led to the appointment by Attorney General Herbert Brownell on August 27, 1953, of a National Committee to Study the Antitrust Laws. I was one of the sixty-one lawyers whom — presumably on Oppie's recommendation — Brownell appointed. The mission of the committee, as announced by President Eisenhower, was "to prepare the way for modernizing and strengthening our laws to preserve American free enterprise against monopoly and unfair competition." Well over a year later, after

---

2. *People ex rel. Christiansen* v. *Connell,* 118 N. E. 2d 262 (Ill. 1954).

numerous meetings with subcommittees and the full committee, on March 31, 1955, the committee issued its comprehensive report, which included several dissenting statements.

The committee was divided into subcommittees, each of which prepared a draft report on one or two subjects, with the committee as a whole voting to endorse certain basic propositions. My subcommittee addressed questions concerning exemptions from the antitrust laws and the interplay between federal regulatory statutes and the antitrust laws. Instead of recommending a single rule applicable to all cases in that area of the law, we concluded, in essence, that each regulatory statute was sufficiently different from the others to require statute-specific analysis. Regulations preventing motor carriers from charging discriminatory rates protected members of the industry from too much competition while some rate regulation in other industries was designed to protect consumers from being overcharged, yet many members of the public assume that all government regulation of rates is motivated by the same objective. In our meetings, we sometimes voted on basic questions, but in the end I think most of the committee's final report was drafted by Bob Bicks, a young lawyer in the Justice Department's Antitrust Division, who later became the head of the division. Because our report was one of the first attempts to summarize the existing rules of antitrust law, I believe the committee made a positive contribution to the law. That conclusion is supported by the fact that about fifteen years later the American Bar Association appointed a second committee to update the original report. The chairman of that committee was Dick McLaren, whose telephone call had led to my first significant profitable work in private practice.

17

Teaching Antitrust Law

I N 1952, JIM Rahl, the Northwestern professor who had taught antitrust when I was a student, took a leave of absence, which led to my
teaching the antitrust course that year. Though I enjoyed leading the class
discussions, I found grading exams difficult and frustrating. Too often
students who had performed well in class made uncharacteristic and sur-
prising errors responding to exam questions. It is almost impossible for a
teacher to administer perfect justice when ranking the standings of his or
her students.

A few years later, I was offered a similar opportunity at the University
of Chicago Law School. When Dean Edward Levi took on additional
responsibilities in university administration, he asked me to substitute
for him in the course "Competition and Monopoly" taught by two professors, an economist and a lawyer. I happily accepted and received an
invaluable education from Aaron Director, who played a key role in the
development of the Chicago school of economics.

Aaron was one of two exceptional scholars in that subject at the University of Chicago; the other, Milton Friedman, was married to Aaron's
sister, the economist Rose Director Friedman, whom I heard was even
more brilliant than either her brother or her husband. Among the pre-
cepts I learned from Aaron is that an agreement among competitors to fix

prices will not succeed unless they are able to limit output as well. My exposure to Aaron's views has made me skeptical about the wisdom of legislation imposing minimum wage levels on an otherwise free labor economy. For just as private conspirators must curtail supply to boost the market price for goods, it would seem that a government rule requiring employers to pay higher wages to their employees would necessarily have an adverse impact on the number of jobs available in the market.

In the following year Aaron and I co-taught a class about patents and antitrust policy; in that course I learned about the immense differences in value among different patents. I also increased my understanding of so-called tying arrangements — conditioning the sale of one item on an agreement to purchase another. A requirement that the licensee of a patent on a printing press use only paper purchased from the patentee is an example. Although such arrangements may violate both the patent laws and the antitrust laws because they are thought to extend the scope of the monopoly granted by a patent, courts sometimes fail to recognize that tying arrangements can also be used as methods of providing bargains to consumers. Whether a steel manufacturer's offer to provide both prefabricated steel and financing to the developer of a housing project is an example of such a bargain, on the one hand, or an abuse of monopoly power, on the other, is the kind of question we addressed in class and that the Supreme Court has answered differently at two stages of the same litigation — compare Justice Black's opinion in *Fortner Enterprises, Inc. v. United States Steel Corp.*[1] with my opinion in *United States Steel Corp. v. Fortner Enterprises, Inc.*[2] I cannot recall the details of Aaron's comments on such cases, but I do recall his meticulous attention to the facts before he expressed his conclusion.

Though I enjoyed my teaching assignments and learned a great deal from them, I never regretted my decision to rely on private practice as my principal source of income. My career choice was, however, tested in a

1. 394 U.S. 495 (1969).
2. 429 U.S. 610 (1977).

different way in early 1961, when Byron White invited me to come to Washington to discuss a job at the Justice Department, where, as the new deputy attorney general, he was restaffing for the new administration. I had always considered the position of assistant attorney general in charge of the Antitrust Division as one of the few government jobs that I would have liked, and, as luck would have it, Byron was then looking for a qualified lawyer for that job.

When I met with him, he told me that Ed Levi had suggested my name. The facts that Byron and I had met at Pearl Harbor during the war; that Sandy Sims, who had sold me one-half of his Terraplane, was a mutual friend; and that we had both been law clerks paved the way to a memorable and pleasant day. Those same facts may also help to explain why I believe my later friendship with Byron was probably closer than my friendship with any other justice. In the afternoon, he took me into Bobby Kennedy's most impressive office for an interview, which turned out to be a flop. I don't think either one of us was favorably impressed with the other. I believe that despite Byron's favorable recommendation, Bobby made the decision to appoint a Minnesota lawyer to the job. I am fairly sure that I would have declined the offer even if it had been made, but the incident came to mind when I later decided to leave private practice for a position with the federal government.

18

People v. Isaacs

THEODORE J. ISAACS, a Chicago lawyer, was the director of the Illinois Department of Revenue from 1961 to 1963. In 1964, an indictment charged that he had violated a state statute by arranging for a corporation that he controlled to provide printing services and supplies to the state. In 1965, the trial judge dismissed the charges against Isaacs, and the state appealed directly to the Illinois Supreme Court. The case was pending before the court for about thirteen months between February 1966 and March 1967. The court then exonerated Isaacs in what appeared to be a unanimous opinion written by Justice Ray Klingbiel. In 1969, a member of the public named Sherman Skolnick challenged the integrity of that judgment.

As my friend Ken Manaster later described Skolnick, he was "the vocal and eccentric leader of a group called the Citizen's Committee to Clean Up the Courts." Although not a lawyer, Skolnick filed numerous lawsuits and made countless public statements accusing judges and other public officials of all sorts of wrongdoing. In early 1969, his group's search of public records uncovered the fact that two of Klingbiel's grandchildren owned one hundred shares of stock in the Civic Center Bank & Trust Company. That fact was presumably the basis for several accusations that Skolnick made in interviews with reporters. One of them telephoned Klingbiel, who, according to the reporter, said he had paid for his grandchildren's shares.

On June 4, 1969, while he was in Springfield to testify in an investigation of organized crime, Skolnick distributed a "fact sheet" listing more stockholders of the bank and noting that Klingbiel was a stockholder when he had authored the court's opinion in *People* v. *Isaacs* and that Isaacs was then the secretary and general counsel of the bank. Skolnick also talked to two reporters whose further investigations generated news stories in which Klingbiel's stock ownership was described as a campaign contribution.

On Wednesday, June 11, 1969, Skolnick filed a written motion requesting the Illinois Supreme Court to revisit its judgment in *People* v. *Isaacs*. The motion alleged that Klingbiel's hundred shares had been given to him by an intermediary (Robert Perbohner) who had received the stock from Isaacs. The motion also added the charge that Roy Solfisburg, the chief justice of the court, was acting as an attorney for the bank. Instead of acting on Skolnick's motion, on Tuesday, June 17, the members of the court decided to create a special commission, including the incoming presidents of the Chicago Bar Association and the Illinois Bar Association, to investigate the integrity of the judgment. The court's order gave the commission the power to subpoena witnesses and documents and to conduct private or public hearings. It also directed the commission "to proceed expeditiously and to file its report on or before August 1, 1969."

On the evening of Thursday, June 19, Henry Pitts, the newly elected president of the Illinois Bar Association, called me at home and asked me to serve as counsel to the commission. I accepted and the next morning on the way to work I bumped into Jerry Torshen on La Salle Street. Because Jerry and I had opposed each other in an earlier case, I knew that he was an excellent lawyer, so I asked him if he would be willing to help. Without any more knowledge of what our work would entail than I had, he readily agreed. We were both fully aware that we would not be paid for our labors, and that the press and general public had already decided that an investigation of the court by practicing lawyers would be a "whitewash." Neither of us, however, had any idea of the magnitude of our task nor of the significance of the court-imposed deadline that allowed us less than six weeks to complete it.

The five members of the commission — all of whom also worked without any compensation — first obtained from the court the authority to expend funds for depositions and for a private investigator. They also persuaded each of four leading law firms and a leading accounting firm to assign an associate to help us with our work. (The lawyers were Ken Manaster, Bill McNally, Nick Sachs, and Joe Coughlin; the accountant was Jim Nussbaum.) To preserve their ability to analyze the evidence impartially, the commissioners decided that they would not personally participate in the investigation unless and until we made a decision to hold public hearings; if we did so decide, they would only consider evidence in the public record.

I was not initially convinced that Skolnick's charges were sufficiently trustworthy to justify public hearings probing into the court's decision-making procedures, so I first decided to take depositions of every member of the Illinois Supreme Court in my office and also to depose Skolnick himself to find out the evidentiary basis for his charges. I also directed our accountant, Jim Nussbaum, and two of our young lawyers (Ken Manaster and Bill McNally) to examine relevant records at the bank and to interview bank officers and employees familiar with its issuance of stock. Not until a week or so had passed did we decide that public hearings were justified and would be appropriate. In the meantime, our delay had magnified the press's and public's assumption that we were engaged in a "whitewash."

Our attempts to get evidence from Skolnick turned out to be counterproductive. He first refused to testify at a deposition unless I provided him with a guarantee of his safety, which I had no power to do. When he steadfastly refused to describe his sources, Jerry Torshen obtained an order holding him in contempt and committing him to the county jail. He ultimately agreed to answer my questions, but his answers were of no help to us. In the meantime, the press thoroughly roasted us; in addition to whitewashing, we were now seen to be punishing the man responsible for the investigation. It was at about that point that Nick Sachs suggested that we should follow the advice: "If you shoot at the king, don't miss." Only after we announced our decision to hold public hearings did the press have any kind words for us.

Some of the evidence we obtained during our investigation was damning and some was completely exculpatory. For example, we found no evidence to support Skolnick's charge that Chief Justice Solfisburg had ever served as an attorney for the bank. To my surprise, however, we learned that the initial vote of the justices had been against Isaacs. We also learned that the court's customary practice was to assign opinions in advance of argument in a predetermined order; following that practice, the *Isaacs* opinion had originally been assigned to Justice Underwood. He wrote a draft that would have reversed the lower court's dismissal order. Justice Schaefer joined that draft, but no other justice did; hence, the case was reassigned. Oddly, instead of assigning the case to the next justice in the predetermined order, the assignment went to Justice Klingbiel. No one, including Justice Byron House, who would have received the assignment if customary procedures had been followed, could explain why Klingbiel received the assignment. Although odd and potentially incriminating, we concluded that the assignment was probably the result of Justice House's routine practice of trading with other justices during hunting season.

At Justice Schaefer's deposition, I was surprised to learn that both he and Justice Underwood had refused to join the new majority opinion written by Klingbiel and that both of them had authored dissents, which were not published — in other words, what appeared to be a unanimous opinion was not. Neither the fact that they had dissented nor their reasons for refusing to join Klingbiel's opinion were known to the public. In their depositions, both correctly noted that on most appellate courts, including the United States Supreme Court, it had long been a practice to limit the publication of written dissents to exceptional cases, a practice believed to enhance the court's reputation for impartially following the law, whereas frequent dissents tend to undermine the public's confidence in their judges. I have never agreed with that view. I then thought, and still think, the public is entitled to know how every judge votes in an argued case. During my entire career on the bench, both on the court of appeals and on the Supreme Court, I followed the practice of either joining a colleague's opinion or writing my own explanation for my vote.

The facts uncovered by our investigation can be briefly stated as follows. The charter of the Civic Center Bank & Trust Company was issued on January 21, 1966, a few weeks after the state filed its appeal to the Illinois Supreme Court in the Isaacs case. The new bank held 15,225 shares of unissued stock as collateral for a $304,500 loan to Isaacs, an officer of the bank. Those shares were to be used to "foster new accounts" but, as the evidence showed, they were issued to persons selected by Isaacs. One of those persons was a member of the commerce commission, who had given one hundred shares to Justice Klingbiel. The list also identified seven hundred shares in the name of "Trust 931," with a parenthetical reference to Roy J. Solfisburg Jr. Before the hearings began, Solfisburg had publicly acknowledged that he had owned stock in the bank, but he never adequately explained why he had placed his shares in a trust for his grandchildren — a trust that lacked any other assets. The inference that he had created the trust to avoid public disclosure of his acquisition of the stock was inescapable. One of the most dramatic incidents during the public hearings occurred when I asked him about Trust 931. As he paused before answering, he reached for a drink of water; while attempting to fill his glass, he poured the water into his lap.

After the hearings ended, we prepared a summary of the evidence and presented oral arguments to the commission. We made it clear that whether or not the justices' ownership of the bank stock influenced their votes in the Isaacs case, their conduct gave rise to an unacceptable appearance of impropriety. As lawyers for the commission, we did not consider it within our role to recommend that the justices resign. Nevertheless, four of the five members of the commission wrote an opinion strongly urging Justices Solfisburg and Klingbiel to do so. After initially refusing, each did resign shortly thereafter.

The Illinois Supreme Court, however, did not vacate its judgment in the Isaacs case. Even though members of my staff had spent countless uncompensated hours, I cannot recall receiving any acknowledgment, let alone thanks, from the court or any of its members. I was, however, elected to be second vice president of the Chicago Bar Association in 1970 and presumably would have become the president of that organization two years later had I not been appointed to the court of appeals. Personally, the most enduring thing to come of the hearings was my lifelong friendship with Ken Manaster, who later wrote a book, *Illinois Justice,* recounting this fascinating episode in the state's history.

19

The Court of Appeals

T HE CONSTITUTION PROVIDES that the president shall appoint
federal judges with the advice and consent of the Senate. For most
of our history, the requirement of senatorial consent has, in effect, given
senators the power to select federal judges in their states. Sometimes that
power has been a source of patronage; sometimes senators make a conscientious effort to find the most qualified lawyers to serve on the bench.

While he was an Illinois Republican senator, Charles Percy made a
serious effort to improve the quality of the federal judiciary in Chicago. A
group of lawyers whom he respected gave him advice about the qualities
of potential judges recommended by others and who suggested the names
of other potential nominees. Among the excellent judges that Percy supported were Phil Tone and Bill Bauer, who both served on the district
court in Chicago and later the Court of Appeals for the Seventh Circuit;
Bob Sprecher, who served on the Seventh Circuit; and Milt Shadur and
Preston Marshall, whom Chuck selected for the district court even
though both were Democrats.

Although we had been friends and classmates at the University of
Chicago, our meeting in Chuck's hotel room on a weekend in 1970 was
probably the first time we had seen each other in well over twenty years. I
had assumed that the purpose of our meeting was to solicit my views

about the qualification of potential nominees to fill two vacancies on the district court and one vacancy on the Seventh Circuit, so I was surprised when, after discussing other candidates, Chuck asked me if I would be interested in going on the Seventh Circuit. My initial reaction was negative because I was extremely happy at Rothschild, Stevens and Barry, and we could foresee a fairly prompt dramatic increase in our firm's earnings. Over the next few days, Chuck advanced three arguments: a court of appeals judgeship was an important and rewarding position; it might lead to an appointment to the Supreme Court; and the opportunity might not be available later. I am truly indebted to his wise counsel, because I have never regretted my decision to accept the opportunity to become a judge.

During the interval between his submission of my name to the Justice Department and the Senate's ultimate confirmation of my nomination, however, I learned that publicity about one's possible transition from the bar to the bench has the unintended consequence of persuading prospective litigants to go elsewhere for their legal representation. I also learned that although I could continue to fly my Cessna, I would longer be able to afford our summer home in Lakeside, Michigan. Interestingly, Bob Sprecher, who was Chuck's excellent choice to fill the next vacancy on the Seventh Circuit, also found it necessary to sell his summer home when he became a federal judge.

A few days after Bob was sworn in, I learned that Harry Blackmun was going to deliver the commencement address at his daughter's graduation from DePauw College in Greensboro, Indiana, on the following Saturday. Not having met any other living justice of the Supreme Court except Byron White, the chance to meet Harry on that occasion — coupled with the fact that Greensboro was within easy flying distance from Howell Airport, where I kept my Cessna — prompted my choice of a new destination for my weekend hobby. I made the flight without difficulty and hitched a ride from the airport to the campus. After Harry's remarks, I introduced myself, explaining that I had recently been appointed to the Seventh Circuit. Harry was characteristically gracious —

so gracious, in fact, that he wrote a nice letter to Bob Sprecher welcoming him to the federal judiciary. Because Harry was always so meticulous in his work at the Court, years later I enjoyed telling my colleagues that Harry had made at least one mistake.

Because my new colleagues already occupied all of the offices on the twenty-seventh floor of the Dirksen Building, where the Seventh Circuit's courtroom was located, I was assigned chambers on the northeast corner of the 26th floor, immediately below the chief judge. With a beautiful view of Lake Michigan to the east, I had one of the most desirable offices in Chicago. My law clerk, Gary Senner, and my secretary, Florence Lundquist, had both worked with me at our law firm, so the transition to a new job went smoothly. One problem that neither of my former partners nor I had foreseen was the need to define my interest in future fees to be paid for work that had begun before my departure. Over eighteen years of practice, we had never prepared a written partnership agreement, but we hired an accountant to define the terms of our separation.

I well remember the three principal benefits associated with my change in occupation: no more time sheets (records of the hours spent working for paying clients); no more work-related travel; and no more long-distance telephone calls during late hours of the night or during dinner. I now had much more control over when and where I would do my work than I had had as a lawyer. And just as the practice of law is a continuing learning experience — as clients keep raising new questions — so does the work of an appellate judge require constant study of previously unfamiliar areas of the law.

When I joined the Seventh Circuit, I was only the second of the seven active judges to have been appointed by a Republican president. My immediate senior on the court, Wilbur Pell, a former president of the Indiana state Bar Association, was the other. (Bob Sprecher soon became the third.) The five judges appointed by Democratic presidents were Chief Judge Luther Swygert, a former prosecutor from Hammond, Indiana, whose Notre Dame classmates called him "Mike" to avoid referring to him by his Protestant first name; Tom Fairchild, who had run an unsuccessful senate campaign against Joe McCarthy before he served on the Wisconsin Supreme Court; Otto Kerner, who had been governor of Illinois and was subsequently convicted of federal offenses (along with Theodore Isaacs, the subject of the chapter on *People* v. *Isaacs*); Walter Cummings, whom I had known and respected as a Chicago lawyer and who had served briefly as the solicitor general of the United States; and Roger Kiley, whom I had known for many years as a good friend of my former partners.

Luther Swygert and Roger Kiley were the other two judges on the panel on my first day of oral argument. We shook hands while we were putting on our robes. I remember thinking that our political backgrounds were entirely irrelevant to our jobs and that all three of us shared an interest in correctly deciding the cases to be argued. Never in the ensuing years on that court did I detect any partisan motivation in the work of any of my colleagues.

After retiring from active service, federal judges may attain senior status, meaning that they remain eligible for judicial service on a voluntary basis. John Hastings was the most respected senior judge on the Seventh Circuit in the early 1970s. We had a long conversation about my new job not long after I arrived. Unlike most of his colleagues, he always wrote the first draft of his opinions and paid particular attention to the statement of facts. "If you do a good job stating the facts," he advised, "the rest of the opinion will write itself." In that conversation, John told me that, as the senior member of the panel in a high-profile case involving a Catholic priest named James Groppi, he had assigned the opinion to Wilbur Pell because "people in Washington might notice the case." Presumably he was referring to people who might participate in the selection of the nominee for the next vacancy on the Supreme Court because it was the kind of case in which the author of the majority opinion would be favorably viewed by officials in the Nixon administration and the author of a dissent would be condemned by the "silent majority" that had favored the impeachment of Chief Justice Earl Warren.

The case arose out of a protest against welfare budget cuts in which

Father Groppi had led a march of about 2,000 people onto the floor of the state assembly while the Wisconsin legislature was in session. The protesters occupied the chamber for about eleven hours. Two days later the assembly passed a resolution holding Groppi in contempt and sentencing him to prison. He had not received any notice or been given any opportunity to participate in the contempt proceedings.

Groppi's lawyers filed habeas corpus petitions in both the Wisconsin state court and the federal district court. The Wisconsin Supreme Court had unanimously denied relief, explaining that there was no need for a separate hearing because the entire legislature had been present when the contempt occurred. The federal district judge had granted relief, but a three-judge panel of the Seventh Circuit, over which Judge Hastings presided, reversed that decision. Then, shortly after my conversation with John, Father Groppi filed a petition for rehearing en banc — a petition asking all of the active judges on the court to rehear the case — which Swygert, Kiley, Kerner, and I voted to grant. Because he was a senior judge, John Hastings was not eligible to vote on the petition and Tom Fairchild was disqualified; rehearing was therefore granted by a four-to-three vote. As a member of the original panel, however, John was permitted to participate in the en banc reargument, and Otto Kerner was persuaded to join the majority, resulting in a five-to-three decision to uphold the contempt finding. I wrote a dissent, which Swygert and Kiley joined.

That was not only my first published opinion, but it also may well have been the most important opinion that I wrote on the Seventh Circuit because it put an end to speculation (engendered by my conversations with Chuck) that I might one day be considered for a vacancy on the United States Supreme Court. That possibility never crossed my mind during the ensuing four years.

Most new federal judges are invited to attend what might be called a school for newly appointed judges where academics and senior members of the judiciary teach them about some aspects of their new positions. For unknown reasons, my participation in those sessions did not occur until March 1973, over two years after I had been sworn in. I had been looking forward to those sessions in Washington because, among other reasons, they would give me the opportunity to meet with Chief Justice Warren Burger, who had authored the unanimous opinion reversing the Seventh Circuit's decision in the Groppi case. When I did meet him at one of the social sessions, I mentioned that I had written the dissent from the Seventh Circuit's en banc decision that the Court had reversed, but I am not sure he remembered that he had authored the Court's opinion. If he had read my dissent, it clearly had not made an indelible impression on him.

Judge Alfred P. Murrah — the judge whose name adorned the federal building in Oklahoma City that Timothy McVeigh bombed in 1995 — presided at a session teaching new judges how to make best use of their law clerks. He endorsed a dress code requiring the clerk to wear a coat and tie — advice that reflected an assumption that most, if not all, law clerks would be male. It was advice that I did not follow. The next clerk that I hired, Steve Goldman, a graduate of Michigan Law School, had worn a coat and tie and had just had his hair cut when I interviewed him. But when he reported for duty after a year at Oxford, I did not recognize the casually dressed man with a head full of long and curly hair. Although the dramatic change in his appearance would surely have prompted a lecture from Judge Murrah, I did not consider withdrawing my job offer. Instead, after learning about his hostility to the Vietnam War, I told him that I would not require him to work on any cases upholding convictions of draftees who refused to report for service in the army. He turned out to be an excellent clerk. Sadly, after a successful career as an employment lawyer and law professor at Catholic University in Washington, D.C., he passed away in 2014. He is one of only two of my former clerks who is no longer living. The other is Matthew Verschelden, who worked with me in the 1981 term at the Court.

While Steve was clerking for me, I dissented in a case in which the majority held that a high school student "had a constitutional right to wear his hair at any length."[1] Needless to say, Steve was not a fan of my

---

1. *Arnold* v. *Carpenter*, 459 F. 2d 939, 944 (CA7 1972).

dissent. Because the dress code excused a child from compliance upon the request of his parents, I thought the child had "no enforceable right to remain unshorn or unwashed without parental consent." Although I believed then, as I do now, that the word "liberty" in the Due Process Clause of the Fourteenth Amendment has substantive content, I was not persuaded that it prevented adults from instructing the young about aspects of "social behavior that the British broadly describe as 'manners.'"

Nor, in my opinion, does the Constitution give a husband the right to stay in the same room with his wife while she is giving birth in a hospital. Unlike my good friend and respected colleague, Bob Sprecher, who dissented in the case, I concluded in *Fitzgerald* v. *Porter Memorial Hospital* [2] that a county hospital's regulation excluding the father from the delivery room during his child's birth did not deprive either parent of "liberty" protected by the Fourteenth Amendment. The plaintiffs were married couples who had trained in the Lamaze method of childbirth, which teaches husbands to play a constructive role in the delivery of their children. As Bob pointed out in his dissent, the record contained uncontradicted expert evidence establishing that the Lamaze method had been used in over 45,000 cases and that qualified experts had concluded that the presence of the husband had beneficial consequences. At the time we were working on the case, my law clerk Jim Whitehead and his pregnant wife were taking a Lamaze class.

Until writing that last sentence, the possibility that Jim's Lamaze studies should have required me to recuse myself from participating in the decision never occurred to me, perhaps because Jim shared my view. Even though the hospital rule struck us as unwise, the Constitution did not give judges the authority to second-guess the medical professionals who had adopted the rule.

I began my opinion by rejecting the argument that the claim should be analyzed as an assertion of a constitutional right to privacy. The relevant Supreme Court precedents did "not deal with the individual's

___
2. 523 F. 2d 716 (CA7 1975).

interest in unwarranted public attention, comment, or exploitation. They deal[t], rather, with the individual's right to make certain unusually important decisions that will affect his own, or his family's destiny. The Court has referred to such decisions as implicating 'basic values,' as being 'fundamental,' and as being dignified by history and tradition."

Although the birth of a child is an event of unequaled importance in the lives of most married couples, "deciding the question whether the child shall be born is of a different magnitude from deciding where, by whom, and by what method he or she shall be delivered." The test that I applied in that case protects a person's right to marry another person regardless of the race or the sex of the chosen spouse; it also protects a pregnant woman's right to decide whether to bear her child. That the Court might decades later extend substantive due process to protect an individual right to bear arms never crossed my mind.

Sam Clapper, a graduate of the University of Chicago Law School who has practiced law in Somerset, Pennsylvania, for the past forty-five years, was my second law clerk and the only one who was ever a passenger in 88 Foxtrot. We had a nice sightseeing flight along the shore of Lake Michigan one Saturday. After I had completed the draft of a dissent that I thought might persuade the third member of a panel to change his vote, I asked Sam to expedite his suggested edits because, as I explained to him, there was still time to change the result. He wasted no time in complying, but only after pointing out that speed might not be all that important because none of my earlier dissents had ever picked up a vote.

The more memorable case on which Sam worked, *Illinois State Employees Union* v. *Lewis*,[3] involved the constitutionality of political patronage. The newly elected Democratic secretary of the state of Illinois had discharged all of his Republican predecessor's employees who refused to switch their allegiance to the Democratic Party, and a group of them had filed suit claiming a violation of their First Amendment rights. When

---

3. 473 F. 2d 561 (CA7 1972).

I first looked at the case I thought the claim was frivolous because patronage had played such an important role in local government since the time of Andrew Jackson. After reading several Supreme Court opinions and reflecting on the issue, however, it dawned on me that the use of government power — here, the power to hire or fire employees — for the sole purpose of providing a benefit to one political party is flatly contrary to the basic duty to govern impartially. Of course, if the employee's party affiliation is relevant to his or her job, it could provide a legitimate basis for an employment decision, but that would not be true for elevator operators, maintenance workers, pilots, typists, mechanics, or other workers who have nothing to do with shaping or implementing policy.

The two other judges on the panel that heard the case were Roger Kiley and William Campbell, the chief judge of the district court in Chicago. (Occasionally the courts of appeals invite either a circuit judge from another circuit or a district judge in the same circuit to participate in cases.) Both of them had been beneficiaries of the patronage system earlier in their careers, and they shared my initial reaction to the case. After the oral argument I explained my first impression at some length before discussing why I had later concluded that the system violated the duty to govern impartially and the plaintiff's First Amendment rights.

Roger apparently misunderstood my remarks during our conference because, when he sent his letter assigning opinions to Bill and me, he incorrectly assigned what he thought would be a unanimous opinion in the patronage case to me. Rather than questioning the assignment, I decided to write out my views. Much to my surprise, my draft persuaded Bill not only to change his vote but to write a separate opinion explaining his own views. Roger, however, adhered to his position and wrote a dissent. When we handed down our judgment on September 18, 1972, I announced an opinion in which no other judge joined. I believe it may have been the first appellate opinion holding that the patronage system is unconstitutional.

Sam left Chicago to start his job in Somerset before I announced our opinion. Because of the importance of the case, he asked Florence, our secretary, to send him clippings of the anticipated comments in the press. A few days later, not having heard a word from Florence, he telephoned to remind her of her promise and expressed surprise when she told him that the press had not even mentioned the decision. My only explanation for that silence is that the Chicago papers then paid a great deal of attention to the work of the federal trial courts but paid little attention to the work of the Seventh Circuit.

The Supreme Court later reviewed the constitutionality of patronage dismissals in several cases, and Justices Sandra O'Connor and Anthony Kennedy helped drive the nails into the coffin in which that unhappy chapter in our history is now buried. In that debate Justice Antonin Scalia first explained an aspect of his jurisprudence that I have often criticized.

He had this to say about patronage: "Thus, when a practice not expressly prohibited by the text of the Bill of Rights bears the endorsement of a long tradition of open, widespread, and unchallenged use that dates back to the beginning of the Republic, we have no proper basis for striking it down."

Although the practice of gerrymandering electoral districts also dates back to the beginning of our republic, that comment would not provide a justification for its preservation because it has been challenged so frequently. What is interesting about gerrymandering, however, is the fact that notwithstanding the complete absence of any argument claiming that the practice serves the public interest, it continues to have an important influence on our government. I first addressed that subject in my second year as a circuit judge in litigation that had been initiated by Sherman Skolnick, the same man who had spurred the inquiry into *People* v. *Isaacs.* In *Cousins* v. *City Council of the City of Chicago,*[4] Tom Fairchild, Walter Cummings, and I reviewed a district court decision dismissing a claim that the defendants had drawn the boundaries of Chicago's fifty legislative districts, or "wards," in violation of the Constitution.

---

4. 466 F. 2d 830 (CA7 1972).

While the majority assumed that a political gerrymandering claim raised a non-justiciable question, it held that the evidence supporting the claim that some of the ward boundaries unnecessarily packed black voters into majority black districts, thus lessening the likelihood that those voters could elect more aldermen, required further proceedings in the district court. After considering alternative approaches to the evaluation of gerrymandering claims, I wrote a long dissent because I disagreed with the view that a stricter standard should be applied to discrimination against racial groups than to discrimination against other identifiable groups of voters: "The mere fact that a number of citizens share a common ethnic, racial, or religious background does not create the need for protection against gerrymandering. It is only when their common interests are strong enough to be manifested in political action that the need arises. Thus the characteristic of the group which creates the need for protection is its political character. It would be anomalous indeed if the characteristic which made constitutional protection necessary should at the same time make it unavailable. Yet that is the logical consequence of an inflexible rule that 'political' gerrymandering is not justiciable."[5]

In my judgment, the fact that political, ethnic, and racial factors were among the criteria considered by the legislators when drawing the ward boundaries in Chicago was not sufficient to establish their invalidity. What was necessary was "a highly improbable shape…inexplicable except by reference to an impermissible gerrymandering purpose." The redistricting of Tuskegee, Alabama, in 1957, which had altered its shape "from a square to an uncouth twenty-eight sided figure,"[6] was an example of such "flagrant gerrymandering."

The federal judicial code provides that certain important cases shall be tried by three-judge courts consisting of a circuit judge and two district judges. I presided over four or five such cases, two of which involved the

---

5. *Id.*, at 852.
6. *Gomillion* v. *Lightfoot*, 364 U.S. 339, 340 (1960).

question whether a state law governing the counting of votes in a federal election violated the Constitution.

In *Dyer* v. *Blair*,[7] Julius Hoffman and Jim Parsons sat with me in a case raising the question whether Illinois had ratified the Equal Rights Amendment. In both branches of the General Assembly a majority had voted in favor of ratification, but the proponents had failed to obtain three-fifths of the vote as required by Illinois law. The plaintiffs correctly argued that the case presented a federal question — specifically what does Article V of the Constitution mean when it says that proposed amendments shall be valid "when ratified by the Legislatures of three fourths of the several States"? Does "ratification" occur when the votes in the ratifying body satisfy a standard prescribed by federal law or does federal law permit the ratifying body to set its own standard, just as that body is apparently free to determine the qualifications of those eligible to vote on the issue and the procedures that shall govern the voting?

The plaintiffs had also correctly argued that the Supreme Court's decision in *Coleman* v. *Miller*[8] had established that a simple majority of the Kansas legislature had been sufficient to ratify the proposed Child Labor Amendment in 1925, and therefore federal law did not *require* a supermajority such as Illinois' three-fifths requirement. After considering all of the aspects of ratification that were left for the states to prescribe, we ultimately concluded that determining how many votes should suffice to constitute a valid ratification could be decided by the states.

Two aspects of that case have puzzled me over the years. Despite its importance, and the fact that competent judges could have decided the case in their favor, the plaintiffs did not appeal. I remain convinced that my opinion reached the correct result, but could it have persuaded the plaintiffs to throw in the towel? I doubt it. The second mystery is provided by the paragraph in Chief Justice Hughes's opinion for the Court in *Coleman* v. *Miller*, which states, "Whether this contention presents a

---

7. 390 F. Supp. 1291 (N. D. Ill. 1975).
8. 307 U.S. 433 (1939).

justiciable controversy, or a question which is political in nature and hence not justiciable, is a question upon which the Court is equally divided and therefore the Court expresses no opinion on that point." Given that all nine justices participated in the case, how could they have been "equally divided"?

Roudebush v. *Hartke*[9] was the other election-related three-judge district court case over which I presided; it arose out of a defeated Senate candidate's request for a recount in the closest race in Indiana's history. The incumbent, Vance Hartke, was declared the winner by a margin of 4,383 votes, or about one vote per precinct. After the Indiana secretary of state had certified that Hartke had been reelected, his opponent, Richard Roudebush, filed petitions for recounts in eleven counties. Hartke objected to the recount on the ground that the Constitution delegates to the United States Senate the power to judge the outcome of the election of its members. An Indiana judge overruled the objection, appointed a three-person recount commission, and directed it to proceed with the recount.

Hartke then filed a complaint in the federal district court in Indianapolis, asking for the appointment of a three-judge court and an injunction barring the recount. A single district judge, without giving notice to the defendant, issued an order temporarily restraining the recount pending the decision by the three-judge court, which was thereafter appointed and over which I presided. After an evidentiary hearing, the two district judges voted to stop the recount. I wrote a short dissent, making three points.

First, I noted that it was improper for the single district judge to have entered a restraining order without giving notice to the defendant when there was no need for expedited relief. I have always been troubled when trial judges make merits rulings without first hearing from the opposing party. Judges often defend that sort of action by pointing out that the preliminary order did not prevent the court from having a full opportunity

---

9. 321 F. Supp. 1370 (S. D. Ind. 1971).

to address the issues later, but that justification overlooks the fact that after any decision-maker has taken a public stand on an issue, he or she is naturally inclined to reach the same result at the end of the matter. I made that point in a footnote because it did not really affect the outcome of the case, but it is a problem that I had encountered so often in private practice that I thought — as I still think — that trial judges should never forget it.

Second, I pointed out that no federal judge had ever enjoined state election officials from conducting a recount of the votes cast in a federal election for a Senate seat. There was no basis for assuming that the Indiana judiciary was incapable of handling the recount litigation without assistance or interference from a federal court. And allowing the recount to proceed would not deprive the parties of their right to have the United States Senate act as the sole judge of the election outcome.

Finally, the evidence clearly established that the Indiana recount procedures had integrity, and that the original ballots were preserved for future review, as was true of all relevant records. There was no proof that the plaintiff would suffer irreparable injury — a prerequisite for injunctive relief. In sum, the work of the Senate would be facilitated rather than impaired by the availability of a fairly conducted recount.

On appeal, by a vote of seven to two, the Supreme Court reversed. In his opinion for the Court, Justice Potter Stewart rejected the arguments that the recount commission would violate federal law when it made judgments about which ballots to count or that there might be accidental destruction of ballots during the recount. He noted that the constitutional grant of power to conduct senatorial elections included broad authority to enact a comprehensive code, and that Indiana, like many other states, had found that the availability of a recount was necessary to guard against irregularity and error in the tabulation of votes. He concluded that "there is no reason to suppose that a court-appointed recount commission would be less honest or conscientious in the performance of its duties than the precinct election boards that initially counted the ballots."[10]

---

10. *Roudebush* v. *Hartke,* 405 U.S. 15, 26 (1972).

Some twenty-eight years later, in *Bush* v. *Gore,* five members of the Supreme Court — without pausing to acknowledge the holding in *Roudebush* v. *Hartke* — prevented Florida election officials from conducting a court-ordered recount of the ballots cast in that state in a presidential election. Justice Antonin Scalia concluded the stay was appropriate because "it is generally agreed that each manual recount produces a degradation of the ballots, which renders a subsequent recount inaccurate."[11] That statement is simply wrong. And it ignores the reasoning in the Court's opinion and in my dissent in *Roudebush.*

---

11. 531 U.S. 1046, 1047 (2000).

20

Two Scandals

T WO NATIONAL SCANDALS that occurred while Richard Nixon
was the president had an important impact on my career. First, on
June 17, 1972, agents of the Committee to Re-elect the President burglar-
ized the Democratic campaign headquarters in the Watergate Hotel, in
Washington, D.C.; and second, on November 10, 1973, Vice President
Spiro Agnew resigned. The second led to Gerald Ford's accession to the
vice presidency; the first led to Nixon's resignation on August 9, 1974,
and Ford's accession to the presidency. In a speech accepting that office
Ford referred to the "long nightmare" that had come to an end.

Two events that occurred during that nightmare were especially
important to me. In a dramatic demonstration of its independence and
ability to act wisely in the public interest, the Supreme Court unanimously decided that Nixon's claim of executive privilege did not justify
his refusal to turn over tapes of his White House conversations. The
taped conversations related to the Watergate break-in and their disclosure
ultimately led to Nixon's resignation. All three Nixon appointees who
participated in the case (Justice Rehnquist was recused) joined the opinion that they knew would produce that result. That case marks the high
point in the nation's respect for its independent judiciary.

The second event occurred in 1973, when I noticed a pain in my left upper arm while walking to the courthouse from Union Station. Doctors — including Bob Jampolis, whom I had known since our days in Delavan, Wisconsin — concluded that my left anterior descending artery was blocked and that I was a candidate for what was then a new procedure known as a coronary bypass. On Bob's recommendation, I went to Palo Alto to consult Norman Shumway, a true pioneer not only in the bypass procedure but also in heart transplants. He performed what has turned out to be an amazingly successful operation. When I was recuperating in the Stanford University Hospital, I watched the televised beginning of Nixon's resignation speech; unfortunately, I fell sound asleep before it ended. As a result of that operation, my pilot's license was temporarily suspended and my judicial workload was reduced for a few weeks.

That operation was also responsible for an important change in my lifestyle. Though I had previously kept in relatively good physical condition, thereafter I made a more serious effort to exercise regularly, with daily calisthenics and more regular time on the tennis court. My doctor advised me that I could safely play doubles, or even singles, if I paused for a rest of a minute or two after every two games. I followed that advice both in Chicago and after moving to Virginia in 1975. In Chicago my favorite opponent was my partner, Ed Rothschild, who had a concrete court at his home and regularly defeated me. After moving to the Washington area, I formed close friendships with singles opponents — Strouse Campbell, Dick Cobb, and Jim Mitchell — and also played fairly regularly in doubles games with a variety of opponents, including Bill Webster, the head of the FBI; Howard Metzenbaum, the senator from Ohio; and Lloyd Bentsen, the senator from Texas — who in a vice-presidential debate in 1988 famously reminded his opponent, Dan Quayle, that he was "no Jack Kennedy." On the one occasion that I was invited to play on the court at the White House, I made far more than my quota of lousy shots.

On November 12, 1975, William O. Douglas, who had served as an active justice for thirty-six years — longer than any other member in the history of the Supreme Court — resigned. A few days later, Bob Sprecher came to my chambers early in the morning to tell me that an FBI agent had interviewed him, asking questions about my qualification for the vacancy created by Douglas's resignation. I remember that visit because Bob seemed even more enthusiastic about my serious consideration than if the FBI had been investigating him.

Newspaper stories speculated about potential successors to Douglas, noting the likelihood that President Ford would nominate the first female justice and stating that the Justice Department had asked a number of law professors to read the opinions of circuit judges under consideration. (I learned later that Larry Tribe, the Harvard law professor and former law clerk to Potter Stewart, read all of my opinions.) Likely choices mentioned in the press included Arlin Adams of Philadelphia, a judge on the Third Circuit Court of Appeals; Bill Webster of St. Louis, whom I had met when the Rahr Malting Company sold its Wisconsin plant to Anheuser Busch; and Cliff Wallace, a judge on the Court of Appeals for the Ninth Circuit favored by Warren Burger. Carla Hills, the Secretary of Urban Development, was the leading female prospect. My good friend Phil Tone, who had succeeded me as one of Justice Rutledge's law clerks and had recently been appointed to the Seventh Circuit, was also under serious consideration. Because the speculation was distracting to both of us, Phil and I agreed that each of us would let the other know if he received any relevant information about the selection process.

On Monday, November 24, President Ford hosted a black-tie dinner at the White House, honoring a selected group of federal judges, presumably including those being considered to fill the vacancy. I first met President Ford at that dinner. While we were finishing our dessert, the president came to our table, pulled up a chair, and introduced himself; we engaged in a friendly conversation about New York City's request for federal assistance to avert an impending bankruptcy. I learned two things about Gerald Ford in that conversation: his command of facts made it obvious that he was a good lawyer; and he was extremely likeable. Neither of us said a word about the vacancy.

On Wednesday, November 26, the White House announced that on the following Saturday, President Ford would be traveling to Alaska and then on to China. Given that the next day would be Thanksgiving, Phil and I agreed that we did not have to be concerned about any word about the vacancy until after the China trip was over. We both welcomed the opportunity to get some work done without wondering whether we might be interrupted by a welcome telephone call.

Although the day after Thanksgiving was a holiday for my secretary, my clerk Sharon Baldwin and I agreed to come to the office to work on an opinion. Late in the morning Sharon answered the phone and handed it to me, saying, "I think you will want to take this call." President Ford was on the line. He told me that he had decided to name me to the Court and wanted to be sure that I would accept the job before he announced his decision. After what was probably an incoherent affirmative and enthusiastic response, followed by thanks for the memorable dinner at the White House earlier that week, he asked me not to disclose his decision until after the public announcement scheduled for late in the afternoon. I told him about my agreement with Phil and asked him for an exception; he responded by saying he was sure that Phil would understand if I told him about his request. I therefore agreed to keep the secret, and left the office to spend the next few hours with my mother.

Moments after my return to the office, I received a call from the White House informing me that the president had asked the caller to let me know that they were about to announce the appointment and that it would be OK to tell Judge Tone. As I hung up the phone and started to call Phil, he walked into my office, telling me that reporters in the building had told him the news and congratulated me. Although the call releasing me from my promise to the president did not come in time to make any difference, it did provide me with incontrovertible evidence of President Ford's decency and thoughtfulness.

Several days later, a lawyer in the Justice Department called to advise me that I should come to Washington to have informal interviews with members of the Senate Judiciary Committee. He told me — and some of the senators whom I later met confirmed — that, after the Senate had voted not to confirm Judge Clement Haynesworth to the Supreme Court in 1969, the committee members had decided that individual senators should meet informally with nominees to the Court before the official hearings began. Apparently some senators had voted against Haynesworth's nomination because they thought his answers to certain questions about an alleged conflict of interest had been evasive when, in fact, he had a speech defect that gave an incorrect impression to people meeting him for the first time. He was a good judge who presumably would have been confirmed if members of the committee had met him briefly before the formal hearings began. The practice of arranging informal prehearing interviews was introduced when Harry Blackmun was nominated in 1970. Although the practice later developed to include more substantive discussions about the nominee's judicial experience and philosophy, most of my interviews were just social occasions to get acquainted.

Senator Barry Goldwater of Arizona, an amateur pilot who had apparently flown every type of plane in the air force, was especially friendly when I told him about my Cessna. I think the fact that I was a licensed pilot convinced him that I would be a good judge. When I visited Strom Thurmond, after shaking hands with everyone on his staff, he invited me into his private office, saying, "Judge Stevens, I want to talk to you about the death penalty." Having decided not to discuss that issue until after I had studied the briefs in relevant pending cases, I expected a possibly hostile exchange, but he went on to say, "I'm not going to ask you for your views on the issue — for that would be improper — but I want to tell you why I think it is a necessary form of punishment." When I visited Senator Edward Kennedy's office, our meeting was entirely social, but one of the members of his staff gave me a book opposing the death penalty that he asked me to read.

My visit with Senator Roman Hruska of Nebraska surprised me for two reasons. In supporting one of Nixon's failed nominations for the vacancy created by Felix Frankfurter's resignation, he had famously argued that not all members of the Court had to be eminent scholars and that average lawyers were entitled to representation on the Court. His comments during our visit demonstrated that he was interested in my views, both about potential injustices to prison inmates and about the scope of federal power under the Commerce Clause. I was impressed that he had obviously read opinions that I had authored about both of those subjects. Indeed, I think he agreed with my opinion for a divided en banc court in *United States* v. *Staszuck*,[1] which upheld the federal conviction of a Chicago alderman who had accepted a $3,000 bribe for not opposing a zoning change that removed an obstacle to the construction of an animal hospital. Because the hospital was never built, the record contained no evidence that either the payment or the zoning change had any effect whatsoever either favorable or unfavorable on interstate commerce. My opinion (as did later opinions after I joined the Supreme Court) had quoted passages from Wiley Rutledge's "Declaration of Legal Faith" to support a broad interpretation of the federal government's power under the Commerce Clause. In later years when other justices sometimes challenged my views about the scope of that power, I often thought about my conversation with the intelligent and conservative senator from Nebraska.

While I was visiting with senators, my former law partners and my friends on the Seventh Circuit were busily assembling answers to detailed questions propounded on behalf of the Judiciary Committee about my former clients and my conduct as a judge that would have revealed whether I had participated in any cases that arguably affected private interests that should have been disclosed. I remember the burdens imposed by those questions — much like the burden of pretrial discovery in major litigation — more clearly than any particular issue. I was also aware of the National Organization for Women's opposition to my nomination, and the need to anticipate some hostile questioning during the hearings. I therefore consulted with Ed Rothschild and we agreed that it would be appropriate for him to appear with me as my lawyer during the formal hearings. The Justice Department had assumed that if I was qualified for a position on the Supreme Court I should not need any special

---

1. 517 F. 2d 53 (CA7 1975).

help in preparing to discuss those qualifications with senators, so having Ed available to discuss potential problems was especially helpful. Among other preparations, we agreed that I should reread my opinions rejecting claims of gender-based discrimination and be prepared to discuss them. As matters developed, no senator asked me a single question about any opinion that I had written.

Perhaps I was fortunate because my dissent in *Sprogis* v. *United Airlines*[2] was particularly controversial. In *Sprogis,* the majority had held that the company's "no marriage rule" — which made married women ineligible for employment as airline stewardesses — violated the statute prohibiting gender-based discrimination. I had reasoned that a company rule would not violate that statute unless the rule provided a benefit to a person of the opposite sex that was not available to the plaintiff. Given the fact that the only position as a cabin attendant that was then open to male employees of United was on flights to Hawaii, the plaintiff would not have been eligible for employment if she had been a man. The rule treated a category of female employees differently from other employees, but that category — namely, cabin attendants on all flights except those to Hawaii — excluded males. Thus, within what I considered the relevant employment category, males rather than females were the disfavored class.

The hearings began on Monday, December 8 and lasted for three days. Chuck Percy had told me that the Democrats, who were then in control of Congress, had made it clear that if I were not confirmed before the end of the year, they would delay the process to confirm Douglas's successor until after the next presidential election. Thus Ed Rothschild and I felt a sense of urgency about the process that was not a matter of public attention. Moreover, unlike every later confirmation hearing, my hearings were not televised. Whereas the first day of every later Senate confirmation hearing has opened with a series of statements by committee

---

2. 444 F. 2d 1194 (CA7 1971).

members explaining how important the hearings are, no such preliminaries took place in 1975.

The principal issue that surfaced as soon as the hearings opened related to my health — given my then recent bypass operation, did I have a sufficient life expectancy to justify the important appointment? That was the issue that occupied the senators' attention even before Ed Levi, speaking for the Justice Department, and the two Illinois senators, Chuck Percy and Adlai Stevenson, endorsed my nomination. A brief interruption related to my health was followed by Warren Christopher's endorsement on behalf of the American Bar Association. Then began my interrogation by individual senators.

Senator Kennedy was my most thorough and — at times — most hostile inquisitor. He asked me whether I saw myself as a person to whom those members of society "with submerged aspirations and suppressed rights would be able to look with confidence and hope?" In my response I told him that I had received letters from prison inmates who had said they were writing to their senators asking them to vote for my confirmation. "I suppose they are about as submerged as any element in our society. So I think I may supply that particular need to some degree at least."[3] My response led to a comment by the senator noting that groups such as the National Organization for Women were opposed to my nomination. Neither he nor any other senator, however, asked me about any specific opinion relating to women's rights.

We spent quite a bit of time going back and forth over whether I should ask the committee to publish my financial statement or whether the committee should simply do so on its own. I had nothing to hide in that area but simply was somewhat embarrassed to have a net worth of only about $171,000 after having been engaged in the successful practice of law for over twenty-eight years.

In another exchange he seemed to be asking me to state that as a judge I would go out of my way to decide cases in favor of disfavored litigants,

---

3. Hrgs. at 15.

and when I declined to do so, he gave me a rather long lecture ending with this exchange:

> **Senator Kennedy:** ... There are many Americans who feel that women, too, have been discriminated against. I was trying to get a statement or comment from you — which I must say has not been forthcoming to this point — that would at least show some sensitivity to this particular kind of a problem. If the answer that you are going to apply the law equally to every citizen is the way you want to leave it, then that is the way the record will stand. However, I believe it is not going to satisfy great numbers of people in this country who feel as I do that there has been a broad sector of our society that has been denied certain rights because there are statutes, ordinances, and regulations which discriminate on the basis of sex. If you want to leave the record just saying that you are going to apply every law equitably, that is the way it will stand.

> **Judge Stevens:** I'd be proud to have the record stand that way.[4]

In addition to women's groups, the opponents of my nomination included an Illinois resident named Anthony Robert Martin-Trigona, who testified in the afternoon of the third day of hearings. His opposition was based on his belief that the investigation of the Illinois Supreme Court's judgment in the Isaacs case was incomplete because we had failed to prove wrongdoing by two members of the court who had not been mentioned in our report. As the witness began his statement, Chairman James Eastland of Mississippi (who was not then presiding) leaned over and asked me if I wanted to listen to the testimony or would prefer to share a glass of bourbon with him in his chambers. Since there was absolutely no need for my presence because Martin-Trigona's speculation was totally unsupported — and demonstrably so — I welcomed and

---

4. Hrgs. at 34.

accepted the invitation. I missed nothing of importance and did gain one nugget of information about the political process during our pleasant conversation. Despite their fundamental differences on matters of policy, Senators Eastland and Kennedy accepted each other's word about matters of procedure, including a commitment that the latter had made concerning the early timing of the committee's vote on my nomination. The hearings concluded on that day, and on the following day the committee voted without dissent to recommend that the Senate confirm my nomination to the Court. The Senate so voted on Friday, December 17, 1975, and two days later I became an associate justice of the Supreme Court.

21

Taking the Oath of Office

GERALD FORD, a member of the bar of the Supreme Court, came to the Court and participated in the ceremony at which Chief Justice Warren Burger administered the oath of office to me. When the Court was called to order at 10:00 a.m., I sat in the "John Marshall Chair" — a chair that the great chief justice had used during his tenure — immediately in front of the clerk of the Court. Attorney General Ed Levi made an oral motion asking the Court's permission to allow the president to present my commission to the clerk. The president then delivered the commission to the clerk, who read it aloud and motioned me to ascend the bench and take the oath, which the chief justice administered. I then took my seat at the left end of the bench, and the Court adjourned.

The ceremony was short and simple, but it was also profoundly significant because it exemplified the independence of the judicial branch. President Ford had followed his constitutional duty to nominate Justice Douglas's successor, and he had come to the Court to see the career of its new member commence. His role in the nomination process had ended, and my career as an independent member of the Supreme Court had begun. The fact that he had been responsible for making that career possible gave him no right to influence my behavior once it had begun. At no time — either before or after I took the oath — did President Ford ever seek to influence my performance of my job.

As I reflect on these events, I'm reminded of an unfulfilled ambition I formed while President Ford was still in office. Concern about my health following my coronary bypass operation had required me to surrender my pilot's license a few months earlier, but after I was sworn in, I renewed my license and a friend flew my plane to Leesburg, Virginia, where I resumed flying on weekends on a regular basis. On one of those flights it occurred to me that President Ford might enjoy joining me on such a Saturday afternoon outing. It would have been especially gratifying to have him aboard because his presence aloft in my plane would have required the redesignation of "Cessna 88-Foxtrot" when communicating with an airport control tower to "Air Force One." I still sometimes wonder whether he might have enjoyed such a flight.

22

The Stevens Court

A s I noted in my book *Five Chiefs,* Byron White was fond of say-ing that each time a justice joins the Court, it creates a new dynamic and a different institution — in effect, a new Court. There is a great deal of truth to that view. In the pages that follow, I reflect on the eleven Courts on which I sat over my thirty-four years as an associate jus-tice, with each section devoted to notable cases and other reflections from each of those Courts. The first is, appropriately enough, the Stevens Court.

October Term 1975 — My First Term

My transition from a judge on the Seventh Circuit to an associate justice of the Supreme Court was far less difficult than might have been expected. Two of my law clerks — Sharon Baldwin and Charles ("Skip") Paul — moved from Chicago to Washington; the third, George Rutherglen, had been hired by Bill Douglas and agreed to finish the term working for me. Although my secretary, Florence Lundquist, who was nearing retirement age, did not want to leave Chicago, my good friend Bob Sprecher allowed me to persuade his secretary, Nellie Pitts, to take that job with me in Washington. (Although the fact had nothing to do with my hiring decision, it is of interest that Nellie was the first African-American secretary at the Court.) Skip and Nellie arrived in Washington a few days before I did and were responsible for assembling the library and most of the furnishings in my new chambers.

It took some time to select the paintings that I was able to borrow from the National Gallery of Art. Three of them — a portrait of Queen Victoria when she was a handsome twenty-two-year-old woman by Franz Winterhalter; a street scene of a town in Corsica by Maurice Utrillo; and a landscape featuring the Salisbury Cathedral — still hang in my chambers today. Those chambers, by the way, are the same ones that I occupied when I arrived at the Court in December 1975. They are on the west side of the building with an unobstructed view of the Capitol and were originally designed to accommodate retired chief justices, but no retired chief was alive when I arrived. Given Bill Douglas's desire to remain in his chambers on the other side of the building, I began my career in the most luxurious offices in the courthouse. Three years later I moved into Tom Clark's office on the north side of the building, and when Potter Stewart retired in 1981 I moved into his chambers in the northeast corner of the building, where I remained for the next quarter century. When Sandra Day O'Connor retired in 2006 (and the Court building was being renovated), I moved into her former chambers on the northwest corner of the building, where I stayed until my retirement in 2010, when I finally moved back to the retired chief justice's chambers. The paintings borrowed from the National Gallery accompanied me on each move, and on one of those moves I was able to persuade the curator to hang the official portrait of Wiley Rutledge in my chambers. Those hangings have been joined by the scorecard that my friend Jim Marsh used to memorialize Babe Ruth's most famous home run, and my favorite snapshot of my wife, Maryan, taken just after our marriage in Leesburg, Virginia.

My new duties were onerous, but far less so than might have been expected because I had had experience with processing certiorari petitions as a law clerk and had received a reasonably broad education in the work of the federal judiciary during the preceding five years. Nevertheless, from day one until my retirement many years later, it was definitely a full-time job. One chore that I had not anticipated was reading the interminable drafts of circulating opinions in *Buckley* v. *Valeo*,[1] the case involving the constitutionality of the campaign finance laws enacted in response to the Watergate break-in in 1972. When announced, the six separate opinions occupied 294 pages in the official reports, and several drafts of each were circulated before they were ultimately released.

Another decision I had to make was whether or not to join the "cert pool," a system for reviewing certiorari, or "cert," petitions that had emerged since my last stint at the Court almost thirty years earlier. Prior to the creation of the cert pool, each justice's chambers reviewed every petition that came to the Court. For example, when I was clerking for Justice Rutledge, my co-clerk, Stan Temko, and I would write memos for Justice Rutledge on each of the paid and some of the in forma pauperis petitions received each week and he would then decide whether to vote to grant or deny the petition based on our memos to him. In October 1972, the Court implemented the cert pool, which transformed that process. All of the petitions were instead divided among the chambers, and each chamber then assigned one law clerk to each petition. That clerk would then evaluate the petition and write a single memo, ranging from two to twenty pages long, for all the justices. At the end of the memo, the clerk would provide a discussion of the arguments for and against granting review in the case and give his or her recommendation. The justices in the pool would then review those memos and decide whether to put a case on the "discuss" list — the set of cases to be considered and voted on at that week's conference.

When I joined the Court, Chief Justice Burger provided me with copies of the pool memos that had been written for upcoming conferences. Although I found the memos thorough, I elected not to join the cert pool. Based on my earlier experience as a law clerk, I thought that I could make an accurate judgment about whether to grant or deny the petition

---

1. 424 U.S. 1 (1976).

more easily by looking at the original papers. I did not discuss that decision with any other justice before making it, but I recall a later conversation with Potter Stewart in which he approved my decision, noting that he thought the pool should not include more than five justices. Indeed, with my initial decision not to participate in the pool, I joined company with Bill Brennan, Potter Stewart, and Thurgood Marshall.

In my view, the cert pool may well have been a reasonable reaction to the increase in the volume of cert petitions over time — from seven or eight per week in 1925 to approximately seventy-five per week in the early 1970s.[2] Over time, I delegated more responsibility to my law clerks in reviewing the cert petitions, but I never seriously considered joining the pool. I recall at least one occasion on which Chief Justice Rehnquist did not put a case on the discuss list but my clerks and I identified it as a candidate for review and added it to the list. (That case, *BMW of North America* v. *Gore*,[3] was ultimately granted, and I wrote the opinion for the Court.) Although any justice could add cases to the discuss list, my independence from the cert pool may have facilitated my addition of cases to the list that otherwise escaped the attention of the justices who participated in the cert pool.

My decision not to join the cert pool was one of three matters on which I disagreed with Chief Justice Burger during my first year on the Court. The other two were quite different. First, in *National League of Cities* v. *Usery*,[4] an important case that I discuss in more detail later and which was decided only six months after I joined the Court, I disagreed with the chief about the outcome. The chief joined Bill Rehnquist's majority opinion, holding that Congress lacked authority under the Commerce Clause to extend its minimum-wage and maximum-hour rules to employees of states and state agencies. In a discussion shortly after I joined the Court, the chief went out of his way to impress on me his

2. See generally Palmer, "The Bermuda Triangle?," *Const. Commentary* 18 (2001): 105, 107.
3. 517 U.S. 559 (1996).
4. 426 U.S. 833 (1976).

strong views about the case, and he may have been disappointed by my failure to agree with him.

The second matter was one that I first discussed with Tom Fairchild, who succeeded Luther Swygert as the Chief Judge of the Seventh Circuit in 1975. During my initial period on the Seventh Circuit, I was reluctant to use the word "we" to describe the statements and holdings of the court from the period before I joined it. Judge Fairchild, however, convinced me that as a judge writing a judicial opinion, I would speak as a member of an institution, not as an individual, making the special contextual use of "we" appropriate. I came to agree that the use of judicial "we" has a special function that justifies its use in this unusual manner. My view therefore differed from that of Chief Justice Burger, who disapproved of the use of "we" for decisions issued before a judge had joined the court in question.

Two memories of my first day of oral argument are still vivid today. When the nine justices lined up in the conference room preparing to ascend the bench in three sets of three — the chief justice and Bill Brennan and Potter Stewart at the head of the line because they would occupy the center seats on the bench, Byron White, Harry Blackmun, and Bill Rehnquist to the right, and Thurgood Marshall, Lewis Powell, and me to the left — a significant division of the Court consisting of five justices in one group and four in the other became apparent. Those over six feet tall — the chief, Byron, Thurgood, Lewis, and Bill Rehnquist — towered over the rest of us. Relative size, however, did not determine voting patterns.

As soon as we had climbed the three steps to the bench and were seated, my neighbor, Lewis Powell — who was concerned about a possible traffic jam when the argument ended — leaned over to ask me to be sure to push my chair back far enough to give Thurgood and him enough space to get off the bench. My only memory of the argument that consumed the next two hours is of my concentration on complying with Lewis's request. When the argument ended, I shoved my chair back so forcefully that I narrowly escaped falling off the back of the bench. My first oral argument might well have been far more memorable than it was.

I have similar memories of my first conferences, the regular meetings of the entire Court at which we conducted our business. My seat was to the right of Bill Brennan, who sat at the end of the table opposite the chief, and to the left of Bill Rehnquist, my immediate senior. When discussing the merits of the cases that had been argued that week, the justices spoke in order of seniority. As the junior, I had the unique responsibility of getting up and responding to any knock on the conference room door — I was what Tom Clark often described as the "highest-paid doorman" in the country. During my first conference, I made the mistake of paying so much attention to the ongoing discussion of the cases that had been argued earlier that week that I did not hear a knock on the door that both of my neighbors got up to answer. No sanction was imposed, but thereafter I never failed to perform my primary duty as the junior justice.

The location of my seat also explains my favorite way of beginning the explanation for my vote in a fair number of difficult cases. I liked starting by saying "I agree with Bill" — my colleagues then had to wait for an explanation of which of my friends I was joining. Two anecdotes will explain why both Bill Brennan and Bill Rehnquist were good friends.

Bill Brennan insisted that as a new member of the Court I should attend the annual white-tie dinner hosted by the members of the press known as the "Grid Iron Club." Because I have never particularly enjoyed formal dinners, my wardrobe did not include a set of tails, and I was not enthusiastic about renting the necessary uniform of the day, so I told Bill that I was not planning to attend. Rather than accept my excuse, he brought his own set of tails to Court and insisted that I borrow them for the occasion. While I would have been able to stuff a pillow in my trousers, they fit well enough to enable me to attend what turned out to be an enormous success because my dinner partner was Ginger Rogers, one of my favorite movie stars. She was just as charming in person as on the screen.

Bill Rehnquist and I had become friends while he was the circuit justice for the Seventh Circuit. He was well liked by all of the judges on the

Seventh Circuit because of his candor in discussing recent decisions of the Court, because he had such a good sense of humor, and also because his wife, Nan, was an extremely gracious person who made friends with everyone so easily. Bill liked to gamble on a variety of different events — the outcome of a forthcoming election, the depth of snow that would accumulate in the courtyard before a storm ended, the Kentucky Derby, and the identity of the winner of the next Washington Redskins football game. As colleagues on the Supreme Court, our bets were modest (usually one dollar), and he was stingy about giving odds, but on every Monday morning during football season our first order of business as we met before going on the bench was either to pay or to collect from the other. That practice continued during his tenure as an associate justice and later as chief — except for the 2000 term, when the Court decided to enjoin the recount of the votes cast in Florida in the presidential election.

Two of the majority opinions that Chief Justice Burger assigned to me were in cases that had first been argued the year before and reargued during the 1975 term, presumably because Bill Douglas's vote might have affected the outcome. (I had been told that the majority had decided not to hand down any opinions during the 1974 term in which he had cast the deciding vote.) Both of those cases challenged the validity of federal statutes that discriminated against immigrants: one made immigrants ineligible for federal welfare benefits for five years after they entered the country and the other allowed federal agencies to refuse to employ noncitizens. We held the latter statute invalid in a divided opinion, but we upheld the former in a unanimous opinion. Why a Court that ultimately decided the case unanimously found it necessary to have the case reargued was never explained to me.

After issuing *Buckley* v. *Valeo,* the major issue confronting the Court during my first term was the constitutionality of the death penalty. Four years earlier, in *Furman* v. *Georgia,*[5] the Court had addressed the

5. 408 U.S. 238 (1972).

constitutionality of Georgia's capital punishment statute. The statute delegated to judges or juries the task of deciding whether a defendant convicted of murder or rape should be sentenced to death but did not prescribe any criteria that would guide the decision-maker's discretion in choosing whether to impose capital punishment on a given defendant. Each of the nine justices had written a separate opinion, and five of them had concluded that the statute was unconstitutional. Bill Brennan and Thurgood Marshall each firmly believed that death was always an impermissible form of cruel and unusual punishment prohibited by the Eighth Amendment; Bill Douglas thought it invalid because, in practice, it was enforced against only a narrow class of indigent persons and members of racial minorities who could not have been expressly targeted for punishment; Potter Stewart considered it as arbitrary as being struck by lightning; and Byron White apparently believed that its uneven and unpredictable application undermined any claim that it was serving a valid punitive purpose. The opinions of the four dissenters — Chief Justice Burger, Harry Blackmun, Lewis Powell, and Bill Rehnquist — essentially argued that even if it was unwise, it was not forbidden by the Constitution. None of them made the argument often advanced today that, because the text of the Constitution provides that any deprivation of "life" must be preceded by "due process," the framers recognized death as a permissible form of punishment, and, so it is argued, what was permissible as a matter of "original intent" must still be permissible today.

Following *Furman*, state legislatures generally had enacted new death penalty statutes, some of which afforded additional procedural protections to defendants, such as separate penalty hearings in which the prosecutor had the burden of proving that aggravating circumstances (evidence establishing the seriousness of the defendant's crime) outweighed mitigating circumstances (evidence tending to excuse or explain the crime) in order to obtain a verdict sentencing the defendant to death. Others sought to limit the risk of arbitrary application by making the punishment of death mandatory for certain crimes. During my first term, the Court granted petitions for certiorari seeking review of five of the new statutes. After the cases were argued, Bill Brennan and Thurgood Marshall voted to invalidate all of them; Chief Justice Burger, Byron White, Harry Blackmun, and Bill Rehnquist voted to uphold all of them; and Potter Stewart, Lewis Powell, and I took a middle position that ultimately determined the outcome of all the cases. We concluded that some of the statutes were valid and others were invalid. Those mandating the imposition of the death penalty if the defendant was found guilty of a capital offense, as the Louisiana and North Carolina statutes did, were invalid, but those permitting the jury to impose that sentence only after a separate hearing were valid.

As the senior justice among the three whose votes determined the outcome of the capital cases that term, Potter Stewart was responsible for assigning the controlling opinions. Instead of designating each of us to author one or more of those opinions, he decided that each of us should be responsible for a separate part of all the opinions: He drafted the explanation for our conclusion that the mandatory penalties in Louisiana and North Carolina were unconstitutional; he assigned to Lewis Powell the drafting of our reasons for upholding the statutes in Georgia, Florida, and Texas; and he asked me to write the statement of facts in all the cases. Contrary to the practice that I followed on both the Seventh Circuit and the Supreme Court, I delegated the task of stating the facts in all of those cases to my clerk Sharon Baldwin, because I thought that the statement of facts would have no impact on our agreed disposition of the cases. That was an unwise decision on my part, because if I had carefully stated the facts in *Jurek* v. *Texas,* I might well have changed my vote in that case. I should then have realized that a jury instruction required by the Texas statute had the practical consequence of converting what at first blush appeared to be a valid discretionary sentencing scheme into an invalid mandatory scheme. Even though a change in my vote probably would not have affected the outcome, I should have voted to invalidate the Texas statute. (My law clerk George Rutherglen urged me to change my vote in that case and I have lived to regret my failure to do so.)

In the years following our decisions in those capital cases, the Court failed to craft or to enforce rules that might have narrowed the category of cases in which the death penalty is permissible. Instead, it actually allowed prosecutors special privileges in selecting capital jurors. In addition, the Court permitted the introduction of emotional "victim impact evidence" during the penalty phase of capital cases that had the perverse effect of increasing, rather than minimizing, the risk of error in the imposition of the death penalty. Whether or not my vote to uphold the validity of capital punishment in 1976 was correct, I am now convinced that the very real risk that an innocent person may be put to death in such a case provides a sufficient reason for ending that form of punishment. I do not recall that risk as having been mentioned by anyone during the arguments in 1976.

I have since learned that Michigan's decision to abolish its death penalty in 1846 was sponsored by a member of the state's legislature who had actually participated in the execution of a man later determined to be innocent. The risk that an innocent man may be wrongfully convicted — and executed — is just as real today as it was in Michigan in 1846. Indeed, the number of wrongfully convicted defendants who have spent years on death row before being exonerated demonstrates the fallibility of our criminal justice system.

The second most significant issue confronting the Court in that year was whether Congress's power to regulate interstate commerce included the power to require states and state agencies to obey the Fair Labor Standards Act, the federal law prescribing minimum wages and maximum hours for employees engaged in work that affects interstate commerce. In *National League of Cities* v. *Usery,*[6] the plaintiffs convinced a five-justice majority that their status as state government agencies provided them with immunity from federal regulation. In Bill Rehnquist's opinion, the Court drew a distinction between action of a state that is comparable to private action, such as operating a railroad, and what it described as the action of a state "qua state," concluding that the latter was immune from

---

6. 426 U.S. 833 (1976).

federal regulation under the Commerce Clause. In a powerful and persuasive dissent, Justice Brennan demonstrated that the majority had departed so dramatically from prior cases that it was guilty of delivering a "catastrophic judicial body blow to Congress' power under the Commerce Clause."

Although I am now convinced that Bill Brennan's dissent was accurate and that his characterization of Bill Rehnquist's majority opinion was fair, my reaction to his draft as the newest member of the Court at the time was concern that it was unnecessarily provocative. I have recently learned from Harry Blackmun's papers at the Library of Congress that his clerk assisting him on the case, who had unsuccessfully tried to persuade him to join Bill Brennan's dissent, had also been critical of the rhetoric in the first few pages. I decided to explain my vote in a short separate opinion, writing,

> The Court holds that the Federal Government may not interfere with a sovereign State's inherent right to pay a substandard wage to the janitor at the state capitol. The principle on which the holding rests is difficult to perceive.

> The Federal Government may, I believe, require the State to act impartially when it hires or fires the janitor, to withhold taxes from his paycheck, to observe safety regulations when he is performing his job, to forbid him from burning too much soft coal in the capitol furnace, from dumping untreated refuse in an adjacent waterway, from overloading a state-owned garbage truck, or from driving either the truck or the Governor's limousine over 55 miles an hour. Even though these and many other activities of the capitol janitor are activities of the State *qua* State, I have no doubt that they are subject to federal regulation.

> My disagreement with the wisdom of this legislation may not, of course, affect my judgment with respect to its validity. On this

issue there is no dissent from the proposition that the Federal Government's power over the labor market is adequate to embrace these employees. Since I am unable to identify a limitation on that federal power that would not also invalidate federal regulation of state activities that I consider unquestionably permissible, I am persuaded that this statute is valid. Accordingly, with respect and a great deal of sympathy for the views expressed by the Court, I dissent from its constitutional holding.[7]

While Harry Blackmun joined Bill Rehnquist's majority opinion, he wrote separately to express concern about its possible implications in areas such as environmental protection. A few years afterward, as I explain in a later chapter, he surprised his colleagues by concluding that *National League of Cities* should be overruled and authored an opinion for the Court so holding. Nevertheless, the central issue raised in those cases remains the subject of debate among members of the Court today. A majority of the Court in recent years has unwisely often agreed with the reasoning in Bill Rehnquist's opinion.

In *Runyon* v. *McCrary*,[8] plaintiffs challenged a private school's policy of refusing to admit qualified black students because of their race. The legal question was whether the Civil Rights Act of 1866 prohibited private discrimination. Byron White favored overruling an earlier case supporting the claim. I firmly believed that Byron's reading of Congress's actual intent was correct. Nevertheless I joined the majority, explaining, "The policy of the nation as formulated by the Congress in recent years has moved constantly in the direction of eliminating racial segregation in all sectors of society." To reverse course on the act's coverage of private discrimination "would be a significant step backwards, with effects that would not have arisen from a correct decision in the first instance."

---

7. *Id.*, at 880–81.
8. 427 U.S. 160 (1976).

Without realizing it, I thus rejected the "original intent" approach to the law that would later be advocated by future attorney general Edwin Meese and my future colleague Antonin Scalia.

That same term, Bill Brennan, Thurgood Marshall, and I voted to hear *Doe* v. *Commonwealth's Attorney for Richmond,* which asked the Court to review a lower-court decision upholding the constitutionality of a Virginia statute punishing sodomy as a felony. Our three votes to hear the case expressed our view that the issue presented was sufficiently important to require full briefing and argument before being decided. But rather than just deny the petition for certiorari, which is not a ruling on the merits and thus has no precedential effect, the Court summarily affirmed, effectively concluding that the lower court's order was so clearly correct that argument was unnecessary. We now know — based on a string of cases beginning with *Lawrence* v. *Texas* in 2003 and culminating with *Obergefell* v. *Hodges* in 2015 — that the summary affirmance was incorrect and failed to appreciate the full aspect of liberty protected by the Fourteenth Amendment. Bill, Thurgood, and I asked that it be noted that we would have set the case for argument,[9] which could be seen as the first step in a long journey that arrived at its goal almost forty years later.

Another case decided during my first term also failed to recognize the nature of the liberty protected by the Constitution. In *Meachum* v. *Fano,*[10] the Court reversed a court of appeals decision holding that three Massachusetts prisoners were entitled to a hearing before they could be transferred from a medium to a maximum security prison. The Court held that their conviction of a crime had sufficiently extinguished the prisoners' interest in liberty "to empower the State to confine them in *any* of its prisons."[11] I would not have objected to the Court's analysis if it had merely held that the transfer had not caused a sufficiently serious harm to constitute a deprivation of liberty within the meaning of the Constitution, but instead it had reasoned that unless the state had conferred a

9. See 425 U.S. 901.
10. 427 U.S. 215 (1976).
11. *Id.,* at 224.

special protection, the prisoners had no interest in liberty meriting any protection at all. I wrote,

> If a man were a creature of the State, the [Court's] analysis would be correct. But neither the Bill of Rights nor the laws of sovereign States create the liberty which the Due Process Clause protects. The relevant constitutional provisions are limitations on the power of the sovereign to infringe on the liberty of the citizen. The relevant state laws either create property rights or they curtail the freedom of the citizen who must live in an ordered society. Of course, law is essential to the exercise and enjoyment of individual liberty in a complex society. But it is not the source of liberty, and surely not the exclusive source.

> I had thought it self-evident that all men were endowed by their Creator with liberty as one of the cardinal unalienable rights. It is that basic freedom which the Due Process Clause protects, rather than the particular rights or privileges conferred by specific laws or regulations.[12]

Sometime after I had begun to write this book, I wrote a letter to all of my surviving law clerks asking them to remind me of events that had occurred during their clerkships. Skip Paul, for instance, recalled sitting alone in my chambers in January 1976 when Bill Rehnquist opened the door after a short knock and introduced himself. "You must be Skip," he said. "I am Bill Rehnquist." Bill then said that he understood that Skip, who was then standing straight-backed at attention, and I played tennis and wondered whether we might also be interested in playing Ping-Pong downstairs with him and his clerk Craig Bradley. Later in the month a date was arranged.

Skip and I walked downstairs wearing street shoes, slacks, dress shirts,

---

12. *Id.,* at 230 (Stevens, J., dissenting).

and ties. In a white-washed brick room in the basement we found tightly tucked a Ping-Pong table and there waiting for us were Bill Rehnquist, who I've previously noted was tall, about six two, and Craig Bradley, who was even taller, both in athletic suits. Both Skip and I are closer to about five nine. Skip recalls that I turned to him and commented, "This is the land of the Giants." But we brought a competitive spirit and, after a robust match, in Skip's words, "the little guys in the business clothes won." No rematch was ever scheduled — or mentioned.

October Term 1976

As I alluded to earlier, members of the Court have long debated whether the Due Process Clause of the Fourteenth Amendment merely requires that fair procedures be followed whenever a state deprives a person of life, liberty, or property, or whether it also prohibits the state from depriving persons of certain liberties. In other words, does the Due Process Clause have substantive as well as procedural content? In two early cases the Court applied what became known as "substantive due process" to invalidate state statutes that prohibited families from sending their children to parochial schools and that prohibited schools from teaching their students German. And in 1905, over the dissent of Justice Oliver Wendell Holmes, the Court applied that doctrine in *Lochner* v. *New York* to invalidate a state statute that limited work hours for bakery employees. The much-criticized *Lochner* decision became the primary example of improper judicial activism. Later cases that rejected *Lochner* and upheld statutes regulating economic activity were sometimes assumed to have entirely rejected the doctrine of substantive due process and sometimes merely to have disapproved of its use to invalidate commercial regulations.

In 1965, Bill Douglas wrote the majority opinion in *Griswold* v. *Connecticut*,[13] which accorded constitutional protection to a married couple's right to use contraceptives. He relied on the notion that "specific

---

13. 381 U.S. 479.

guarantees in the Bill of Rights have penumbras, formed by emanations from those guarantees that help give them life and substance."[14] In his view, the right to privacy was one such "penumbral right," and it entitled married couples to use contraception. Although Douglas's opinion was much maligned, he had avoided reliance on the controversial doctrine applied too broadly in *Lochner.* In contrast, in a concurring opinion, the second Justice John Harlan relied on substantive due process to reach the same result.

Eight years later, in *Roe* v. *Wade,*[15] seven justices joined Harry Blackmun's opinion invalidating a Texas statute that made it a crime for a woman to obtain an abortion. *Roe* was not nearly as controversial when it was decided as it later became. Notably, during my Senate confirmation hearings just two years after *Roe,* the subject of abortion was not even mentioned. And Clarence Thomas, during his Senate hearings, testified that abortion had not been the subject of much discussion or debate among Yale law students in the years immediately after the opinion was handed down. In the opening section of his opinion in *Roe,* Harry quoted an excerpt from Holmes's "vindicated" *Lochner* dissent. Like Bill Douglas in *Griswold,* he thus made a point of avoiding simple reliance on substantive due process; instead his opinion held that a "right of privacy," unmentioned in the text of the Constitution, was "broad enough to encompass a woman's decision whether or not to terminate her pregnancy."[16] I have always had my doubts about the validity of that rationale and believe it may have made the arguments of the opinion's critics more persuasive than if he had simply relied squarely on substantive due process as Potter Stewart did in his concurring opinion. Potter explained that "freedom of personal choice in matters of marriage and family life is one of the liberties protected by the Due Process Clause of the Fourteenth Amendment.... That right necessarily includes the right of a woman to decide whether or not to terminate her pregnancy."[17]

---

14. *Id.,* at 484.
15. 410 U.S. 113 (1973).
16. *Id.,* at 153.
17. *Id.,* at 169–70.

A case argued early in my second term on the Court, *Whalen* v. *Roe*,[18] gave me the opportunity to endorse Potter Stewart's correct rationale for the Court's earlier decision in *Roe* v. *Wade*. In *Whalen*, a district court had invalidated a New York statute that created a computerized record of the names and addresses of all persons who had obtained, pursuant to a doctor's prescription, certain drugs for which there is both a lawful and an unlawful market. The court had relied squarely on the "right to privacy" as the basis for its decision. We reversed and upheld the statute. In my opinion for a unanimous Court, I explained that "cases sometimes characterized as protecting 'privacy' have in fact involved at least two different kinds of interests. One is the interest in avoiding disclosure of personal matters, and another is the interest in making certain kinds of important decisions."[19] The term "privacy" appropriately describes the first category, but the word "liberty" better describes the latter. I cited *Roe* as the first example of cases in the second category. I thus endorsed the separate opinions of John Harlan in *Griswold* and Potter Stewart in *Roe* — both of whom had relied on "liberty" rather than "privacy" — as the correct basis for their concurring votes.

Criticism of *Roe* became more widespread perhaps in part because opponents repeatedly made the incorrect argument that only a "right to privacy," unmentioned in the Constitution, supported the holding. Correctly basing a woman's right to have an abortion in "liberty" rather than "privacy" should undercut that criticism.

My experience on the Seventh Circuit must explain four opinions that I wrote in my second term. In the first, *Estelle* v. *Gamble*,[20] I disagreed with an otherwise unanimous Court that rejected a prison inmate's claim that the medical treatment of his painful back injury by several different state officials constituted cruel and unusual punishment that violated the Eighth Amendment. The Seventh Circuit had allowed the prisoner's

18. 429 U.S. 589 (1977).
19. *Id.,* at 598–599.
20. 429 U.S. 97 (1976).

complaint to go forward. The Supreme Court reversed, concluding that the prisoner's allegations might well have been sufficient to describe tortious malpractice but did not violate the Constitution because he did not "allege acts or omissions sufficiently harmful to evidence deliberate indifference to serious medical needs."[21]

As I remember the vote at conference, the majority had decided that the Seventh Circuit should have simply affirmed the district court's order dismissing the case entirely. When Thurgood Marshall was assigned the majority opinion, however, after reviewing the record he merely held that the case against the medical director of the prison should have been dismissed but allowed the Seventh Circuit an "opportunity to consider, in conformity with this opinion, whether a cause of action has been stated against the other prison officials."[22] Thurgood's papers suggest that he originally wanted to remand the case directly to the district court for a hearing, but other justices persuaded him to permit the Seventh Circuit to first decide if a hearing was even necessary. The papers also show that the majority opinion was the product of compromise, shaped particularly by comments from Bill Rehnquist and Lewis Powell that forced Thurgood to narrow the opinion's support for a constitutional right to medical care for prisoners.[23]

I adhered to my dissenting vote because the opinion failed to respect the settled practice of liberally construing complaints drafted by prison inmates, failed to explain why the case had sufficient importance to justify review in our Court, and improperly attached significance to the subjective motivation of prison officials in deciding whether they had inflicted cruel and unusual punishment on a prisoner. My opposition to granting cert in *Estelle* was influenced not only by my view that the case involved nothing more than the application of well-settled law by three fine judges (including the retired Justice Tom Clark) but also by my opposition to Chief Justice Burger's support for the creation of a new federal

---

21. *Id.*, at 106.
22. *Id.*, at 108.
23. See Christopher E. Smith, *The Supreme Court and the Development of Law: Through the Prism of Prisoners' Rights* (New York: Palgrave Macmillan, 2016), 130–44.

court to process cert petitions. Instead of focusing on the importance of being more selective in decisions to grant cert, he favored the rather drastic remedy of creating an entirely new tribunal to perform that function.

On the merits, I thought that the question "whether the constitutional standard has been violated should turn on the character of the punishment rather than the motivation of the individual who inflicted it."[24] To illustrate my point, I referenced the notorious Civil War prisoner-of-war camp in Andersonville, Georgia, where 13,000 Union troops died from poor conditions and disease. "Subjective motivation may well determine what, if any, remedy is appropriate against a particular defendant....[But] [w]hether the conditions in Andersonville were the product of design, negligence, or mere poverty, they were cruel and inhuman."[25] The case is memorable because I believe it was the only one in which I would have given greater protection to a prison inmate's constitutional rights than Thurgood Marshall did.

The second case, *General Electric Co.* v. *Gilbert*,[26] raised a question of special interest to those who had opposed my confirmation on the ground that I would not be sympathetic to claims of discrimination against females. The question was whether the exclusion of pregnancy benefits from General Electric's otherwise comprehensive disability insurance plan for its employees violated a statutory prohibition against discrimination on the basis of sex. Two years earlier, the Court had held that a similar exclusion for pregnancy disabilities contained in California's disability insurance plan for state employees did not violate the Equal Protection Clause. The Court had reasoned that men and women were treated equally because neither class was protected against the risk of pregnancy. "There is no risk from which men are protected and women are not. Likewise there is no risk from which women are protected and men are not."[27]

24. 429 U.S., at 116.
25. *Id.,* at 116–17.
26. 429 U.S. 125 (1976).
27. *Geduldig* v. *Aiello,* 417 U.S. 484, 496–97 (1974).

That reasoning was again endorsed by Bill Rehnquist in his opinion for the Court in *Gilbert*.

Bill Brennan, joined by Thurgood Marshall, wrote a thorough dissent discussing the company's motives, the expertise of the Equal Employment Opportunity Commission, and the policy supporting the statutory prohibition against sex discrimination. I wrote a brief dissent concluding that "the language of the statute plainly requires the result which the Courts of Appeals have reached unanimously" — that is, a company may not exclude pregnancy benefits from an otherwise comprehensive disability insurance plan.[28] The issue turned on the answer to this simple question: "Does a contract between a company and its employees which treats the risk of absenteeism caused by pregnancy differently from any other kind of absence discriminate against certain individuals because of their sex?" The answer was obviously yes, because "it is the capacity to become pregnant which primarily differentiates the female from the male." Congress reacted to the Court's patently incorrect decision by enacting the Pregnancy Discrimination Act in 1978.

My third separate opinion was in *Craig* v. *Boren*,[29] which also involved sex discrimination. In that case, however, males were the disfavored class, and the issue involved the constitutionality of a statute rather than a dispute about its coverage. An Oklahoma statute prohibited the sale of 3.2 percent beer to males between the ages of 18 and 21 but permitted sales to females in that age bracket. Only Chief Justice Burger and Bill Rehnquist dissented from the Court's holding that the statute violated the Equal Protection Clause.

Prior to the Court's decision in that case, its opinions had seemed to divide statutes discriminating between different classes of persons into two categories: those requiring "strict scrutiny" and those merely requiring the legislature to have a "rational basis" for its decision. Statutes that triggered strict scrutiny were always invalidated, while those reviewed

---

28. 429 U.S., at 162.
29. 429 U.S. 190 (1976).

under the "rational basis" standard were almost always upheld. Whether sex discrimination should be reviewed under strict scrutiny or rational basis had been an open question after the Court unanimously invalidated a state statute giving males priority over females in qualifying as executor of a decedent's estate in *Reed* v. *Reed* in 1971. In *Craig* v. *Boren,* Bill Brennan's discussion of the showing required to justify a gender-based classification — it "must serve important governmental objectives and must be substantially related to achievement of those objectives"[30] — seemed to create an intermediate category of equal protection analysis.

As a Seventh Circuit judge I had struggled to understand the two-tiered approach to interpreting the Equal Protection Clause, particularly when trying to decipher the cases involving political gerrymanders, and concluded that it created more questions than answers. Accordingly, while I agreed with the conclusion in Bill Brennan's opinion in *Craig* v. *Boren,* I wrote separately, stating in part, "There is only one Equal Protection Clause. It requires every State to govern impartially."[31] I am still convinced that carefully analyzing in each case the reasons why a state enacts legislation treating different classes of its citizens differently is far wiser than applying a different level of scrutiny based on the class of persons subject to disparate treatment.

My fourth separate opinion was my solo dissent in *Delaware Tribal Business Committee* v. *Weeks,*[32] a case illustrating the diversity of issues confronting federal judges. In 1856 and 1857 the United States breached a treaty with the Delaware Indians by making private sales — rather than holding auctions — of reservation lands. Approximately one hundred years later, two groups representing the entire Delaware Tribe filed claims before the Indian Claims Commission establishing that the private sales had realized $1,385,617.81 less than the tribe would have collected from public auctions. Plus interest, the difference amounted to $9,168,171.13. Congress enacted a statute appropriating that sum and directing how it

30. *Id.,* at 197.
31. *Id.,* at 211.
32. 430 U.S. 73, 78 (1977).

should be distributed, but those directions omitted any provision for payment to the "Kansas Delawares." A member suing on behalf of that specific group persuaded a district court to enjoin any distribution of funds unless either the secretary of the interior or Congress included the Kansas Delawares in the award. The government appealed directly to our Court, which reversed by an eight-to-one vote.

Bill Brennan's opinion for the Court gave three reasons for his conclusion that Congress's omission of the Kansas Delawares was "tied rationally to the fulfillment of Congress's unique obligation toward the Indians." First, about ten years after the breach of the treaty obligation to sell the lands at auction, the ancestors of the Kansas Delawares had exercised their right to sever relations with the tribe and become American citizens, retaining their interest only in a proportionate share of the cash value of assets "then held" by the tribe. Second, in 1904 Congress had also excluded the Kansas Delawares from participation in a distribution of assets acquired by the tribe as compensation for another breach of the treaty. Third, limiting the award would avoid potential delay and the burden of resolving disputes about individual claims.

My dissent began by pointing out that the ancestors of the Kansas Delawares had suffered precisely the same wrong as those whose descendants will share in the award on a per capita basis and that it was clear that their exclusion was the consequence of a malfunction of the legislative process rather than a deliberate decision by Congress. Each of the three hypothetical justifications for the exclusion of the Kansas Delawares advanced by the majority opinion merely emphasized the absence of any rational explanation for the legislative malfunction, either because the justification did not exclude other Indians who should have been excluded under the same rationale or because the purported justification did not in fact describe the position of the Kansas Delawares. After explaining why there was no reason to believe that the discrimination was the product of an actual legislative choice, I concluded by quoting a phrase from an article by Professor Hans Linde — there had been a deprivation of property without the "due process of lawmaking" that the

Fifth Amendment guarantees.[33] In that and other cases, Linde's writing further supported my view that a study of legislative history can be valuable in trying to decipher the meaning of ambiguous statutes.

October Term 1977

During my early years on the Court, my colleagues granted review in many more cases than I thought wise. Instead of giving priority to claims that constitutional rights were being denied, the Court seemed to have a special interest in making sure that lower courts were allowing the police sufficient leeway in their enforcement of the criminal law — possibly reflecting a reaction by the four justices appointed by President Nixon to the dramatic decisions announced a few years earlier when Earl Warren had been the chief justice. An example of the Court's activism occurred early in my third term.

In *Pennsylvania* v. *Mimms*,[34] the Supreme Court of Pennsylvania had reversed a Muslim's conviction for carrying a concealed firearm without a license. While on routine patrol, two Philadelphia police officers had observed Henry Mimms driving with an expired license plate. They stopped the vehicle for the purpose of issuing a traffic summons. When one of the officers approached the car, he asked the driver to get out and produce his driver's license. As the driver was getting out of the front seat, the officer noticed a large bulge in his jacket, which prompted a frisk and the discovery of the weapon.

The state supreme court ruled that, given the absence of any evidence or even suspicion "that criminal activity was afoot or that the occupants of the vehicle posed a threat to police safety," the officers' order to Mimms to get out of his car was an unconstitutional seizure.

Bill Rehnquist persuaded a majority of our Court to summarily reverse the Pennsylvania Supreme Court's decision without full briefing

---

33. See "Due Process of Lawmaking," *Neb. L. Rev.* 55 (1976): 197.
34. 434 U.S. 106 (1977) (per curiam).

and oral argument. I dissented because I thought the Pennsylvania Supreme Court had reached the correct result, and, more importantly, because I thought it unwise to establish, without full briefing and argument, a categorical rule allowing every police officer to require drivers to get out of their cars. The new rule was supposedly justified by the interest in protecting the safety of the officer, despite the fact that professional studies had concluded that officer safety was better protected by requiring the driver to remain in the car.

Not only did the majority exaggerate the new rule's potential benefit to officer safety, but it largely ignored the rule's burden on the public. This aspect of the decision especially troubled me. I commented in my dissent that the "Court cannot seriously believe that the risk to the arresting officer is so universal that his safety is *always* a reasonable justification for ordering a driver out of his car."[35] "The commuter on his way home to dinner," I noted, "hardly pose[s] the same threat as a driver curbed after a high speed chase through a high crime area late at night."[36] "Nor is it universally true that the driver's interest in remaining in the car is negligible."[37] Among other examples I provided was the person who may have "left home in haste to drive children or spouse to school or to the train [and who] may not [have been] fully dressed."[38] My broader point was that, "[w]hether viewed from the standpoint of the officer's interest in his own safety, or from the citizen's interest in not being required to obey an arbitrary command, it is perfectly obvious that the millions of traffic stops that occur every year are not fungible."[39] I later dissented again, this time joined by Anthony Kennedy, in *Maryland* v. *Wilson*,[40] which extended *Mimms* to passengers as well as drivers.

The Court's construction of the Fourth Amendment in *Mimms* did not require state courts to adopt the same rule when construing their

35. *Id.*, at 120.
36. *Ibid.*
37. *Ibid.*
38. *Id.*, at 121.
39. *Ibid.*
40. 519 U.S. 408 (1997).

own constitutions, but most of them did. Some twenty-two years later, however, the Massachusetts Supreme Judicial Court took a fresh look at the issue in *Commonwealth* v. *Gonsalves*.[41] A majority of that court, over a lengthy dissent by Justice Charles Fried (who had been the solicitor general in Ronald Reagan's administration), agreed with the position I and the other dissenters endorsed in *Mimms* and *Wilson*. Before quoting my *Mimms* dissent, the *Gonsalves* majority noted that the simple fact that "a small percentage of routine traffic stops may result in the detection of more serious crime is no reason to subject the vast majority of citizens to orders to get out of their vehicles" and that "[s]uch an intrusion into a driver or a passenger's privacy is not minimal."[42] Other state supreme courts, including those of Vermont and Hawaii, have likewise rejected the *Mimms* rule as a matter of state constitutional law and held that an exit order must be supported by reasonable suspicion that a crime has been committed or that the driver or passenger presents a safety risk. Reasonable minds can disagree over the wisdom of the *Mimms* rule, but the fact that it was made without the benefit of full argument and briefing still troubles me.

Shortly before the Court announced *Mimms,* it heard argument in *Regents of the University of California* v. *Bakke*.[43] In that case, the California Supreme Court had invalidated the University of California Medical School's affirmative action program, holding that the program, which reserved sixteen places out of one hundred for minority students, violated the federal and state constitutions and Title VI of the Civil Rights Act of 1964.

In his opinion announcing the judgment of our Court, Lewis Powell stated that he was deciding two different legal issues: (1) whether the state court judgment holding the California program unlawful and directing that applicant Allan Bakke be admitted should be affirmed; and (2) whether the portion of the judgment enjoining the school "from

---

41. 711 N. E. 2d 108 (Mass. 1999).
42. *Id.,* at 112.
43. 438 U.S. 265 (1978).

according any consideration to race in its admissions process must be reversed."[44] I wrote a separate opinion, which Chief Justice Burger, Potter Stewart, and Bill Rehnquist joined, agreeing with Lewis's affirmative answer to the first question, but we did not think the record supported his view that the state court's judgment precluded the university from using its race-based admissions program in cases other than Bakke's. Writing separately, Bill Brennan, Byron White, Thurgood Marshall, and Harry Blackmun joined his answer to the second question. In short, the Court held that the university's affirmative action program was invalid but that the use of race might be permissible in other situations. Specifically, it endorsed the Harvard program that was quoted in full as an appendix to Lewis's opinion. The university's interest in having a diverse student body could justify the use of race in some circumstances but did not justify the quota system applied in Bakke's case.

The primary point of my separate opinion was based on the long-settled proposition that the Court should avoid deciding constitutional questions "unless such adjudication is unavoidable." I and the justices who joined my opinion were convinced that California's program violated the 1964 Civil Rights Act's prohibition of discrimination "on the ground of race" in the administration of any program receiving federal financial assistance and that it was therefore unnecessary to decide whether the program also violated the Constitution. In our view it was also unnecessary to discuss the question whether race could be a factor in any other admissions decision by the university because we did not agree with Lewis's view that the state court judgment had ruled on that hypothetical question.

The other opinions had construed the Civil Rights Act as prohibiting only those acts of discrimination that violated the Equal Protection Clause, which meant that they had to answer the constitutional question in order to determine what the statute meant. I still find their reasoning on this point unconvincing. I remain persuaded that Congress intended the relevant provisions of the Civil Rights Act to prohibit federal

---

44. *Id.*, at 272.

financial assistance to any program that discriminated against whites as well as nonwhites. It also still seems unlikely to me that Congress intended the meaning of the act to depend entirely on the outcome of the Court's future cases interpreting the Constitution.

Putting aside the debate about the legal issues that determined the outcome of *Bakke,* two aspects of those opinions merit special comment. First, Thurgood Marshall's opinion should be required reading for every high school in the country, for it tells a story that should be, but regrettably is not, familiar to many Americans. In that opinion, he summarized the impact of the Constitution as originally enacted on black Americans as well as the Supreme Court's role in reducing the force of the three amendments adopted after the Civil War. Second, Lewis Powell's description of the benefits provided to American students by the presence of diversity in the classroom provides an acceptable rationale for affirmative action in educational institutions that does not apply with the same force in the employment context.

During my third term, Lewis Powell also wrote for a divided Court in an important First Amendment case holding that the Constitution protects a corporation's right to spend money to influence the vote on a state referendum. I was one of the five votes supporting his opinion in *First National Bank of Boston* v. *Bellotti.*[45] That opinion includes a footnote stating that "our consideration of a corporation's right to speak on issues of general public interest implies no comparable right in the quite different context of participation in a political campaign for election to public office."[46] I had requested that footnote to make clear that the Court's holding did not affect the validity of rules regulating the financing of campaigns between rival candidates for public office — the important public interest in providing an equal playing field for rival candidates was not at issue in that case. In later years, justices who were not on the Court when *Bellotti*

---

45. 435 U.S. 765 (1978).
46. *Id.,* at 787n28.

was decided have occasionally cited that opinion as having ruled on the very issue that Powell put to one side in that footnote.

Probably the most consequential case of the 1977 term was *Monell* v. *New York City Dept. of Social Servs.*[47] That case involved a lawsuit brought under Section 1983 of Title 42 of the U.S. Code, the codified version of Section 1 of the Civil Rights Act of 1871. That act is sometimes referred to as the Ku Klux Klan Act because Congress enacted it in response to outrageous violence the Klan committed against former slaves in the mid-nineteenth century, though today Section 1983 provides the primary vehicle by which constitutional claims are litigated against state and local governments. While debating the act, Senator Sherman of Ohio (better known today for the antitrust statute bearing his name) proposed an amendment that would have imposed liability on municipal corporations for damages inflicted on its residents by Klan members. Some have incorrectly viewed Congress's rejection of that proposed amendment as providing support for *Monroe* v. *Pape*,[48] which held that municipal corporations cannot be sued under Section 1983.

The principal question in *Monell* was whether the City of New York could be sued under Section 1983 for allegedly violating the Constitution based on its policy of compelling pregnant city employees to take unpaid absences before such leaves were medically necessary. The Court held that the city could be sued under Section 1983 and therefore concluded that *Monroe* v. *Pape* must be overruled, in part because that opinion had misconstrued the deliberations over the Sherman Amendment in 1871 and because nothing in the legislative history precluded a construction of the statute that permitted suits against municipalities. I fully agreed with that analysis.

But in Part II of *Monell*, which I wisely refused to join, the Court gratuitously and surprisingly concluded that the refusal to adopt the Sherman Amendment supported the conclusion "that a municipality cannot

---

47. 436 U.S. 658 (1978).
48. 365 U.S. 167 (1961).

be held liable *solely* because it employs a tortfeasor — or, in other words, a municipality cannot be held liable under Section 1983 on a respondeat superior theory."[49] (Ironically, even though the Court overruled *Monroe*, the majority's reasoning in Part II would have justified *Monroe's* refusal to impose liability on the City of Chicago for the wrongful conduct of its police officers in that earlier case.) The *Monell* majority further concluded that a local government may be sued only "when execution of a government's policy or custom, whether made by its lawmakers or by those whose edicts or acts may fairly be said to represent official policy, inflicts the injury that the government as an entity is responsible under § 1983."[50] I remain skeptical of that conclusion.

My opinion for the Court in the antitrust case *National Soc. of Professional Engineers* v. *United States*[51] gave me the opportunity to share with the public two propositions that my students had learned when I taught the course in antitrust law years earlier. First, Section 1 of the Sherman Act is an example of a statute "that cannot mean what it says. The statute says that 'every' contract that restrains trade is unlawful. But, as Justice Brandeis perceptively noted, restraint is the very essence of every contract; read literally, Section 1 would outlaw the entire body of private contract law. Yet it is that body of law that establishes the enforceability of commercial agreements and enables competitive markets — indeed, a competitive economy — to function effectively."[52] Second, contrary to its name, the Rule of Reason — under which the proper inquiry is whether the challenged agreement is one that promotes, or one that suppresses, competition — "does not open the field of antitrust inquiry to any argument in favor of a challenged restraint that may fall within the realm of reason. Instead, it focuses on the challenged restraint's impact on competitive conditions."[53]

---

49. 436 U.S., at 691.
50. *Id.,* at 694.
51. 435 U.S. 679 (1978).
52. *Id.,* at 687–88.
53. *Id.,* at 688.

*   *   *

My third term did not end until July 3, 1978, when Chief Justice Burger announced the judgment in *Lockett* v. *Ohio*.[54] In *Lockett*, the Ohio Supreme Court had affirmed the death sentence imposed on Sandra Lockett, a twenty-one-year-old who had participated in the planning and execution of the robbery of a pawn shop. She had been seated in a car when two of her accomplices entered the shop armed with a gun. The robbery proceeded according to plan until one of the robbers announced the "stickup," at which point the pawnbroker grabbed the gun. The gun went off, firing a fatal shot into the pawnbroker. Although Sandra neither intended nor expected the killing to occur, under Ohio law she had committed a capital offense. She was found guilty and sentenced to death.

One of Lockett's arguments challenging the constitutionality of Ohio's death penalty statute was that it did not permit the sentencing judge to consider as mitigating factors her lack of specific intent to cause death and her relatively minor part in the crime. Chief Justice Burger was convinced; he noted that the concept of individualized sentencing, although not constitutionally required, had been accepted for many years in noncapital cases and favorably noted in death cases as well. He quoted with approval an excerpt from the opinion that Potter Stewart, Lewis Powell, and I had announced two years earlier stating that "the fundamental respect for humanity underlying the Eighth Amendment… requires consideration of the character and record of the individual offender and the circumstances of the particular offense as a constitutionally indispensable part of the process of inflicting the penalty of death."[55] Chief Justice Burger noted that the foregoing declaration "rested 'on the predicate that the penalty of death is qualitatively different' from any other sentence" and "calls for a greater degree of reliability when the death sentence is imposed."[56] He then added this profoundly important

---

54. 438 U.S. 586.
55. See 438 U.S., at 604, quoting *Woodson* v. *North Carolina*, 428 U.S. 280, 304 (1976) (plurality opinion).
56. *Ibid.*

statement: "The need for treating each defendant in a capital case with that degree of respect due the uniqueness of the individual is far more important than in noncapital cases.... The nonavailability of corrective or modifying mechanisms with respect to an executed capital sentence underscores the need for individualized consideration as a constitutional requirement in imposing the death sentence."[57]

Accordingly, the sentencer in a capital case must not be precluded from considering as a mitigating factor any aspect of a defendant's character or record and any of the circumstances of the offense that the defendant proffers as a basis for a sentence less than death. When *Lockett* was written, the risk of error in capital cases was not as well recognized as it is today, but that recognition makes Chief Justice Burger's emphasis on the "nonavailability of corrective or modifying mechanisms with respect to an executed capital sentence" an equally powerful reason for abolishing the death penalty altogether.

October Term 1978

My fourth term on the Court began a month before Jimmy Carter defeated Gerald Ford in the 1978 presidential election. While I have always thought that Ford's decision to pardon Richard Nixon was correct because it helped the country recover from the Watergate "nightmare," I also suspect that decision may have been so unpopular that it determined the outcome of the election. One of the many reasons why I admire President Ford so much is my conviction that when he decided to pardon Nixon he was fully aware of its likely adverse impact on his own political future, but he nevertheless made the decision that he rightly believed would best serve the country.

Jimmy Carter was inaugurated at a ceremony on the east side of the Capitol — a setting far less imposing than the balcony on the other side facing the Washington Monument and the Lincoln Memorial. I nevertheless have a vivid memory of the occasion, partly because of my respect

---

57. *Id.*, at 605.

for Ford but more importantly because the event that transferred the leadership of the most powerful country in the world from a member of one political party to another was conducted with such dignity, courtesy, and respect.

Not long after the inauguration, the Carters invited the members of the Court and their wives to an informal dinner at the White House. It was a small gathering, with all of us seated at two tables — the president at one and the first lady at the other. Halfway through the meal they changed places, giving every guest an opportunity to socialize with both of them. I have indistinct memories of the president commenting on some reading he had just finished and stating that he felt well prepared for his new job. Except for the occasion of the pope's visit to Washington a year later, I remember no other contact with him while he was in office. Though he wisely selected Ruth Ginsburg and Stephen Breyer to fill vacancies on the District of Columbia and First Circuit Courts of Appeals, respectively, he did not have an opportunity to make any appointments to the Supreme Court.

Early in the term, the Court heard argument in an interesting and unusual case involving a state's claim of sovereign immunity, *Nevada* v. *Hall*.[58] The plaintiffs were California residents who were severely injured in an automobile accident in California. The allegedly negligent driver of the other car, who was killed in the collision, was an employee of the University of Nevada engaged in state business in a state-owned car. The plaintiffs sought recovery from the state of Nevada in a California court; Nevada claimed that as a sovereign state it was not subject to suit in the courts of another state. The California courts rejected that defense, and we granted certiorari to decide whether federal law protected Nevada from liability. Chief Justice Burger, Harry Blackmun, and Bill Rehnquist thought it did, but six justices concluded that federal law did not provide a sovereign immunity defense to a state sued in the courts of another state; instead, whether California recognized the defense was a matter of

---

58. 440 U.S. 410 (1979).

California law to be decided by California judges. Because the chief was in dissent, Bill Brennan, as the senior member of the majority, assigned the opinion to me.

Although the doctrine of sovereign immunity was older than our country, I was surprised to learn that, despite its importance, the question whether one state may claim immunity from suits in another state's courts had never been considered by our Court. The Court, however, had considered another aspect of the sovereign immunity doctrine — namely, a sovereign's power to decide whether it will allow itself to be sued in its own courts. When a sovereign creates its own judicial system, it obviously may decide whether it will permit itself to be sued or, in the alternative, grant itself immunity from suit in its courts. Justice Holmes was discussing this concept of sovereign immunity when he said "that there can be no legal right as against the authority that makes the law on which the right depends."

The origins of that concept may have been based on the fiction that the king could do no wrong or more probably on the structure of the feudal system. No lord could be sued by a vassal in the lord's court, while each petty lord was subject to suit in the courts of a higher lord. Since the king was at the apex of the feudal pyramid, there was no higher court in which he could be sued. But neither the feudal structure nor the fiction that the king was infallible would provide any justification for recognizing an immunity that would prevent a California court from adjudicating a claim against the state of Nevada.

As a matter of comity, however, some sovereigns have extended immunity to other sovereigns in exchange for either an express agreement — or at least a reasonable expectation — that they will receive a comparable immunity if they are sued in the courts of the other sovereign. If it had chosen to do so, California might have granted its sister states sovereign immunity hoping all of them would reciprocate, but California had not done so. The question we faced, therefore, was whether there is any basis in the Constitution or any federal statute for imposing a requirement that state courts must grant immunity to all of their sister states. No such statute exists and the Constitution is silent on the question. Nevertheless, Nevada argued that such a rule was implicit in the Constitution when it was adopted.

My opinion for the Court categorically rejected that argument and held that each state was free to determine whether to grant immunity to a sister state. In his dissent, Bill Rehnquist did not rely on anything in the text of the Constitution; rather he relied on notions of a constitutional plan — "the implicit ordering of relationships within the federal system necessary to make the Constitution a workable governing charter and to give each provision of the document the full effect intended by the Framers." He quoted Alexander Hamilton's statement in the Federalist Papers that "[it] is inherent in the nature of sovereignty not to be amenable to suit of an individual *without its consent*." He did not consider, however, the difference between a sovereign's reliance on the immunity defense in its own courts and such reliance in another sovereign's courts. Moreover, neither in that dissent nor in later opinions that extended the doctrine to protect state officials from actions seeking to enforce federal legislation did Bill Rehnquist attempt to explain why the ancient doctrine of sovereign immunity should be kept alive in a democratic country.

Later in the term, Bill Rehnquist wrote his opinion for a unanimous Court in *Leo Sheep Co.* v. *United States*.[59] He characterized the issue in the case as "mundane": whether the federal government had an implied easement to build a road across land that was originally granted to the Union Pacific Railroad as part of a scheme to subsidize the construction of a transcontinental railroad. Far from being mundane, however, his opinion is a fascinating example of the use of history to shed light on the meaning of an Act of Congress; in that case it was the history of the country rather than merely an account of the legislative deliberations that produced ambiguous statutory language. Like Thurgood Marshall's illuminating discussion of the development of racial segregation both before and after the Civil War in his separate *Bakke* opinion, Bill's

---

59. 440 U.S. 668 (1979).

account of the development of Congress's power to make "internal improvements" — such as land grants for a road between Columbus and Sandusky, Ohio — sheds important light on aspects of our history that are not as well known as they should be. The Civil War apparently helped break a political impasse in Congress that had frustrated attempts to determine the routes of railroads from the Mississippi River to California. Few readers will recognize the names of two Civil War battles — the Battle of Picacho Pass and the Battle of Glorietta Pass — that led to the transfer in the spring of 1862 of Tucson, Arizona, and portions of Colorado from Confederate forces to the Union. But after reading Bill's opinion they may be convinced that those battles, or at least the Civil War itself, played a significant role in making "some impression upon Congress of the necessity for being able to transport readily men and material into that area for military purposes."[60]

In later cases involving statutory construction as well, Bill Rehnquist made effective use of legislative history. While I did not participate in the case upholding the affirmative action program adopted by the Kaiser Aluminum & Chemical Corporation in 1974 (because Bob Turner, my close friend from the navy and from law school, was the general counsel of Kaiser and presumably one of the architects of the plan), I admired Bill Rehnquist's thorough analysis of the legislative history of Title VII of the Civil Rights Act of 1974 in that case. Kaiser's program resulted from a collectively bargained agreement that reserved for black employees 50 percent of the openings in an in-plant training program until the percentage of black workers in the plant was commensurate with the percentage of blacks in the local labor force. The majority opinion written by Bill Brennan upheld the validity of the program — a result that has served the public interest in the long run. Nevertheless, Bill Rehnquist's thirty-five-page dissenting opinion convinced me that Congress actually intended to prohibit programs like Kaiser's because they discriminated against white employees on the basis of their race. I still think the dissent had the

---

60. *Id.*, at 674.

better of the argument. I mention the case because, like the *Leo Sheep* case, it illustrates the fact that Bill Rehnquist endorsed the use of legislative history as a tool of statutory construction — an increasingly controversial proposition for some on the Court today.

In February 1979, I was one of the three judges hearing a moot court competition at Notre Dame Law School. Sitting with me were Arthur England, the chief justice of the Supreme Court of Florida, and Cornelia Kennedy, who was at the time the chief judge of the U.S. District Court for the Eastern District of Michigan and who later became a judge on the Court of Appeals for the Sixth Circuit. Cornelia and I had first met in 1970 when both of us attended the Senate Judiciary Committee hearing that preceded our appointment to the federal bench. We were good friends. All of the student participants in the argument were women, and all were excellent advocates. I have referred to the argument on many occasions as the best moot court that I attended during my years on the bench. It was an important occasion for reasons that have seldom been recognized.

During the argument all of the participants addressed Cornelia as "Madame Justice." I noticed that she did not seem to welcome that form of address; nevertheless, I was surprised by her response during the fourth advocate's argument. Obviously unhappy with the fact that all the female advocates had addressed her as "Madame Justice," she ultimately interrupted the final advocate with this question: "Why do you address me as 'Madame Justice'? The word 'Justice' is not a sexist term." At our conference with Justice England after the argument, I commented on the obvious strength of Cornelia's adverse reaction to the use of the term "Madame Justice," and she forcefully restated views that she must have formed during her tenure as one of the few female jurists on the federal bench for many years — indeed, one of only seven when she was appointed in 1970.

After my return to Washington, at the next Court conference that I attended, I described the incident to my colleagues. Potter Stewart responded by stating that sooner or later we were going to have women serving on the Court and that it would be wise to anticipate that change by substituting the simple term "Justice" for the term "Mr. Justice" that had until then been the only accepted form of address to a member of the Court and which then appeared on a brass nameplate on the door to every justice's chambers. Potter's suggestion was promptly endorsed, and by an eight-to-one vote put into effect. Thanks to the firm views expressed by Cornelia Kennedy, one of the pioneer female members of the federal judiciary, an all-male institution avoided one of the problems that might have confronted Sandra O'Connor (and the rest of us) when she later joined the Court.

October Term 1979

Supreme Court terms begin on the first Monday of October. Before Harry Blackmun joined the Court in 1970, the first week of each term was reserved for the consideration of certiorari petitions that had been filed during the summer; oral arguments did not take place until the following week. At Harry's suggestion, however, the Court began holding its first fall conference during the last week in September, and hearing arguments beginning on the first Monday in October. In October 1979, an unusual event followed the first week of argument — Pope John Paul II visited Washington, D.C., and the members of the Court were invited to meet him.

They joined some fifty or sixty other invited guests who were lined up outside the White House on a cloudy morning awaiting the arrival of the "popemobile." When the vehicle arrived, the sun suddenly broke through the clouds, its beams dramatically focused on the pope, as though a Hollywood director (or perhaps the good Lord) had planned the scene.

After the pope alighted, he was escorted by President Carter down the line, greeting and shaking hands with each of the invited guests. As they approached my daughter Sue and me, and the president mentioned my name, the pope graciously suggested that I might be "John Paul the

Third." Lewis Powell's wife, Jo, was standing next to Sue and responded, "No, he is our John Paul the First." Her remark surprised me as much as it surprised the pope, but I have always remembered that incident as evidence of my close friendship with Lewis and his especially kind spouse.

Lewis had served in England during World War II; he was responsible for providing senior air force and other combat officers with intelligence derived from the decryption of German communications. Because of the ever-present risk of capture, he used fictional explanations for his sources of information. Our duties were quite different, but those experiences were among the shared circumstances that enhanced our friendship and mutual respect. During the entire time that we were both on the Court, we sat next to each other during oral arguments. On more than one occasion he greeted me with a compliment on a dissent that I had just circulated, sometimes even stating that he wished that he had read it before joining the majority.

Later that term he authored the dissent, which Bill Brennan, Thurgood Marshall, and I joined, in an important case in which the defendant challenged the constitutionality of his life sentence for committing three relatively minor property offenses. In 1964 William Rummel pleaded guilty to the fraudulent use of a credit card to obtain eighty dollars in goods and services; in 1969 he pleaded guilty to passing a forged check in the amount of $28.36; and in 1973 he was found guilty of obtaining $128.75 by false pretenses. Under Texas's recidivist statute, the trial judge sentenced him to life in prison. The Texas courts and the federal district court rejected his claim that the sentence violated the constitutional prohibition against cruel and unusual punishment.

In our Court, Rummel stressed the absence of any violence and the small amounts of money involved to support his argument that there was no precedent for imposing such a severe penalty for such minor offenses. Writing for the majority in *Rummel* v. *Estelle*,[61] however, Bill Rehnquist essentially held that legislatures rather than courts should make the

---

61. 445 U.S. 263 (1980).

"subjective" decisions setting sentence limits — although he appeared willing to assume that a life sentence for illegal overnight parking might be too much. In his dissent, Lewis Powell first endorsed the proposition that "the Cruel and Unusual Punishments Clause extends not only to barbarous methods of punishments, but also to punishments that are grossly disproportionate." He then cogently explained why Rummel's sentence was excessive, whether compared to other Texas sentences, to sentences in other states, or to basic notions of fairness. I have long shared the view that the Eighth Amendment contains a proportionality principle, which sentences of excessive length may violate.

Also in the 1979 term, Lewis Powell authored the dissent from my opinion for the Court in *Branti* v. *Finkel,*[62] which held that assistant public defenders who were satisfactorily performing their jobs could not be discharged solely because of their political beliefs. My opinion relied almost entirely on Bill Brennan's opinion in *Elrod* v. *Burns,*[63] which in turn had followed the reasoning of my opinion as a Seventh Circuit judge in *Illinois State Employees* v. *Lewis.*[64] Lewis's dissent, however, was the first to advocate the preservation of the patronage system on its merits, rather than simply arguing that it was an important part of the country's history that should be kept alive for that reason. Our rejection of his thoughtful dissent was an important step in the development of the law.

A few terms earlier, Lewis had authored a cogent concurrence in *United States* v. *Watson,*[65] which held for the first time that a law enforcement officer need not obtain a warrant, even if he has time to do so, to make a valid arrest in a public place. He pointed out that the Court had not decided the more difficult question whether, in the absence of exigent circumstances, officers having probable cause to arrest a suspect may enter his home to take him into custody without a warrant. That question was

---

62. 445 U.S. 507 (1980).
63. 427 U.S. 347 (1976).
64. 473 F. 2d 561 (CA7 1972).
65. 423 U.S. 411 (1976).

presented to the Court in *Payton* v. *New York*,[66] a case decided during the 1979 term.

Neither English common law judges, nor the state courts, nor scholars had reached a consensus on the issue. Over the dissent of Byron White, the author of *Watson,* the Court decided that the police must obtain a warrant before entering a home to make an arrest. My opinion for the majority in *Payton* relied primarily on "the overriding respect for the sanctity of the home that has been embedded in our traditions since the origins of the Republic." In a footnote, I quoted from William Pitt, Earl of Chatham, who had famously said in 1763, "The poorest man may in his cottage bid defiance to all the forces of the Crown. It may be frail; the roof may shake; the wind may blow through it; the storm may enter; the rain may enter; but the King of England may not enter — all his force dares not the threshold of the ruined tenement." My law clerk Peter Isakoff recalled *Payton* as his favorite case of the 1979 term, and he also reminded me that I had not only been able to hold the five original votes from conference, but I was also able to steal Harry Blackmun away from Byron's dissent, yielding a solid six-to-three majority. *Payton* remains good law today.

Three additional opinions that I wrote toward the end of the 1979 term must be mentioned: my dissent in *Harris* v. *McRae;*[67] my dissent in *Fullilove* v. *Klutznick;*[68] and my opinion announcing the judgment of the Court in the "benzene case," *Industrial Union Dept., AFL–CIO* v. *American Petroleum Institute.*[69]

In 1977, I had joined the majority opinion in *Maher* v. *Roe,*[70] holding that the Constitution does not require the government to pay for nontherapeutic abortions even though it subsidizes the costs of childbirth for indigent women. The fact that earlier cases protected a woman's freedom

---

66. 445 U.S. 573 (1980).
67. 448 U.S. 297 (1980).
68. 448 U.S. 448 (1980).
69. 448 U.S. 607 (1980).
70. 432 U.S. 464.

to choose abortion over natural birth did not include a constitutional right to have the government pay for a medically unnecessary abortion. In *Harris* v. *McRae,* Potter Stewart's opinion for the majority extended that holding to enforce the Hyde Amendment's prohibition on the use of federal funds to pay for abortions even though the abortion was medically necessary and the patient was indigent and eligible for Medicare benefits. (Although I dissented from the majority opinion in *Harris,* a remarkable and commendable feature of the opinion is the fact that it does not mention a right to privacy and its discussion of the constitutional right at stake is phrased entirely in the language of "liberty.")

In my dissent, I noted that the majority decision was a product of a flawed method of equal protection analysis based on "levels of scrutiny" rather than comparing the weight of the individual's interest in inclusion in the protected class with the government's interest in keeping her out. Since the Court had already decided that the individual interest in the freedom to have an abortion and the government's interest in protecting maternal health both outweighed the government's interest in protecting life prior to viability, the Court's equal protection analysis was "doubly erroneous."[71]

In *Fullilove,* by a vote of six to three, the Court upheld the constitutionality of a requirement in a congressional spending program that 10 percent of the federal funds granted for local public works projects must be used by the local grantee to procure services or supplies from businesses owned and controlled by members of one of six defined groups of American citizens: "Negroes, Spanish-speaking, Orientals, Indians, Eskimos, and Aleuts." Potter Stewart, joined by Bill Rehnquist, dissented on the ground that the Constitution flatly prohibits discrimination on the basis of race.

I also dissented, but unlike those two justices, I was not convinced that the constitutional provisions that require the government to govern impartially contain an absolute prohibition against any statutory classification

---

71. 448 U.S., at 352n4.

based on race. I did, however, believe that the Constitution required special scrutiny of any governmental decision-making that drew nationwide distinctions between citizens on the basis of their race and incidentally also discriminated against noncitizens in each of the preferred racial classes. The fact that Congress for the first time in its history had created a broad classification for entitlement to special benefits based solely on racial characteristics identified a dramatic difference between this act and the thousands that had preceded it; yet that fact was not even mentioned in the act's statement of purposes or in the reports of either the House or the Senate committee that processed the legislation. Nor had the legislation's unprecedented nature been the subject of any testimony or inquiry in any legislative hearing on the bill that was enacted. The sparse deliberation that preceded enactment was comparable to Congress's mistreatment of the Delaware Indians that had prompted my dissent a year earlier. In sum, I thought the statute invalid because it was not "narrowly tailored." In a footnote, I identified some of the questions that Congress had failed to address:

> For example, why were these six racial classifications, and no others, included in the preferred class? Why are aliens excluded from the preference although they are not otherwise ineligible for public contracts? What percentage of Oriental blood or what degree of Spanish-speaking skill is required for membership in the preferred class?[72]

I thought the statutory preference for each of the racially defined classes could not be upheld either as an appropriate remedy for victims of unfair treatment in the past or on an assumption that they would be less able to compete with nonmembers in the future.

The same day that *Fullilove* was announced — July 2, 1980 — I also announced the judgment of the Court in a case invalidating regulations

---

72. 448 U.S., at 552n30.

adopted by the secretary of labor to minimize the health risks resulting from the exposure to benzene in the workplace. My opinion contains a comprehensive and uninteresting discussion of the voluminous evidence in the record that we found insufficient to support the extremely burdensome regulation at issue. In that opinion I relied heavily on the study of the record by my law clerk Michele Odorizzi, whose pregnancy was threatening to produce her first child before her analysis of the evidence was completed. As it developed, we completed our opinion before the baby arrived, but just a few days after his delivery she was well enough to appear in open court when I descended from the bench to move her admission to the Supreme Court bar. Over the years we have frequently recalled that event as the most important accomplishment of the October 1979 term.

In his response to my request for comments on the term, Peter Isakoff, Michele's co-clerk, noted that 1979 was a particularly happy year because it was the year that I married Maryan. It was also the year when Bob Woodward and Scott Armstrong's book *The Brethren* came out. Peter recalled that while the book might seem tame now, particularly as the Court is a more open institution than it used to be, *The Brethren*'s release was anticipated with dread. Despite the stern admonition that law clerks and all Court personnel receive about secrecy, it was apparent from the book's contents that several people at the Court, including law clerks and possibly even a justice or two, had spoken with the authors. At the height of the tension surrounding the book, Peter recalled that I walked into his and Michele's office with the book in hand, reading out loud from the chapter concerning the 1975 term, the only place in the book where I was mentioned. The book is written with an omniscient third-person narrator who purports to quote the justices' inner, unexpressed thoughts. Peter recalls that I laughed uproariously, ridiculing the authors' attempt to capture my own thoughts, which helped diffuse much of the tension surrounding the book.

At the time, I was the only justice who had only two law clerks, and Chief Justice Burger made it known to Peter and Michele when he had lunch with them that he was openly skeptical of the two-clerk practice, because it risked creating a bottleneck for the Court. As Michele's pregnancy progressed, I asked Peter whether he and Michele would be able to handle the assigned workload. He assured me that they would be able to handle it, which of course they did.

October Term 1980

On November 4, 1979, the American embassy in Tehran had been seized and our diplomatic personnel captured and held hostage. Ten days later President Carter declared a national emergency and froze the assets of the Iranian government and its central bank; he later issued regulations that authorized creditors of Iran to initiate legal proceedings against Iranian entities. Pursuant to those regulations Dames & Moore, an American company claiming that it was owed $3,436,694.30 plus interest under a contract to conduct site studies for a nuclear plant in Iran, brought suit in a federal court in California and obtained an attachment against Iranian property to secure any judgment that it might obtain.

On January 19, 1981, the day before Ronald Reagan succeeded President Carter, the government of Algeria announced the terms of an agreement between Iran and the United States that provided for (1) the release of the American hostages on the following day; (2) the termination of all litigation between Iran and the United States and citizens of either country, including the nullification of all attachments and judgments obtained in such litigation; (3) the establishment of an Iran–United States arbitration tribunal to make final and binding awards of all claims that were not settled within six months; and (4) the return to Iran of all frozen assets except for $1 billion to be deposited in the Bank of England and used to pay awards rendered against Iran by the new arbitration tribunal. On the day that the Algerian government announced the settlement, President Carter issued a series of executive orders carrying out our government's obligations under the agreements, and on February 24, President Reagan issued another executive order ratifying what his predecessor had done.

Thereafter Dames & Moore challenged the validity of the executive orders and regulations implementing the settlement. On May 28, 1981, the district court entered an order upholding the presidents' actions. Five days later, Dames & Moore filed a notice of appeal in the court of appeals, followed promptly by a petition in the Supreme Court that we issue a writ of certiorari without waiting for the court of appeals to consider the case. We granted that petition, adopted an expedited briefing schedule, and set the case for oral argument on Wednesday, June 24, 1981. At that argument, the solicitor general informed us that unless the government acted on its obligations under the settlement by July 19, 1981, Iran could consider the United States to be in breach of its agreement.

At the justices' conference after that argument we all agreed that the president had the constitutional authority that both Jimmy Carter and Ronald Reagan had exercised in agreeing to the settlement with Iran. That conclusion was supported by an act of Congress — the International Emergency Economic Powers Act of 1976 — as well as by the fact that the United States, like other nations, had frequently engaged in the practice of settling claims by the nationals of one state against another, and by statements in our earlier opinions that the president's power over foreign affairs is at its zenith when it is supported by Congress. Congress had held hearings on the agreement and, far from disapproving any aspect of it, had characterized the new arbitration tribunal as "of vital importance to the United States." We assumed that the creation of the international arbitration procedure would produce the fair resolution of disputed claims.

Recognizing the need for a prompt and lucid opinion, Chief Justice Burger — instead of assigning the preparation of the Court opinion to himself as might well have been appropriate in such an important case — requested the justice he thought best qualified for the task to take the assignment. Bill Rehnquist did that job. His scholarly thirty-five-page opinion, concluding with the directive that "the mandate shall issue forthwith," was announced on July 2, 1981, just eight days after the Court heard argument in the case.

*　　*　　*

In two cases decided during the 1980 term — the last term in which all of the justices were males — the Court considered the constitutionality of two state statutes of special interest to females. In *H. L.* v. *Matheson*,[73] a Utah statute regulated pregnant teenagers' access to abortion, and in *Michael M.* v. *Superior Court, Sonoma Cty.*,[74] a California statute was designed to minimize teenage pregnancies. In both cases six justices rejected the challenges to the statutes, and in both I wrote separate opinions.

H.L. was one of a series of cases involving the constitutionality of state statutes limiting the rights of young women to obtain abortions. In 1978, H.L. was an unmarried fifteen-year-old girl living with her parents in Utah and dependent on them for support. After discovering that she was pregnant, she consulted with a social worker and a physician who advised her that an abortion would be in her best medical interest. The doctor, however, refused to perform the procedure because a Utah statute required him to notify her parents before performing the abortion. For undisclosed reasons, H.L. refused to notify her parents and, while still in the first trimester of her pregnancy, brought a class action challenging the validity of the Utah statute. Suing on behalf of a class of unmarried minor women suffering from unwanted pregnancies that they were unable to terminate because of the statute, she sought a declaration that the statute was invalid and an injunction against its enforcement.

The majority decided that H.L. did not have standing to sue on behalf of the entire class that she represented, but upheld the statute as applied to an unemancipated minor who is dependent upon her parents and has made no showing "as to her maturity or as to her relations with her parents."[75] As explained in Lewis Powell's concurring opinion, the Court left open the question whether the statute could be enforced in cases involving "a mature minor or a minor whose best interests would not be served by parental notification."[76]

73.　450 U.S. 398 (1981).
74.　450 U.S. 464 (1981).
75.　450 U.S., at 407.
76.　*Id.,* at 414.

I concurred in the judgment. A few years earlier, the Court had invalidated a Missouri statutory provision that required an unmarried woman under the age of eighteen to secure her parents' consent before she could obtain an abortion. Because it was so well settled that the law may prevent minors from entering into binding contracts and making a variety of other less important decisions on their own, I thought the parental consent requirement was valid and had dissented from that holding. The Utah statute challenged by H.L. merely required the doctor to notify the parents of his patient before performing the procedure, but did not forbid him from proceeding with or without their consent. The Utah Supreme Court had correctly distinguished the earlier case and simply rejected H.L.'s challenge without questioning her standing to sue on behalf of the class. For the reasons given in my dissent in the earlier case, I would have simply affirmed the Utah court's decision. In my judgment a statute merely requiring a doctor to notify parents that he was about to perform a serious medical procedure on their child was clearly valid. As I had written in my earlier dissent, "The State's interest in protecting a young person from harm justifies the imposition of restraints on his or her freedom even though comparable restraints on adults would be constitutionally impermissible."[77]

In *Michael M. v. Superior Court, Sonoma Cty.,*[78] a seventeen-year-old male who had had sex with a sixteen-year-old female was accused of violating California's "statutory rape" law. The statute prohibited "an act of sexual intercourse accomplished with a female...under the age of 18 years."[79] The defendant claimed that the statute was unconstitutional because the law punished only men for the act of sexual intercourse. The California Supreme Court held that the statute did not violate the Equal Protection Clause because only males can "physiologically cause the result which the law properly seeks to avoid" — namely, teenage pregnancy. While no member of our Court seemed to agree with that notion,

---

77. *Planned Parenthood of Central Mo. v. Danforth,* 428 U.S. 52, 102 (1976).
78. 450 U.S. 464 (1981).
79. *Id.,* at 466.

the majority did uphold the statute. For the majority the fact that females suffer most of the burdens of pregnancies justified a rule that excluded them from criminal responsibility for their participation in the risk-creating conduct.

Writing for himself and Byron White and Thurgood Marshall, Bill Brennan dissented on the ground that the state had failed to show that its gender-based discriminatory rule was substantially related to the achievement of its admittedly valid state interest in preventing teenage pregnancy. For me the statute was invalid for a more fundamental reason — as applied to two teenagers of the same age voluntarily engaging in sexual activity, it required that "one, and only one, of two equally guilty wrongdoers be stigmatized by a criminal conviction." Such a rule "violates the essence of the constitutional requirement that the sovereign must govern impartially."

During the 1980 term the Court decided an important patent case that led to a significant increase in the number of granted patents in later years. The case, *Diamond* v. *Diehr,*[80] involved the patentability of a process for molding uncured synthetic rubber into permanent products under heat and pressure. The process measured the temperature inside the mold and, applying a familiar formula, used a computer to ascertain the precise time when all parts of the object would be cured and it was time to open the molding device. Recognizing that laws of nature, natural phenomena, algorithms, and abstract ideas are excluded from patentable subject matter, by a five-to-four vote the Court nevertheless held that the patent on the rubber-curing process was valid.

I had written many patent decisions as a Seventh Circuit judge, and had authored the opinion for the Court in *Parker* v. *Flook*[81] — a case invalidating a somewhat similar patent — two years earlier. I felt strongly that the majority was taking an important step in the wrong direction. I therefore dissented at some length, beginning with a description of the then

---

80. 450 U.S. 175 (1981).
81. 437 U.S. 584 (1978).

relatively young computer industry and the fact that prior to 1968 "well-established principles of patent law probably would have prevented the issuance of a valid patent on almost any conceivable computer program."[82] I noted that in 1965 the president's Commission on the Patent System had recommended that computer programs should be expressly ineligible for patent coverage, and I explained in detail why a correct interpretation of our decision in *Flook* required the same result in this case.

The disagreement between the majority and the dissenters stemmed from their differing understandings of what the inventors claimed to have discovered: the majority thought that the inventors had discovered a method of constantly measuring the actual temperature inside a rubber molding press whereas I read the patent as claiming the discovery of an improved method of calculating the time that the mold should remain closed during the curing process. Among my reasons for rejecting the majority's understanding was the fact that an ordinary back porch thermometer qualified as a device "for constantly measuring actual temperatures."

The question that the case actually presented, then, was whether a new method of programming a digital computer qualifies as patentable subject matter. My negative answer to that question has been shared by several Commissioners of Patents and Trademarks.

Connie Trela and Jeff Tone, my clerks during the 1980 term, recalled that the cases on which they worked were less notable than events outside the Court, such as the attempted assassination of President Reagan. The majority opinions assigned to me that term reflected my status as a junior justice; that is, they were not very interesting. This meant that the most interesting opinions they helped me with were my concurrences and dissents, at least a few of which later became controlling law, such as my dissent in *Diamond* v. *Diehr,* which was largely adopted by the Court years later in *In re Bilski, Mayo* v. *Prometheus,* and *CLS Bank* v. *Alice Corporation.*

---

82. 450 U.S., at 195.

That was also true of my separate opinions in *Robbins* v. *California*,[83] which held that the Fourth Amendment required a warrant be obtained to open opaque sealed packages found in the trunk of a car, and *New York* v. *Belton*,[84] decided the same day, which held that a warrant was *not* required for the search of a jacket found in the back seat of a car because the search was incident to a "lawful custodial arrest." I dissented in *Robbins* and concurred in the judgment in *Belton;* in the very next term, in *United States* v. *Ross*,[85] the Court, in an opinion I authored, adopted the view set forth in my *Robbins* dissent.

And in *Eddings* v. *State of Oklahoma*,[86] the Court initially voted to deny the petition involving a defendant who committed murder when he was sixteen years old and was sentenced to death after the state courts ruled that his youth would not be considered a mitigating factor. I circulated a draft dissent from the denial, arguing that consistent with the principles of the Eighth Amendment and evolving standards of decency, a civilized nation would not approve the execution of a juvenile. The Court ultimately granted the petition, and in a five-to-four decision by Lewis Powell vacated the death sentence. Although that opinion did not go as far as my dissent, my view that the Eighth Amendment did not permit the execution of a juvenile later became the law in *Roper* v. *Simmons*.[87]

83. 453 U.S. 420 (1981).
84. 453 U.S. 454 (1981).
85. 456 U.S. 798 (1982).
86. 455 U.S. 104 (1982).
87. 543 U.S. 551 (2005).

23

The O'Connor Court

October Term 1981

After President Ford nominated me and before my Senate confirmation hearings began, Harry Blackmun thoughtfully sent me a copy of the transcript of his own confirmation hearings to enable me to get a feel of what I might soon expect. When President Reagan kept his campaign promise and nominated the first woman justice, I thought it appropriate to follow Harry's example and offered to send Sandra Day O'Connor a copy of the transcript of my hearings. Her prompt reply illustrated two characteristics that were repeated over and over again during our later years as colleagues: She was gracious and friendly, and she had the foresight to have already obtained and read the transcript.

One of my memories of Sandra's first term on the Court involved the reference to her appointment in President Reagan's first State of the Union address. Years earlier, the members of the Court, led by Chief Justice Earl Warren, had risen and joined the enthusiastic applause responding to President Johnson's announcement of his support for new civil rights legislation. News accounts of the Court's reaction described it as the equivalent of a Court decision upholding the constitutionality of the president's proposal. Following that event, the members of the Court had uniformly and consistently adhered to a practice of maintaining complete silence during the State of the Union. We abandoned that self-imposed rule when we were given the opportunity to stand and applaud President Reagan's reference to having fulfilled his campaign promise. With the possible exception of Harry Blackmun, who viewed any Reagan nominee as a threat to the longevity of his opinion in *Roe* v. *Wade,* all of us warmly welcomed Sandra as a new colleague.

While I shared Harry's concern about Sandra's legal views, partly because the new administration urged the Court to reexamine its earlier decisions protecting women's liberty interests and partly because Sandra more often supported the prosecutor's position in death penalty cases than I did, I never had any doubts concerning either her judicial skills or her intellectual integrity. She was a fitting successor to Potter Stewart, a justice whom I especially admired notwithstanding our frequent disagreements. Sandra never complained about the inconvenient need to return to her chambers during recesses in which her colleagues had access to the male-only bathroom facilities — an inconvenience that was corrected only after I called it to the attention of the chief justice. She succeeded me as the country's highest paid doorman in responding to knocks on the conference room door, and flawlessly handled the junior justice's post-conference task of promptly reporting the results of our deliberations to the clerk of the Court and his assistants. Although Sandra was inevitably the subject of extraordinary media attention, such distractions never impeded her thorough preparation for oral arguments or her participation in our conference deliberations. In sum, I have always been convinced that Sandra was superbly qualified not only to be a Supreme Court justice but specifically to take on the challenging role as the first female Supreme Court justice.

Sandra's first term on the Court was an especially busy one, even for that period. We issued 184 opinions, including her first dealing with gender discrimination — *Mississippi University for Women* v. *Hogan*[1] — in which

---

1. 458 U.S. 718 (1982).

a male nursing supervisor living in Columbus, Mississippi, sought admission to the state-supported School of Nursing of the Mississippi University of Women. He claimed a constitutional right to attend school in his hometown, even though he was eligible for admission to other schools elsewhere in the state. Sandra, who had been refused employment except as a secretary by leading law firms in California despite her superb academic record at Stanford Law School, wrote a straightforward opinion for the Court upholding his claim. The four justices appointed by President Nixon dissented, relying heavily on the long and respected history of single-sex schools. They correctly predicted that Sandra's opinion, even though narrowly written, would have a profound effect on single-sex educational institutions thereafter.

On July 2, 1982 — the day after I joined Sandra's five-to-four opinion for the Court in the gender discrimination case — we were on opposite sides of the five-to-four decision in *Enmund* v. *Florida*,[2] in which one of my former law clerks, Jim Liebman, convinced the majority, including me, that the Eighth Amendment prohibited imposing the death penalty on a defendant who did not himself kill, attempt to kill, or intend to kill. In his opinion for the Court, Byron White relied on both the holding and the reasoning in our prior opinion invalidating the death penalty for the rape of an adult woman: The Court had "looked to the historical development of the punishment at issue, legislative judgments, international opinion, and the sentencing decisions juries have made before bringing its own judgment to bear on the matter."[3] While I continue to endorse Byron's reasoning in that case, some critics have argued that American justices should place no weight on either international opinion or their own judgment.

On that same day, July 2, 1982, I announced one of the opinions of which I have always been most proud — *National Association for the Advancement of Colored People* v. *Claiborne Hardware Co.*[4] Thurgood

---

2. 458 U.S. 782 (1982).
3. *Id.*, at 788–89.
4. 458 U.S. 886 (1982).

Marshall did not participate in the case, and Bill Rehnquist merely concurred in the result, but otherwise the opinion was unanimous. We reversed a judgment of the Mississippi Supreme Court awarding damages of $1,250,699 against ninety-two of the participants in a seven-year boycott (from 1966 to 1972) of twelve white merchants in Claiborne County, Mississippi. They had been held liable for all damages resulting from the boycott on the ground that they had agreed to use force, violence, and threats to enlist support for the boycott from reluctant black citizens and to induce the white merchants to accommodate their demands.

The petition describing those demands shed a revelatory light on the status of race relations in Mississippi in the 1960s and 1970s. The petition "called for the desegregation of all public schools and public facilities, the hiring of black policemen, public improvements in black residential areas, selection of blacks for jury duty, integration of bus stations . . . and an end to verbal abuse by law enforcement officers."[5] It stated that "Negroes are not to be addressed by terms as 'boy,' 'girl,' 'shine,' 'uncle,' or any other offensive term, but as 'Mr.,' 'Mrs.,' or 'Miss,' as is the case with other citizens."[6] An additional demand that all stores employ black clerks and cashiers was later added. The failure to make a favorable response to the demands by an April 1 request led to a meeting at which several hundred black people voted unanimously to begin the boycott.

As a legal matter the case was difficult because it involved the well-settled rules imposing broad joint and several liability on participants in unlawful conspiracies, as well as the conflicting First Amendment rules protecting the rights of individuals to engage in concerted action to advance their political goals. And as a factual matter, despite the persuasive evidence supporting the merits of the defendants' grievances and the arbitrary character of the plaintiffs' refusal to accommodate any of their demands, there was credible evidence that organizers and supporters of

---

5. *Id.,* at 899.
6. *Ibid.*

the boycott had engaged in threats and violent acts against individuals who had refused to support the boycott. There was also strong, provocative language in a speech delivered by Charles Evers, a leader of the boycott.

We concluded that the damages award had to be set aside because the causal connection between the defendants' relatively small number of unlawful acts and the proven injuries to the plaintiffs was so remote. In the final paragraphs of the opinion, I wrote:

> The taint of violence colored the conduct of some of the petitioners. They, of course, may be held liable for the consequences of their violent deeds. The burden of demonstrating that it colored the entire collective effort, however, is not satisfied by evidence that violence occurred or even that violence contributed to the success of the boycott. A massive and prolonged effort to change the social, political, and economic structure of a local environment cannot be characterized as a violent conspiracy simply by reference to the ephemeral consequences of relatively few violent acts.... The burden of demonstrating that fear rather than protected conduct was the dominant force in the movement is heavy. A court must be wary of a claim that the true color of a forest is better revealed by reptiles hidden in the weeds than by the foliage of countless free-standing trees.[7]

The opinion was well received by civil rights advocates and by the media. The *New York Times* recounted the emotional celebration that broke out at the NAACP's annual convention when delegates learned of the decision. The *Times* also published a separate editorial that praised the opinion as a "ringing affirmation of the constitutional right of all citizens to organize boycotts to achieve political, economic and social

---

7. *Claiborne Hardware Co.*, 458 U.S., at 932–34 (footnote omitted).

change." It further predicted that the opinion would "become a mile-stone of American constitutional history."

In November 1981, Maryan and I were among about 125 guests at a black-tie dinner at the French embassy, following a concert performed by the Orchestre National de France at the Kennedy Center. Leonard Bernstein had conducted the concert and was the guest of honor at the dinner. Two of my seniors on the Court, Byron White and Harry Blackmun, and their wives were among the guests. For reasons that were not explained to us, instead of asking either of those couples to sit at the head table with the guest of honor and his young male companion, the ambassador and his wife invited Maryan and me to join them. I have always assumed that we were preferred over other more eligible guests because Maryan was easily the most beautiful woman at the party.

She particularly enjoyed the occasion because she was an accomplished pianist, frequently played classical music, and conversed comfortably with Bernstein, who was seated next to her. Their exchange included comments on the emotions that the director experiences as he leads the orchestra to the climax of the performance of a masterpiece. When asked how he felt as he animatedly gestured with his baton in such moments, without a second's hesitation, Bernstein replied, "It's like fucking in a cathedral."

October Term 1982

In the 1982 term, the Court decided *EEOC* v. *Wyoming*,[8] a case raising an issue similar to that decided in its earlier unfortunate decision in *National League of Cities* v. *Usery*.[9] As recounted in earlier chapters, in that earlier case, Bill Rehnquist had concluded that principles of state sovereignty prevented Congress from requiring state employers to abide

---

8. 460 U.S. 226 (1983).
9. 426 U.S. 833 (1976).

by certain minimum wage and maximum hour provisions of the Fair Labor Standards Act, notwithstanding the fact that the act was otherwise a valid exercise of Congress's power to regulate commerce. The question in *Wyoming* was whether Congress had acted constitutionally when, in 1974, it had extended the definition of "employer" under the Age Discrimination in Employment Act to include state and local governments. Harry Blackmun supplied the fifth vote supporting Bill Brennan's opinion upholding the statute. As had been true in *National League of Cities,* I had doubts about the wisdom of the legislation but nevertheless wrote a separate opinion supporting the majority because I thought it important to emphasize that the Commerce Clause was the framers' response to the central problem that gave rise to the Constitution itself; namely, the need to prohibit trade barriers among the states.

I quoted the following excerpt from Justice Rutledge's "Declaration of Legal Faith," as I had done in an opinion that I had written as a Seventh Circuit judge, and as I would do again on the Supreme Court:

> If any liberties may be held more basic than others, they are the great and indispensable freedoms secured by the First Amendment. But it was not to assure them that the Constitution was framed and adopted. Only later were they added, by popular demand. It was rather to secure freedom of trade, to break down the barriers to its free flow, that the Annapolis Convention was called, only to adjourn with a view to Philadelphia. Thus the generating source of the Constitution lay in the rising volume of restraints upon commerce which the Confederation could not check. These were the proximate cause of our national existence down to today. As evils are wont to do, they dictated the scope and character of their own remedy. This lay specifically in the commerce clause. No prohibition of trade barriers as among the states could have been effective of its own force or by trade agreements. It had become apparent that such treaties were too difficult to negotiate and the process of securing them was too complex for this

method to give the needed relief. Power adequate to make and enforce the prohibition was required. Hence, the necessity for creating an entirely new scheme of government. So by a stroke as bold as it proved successful, they founded a nation, although they had set out only to find a way to reduce trade restrictions. So also they solved the particular problem causative of their historic action, by introducing the commerce clause in the new structure of power.[10]

I argued that it was "so plain that *National League of Cities* not only was incorrectly decided, but also is inconsistent with the central purpose of the Constitution itself, that it is not entitled to the deference that the doctrine of stare decisis ordinarily commands for this Court's precedents."[11]

My separate opinion prompted Lewis Powell to "record a personal dissent from [my] novel view of our Nation's history." He wrote a thoughtful opinion explaining how principles of federalism had formed the basis for the assertions of states' rights throughout our history. I did not think, however, that he appreciated the force of the argument regarding the paramount importance of the Commerce Clause in the decision to form a new nation, or of the critical importance of the Supremacy Clause when questions arise as to the relative importance of conflicting federal and state policies. The debate between our two views about the relative importance of state and federal rules remains very much alive today.

Later in that term I wrote my separate opinion in *Karcher* v. *Daggett*.[12] I was one of the five justices who agreed that the map of New Jersey's congressional districts was unconstitutional. As explained in Bill Brennan's opinion, four justices relied on the principle, found in Article I, Section 2, that congressional districts must provide roughly equal representation for equal numbers of people. In contrast, I thought — and still think — that

---

10. 460 U.S., at 244–45, quoting W. Rutledge, *A Declaration of Legal Faith* (Lawrence: University of Kansas Press, 1947), 25–26.
11. *Id.,* at 249–50.
12. 462 U.S. 725 (1983).

the Equal Protection Clause provides just as clear if not clearer prohibition on political gerrymandering.

That clause, as I explained in my concurrence, "requires every State to govern impartially. When a State adopts rules governing its election machinery or defining electoral boundaries, those rules must serve the interests of the entire community. If they serve no purpose other than to favor one segment — whether racial, ethnic, religious, economic, or political — that may occupy a position of strength at a particular point in time, or to disadvantage a politically weak segment of the community, they violate the constitutional guarantee of equal protection." It seems to me that the bizarre shapes of most of the districts shown on the map provided sufficient evidence of gerrymandering to require the state to offer some neutral explanation for drawing them; its complete failure to do so justified finding them unconstitutional.

Because the colored map provided the most persuasive evidence supporting my view of the law, I requested the Court's printer to include it in the official report of the case. At first, Chief Justice Burger objected because he thought the expenditure was excessive, but he ultimately withdrew his objection when I pointed out that I had saved the Court much more than the amount at issue by employing only two law clerks while all of my colleagues employed three or more. Preserving that map for posterity was a small victory when compared with my lack of success in persuading some of my colleagues of the pernicious and unconstitutional harm partisan gerrymandering causes.

Following a White House dinner at which Maryan sat next to Charles Zwick, the director of the United States Information Agency, we received an invitation to represent the United States at a meeting celebrating the fortieth anniversary of the Finnish-American Society in Helsinki in the early summer. I was asked to deliver a speech and decided to recommend that the Finns emulate the federal judiciary by providing their judges with life tenure. After preparing a draft of my talk, my clerk Carol Lee advised me that the Finnish judges were already appointed for life, so I revised my draft to compliment my hosts on the wisdom of their practice and contrast it with the unfortunate consequences of judicial elections that are held in most of our states.

In that speech, after discussing a few cases that supported the general proposition that the work of judges is necessarily often disliked by the public, I made these comments:

> The somewhat random selection of cases that I have mentioned has repeatedly reminded us that the work product of the independent judiciary is often unpopular. A question that one may properly ask is how an institution that characteristically behaves in an unpopular way has survived for almost two centuries. Several different factors may provide the answer.
>
> Perhaps of greatest importance is the general realization that individual freedom in a complex society cannot survive without rules that both grant power to the Government and place limits on the way in which that power may be exercised. The French Revolution taught us that the dangers of oppression by the ruling class may exist not only under an absolute monarch, but under a government representing the views of the majority as well. The history of the United States, as of most other countries, teaches us that majority status is transient — that today's majority may be tomorrow's minority. Thus, when we speak of a government under law we have in mind a set of rules that do more than merely serve the interests of those in power at any given point in time.
>
> No set of rules can be completely self-executing. No matter how diligent and thorough the lawmaker may be, questions of interpretation and administration will remain for judges to answer. If those answers are provided by men and women beholden to the political party in power, or to the popular majority, the law itself tends to become an instrument of policy rather than an indepen-

dent guide to the conduct of individual affairs. The role of the impartial judge is thus like the role of the rule of law itself. The tenure provided to the independent judiciary is simply a method of guaranteeing the impartiality that is essential to the evenhanded administration of justice.

It may be true that in final analysis no rule of law — whether domestic or international — can be enforced without the power to inflict physical or economic punishment upon transgressors. It is nevertheless worthy of note that the power of the independent judiciary in the United States has survived the criticism and the occasional hostility of the Executive and Legislative Branches even though the entire control of the physical and economic resources of the Government is possessed by those two Branches. The weakest of the three Branches of the American Government is able to function effectively largely because the impartiality of the Federal Judiciary is virtually never questioned.

Disagreement concerning the wisdom of particular decisions contains no suggestion of improper motivation, bad faith, or the quest for political advantage. An honest mistake by an independent judge is less dangerous than a popular decision by a tribunal beholden to the party of power.[13]

During our visit, the American ambassador arranged a press conference with the Finnish press. One after another of the reporters asked me why the United States still had the death penalty. My attempts to explain that practice left them totally unimpressed and reminded me of how far out of step our country was. After our time in Finland, we spent two days in Leningrad, where (as I had been warned by the CIA) our luggage was

---

13. "The Independent Judiciary," pp. 15–17, remarks by Justice John Paul Stevens at the "America Days" Celebration of the Fortieth Anniversary, Finlandia Hall, August 20, 1983, Helsinki, Finland.

obviously searched during one of our absences from our hotel room. I was surprised to find that there were no bicycles in the streets and few if any small boats in the Neva River. Dining in our hotel was slow and unappetizing, but we thoroughly enjoyed the ice cream sold by street vendors and our visit to the Gold Room in the Hermitage Museum.

Three minor details about our departure from the Leningrad Airport still puzzle me. First, after our arrival at the terminal, we were placed on a bus that encircled the airport and then deposited us at the same spot where we had arrived; second, a heavily made-up, attractive young stewardess greeted us as we entered the aircraft but was never seen again; and third, our pilot, instead of first taxiing to the end of one of the runways, began his takeoff run from the middle of the runway closest to the terminal. I was not favorably impressed by my one flight on an Aeroflot plane.

October Term 1983

Four cases decided during October term 1983, my ninth term on the Court, had an especially important impact on the law.

The issue in *Pennhurst State School and Hospital* v. *Halderman*[14] was whether a federal court has the power to issue an injunction prohibiting state officials from violating state law. The case concerned the conditions at the Pennhurst State School and Hospital, a Pennsylvania institution for the care of those with intellectual disabilities. Terri Lee Halderman, a resident of Pennhurst, had brought a class action alleging that the institution's treatment of its residents violated both state and federal law. At the conclusion of the trial, the district court had entered detailed findings supporting its determination that Pennhurst had been operated in violation of state and federal law for several years. The court ordered Pennsylvania to remove Pennhurst's residents from the institution and to provide them with alternative, suitable community living arrangements.

The conditions at Pennhurst were, to say the least, disturbing. Among

---

14. 465 U.S. 89 (1984).

other equally shocking facts, "Infectious diseases were common and minimally adequate health care was unavailable. Residents of Pennhurst were inadequately supervised, and as a consequence were often injured by other residents or as a result of self-abuse. Assaults on residents by staff members, including sexual assaults, were frequent."[15]

The Court of Appeals for the Third Circuit, sitting en banc, unanimously affirmed the district court's findings and most of its remedy, except as to the order that Pennhurst be closed. In affirming the remedial order, the Third Circuit relied on a provision of federal law. We granted certiorari in the 1980 term and reversed on the ground that the federal provision the court relied upon did not create any substantive rights. Our Court remanded the case to the appellate court, however, to consider whether state law or another provision of federal law could support its judgment. On remand, the Third Circuit determined that a state statute supported its prior decision.

Our Court again granted certiorari. This time, the question presented was whether the federal district court had overstepped its authority by ordering Pennsylvania officials to bring the conditions at Pennhurst into compliance with state law. More generally, Pennsylvania argued that under the Eleventh Amendment federal courts lacked the power to order state officials to act in accordance with state law.

The Eleventh Amendment previously had been interpreted by the Supreme Court to protect state sovereign immunity, that is, that a state, as sovereign, may not be sued without its consent for violations of its own law. The Supreme Court, however, had long recognized a critical exception to that doctrine: a suit challenging the legality of a state official's action was not considered a suit against the state itself. This exception reflects the idea that when a state official acts in violation of state or federal law, the official does not exercise power delegated by the state but rather engages in ultra vires conduct. Since the "sovereign could not and would not authorize its officers to violate its own law," the official who

15. *Id.*, at 127n1 (Stevens, J., dissenting).

acts illegally is stripped of his or her official capacity and may be sued for injunctive relief.[16] Yet in *Pennhurst,* a majority of the Court disregarded this well-established principle and instead held that the doctrine of sovereign immunity barred federal courts from ordering state officials to conform their conduct to state law. In his opinion for the Court, Lewis Powell reasoned that federal courts may enjoin state officials only from violating federal law; the federal judiciary has no power to hold state officials to their state-law obligations.

In addition to revealing the alarming conditions at the Pennhurst State School and Hospital, the case exposed the willingness of a majority of the Court to cast aside over a century of jurisprudence — consisting of at least twenty-eight cases — to effect a dramatic, unprecedented expansion of sovereign immunity. The majority's conclusion that the Eleventh Amendment permits federal courts to enjoin state officials from violating federal law but prohibits such injunctions on the basis of state law lacked justification in either logic or precedent. As I explained in my dissent, "Since a state officer's conduct in violation of state law is certainly no less illegal than his violation of federal law, in either case the official, by committing an illegal act, is 'stripped of his official or representative character'" and is subject to suit, for "in all such cases the [state officer's] conduct is of a type that would not be permitted by the sovereign and hence is not attributable to the sovereign under traditional sovereign immunity principles."[17] "The majority's position that the Eleventh Amendment does not permit federal courts to enjoin conduct that the sovereign State itself seeks to prohibit thus" was, in my view, "inconsistent with both the doctrine of sovereign immunity and the underlying respect for the integrity of state policy which the Eleventh Amendment protects."[18]

The unprincipled nature of the majority's holding was further highlighted by the fact that the Court's disposition of the case in 1981 — remanding for the Third Circuit to consider whether state law supported

---

16. *Pennhurst,* 465 U.S., at 158 (Stevens, J., dissenting).
17. *Id.,* at 147, 150.
18. *Id.,* at 150–51.

the district court's injunction — would have been impermissible under the majority's novel theory of sovereign immunity. As I said in both the first and final sentences of my dissent, the case "illuminated the character of an institution."[19]

Bill Brennan and Thurgood Marshall were usually the only dissenters in cases upholding death sentences, but I joined them in *Spaziano* v. *Florida*,[20] and Bill asked me to write the opinion explaining my vote. The case presented the question whether a Florida statute authorizing the judge to impose a death sentence notwithstanding the jury's recommendation of a life sentence violated the Eighth Amendment. Harry Blackmun, writing for the majority, correctly noted that we had previously upheld the Florida capital sentencing scheme without specifically addressing the narrower issue presented in the *Spaziano* case and that sentencing was generally the business of judges rather than juries.

In my thirty-seven-page dissent, I explained why I was convinced that the reasons why death was different from all other forms of punishment supported the conclusion reached by most states that gave juries the final say on the question whether that penalty should be imposed in any particular case. Unlike the justifications for punishing other crimes, which include rehabilitation of the offender, preventing him from engaging in future criminal activity, and deterring others from committing crimes, the principal justification for imposing a death sentence is retribution — an expression of society's moral outrage in response to particularly offensive conduct. "And if the decision that capital punishment is the appropriate sanction in extreme cases is justified because it expresses the community's moral sensibility — its demand that a given affront to humanity requires retribution — it follows, I believe, that a representative cross section of the community must be given the responsibility for making that decision."[21]

The majority's decision in *Spaziano* was followed for several years but

---

19. *Id.,* at 126.
20. 468 U.S. 447 (1984).
21. *Id.,* at 481.

in time the Court came to agree with the view that I expressed and, in *Hurst* v. *Florida,* the Court overruled *Spaziano* to the extent it "allow[ed] a sentencing judge to find an aggravating circumstance, independent of a jury's factfinding, that is necessary for imposition of the death penalty."[22]

In *Sony Corp. of America* v. *Universal City Studios, Inc.,*[23] the Court held that Sony's sale of home videotape recorders did not constitute contributory infringement of television program copyrights. The primary use of Sony's videotape recorders — known as "Betamax" recorders — was a practice known as "time-shifting," whereby consumers record a television program for later viewing at a more convenient time and thereafter erase it. The case concerned the private, home use of Betamax recorders to record programs broadcast free of charge on the public airwaves.

Universal City Studios and Walt Disney Productions argued that the use of Betamax recorders to record its copyrighted television programs constituted infringement, and that Sony — as the manufacturer and marketer of the Betamax device — was liable for contributory infringement. The district court had ruled in favor of Sony, but the Court of Appeals for the Ninth Circuit reversed, ruling that Universal and Disney were entitled to enjoin the distribution of Betamax recorders, collect royalties on the sale of the device, or obtain other relief.

Our Court reversed. I wrote the majority opinion rejecting Universal and Disney's "unprecedented attempt to impose copyright liability upon the distributors of copying equipment."[24] Central to this result was the district court's finding that time-shifting in fact enlarges the audience for the copyrighted television programs, and thus neither impairs the commercial value of the copyrights nor creates any likelihood of future harm. Our narrow, five-justice majority shared the district court's view that the public benefits of home time-shifting outweighed any potential injury to the owners of copyrighted programs and constituted a fair use of the copyrighted works.

---

22. 136 S. Ct. 616, 624 (2016).
23. 464 U.S. 417 (1984).
24. *Id.,* at 421.

The case was first argued on January 18, 1983, and the Court avoided affirming the Ninth Circuit by the narrowest possible margin. After oral argument, Harry Blackmun was assigned to write an opinion for the Court affirming the Ninth Circuit's holding that Sony was liable for contributory infringement. With him in the majority were Thurgood Marshall, Lewis Powell, Bill Rehnquist, and Sandra O'Connor. Expecting to be in dissent, I circulated a memorandum to the conference outlining my position that, under a careful reading of the Copyright Act, making a single copy of a copyrighted work for a purely private, noncommercial use would not constitute an infringement. Since that is all that time-shifting entailed, in my view Sony could not be held liable for contributory infringement. I noted that while Congress could always amend the statute if it wished to enact a different policy, a contrary decision by our Court would force the judiciary to fashion a detailed series of remedies that could be much better addressed by the legislature. In light of the views expressed in my memorandum, Chief Justice Burger (who also favored reversal) assigned me the dissent. He noted in his memorandum assigning me the opinion that we had "a chance of changing some of those in the precarious majority over to the reversal side." Indeed, a few days later Lewis Powell notified the conference that my memorandum had convinced him that the issue was more difficult than Harry had assumed and that he would be going "back to the 'books'" to consider the question further.

Several months later, Harry and I circulated our respective draft opinions to the conference. Sandra expressed concerns with Harry's draft and additional back-and-forth ensued without resolution. At that point, there were only a few weeks remaining in the term, and Byron White proposed that the case be set for reargument. The conference agreed. After the case was reargued the following term, Sandra changed her vote to reverse. Harry and I then traded places: I was assigned the majority opinion, which was joined by the chief, Bill Brennan, Byron, and Sandra. Harry authored the dissent. Few, if any, of my opinions for the Court have been as gratifying as the result in that case.

*   *   *

Chevron U.S.A. Inc. v. *Natural Resources Defense Council, Inc.,*[25] is the most frequently cited opinion I authored during my tenure on the Court; indeed, by some accounts, it is the most cited Supreme Court opinion ever. That decision firmly established the proposition that Congress may delegate its power to make policy decisions to agencies created to administer its programs. Congress may make that delegation by leaving the meaning of key words in a statute ambiguous.

The importance of the decision was not recognized when the case arrived at the Court. The question it presented was whether a regulation promulgated by the Environmental Protection Agency requiring states to establish permit programs for new or modified major "stationary sources" of air pollution allowed a state to adopt a plant-wide definition of that term instead of treating each pollution-emitting device as a separate source.

The Court of Appeals for the D.C. Circuit found that neither the text nor the legislative history of the controlling statute indicated whether states could treat all pollution-emitting devices within the same industrial grouping as though they were encased within a single "bubble." Following two of its earlier decisions, the court concluded that the bubble concept was appropriate in programs designed merely to maintain existing air quality but inappropriate in programs enacted to improve air quality. It therefore set aside the regulation as contrary to law.

The EPA and two manufacturers filed petitions for certiorari first considered at the Court's conference on May 19, 1983. At that conference only Byron White and Bill Rehnquist voted to grant. Sandra O'Connor voted to "join three" — meaning that she would make the fourth vote to grant if three other justices so voted. After listening to the discussion, Lewis Powell asked to have the case relisted for the next conference. He then cast his vote to grant, making Sandra's "join three" the decisive vote. Later Thurgood Marshall, Bill Rehnquist, and Sandra concluded that

---

25. 467 U.S. 837 (1984).

they had to disqualify themselves. In sum, of the six justices who ultimately decided the merits of the case, only two (Byron White and Lewis Powell) had voted to grant certiorari.

After the oral argument, our conference discussion was almost as inconclusive as our deliberations at the preargument conferences. Chief Justice Burger and Bill Brennan both voted to affirm, and the remaining four votes were tentatively to reverse. Being the senior among those four, Byron asked me if I would like to try my hand at producing a majority opinion. I agreed, studied the case even more thoroughly than before and became firmly convinced that the D.C. Circuit had erred when it construed the statute as commanding different results for programs designed to reduce air pollution as compared to those merely maintaining the existing level of pollution; that result was inconsistent with the understanding that Congress had left the meaning of the term "stationary source" ambiguous. As I explained in the most frequently quoted passage in the opinion,

> When a court reviews an agency's construction of the statute which it administers, it is confronted with two questions. First, always, is the question whether Congress has directly spoken to the precise question at issue. If the intent of Congress is clear, that is the end of the matter; for the court, as well as the agency, must give effect to the unambiguously expressed intent of Congress. If, however, the court determines Congress has not directly addressed the precise question at issue, the court does not simply impose its own construction on the statute, as would be necessary in the absence of an administrative interpretation. Rather, if the statute is silent or ambiguous with respect to the specific issue, the question for the court is whether the agency's answer is based on a permissible construction of the statute.[26]

---

26. *Id.,* at 842–43.

The logic of the decision rested in part on the limited role that judges play when confronting ambiguous portions of regulatory statutes. As described in the following two paragraphs of the opinion,

> Judges are not experts in the field, and are not part of either political branch of the Government. Courts must, in some cases, reconcile competing political interests, but not on the basis of the judges' personal policy preferences. In contrast, an agency to which Congress has delegated policymaking responsibilities may, within the limits of that delegation, properly rely upon the incumbent administration's views of wise policy to inform its judgments. While agencies are not directly accountable to the people, the Chief Executive is, and it is entirely appropriate for this political branch of the Government to make such policy choices — resolving the competing interests which Congress itself either inadvertently did not resolve, or intentionally left to be resolved by the agency charged with the administration of the statute in light of everyday realities.

> When a challenge to an agency construction of a statutory provision, fairly conceptualized, really centers on the wisdom of the agency's policy, rather than whether it is a reasonable choice within a gap left open by Congress, the challenge must fail. In such a case, federal judges — who have no constituency — have a duty to respect legitimate policy choices made by those who do. The responsibilities for assessing the wisdom of such policy choices and resolving the struggle between competing views of the public interest are not judicial ones: Our Constitution vests such responsibilities in the political branches. *TVA* v. *Hill,* 437 U.S. 153, 195 (1978).[27]

---

27. *Chevron U.S.A.,* 467 U.S., at 865–66.

Despite his original vote to affirm, Chief Justice Burger joined my opinion shortly after it was circulated, but Bill Brennan did not come aboard until after we had exchanged letters and I had a meeting with him in his office. I believe that was the only case in which I visited another justice for the purpose of trying to persuade him or her to join one of my opinions.

My law clerk Larry Rosenthal, who is now on the faculty at Chapman University, recalled that, by this term, a majority of the Court had formed the view that its mission was to roll back the Warren Court's procedural protections for criminal defendants. In the previous term, for example, the Court had announced that it would reexamine the exclusionary rule, which provides that evidence obtained in violation of the Fourth Amendment must be suppressed, when it ordered reargument in *Illinois* v. *Gates*,[28] only to conclude that the case was not an appropriate vehicle for addressing that question. Granting two different cases that had been held for *Gates* — *Massachusetts* v. *Sheppard*[29] and *United States* v. *Leon*[30] — made it clear that the Court was bound and determined to roll back the exclusionary rule.

Larry remembers thinking that I was more troubled by the injudiciousness of the Court's forced march against the exclusionary rule than by the outcome in these cases. The Court often declines to grant cert in cases with "vehicle problems," meaning issues that might complicate the Court's review of the question presented in the case, such as a petitioner who may not have standing to bring his or her claim. Both *Sheppard* and *Leon* had such problems in that it was doubtful that there had been a violation of the Fourth Amendment in either. The prosecution in both cases, however, conceded that the Fourth Amendment had been violated because they were focused on attacking the exclusionary rule, and the Court's majority was willing to let this tactic succeed. In my dissent in *Leon,* I highlighted the Court's departure from adherence to judicial restraint, observing that

---

28. 462 U.S. 213 (1983).
29. 468 U.S. 981 (1984).
30. 468 U.S. 897 (1984).

"when the Court goes beyond what is necessary to decide the case before it, it can only encourage the perception that it is pursuing its own notions of wise social policy, rather than adhering to its judicial role."[31]

The term produced several other decisions retreating from Warren Court precedents, decisions from which I dissented, including *Minnesota v. Murphy*,[32] which restricted the scope of *Miranda* by holding that a probationer who had been required to attend a meeting with his probation officer, who wished to question him about a murder, need not have been given *Miranda* warnings; *Oliver v. United States*,[33] which held that drug officers who trespassed onto private property by passing a locked gate with a no trespassing sign had not conducted a "search" under the Fourth Amendment; *Segura v. United States*,[34] which held that an eighteen-to-twenty-hour warrantless occupation of a private apartment did not require the suppression of evidence found during that occupation because a warrant was later issued; *INS v. Lopez-Mendoza*,[35] which held that the exclusionary rule did not apply to deportation proceedings, leaving immigration officials effectively unconstrained by the Fourth Amendment; and *New York v. Quarles*,[36] which recognized a "public safety" exception to *Miranda*. Of all the cases of this type, Larry remembers that I was particularly bothered by *Hudson v. Palmer*,[37] which held that the Fourth Amendment did not protect prisoners against unreasonable searches and seizures. I was so troubled that I announced my dissent from the bench, and wrote, "To hold that a prisoner's possession of a letter from his wife, or a picture of his baby, has no protection against arbitrary or malicious perusal, seizure, or destruction would not, in my judgment, comport with any civilized standard of decency."[38]

---

31. 468 U.S., at 963.
32. 465 U.S. 420 (1984).
33. 466 U.S. 170 (1984).
34. 468 U.S. 796 (1984).
35. 468 U.S. 1032 (1984).
36. 467 U.S. 649 (1984).
37. 468 U.S. 517 (1984).
38. *Id.*, at 546.

October Term 1984

Constitutional rules adopted for a specific, relatively narrow purpose occasionally endorse a much wider proposition. The point is well illustrated by the Court's treatment of statutes enacted by the state of Alabama authorizing a one-minute period of silence in all public schools for meditation or voluntary prayer.[39] The district court upheld the validity of three such statutes, reasoning that the Establishment Clause of the First Amendment did not bar the states from establishing a religion. Not surprisingly, the Court of Appeals for the Eleventh Circuit reversed, and our Court ultimately agreed that the statutes were invalid.

In my opinion for the Court, I reviewed some of the history of the adoption of the First Amendment, specifically noting the framers' primary interest in avoiding all rivalry among Christian sects and the absence of any evidence of intent to protect non-Christian sects from discrimination. I then explained:

> Just as the right to speak and the right to refrain from speaking are complementary components of a broader concept of individual freedom of mind, so also the individual's freedom to choose his own creed is the counterpart of his right to refrain from accepting the creed established by the majority. At one time it was thought that this right merely proscribed the preference of one Christian sect over another, but would not require equal respect for the conscience of the infidel, the atheist, or the adherent of a non-Christian faith such as Islam or Judaism. But when the underlying principle has been examined in the crucible of litigation, the Court has unambiguously concluded that the individual freedom of conscience protected by the First Amendment embraces the right to select any religious faith or none at all. This conclusion derives support not only from the interest in respecting the individual's freedom of conscience, but also from

---

39. *Wallace* v. *Jaffree,* 472 U.S. 38 (1985).

the conviction that religious beliefs worthy of respect are the product of free and voluntary choice by the faithful, and from recognition of the fact that the political interest in forestalling intolerance extends beyond intolerance among Christian sects—or even intolerance among "religions"—to encompass intolerance of the disbeliever and the uncertain.[40]

The majority's recognition of the broad tolerance embraced by the Establishment Clause made it clear that the Alabama law, which characterized prayer as a favored practice, could not stand.

Occasionally the facts that justified the enactment of a statute cease to exist. The Court was presented with such a case during my tenth term. It is a misuse of judicial resources to preserve useless laws, but that is exactly what Bill Rehnquist did in his opinion for the Court in *Walters* v. *National Association of Radiation Survivors*.[41] The case upheld a federal statute prohibiting any lawyer from charging more than ten dollars for services provided to a veteran seeking federal benefits for a service-related death or disability.

The majority reasoned that Congress intentionally designed an administrative scheme that relies on veterans' organizations to provide trained (non-lawyer) service representatives to help veterans navigate the benefits process free of charge. Bill's opinion placed great weight on the legitimacy of the governmental interest in ensuring a benefits scheme that is sufficiently informal that professional legal assistance remains unnecessary and veterans need not lose a portion of their award to legal fees.

To my mind, though, that rationale was a thinly veiled attempt to provide a contemporary justification for a sorely anachronistic provision. To be sure, when the ten-dollar fee limitation was enacted in 1864, Congress presumably considered it reasonable. The legal work involved in preparing a veteran's claim consisted of little more than filling out a form, and

---

40. *Id.,* at 52–55.
41. 473 U.S. 305 (1985).

the ten-dollar fee was roughly the equivalent of $580 today. The law was originally aimed at unscrupulous attorneys, and it made them subject to imprisonment for overcharging. But in 1984, when the case was decided, the statute effectively denied every veteran access to any lawyer charging a reasonable fee for his or her services. The paternalistic interest in protecting veterans from exploitation by unscrupulous lawyers and the bureaucratic interest in minimizing the cost of processing claims fell far short of warranting the restraint on veterans' freedom to access legal counsel — especially as no one denied that complicated claims arose from time to time for which the services of a lawyer could make a critical difference.

My dissent began by explaining that I thought the fee limitation was unwise, and that it was an insult to the legal profession to assume lawyers would bring confusion rather than clarity to benefits proceedings. But the focus of my opinion was on the importance of the broader right at stake: the citizen's right to counsel in a contest with the sovereign. The majority opinion seemed to me to exhibit an "unawareness of the function of the independent lawyer as a guardian of our freedom."[42] I closed with the following comment:

> In my view regardless of the nature of the dispute between the sovereign and the citizen…the citizen's right to consult an independent lawyer to speak on his or her behalf is an aspect of liberty that is priceless. It should not be bargained away on the notion that a totalitarian appraisal of the mass of claims processed by the Veterans' Administration does not identify an especially high probability of error.[43]

The same day that the Court announced its decision in *Walters,* it also decided a case that expanded protection for state employees who violate federal law. *Atascadero State Hospital* v. *Scanlon*[44] involved a suit brought under the federal Rehabilitation Act of 1973, which prohibited any program receiving federal financial assistance from engaging in employment

---

42. *Id.,* at 371.
43. *Id.,* at 371–72.
44. 473 U.S. 234 (1985).

discrimination against individuals with disabilities. Douglas Scanlon, who was blind in one eye, brought an action for damages against a California state hospital, alleging that it had refused to hire him in violation of the act. In an opinion written by Lewis Powell, the Court assumed that the complaint had alleged a violation of the federal statute but nevertheless held that the action must be dismissed because Congress had not made its intention to abrogate the states' sovereign immunity "unmistakably clear" in the language of the statute itself.[45]

Perhaps the most remarkable feature of the majority opinion was the fact that, after announcing its brand-new "clear statement" requirement, the Court then applied it to the statute at issue to determine whether Congress had "chosen to override the Eleventh Amendment" — notwithstanding, of course, that Congress had no reason to know of such a stringent requirement when it had drafted the Rehabilitation Act.[46] One paragraph in particular epitomizes the extreme nature of the Court's new rule: despite language in the statute providing for remedies against "*any* recipient of Federal assistance," the Court insisted that states in fact "are not like any other class of recipients of federal aid," and thus a "general authorization for suit in federal court is not the kind of unequivocal statutory language sufficient to abrogate the Eleventh Amendment. When Congress chooses to subject the States to federal jurisdiction, it must do so specifically."[47]

Thurgood Marshall, Harry Blackmun, and I joined Bill Brennan's masterful dissent, which not only refuted the majority's interpretation of the Rehabilitation Act but also set forth a painstaking account of the drafting and ratification of the Eleventh Amendment. That history reveals that the amendment was never intended to constitutionalize the doctrine of state sovereign immunity or to impose the doctrine as a limit on the judicial power of federal courts. I also joined Harry's brief dissent observing that the Court had taken an egregiously wrong turn in 1890

45. *Id.,* at 242.
46. *Id.,* at 244.
47. *Id.,* at 246.

when it decided, in *Hans* v. *Louisiana*,[48] to expand the scope of the Eleventh Amendment far beyond its actual text — which does not prohibit suits against states but rather restricts federal court jurisdiction only over suits against a state by citizens of another state or of a foreign country.

Writing only for myself, I published a brief dissent explaining that while I had previously decided to abide by sovereign immunity precedents with which I disagreed, it had become clear that a majority of the Court did not feel "constrained by stare decisis in its expansion of the protective mantle of sovereign immunity."[49] That circumstance, combined with my deepening appreciation for how "egregiously incorrect" those precedents were, had convinced me that a fresh approach to the Court's sovereign immunity jurisprudence was imperative.

Incidentally, one unintended consequence of *Atascadero's* holding was a bar to recovery for patent and copyright holders in infringement actions against state agencies. I do not recall any discussion among my colleagues regarding that particular impact of the Court's decision and suspect that it escaped our notice when the case was decided.

In my judgment, Bill Rehnquist's plurality opinion in *Oklahoma City* v. *Tuttle*[50] is one of the worst decisions announced during my years on the Court. The district court, affirmed by the Court of Appeals for the Tenth Circuit, had held that Oklahoma City was liable for a police officer's fatal shooting of the plaintiff's husband. Relying on dicta in *Monell* v. *New York City Dept. of Social Services*,[51] the plurality determined that a municipality cannot be held liable under the Civil Rights Act, 42 U.S.C. § 1983, for violating an individual's constitutional rights unless the individual establishes that the violation was committed pursuant to a municipal "custom or policy."

The plaintiff in *Tuttle* had attempted to show that the police's use of force against her husband had been so extraordinarily excessive that it

---

48. 134 U.S. 1 (1890).
49. 473 U.S., at 304.
50. 471 U.S. 808 (1985).
51. 436 U.S. 58 (1978).

evidenced a policy of inadequate police training or supervision on the part of the municipal officials in charge. The plurality rejected this theory of liability on the ground that a municipal custom or policy cannot be established on the basis of a single incident of unconstitutional activity, no matter how extreme. The plurality further determined that a "policy" constitutes a course of action consciously chosen from among various alternatives, such that a policy of inadequate training could only be established through proof that "policymakers deliberately chose a training program which would prove inadequate."[52] Concurring in the judgment, Bill Brennan, joined by Thurgood Marshall and Harry Blackmun, agreed that a single incident did not suffice to prove a municipal policy that would support liability.

As the lone dissenter, I set forth my view that if a municipal officer violates the Constitution while engaged in the performance of his official duties, federal law provides a remedy against both the individual officer and the municipality that employs him. This conclusion followed in a straight line from the text and legislative history of 42 U.S.C. § 1983, as well as entrenched principles of tort law at the time Section 1983 was enacted. Under those principles, an agent or employee's wrongful conduct performed in the course of official duty was attributable to his or her employer — including a municipal employer — in a suit for damages. The Court's novel "policy requirement" lacked support in the statute's text and history and amounted to "judicial legislation of the most blatant kind."[53]

My opinion for a unanimous Court in *Aspen Skiing Co.* v. *Aspen Highlands Skiing Corp.*[54] upheld a jury verdict finding that the company that owned three of the four skiing facilities in the vicinity of Aspen, Colorado, had violated Section 2 of the Sherman Act by terminating and refusing to renew a long-standing marketing arrangement that allowed skiers to purchase six-day tickets usable on any given day at any of the four

---

52. 471 U.S., at 823.
53. *Id.,* at 842.
54. 472 U.S. 585 (1985).

mountains in the Aspen market. The case is memorable, not only because it was the only opinion involving a violation of Section 2 that was decided during my thirty-five years on the Court but also because it reminds me of especially enjoyable visits to Aspen, including the winter when I first learned to ski, the seminars conducted in the summer by the Aspen Institute's Justice and Society Program directed by Alice Henkin, and a special round of golf with Maryan.

As a beginner on the slopes, I was taught to "snowplow" going downhill to avoid the risk of accelerating to a speed that was too dangerous. The snowplow involved skiing from left to right at an angle that was almost horizontal, then turning to ski from right to left at a similar angle, thus progressing gradually down the slope. My main problem was unintentional acceleration that would send me hurtling into the woods before I could make the turn in the other direction. Eventually, having mastered the snowplow, I took my ten-year-old daughter Liz to an intermediate slope, where I planned to meet her near a tree halfway down the mountain after snowplowing to our destination. Instead of following my instructions to make a gradual descent to the tree, she said "OK, Dad," then made a direct high-speed run to the rendezvous where I caught up with her about ten minutes later. Eventually I did learn to ski, but I never qualified as a teacher of younger and more fearless athletes.

On several occasions Alice's husband, Lou Henkin, and I co-taught a seminar about justice at Aspen. Lou was a former law clerk to Judge Learned Hand and Justice Felix Frankfurter, and the country's leading scholar on international law, not to mention an extremely nice guy. As had been true of my co-teaching with the economist Aaron Director at the University of Chicago Law School years earlier, I am sure I learned much more from Lou than our students learned from me. Indeed, recalling that we had an impressive array of participants in our discussion sessions — people such as Newt Minow (former chairman of the Federal Communications Commission who became famous for referring to the television audience as a "vast wasteland"), Sandy d'Alemberte (later to become president of the American Bar Association and the University of

Florida), former solicitor general Wade McCree (a gifted poet who closed each session with a freshly composed limerick), and Bryan Stevenson (a brilliant young lawyer who had begun his career performing pro bono legal work for indigent defendants in Alabama when he could have earned a fortune as a Wall Street lawyer) — I think Lou and I both may have learned more than we contributed to our sessions.

One afternoon Maryan and I played a round of golf on the course at Snowmass by ourselves. On the par 3, 170-yard eleventh hole, I hit a four-iron shot that bounced on hard ground in front of the green and trickled into the hole. Except for Maryan, the only witness to that event was a traveling vendor of soft drinks who provided us with free Cokes to celebrate my shot. After we returned to our cottage, Lou and Alice Henkin walked by while Maryan was inside, and I proudly recited my once-in-a-lifetime achievement. When Maryan came out of the kitchen, Lou exclaimed: "That was a pretty exciting event for John!" Her deadpan response was, "What are you talking about?"

October Term 1985

On November 11, 1985, Maryan, and I were guests of the National Gallery of Art at a black-tie dinner celebrating an exhibition of British masterpieces. I have no memory of any of the works of art displayed on that occasion, but I vividly recall meeting Princess Diana and her then husband, Prince Charles. Diana, an unforgettably beautiful and gracious woman, was the center of attention for one group of admirers after another. I remember standing with Charles nearby as he remarked about his second-class appeal whenever he and Diana were in joint attendance at similar events.

A year later we attended a similar dinner celebrating an exhibition of paintings by Spanish artists. Maryan and I were seated at tables in different rooms. Her dinner partner was Jaime Ortiz-Patino, who was then the president of the World Bridge Federation and a good friend of Robert Trent Jones, a well-known architect of excellent golf courses. During

My mother, Elizabeth Street Stevens.

My father, Ernest James Stevens.

My father, Ernest J. Stevens, with his four sons (*left to right*): me, William Kenneth, Richard James, and Ernest Street — John, Bill, Jim, and Ernie, 1923.

Working on a jigsaw puzzle with my older brothers, Bill and Jim, in the Stevens Hotel, 1928.

My father — Ernest J. Stevens.

On Oahu during World War II, 1943.

1947: Law clerks on the Supreme Court front steps. Not until 1947 were associate justices authorized to employ two law clerks. Only four of them did. All of those serving in the '47 term — except Frank Allen, who clerked for Chief Justice Vinson — are shown in this picture. *Front row, left to right:* Stan Temko (Rutledge), Larry Ebb (Vinson), John Thompson (Vinson), and Bob von Mehren (Reed); *second row, left to right:* Jim Marsh (Jackson), Al Rosenthal (Frankfurter), Jim Lake (Burton), me (Rutledge), and Bob Spitzer (Reed); *third row, left to right:* Bruce Griswold (Burton), Bill Joslin (Black), Gene Gressman (Murphy), Irving Helman (Frankfurter), and Stan Sparrow (Douglas).
Collection of the Supreme Court of the United States

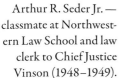

Arthur R. Seder Jr. — classmate at Northwestern Law School and law clerk to Chief Justice Vinson (1948–1949).

The three partners in the law firm of Rothschild, Stevens & Barry, 1952. *Left to right:* Edward I. Rothschild, me, and Norman J. Barry.

With President Gerald Ford and Chief Justice Warren Burger, December 19, 1975, after being sworn in as a member of the Court.
Collection of John Paul Stevens; photographer unknown

With Maryan after our marriage in Leesburg, Virginia, on December 1, 1979.

Cartoon by Herb Block published in the *Washington Post* in response to my opinion for the Court in *Payton* v. *New York,* 445 U.S. 573, 1980. *A 1980 Herblock Cartoon, copyright The Herb Block Foundation*

To Justice John Paul Stevens
With deepest appreciation for your unselfish service to the people
of the United States and to their laws. Ronald Reagan

In the Conference Room at the Supreme Court swearing-in ceremony for Justice O'Connor on September 25, 1981. *Left to right:* Harry Blackmun, Thurgood Marshall, William J. Brennan, Warren Burger, President Ronald Reagan, Sandra Day O'Connor, Byron White, Lewis Powell, William Rehnquist, and me.
Courtesy Ronald Reagan Library

The justices leaving the Conference Room on the day of Justice Sandra Day O'Connor's investiture, September 25, 1981. *Left to right:* Chief Justice Burger, Justices Brennan, White, Marshall, and Powell, me, and Justices Blackmun and Rehnquist.
Michael Evans, The White House

Ronald Reagan greeting me at the White House reception for the Supreme Court justices on October 1, 1985, with (*background, left to right*) Justices Byron White and Potter Stewart and Attorney General Edwin Meese.
Courtesy Ronald Reagan Library

My children at Sue's wedding on August 25, 1990. *Left to right:* Kathryn (Jedlicka), John Joseph, Susan Roberta (Mullen), and Elizabeth Jane (Sesemann).

Herb Block cartoon, March 31, 2000, after the decision considering whether nude dancing is protected by the First Amendment. *A 2000 Herblock Cartoon, copyright The Herb Block Foundation*

Chief Justice Rehnquist congratulating me after presentation of medal evidencing twenty-five years of service at the Supreme Court on May 21, 2001.
Photograph by Franz Jantzen, Collection of the Supreme Court of the United States

their cordial dinner conversation, in answer to Ortiz-Patiño's question about whether we were members of the Coral Ridge Country Club in Fort Lauderdale, Florida, Maryan's negative reply was accompanied by the explanation that a federal judge's salary would not support such a luxury. He assured her that he would persuade Mr. Jones, the owner of the club, to provide us with an honorary membership. After the dinner, when she relayed their conversation to me, I expressed my skepticism by asking whether he had also promised her a Hollywood movie contract. After we arrived in Florida a few days later, I was astounded when I received a telephone call that confirmed Maryan's confidence in the reliability of her dinner companion's trustworthiness and Mr. Jones's generosity.

During the ensuing years the acceptance of such honorary club memberships by members of the judiciary has been frequently and repeatedly criticized by members of Congress and the press, apparently on the principal ground that the memberships may generate disqualifying conflicts of interest and the exposure to unduly conservative points of view. I have never been convinced that those concerns had sufficient merit to outweigh the obvious and substantial health benefits from regular physical exercise that free athletic facilities provide to overworked judges. And conflicts of interest can always be dealt with if and when they in fact arise through recusal of the judge from a particular case.

As members of the Coral Ridge club, Maryan and I made several good friends, some of whom I still see occasionally. Among them are Ray and Mitzi Doumar, with whom we frequently played both golf and tennis. Their son Ray graduated from law school not long after we joined the club and began his successful law practice in Augusta, Georgia, where he met some members of the Augusta National Golf Club, which hosts the best-known professional golf tournament in the country every spring. He persuaded two club members — Hale Barrett and Jay Johnson — both of whom were practicing lawyers, to invite Maryan and me to join them in a round of golf at Augusta on April 15, 1994. That was truly a memorable day, not only because we had previously watched so many tournaments on the beautiful golf course during prior years, but also because — following the instructions of an expert caddy — I managed to break 100. Ray and his wife hosted a celebratory party that evening; I kept the card recording my score of 97 in my briefcase for many years.

The absence of language in the Constitution identifying exactly what liberties are protected by the doctrine of substantive due process makes Court decisions about its scope especially important. As I note in earlier chapters, in *Lochner* v. *New York,* a closely divided Court held that the doctrine protected a baker's claimed right to contract with his employees to work more than ten hours a day. In my eleventh term on the Court, I wrote an opinion that refused to recognize a novel substantive due process claim but accepted the doctrine itself.

In *Regents of the University of Michigan* v. *Ewing,*[55] we reversed a decision of the Court of Appeals for the Sixth Circuit that had held that a student in a six-year program of combined undergraduate and medical education had a constitutional right to retake an important written exam that he had failed. Relying primarily on the fact that the university had previously given students who failed the exam at least one second chance, the court of appeals concluded that its action in Ewing's case was arbitrary. We unanimously disagreed, essentially holding that the substance of academic decisions were either not reviewable at all by judges or that their review at most merely required judges to be satisfied that the faculty had exercised a professional judgment, which it unquestionably had done in this case. While construing the doctrine of substantive due process narrowly, no member of the Court disagreed with my quotation of Byron White's earlier comment "that the Court regularly proceeds on the assumption that the Due Process Clause has more than a procedural dimension."[56]

The first black teacher in the public schools of Jackson, Michigan, was hired in 1954. Fifteen years later, in 1969, only 3.9 percent of the public

---

55. 474 U.S. 214 (1985).
56. *Id.,* at 225.

school teachers in Jackson were black. In that year, the Michigan Civil Rights Commission found that the Jackson School Board had engaged in various discriminatory practices, including racial discrimination in the hiring of teachers. As a part of its settlement with the commission, the school board took affirmative action to employ more black teachers, and in two years the percentage increased to 8.8 percent. In 1971, however, economic conditions required the board to discharge a number of teachers, and, following settled practice, the teachers with the least seniority were the first to be laid off, which meant that almost all of the newly hired black teachers were fired. Thereafter, the school board recognized that a freeze on the discharge of minority teachers might be necessary to preserve the benefits of the affirmative action program, but the teachers' union sought to retain the "last hired first fired" rule. Ultimately the parties reached a compromise that prohibited any minority discharges that would reduce their percentage of teachers employed at the time of the layoff. That compromise was accepted by an overwhelming majority of the teachers in six successive collective bargaining agreements.

In 1982, however, when economic conditions once again forced a significant layoff, Wendy Wygant and another recently hired white teacher lost their jobs as a result of the compromise. They brought suit in federal district court, alleging that their discharges violated the Equal Protection Clause. The district court and the Court of Appeals for the Sixth Circuit rejected their claims, holding that the racial preferences granted by the school board need not be justified by a finding of prior discrimination but were permissible as an attempt to remedy societal discrimination by providing "role models" for minority schoolchildren.

In 1985, the Supreme Court granted the white teachers' petition for certiorari. During the week before the oral argument of the case, I had a meeting with Lewis Powell in his office to discuss another matter. As I was leaving, I made the observation that at long last during the following week we were going to hear an easy case involving an affirmative action issue. He agreed with my assessment of the difficulty of the case, but neither of us realized that we did not agree on how the case should be decided. Indeed, neither of us expected the case to produce so many opinions. As the headnote to the case explained:

> On certiorari, the United States Supreme Court reversed. Although unable to agree on an opinion, five members of the court agreed that the layoffs were in violation of the equal protection clause. It was also agreed by five members of the court that the equal protection clause does not require a public employer's voluntary affirmative action plan to be preceded by a formal finding that the employer has committed discriminatory acts in the past.[57]

There were three opinions supporting the result: Lewis Powell's lead opinion, joined by Chief Justice Burger and Bill Rehnquist; and separate opinions by Byron White and Sandra O'Connor. There were two dissents: an opinion by Thurgood Marshall, joined by Bill Brennan and Harry Blackmun; and my solo dissent. In his opinion, Lewis correctly noted that, in its earlier cases, "the Court has insisted upon some showing of prior discrimination by the governmental unit involved before allowing limited use of racial classifications in order to remedy such discrimination."[58] In his dissent, Thurgood argued that the record contained sufficient evidence of prior discrimination to justify accepting the compromise between the union and the school board and that a remand for further evidence would make it possible to develop an adequate record that would fully justify a race-based remedy. My dissent took a fundamentally different approach. I argued that "it is not necessary to find that the Board of Education has been guilty of racial discrimination in the past to support the conclusion that it has a legitimate interest in employing black teachers in the future. Rather than analyzing a case of this kind by asking whether minority teachers have some sort of entitlement to jobs as a remedy for sins that were committed in the past, I believe we should

---

57. *Wygant v. Jackson Bd. of Educ.*, 476 U.S. 267 (1986).
58. *Id.*, at 274.

first ask whether the Board's action advances the public interest in educating children for the future." I then explained why I believed that an integrated faculty would benefit the entire student body rather than merely providing role models for minority students. That opinion made a positive contribution to the adoption and approval of later affirmative action plans, including those adopted by the U.S. armed forces.

On January 27, 1986, the Court decided *Midlantic National Bank* v. *New Jersey Department of Environmental Protection,*[59] which presented the question whether a bankruptcy trustee may abandon property in contravention of local laws that protect the public's health and safety. A recent article in the *Journal of Supreme Court History* reminded me of the complicated nature of the Court's decision-making in this otherwise prosaic case.[60]

The facts involved a waste-removal company that had amassed nearly 500,000 gallons of toxic oil at its New York and New Jersey facilities. After the company declared bankruptcy, the bankruptcy trustee wished to abandon the facilities because the estimated cost of disposing of the toxic oil rendered the property a net burden to the estate. But state and local entities objected to the abandonment of the site without cleanup as violating state and local laws. By the time the case reached the Court, New York had already acted to decontaminate the facilities, so the ultimate issue was whether the bankrupt company would have to reimburse the state for its efforts. The Court of Appeals for the Third Circuit had held that abandonment would be impermissible because of the conflict with state law.

Lewis Powell wrote an opinion for the Court that Bill Brennan, Thurgood Marshall, Harry Blackmun, and I joined. It was crucial to our decision that, prior to the enactment of the new Bankruptcy Code in 1978, the trustee's abandonment power had been a matter of judge-made law.

---

59. 474 U.S. 494.
60. Ronald Mann, "Balancing Bankruptcy and Environmental Law: *Midlantic National Bank v. New Jersey Department of Environmental Protection,*" *J. of Sup. Ct. Hist.* 42, no. 1 (2017): 101–17.

Although the relevant provision of the code contained no express limitations on the trustee's abandonment power, we reasoned that the code impliedly incorporated a preexisting common-law doctrine, embodied in a few lower court cases, which prohibited a trustee from exercising the power to abandon in violation of state and federal laws. "The normal rule of statutory construction is that if Congress intends for legislation to change the interpretation of a judicially created concept, it makes that intent specific. If Congress wishes to grant the trustee an extraordinary exemption from nonbankruptcy law, the intention would be clearly expressed, not left to be collected or inferred from disputable considerations of convenience in administering the estate of the bankrupt."[61] Bill Rehnquist wrote a dissenting opinion, joined by Chief Justice Burger, Byron White, and Sandra O'Connor.

What is especially interesting about the case is that at conference I had originally voted to reverse the Third Circuit's judgment. Bill Rehnquist circulated a draft that was expected to become the majority opinion, holding that the code permitted abandonment without regard for state environmental regulations. But as I considered the case further, I realized that the abandonment decisions at issue were not just adjustments in creditors' rights that gave the state a priority claim for the cleanup costs. Rather, state law prohibited the trustee's conduct because of the consequences for public health and safety.

Ultimately, I felt I had to change my vote, and I offered a number of comments to Lewis Powell concerning his draft dissent — now the majority opinion. My memoranda to Lewis Powell reveal the concerns I had even after changing my vote. I wrote: "I found that I could not subscribe to Bill Rehnquist's proposed disposition because it seemed to authorize the trustee to abandon without any constraint whatsoever imposed by state law. You have convinced me that position is untenable. I am inclined to believe that the opposite extreme would be equally unsatisfactory. Specifically, I could not subscribe to a holding that the State could veto any

---

61. 474 U.S., at 501.

abandonment, no matter how many safety precautions were taken and no matter how much money the estate had spent in an effort to rectify the problem."[62] My concerns about the scope of Lewis Powell's draft opinion were eventually embodied in certain reservations in the final paragraph of the opinion, which noted that "[t]he abandonment power is not to be fettered by laws or regulations not reasonably calculated to protect the public health or safety from imminent and identifiable harm."[63]

The case is a good example of understanding the purpose of a statute without much help from pure text. My eventual vote was informed by my realization that, because of the serious public health implications, Congress's general authorization of abandonment could not be read to grant the trustee unmitigated power to violate state law and endanger local populations. The case is also a good example of the influence that an undecided vote can exert over the potential breadth of the Court's final disposition.

Congress enacted the Federal Tort Claims Act in 1946, waiving the federal government's preexisting sovereign immunity in actions to recover damages caused by the negligence of the federal government or its employees. In a case decided in 1986, *United States* v. *James,*[64] the Court held — over my dissent joined by Thurgood and Sandra — that the statute did not allow recovery on behalf of plaintiffs who had drowned or been seriously injured due to the federal government's negligent failure to warn them of the dangers from the release of floodwaters from two federal flood-control projects. The decision was based on the majority's interpretation of a statutory provision enacted in 1928, well before Congress subjected the federal government to tort liability.

In response to a disastrous flood, as well as to perennial threats posed by recurrent floods to landowners in the alluvial valley of the Mississippi River, Congress enacted the Mississippi Flood Control Act of 1928, which authorized the Army Corps of Engineers to design and build a

---

62. Memorandum to Justice Powell (January 7, 1986).
63. 474 U.S., at 507n9.
64. 478 U.S. 597.

system of levees and other flood-control works. As part of that undertaking, the statute directed the secretary of war and the chief of engineers to acquire lands subject to overflow along the riverbanks, where it was impracticable to construct levees. Although the federal government retained its sovereign immunity to tort liability at that time, there was a risk that those acquisitions might be considered takings of property without just compensation and therefore increase the cost of the project. To foreclose that risk, in the section of the act containing the direction relating to "lands so subjected to overflow and damage," this sentence appears: "No liability of any kind shall attach to or rest upon the United States for any damage from or by floods or flood waters at any place."

The key to my dispute with the majority turned on the difference between the meaning of the words "damage" and "damages." I thought — and still think — it clear that the term used in the statute (as it had been construed for centuries) described injury to property whereas "damages" describes the value of the harm to either person or property that an injured party suffers. By that reading, the statute's reference to "damage" did not immunize the federal government from responsibility for harms to persons. When the Flood Control Act was enacted, there was no need to protect the government from tort liability at all because the Federal Tort Claims Act did not yet exist.

In their treatise on statutory construction, Nino Scalia and Bryan Garner made this comment on that case:

> The Court's [majority] opinion glossed over the distinction between *damage* (harm to property) and *damages* (money awarded in a court judgment) and used them interchangeably.... [That reasoning is] similar to equating *desert* (a dry place) with *deserts* (what one deserves) or *premise* (logical foundation) with *premises* (property) or *specie* (coinage) with *species* (category under genus).

> Justice John Paul Stevens filed an admirable textualist and originalist dissent, noting that in a proviso to the immunity, the statute

twice referred to lands 'subjected to overflow and damage.' He distinguished *damage* from both *injury* (personal injury) and *damages* (compensation), citing legal dictionaries and encyclopedias from the appropriate era.... Alas, Justice Stevens's reasoning did not carry the day, and the surviving spouses recovered nothing.

In 1982, Pennsylvania enacted a mandatory minimum sentencing law providing that anyone convicted of certain felonies was subject to a sentence of at least five years if the sentencing judge found by a preponderance of the evidence that the defendant "visibly possessed a firearm" during the commission of the offense. A Pennsylvania judge found the statute unconstitutional. The Pennsylvania Supreme Court reversed, and our Court granted certiorari in *McMillan* v. *Pennsylvania*.[65]

In his opinion for a majority of the Court, Bill Rehnquist upheld the statute over the dissents of four justices. He reasoned that the requirement of proof beyond a reasonable doubt applied only to facts defining the crime charged in the indictment and did not apply to a sentencing factor that only came into play after the jury had found the defendant guilty. In reaching this conclusion, Bill relied on the fact that the sentencing factor did not raise the maximum penalty for any crime but rather required the sentencing judge to impose a particular minimum penalty within the range already prescribed by statute.

But, as I argued in my dissent, there is a vast difference between sentencing factors that bear on a discretionary decision to select a punishment within the range authorized by statute and elements of a crime mandating a higher minimum sentence. The *McMillan* majority's broad conception of sentencing factors allowed the states to evade the fundamental rule that "the Due Process Clause protects the accused against conviction except upon proof beyond a reasonable doubt of every fact necessary to constitute the crime with which he is charged."[66]

---

65. 477 U.S. 79 (1986).
66. *In re Winship,* 397 U.S. 358, 364 (1970).

The importance of the distinction between elements and sentencing factors was magnified by the adoption of mandatory sentencing guidelines in the Sentencing Reform Act of 1984. Under the mandatory guidelines, judges retained discretion to select a sentence within a given range that was determined by objective criteria, such as the type of offense and the defendant's criminal history. A fact that required a judge to impose a sentence within a higher range would be comparable to an element of the crime that increased a mandatory minimum sentence. Under the Pennsylvania statute in *McMillan,* a defendant's visible possession of a firearm increased the mandatory minimum, whereas under the guidelines comparable aggravating facts moved a convicted defendant's range of permissible sentences into a higher category that had both a higher mandatory minimum and a higher maximum.

It was not until 2013 that the Court finally abrogated its unfortunate decision in *McMillan* in *Alleyne* v. *United States.*[67] The Court held that facts that increase the mandatory minimum sentence must be submitted to the jury and proven beyond a reasonable doubt.

My good friend Byron White and I engaged in important debates in two cases decided in the 1985 term: *Thornburgh* v. *American College of Obstetricians and Gynecologists,*[68] in which the Court invalidated several provisions of a Pennsylvania statute regulating abortions, and *Bowers* v. *Hardwick,*[69] in which Byron wrote the opinion upholding Georgia's law prohibiting sodomy. I have always thought Byron made the most persuasive argument for overruling *Roe* v. *Wade* in *Thornburgh* because he recognized that the issue depended on an interpretation of the substantive content of the word "liberty" in the Fourteenth Amendment, rather than the argument that the word "privacy" does not appear in the Constitution. On the other hand, his attempt in *Bowers* to defend a statute that by its terms applied without exception to all persons — including not only

---

67. 570 U.S. 99.
68. 476 U.S. 747 (1986).
69. 478 U.S. 186 (1986).

heterosexuals but married couples as well — which the state tried to save by announcing that it would only enforce it against homosexuals — was never persuasive and predictably overruled years later.

On June 17, 1986, Warren Burger sent a letter to President Reagan requesting to be relieved of his duties as chief justice effective July 10, 1986, or as soon thereafter as his successor was confirmed. He gave an unusual reason for resigning: He needed more time to perform his duties as chairman of the Commission on the Bicentennial of the Constitution. I am sure he was sincere in making that explanation, but I remain somewhat perplexed by his decision to treat that temporary assignment as more important than his responsibilities as our chief. In any event, a few days later the president decided to appoint Bill Rehnquist to become the new chief and Antonin Scalia to join the Court as an associate justice.

Although Nino was confirmed unanimously, Bill's nomination as our new chief, which all of us heartily supported because we knew that he would do a significantly better job than Burger had, oddly generated thirty-three negative votes in the Senate. I do not remember exactly when Nino and I first met, but we had many mutual acquaintances, including former attorney general Ed Levi, my former Seventh Circuit colleague Luther Swygert, and Bill Rehnquist, all of whom enthusiastically supported his nomination, as did my former law partner Ed Rothschild.

Telephone conversations with Ed at the time prompted me to call Nino and provide him with the unsolicited advice that he should ask another lawyer to represent him during the hearings. I remember telling him that I thought it would be a mistake to rely entirely on Justice Department personnel because their interests during the hearings might diverge from his in unexpected ways. As it developed, he had no need for such advice, but I think he appreciated the spirit that motivated it. We became good friends as soon as he joined the Court.

Nino was one of the two justices (Bill Brennan was the other) who attended the dinner celebrating the wedding of my youngest daughter, Sue, at the Washington Golf and Country Club on September 26, 1986.

Everyone enjoyed meeting them because they were both so friendly and had such contagious senses of humor. Nino established a special relationship with my son John and my oldest daughter Kada, both of whom were smokers. Somehow Nino became aware of the fact that they were indulging their bad habit just outside the clubhouse and, not having brought any cigarettes with him because he had recently decided to give up smoking, accepted an invitation to join them. Their agreement with his request that they not tell his wife, Maureen, gave their newly formed friendship a special quality.

24

The Scalia Court

October Term 1986

At our first conference with Bill Rehnquist as our new chief justice, he invited us to continue to address him by his first name — a suggestion that we immediately and unanimously rejected. Our settled custom of referring to the "CJ" as either "Chief" or "Mr. Chief Justice" was too important a tradition to change. Other changes were, however, immediately apparent under our new chief. The first conference during a new term, which mostly involves the disposition of the certiorari petitions that had accumulated over the summer, had usually taken almost three days. With the new chief at our helm, I think we had almost finished the list on Monday before we broke for lunch.

Bill was a much more efficient and orderly presiding officer than his predecessor had been. He gave each member of the Court a full opportunity to speak on each case for as long as the speaker desired, but discouraged repetition and reargument of points already covered. He was completely fair to those who disagreed with him as well as those supporting his views, and he never seemed at all confused about the positions espoused by any of his colleagues. I have no recollection of any problems with his assignment of opinions.

That term was, of course, also Nino Scalia's first. One of his first opinions initiated a debate between us over the relevance of legislative history in statutory interpretation that persisted as long as we were both on the Court. His opinion concurring in the judgment in *INS* v. *Cardoza-Fonseca*[1] severely criticized my majority opinion for its reliance on legislative history rather than just statutory text and, more importantly, for misapplying the rule announced in *Chevron*, which I had authored four years earlier. Despite his criticism, I thought — and still think — it clear that our holding was governed by the passage in *Chevron* stating that the judiciary "must reject administrative constructions which are contrary to clear congressional intent."[2]

My law clerk Larry Marshall, who now teaches at Stanford, commented that the most significant case of the term in his view was *McCleskey* v. *Kemp*.[3] Warren McCleskey challenged Georgia's capital punishment system on the ground that it was discriminatory based on the race of the victim and, to a far lesser extent, the race of the defendant. Of course, in *Gregg* v. *Georgia*,[4] the Court had accepted the state's arguments that they had "fixed" the capital punishment system and it therefore effectively reinstated the death penalty. Based on a sophisticated multiple regression study conducted by Professor David Baldus and his colleagues, McCleskey was now claiming that the system had not been fixed after all. Many at the time thought that a decision in McCleskey's favor would put an end to the death penalty, whereas a contrary decision would mean the failure of the last wholesale challenge to the modern capital punishment system.

He also recalls that tensions were very high among the clerks — especially when it was learned that the five "conservative" justices had caucused alone before the oral argument. Many of the clerks in the other chambers were devastated when they learned that Lewis Powell, the swing vote, had voted against McCleskey. But he also recalls that not all

---

1. 480 U.S. 421, 452 (1987).
2. *Chevron* v. *Natural Resources Defense Council,* 467 U.S. 837, 843n9 (1984).
3. 481 U.S. 279 (1987).
4. 428 U.S. 153 (1976).

law clerks in the building agreed on the case's importance; when one clerk walked by as Larry and others were having an animated conversation about the case, the clerk asked what the hubbub was about, but was surprised when Larry told him that it was about McCleskey. The law clerk looked dismayed, informing Larry that it was clear to him that the most important case of the term was one of the takings cases the Court had decided in favor of the government. Larry still remembers that conversation and how it demonstrates the different priorities and perspectives people bring to various problems.

I profoundly disagreed with my colleagues in two cases presenting stare decisis issues that term. The question concerned the arguable duty of the Supreme Court to follow a rule of federal law established only by lower court decisions interpreting an ambiguous federal statute, rather than make its own determination of wise policy. The first was an uninteresting tax opinion written by Lewis Powell, *Commissioner* v. *Fink*,[5] in which I was the only dissenter. The second was a fascinating mail fraud case written by Byron White, *McNally* v. *United States*,[6] in which Sandra O'Connor joined most of my dissent.

The question in *Fink* was "whether a dominant shareholder who voluntarily surrenders a portion of his shares to the corporation, but retains control, may immediately deduct from taxable income his basis in the surrendered shares."[7] That very question had been answered by the Board of Tax Appeals over forty-five years earlier and its answer had been consistently followed in decisions in which the Internal Revenue Service had announced its acquiescence. Although Congress had dramatically revamped the tax code in 1954, the IRS made no attempt to modify the Tax Court's approach to this issue until 1977 after the Finks had transferred their stock. The IRS failed to persuade the Court of Appeals for the Sixth Circuit to change the established rule, but eight members of our

---

5. 483 U.S. 89 (1987).
6. 483 U.S. 350 (1987).
7. 483 U.S., at 89.

Court agreed with the IRS's new rule that the shareholder could not deduct the loss until he disposed of his remaining shares.

In my dissent, I did not consider whether the old or the new rule represented better policy. I believed instead that fairness to the taxpayers and, more importantly, to the process of interpreting statutes should have led to a different result. I wrote: "The relationship between the courts or agencies, on the one hand, and Congress, on the other, is a dynamic one. In the process of legislating it is inevitable that Congress will leave open spaces in the law that the courts are implicitly authorized to fill. The judicial process of construing statutes must therefore include an exercise of lawmaking power that has been delegated to the courts by Congress. But after the gap has been filled, regardless of whether it is filled exactly as Congress might have intended or hoped, the purpose of the delegation has been achieved and the responsibility for making any future change should rest on the shoulders of the Congress."[8]

The question in *McNally* was whether the federal statute prohibiting the use of the mails to defraud prohibited only schemes to deprive victims of money or property or also the intangible right of the citizenry to honest government. When the statute was enacted in 1872, its sparse legislative history revealed an interest in protecting people from schemes to protect their property without any mention of a broader purpose. Likewise, the first Supreme Court case construing the statute held that its terms should be interpreted broadly with respect to property rights but was silent about intangible rights. A significant number of court of appeals decisions, however, had held that the statute also prohibited schemes to deprive citizens of honest government. *McNally* itself was such a case in the Sixth Circuit. The defendant had control of Kentucky's award of workers' compensation contracts and accepted payments for awarding business to his associates, conduct that would unquestionably have been criminal under the statute's construction in a host of intermediate court decisions.

---

8. *Id.*, at 104.

In his opinion holding that the statute simply did not apply to honest-services fraud, Byron White gave no deference whatsoever to the views of the many court of appeals judges who had come to a contrary conclusion. His decision was quite wrong on the merits of the case before the Court, but in my opinion even more wrong in its blithe disrespect for the thoughtful views of so many other judges. Congress promptly disapproved of the decision by enacting an amendment that reinstated the pre-*McNally* rule, but of course it could not require the Court to implement my views about stare decisis thereafter.

Another important case released in June of that term was *Turner v. Safley*,[9] which construed two Missouri prison regulations — one permitting correspondence between inmates at different institutions only if they are immediate family members, and the other allowing an inmate to marry only with the permission of the prison superintendent. Sandra O'Connor wrote the opinion for the Court, striking down the marriage regulation as unconstitutional but upholding the restriction on inmate-to-inmate correspondence. While I agreed with the Court's disposition of the marriage restriction, I wrote an opinion — joined by Bill Brennan, Thurgood Marshall, and Harry Blackmun — that expressed my disagreement with the Court's approval of the inmate correspondence restriction.

The most notable aspect of Sandra's majority opinion was that it laid out a rational basis test that justified upholding the correspondence regulation and that would frequently be applied to prisoners' constitutional claims going forward. The test included four considerations. "First, there must be a 'valid, rational connection' between the prison regulation and the legitimate governmental interest put forward to justify it." Second, a court must ask whether " 'other avenues' remain available for the [inmate's] exercise of the asserted right." The third consideration was "the impact accommodation of the asserted constitutional right will have on guards and other inmates." Specifically, "[w]hen accommodation of an asserted

---

9. 482 U.S. 78 (1987).

right will have a significant 'ripple effect' on fellow inmates or on prison staff, courts should be particularly deferential to the informed discretion of corrections officials." Finally, "the absence of ready alternatives is evidence of the reasonableness of a prison regulation," whereas "the existence of obvious, easy alternatives may be evidence that the regulation is not reasonable."[10]

I thought the test was an insufficiently weak safeguard for prisoners' rights. I explained my concerns about this lenient standard of review in my dissenting opinion: "[I]f the standard can be satisfied by nothing more than a 'logical connection' between the regulation and any legitimate penological concern perceived by a cautious warden, it is virtually meaningless. Application of the standard would seem to permit disregard for inmates' constitutional rights whenever the imagination of the warden produces a plausible security concern and a deferential trial court is able to discern a logical connection between that concern and the challenged regulation."[11]

Later scholarly consideration of the impact of the *Turner* standard supports my view at the time. As one political science professor has written: "Although the explication of factors to be used in applying the *Turner* test would be helpful to the lower courts, the majority's preference for judicial restraint and a lower level of scrutiny of prisoners' constitutional claims could have only one consequence — diminished protection for prisoners' rights."[12]

In the last month of his eighteen-year career on the Supreme Court, Lewis Powell wrote the opinion in *Booth* v. *Maryland*,[13] invalidating Maryland's statute authorizing the use of "victim impact statements" in capital cases. The opinion was faithful to the reasoning in the earlier cases

10. *Id.*, at 89–91.
11. *Id.*, at 100–101.
12. John A. Fliter, *Prisoners' Rights: The Supreme Court and Evolving Standards of Decency* (Westport, CT: Greenwood Press, 2001), 159; see also Christopher E. Smith, *The Supreme Court and the Development of Law: Through the Prism of Prisoners' Rights* (New York: Palgrave Macmillan, 2016), 116.
13. 482 U.S. 496 (1987).

that he, Potter Stewart, and I had written in 1976, in which we upheld the death penalty on the understanding that the jury's discretion would be "suitably directed and limited so as to minimize the risk of wholly arbitrary and capricious action."[14] Our reasoning in those cases required the exclusion of evidence unrelated to the defendant's record or the circumstances of the defendant's crime. But the victim impact statement in the *Booth* case included detailed information about the commendable personal characteristics of the two elderly people that the defendants had murdered, and the serious emotional impact of their deaths on the members of their family, as well as the family members' opinions about the crimes. All of the facts in the statement were wholly unrelated to the blameworthiness of the defendants.

The admission of such evidence obviously would have increased the risk of arbitrariness in imposition of the death penalty, which Potter had compared to the risk of being struck by lightning. Bill Brennan, Thurgood Marshall, Harry Blackmun, and I joined Lewis's opinion. But those justices (other than Harry) who had agreed with Byron White, and disagreed with Lewis, Potter, and me, in *Gregg*— as well as Nino Scalia who had replaced Chief Justice Burger a year earlier — dissented. In my judgment Lewis's opinion represented the last chapter in our effort to require that any decision to impose a death sentence must "be, and appear to be, based on reason rather than caprice or emotion" as the three of us had written in 1977 in *Gardner* v. *Florida*.[15]

At our conference on the last day of the term, Lewis Powell told us that he was resigning— an announcement that we all regretted and which produced a few tears from Sandra. President Reagan nominated Robert Bork to fill the vacancy. Bob had been a friend of mine since the days when we were both practicing law in Chicago. I knew that he was an excellent lawyer, had served honorably in the Marine Corps, and was an extremely

---

14. *Gregg* v. *Georgia,* 428 U.S. 153, 189 (1976).
15. 430 U.S. 349 (1977).

likeable person. I have always ranked him as the most persuasive solicitor general who represented the United States before the Supreme Court while I was a justice. I thought, and still think, that he was eminently qualified for the position, and I said as much in response to a question at the Eighth Circuit Judicial Conference in the summer of 1987.

When Bob testified before the Senate Judiciary Committee, however, he offended some Committee members and many listeners in the television audience. He had also grown an unruly beard. He frankly stated his opinion on a variety of legal issues — mentioning, for example, that he shared my views about the Equal Protection Clause, which many critics thought idiosyncratic. He also shared his adherence to earlier scholarly writings with which some liberals disagreed. Liberal scholars testified against him and liberal politicians opposed him and, in the end, the Senate Committee (by a vote of 5–9) and the entire Senate (by a vote of 42–58) rejected his nomination.

The tactics of Bork's opponents included misstatements about his views and a certain amount of unfair comment on his character, motivated in part by a fear that his approval might lead to the reexamination and possible overturning of *Roe* v. *Wade*. Bob's later writings seemed to confirm that fear, but I have never been convinced that his actual work as a justice would necessarily have paralleled those writings. There is a world of difference between a judge's duty to rule impartially and a citizen's freedom to express his or her own views. In any event, one of the unfortunate consequences of the Bork hearings is that we will never know what kind of a justice he would have been even though we do know that he was an excellent circuit judge. A second unfortunate consequence of those hearings is that they have given the public, as well as some senators, the impression that the political views of nominees to the Supreme Court are more important than their judicial qualifications. That impression, in turn, undermines the public's confidence in judges as impartial guardians of the rule of law.

It was also during the 1986 term that Lewis Powell declined David Lloyd Kreeger's invitation to judge a moot court competition at American

University in Washington, D.C., on the question whether William Shakespeare was the true author of the plays he is supposed to have written. Bill Brennan and Harry Blackmun had already agreed to serve when, at Lewis's suggestion, Kreeger called on me to discuss the question that he had been pondering for many years as he read and reread the plays in the Shakespeare canon. At that meeting, he explained that two law professors were researching the issue in preparation for the argument, which was scheduled for September, shortly before our next term would begin. I accepted his invitation.

Before the oral argument, Bill, Harry, and I decided that the lawyer challenging the orthodox view that Shakespeare really wrote the plays should shoulder the burden of proof under the "beyond a reasonable doubt" standard, which seemed appropriate in a case involving the "BARD." That lawyer's arguments included persuasive evidence supporting the view that Edward de Vere, the seventeenth Earl of Oxford, was the actual author and even more persuasive evidence that the man whose almost illegible signature "Shaksper" appeared on William Shakespeare's will (which left his "second best bed" to his widow) was not. After the argument, we promptly announced our judgment upholding the status quo, but Harry and I both confessed to having some doubt concerning our verdict.

The arguments identified skeptics — such as Mark Twain, Walt Whitman, Henry James, John Galsworthy, and Sigmund Freud — who had opined that William Shakespeare was a pseudonym for a well-educated nobleman who had written the plays. The arguments also noted the complete absence of any contemporary correspondence with the author during his lifetime and the striking difference between the spelling (and legibility) of his few actual signatures and the name "Shakespeare." They also described the research of an English teacher (unfortunately named "Looney") who had first developed the thesis that de Vere was the true author. I do not recall any reference in the argument to the fact that particularly impressed Maryan and me later that year when we visited Shakespeare's home in Stratford-upon-Avon: We found no evidence whatsoever that the house ever contained a library. The man who wrote those plays must have owned some books.

Before our return to the United States after that visit, we spent a few pleasant days at the Grand Hotel in Cabourg on the Normandy coast of France. We had the opportunity to enjoy watching equestrians on the shore during the early morning, topless sunbathers during the day, and a well-behaved dog who sat at a table in the hotel dining room with his owners during dinner. We decided not to play in a duplicate bridge game in the hotel because the volume of cigarette smoke was so dense. Our visit to the military cemetery overlooking the bluff that our invading soldiers had climbed after coming ashore on June 6, 1944, was particularly moving. Indeed, it was an unforgettable experience that I thought of while writing my dissents in cases involving the constitutionality of burning the American flag to convey a message of protest.

25

The Kennedy Court

October Term 1987

Despite the partisan character of the debate over Bob Bork's confirmation, on February 3, 1988, the Senate, which then had a Democratic majority, unanimously confirmed Ronald Reagan's nomination of Tony Kennedy. Tony had earlier been appointed by Gerald Ford to serve on the Court of Appeals for the Ninth Circuit and was a well-respected judge whom all of us welcomed. I attended his swearing-in ceremony at the White House and remember being so offended by the partisan character of Ronald Reagan's remarks on that occasion that I decided not to attend comparable events at that location in the future. I came to believe that the swearing-in of members of the Court was a judicial ceremony that should take place at the Court, where the president may participate in the proceedings if he is a member of our bar (as Ford did when I was sworn in) or merely witness the event (as Reagan did when Sandra was sworn in). Holding the event at the White House conveys the incorrect message to the public that the new justice will have some sort of ongoing relationship with the executive instead of commencing an entirely new career.

Shortly after Tony was sworn in, we heard argument in *Patterson* v.

McLean Credit Union,[1] a case presenting the question whether racial harassment of a black employee violated 42 U.S.C. § 1981, which provides that all persons "have the same right to make and enforce contracts…as is enjoyed by white persons." At our conference following the argument, after explaining that he was not entirely sure about the answer, Tony voted somewhat tentatively in favor of the plaintiff, thus providing the majority for the result favored by Bill Brennan, Thurgood Marshall, Harry Blackmun, and me. Instead of assigning the opinion to Tony — who would have been in the majority even if he changed his mind — Bill decided to write the majority himself, and, as it developed, failed to persuade Tony to adhere to his original vote. The case was set for reargument in the following term, and Tony ultimately wrote the Court opinion for the opposite result, finding that the employee's racial harassment claim was not actionable under Section 1981. I thought at the time — and still think — that Bill would have been much wiser to allow Tony to prepare the first draft of an opinion favoring the plaintiff. He was more likely to be convinced by his own reasoning than by Bill's. I repeatedly recalled that case years later when I had the responsibility for assigning majority opinions.

Three other cases considered during the 1987 term stand out in my memory: *Morrison* v. *Olson,*[2] upholding the constitutionality of the independent counsel provisions of the Ethics in Government Act of 1978; *Boyle* v. *United Technologies Corp.,*[3] creating an entirely new defense for negligent government contractors; and *Thompson* v. *Oklahoma,*[4] prohibiting the execution of a defendant who was a 15-year-old at the time of his crime.

Although I did not share his evaluation, I have a firm impression that Nino Scalia regarded his solo dissent in the *Olson* case as one of his best opinions. A few days before it was announced, at an afternoon party at the Court attended by all the clerks and justices, Nino joined Byron and

1. 491 U.S. 164 (1989).
2. 487 U.S. 654 (1988).
3. 487 U.S. 500 (1988).
4. 487 U.S. 815 (1988).

me while we were recalling that Justice John Harlan II had been an advocate of having at least one dissenting opinion announced orally each term. As I remember the conversation, Nino said he was unaware of the custom and both Byron and I suggested that he should adopt that practice with respect to his *Olson* dissent. He accepted our suggestion and his oral statement received extensive favorable comment in the press. I think it may well have helped to persuade Congress not to reenact similar legislation thereafter.

Nino's opinion remains the subject of debate today. In a recent opinion piece in the *New York Times,* Eric Posner, the University of Chicago Law School professor, provided the following observation:

> In 1978, Congress believed that an independent counsel was necessary and proper for preventing the president from breaking Congress's laws. Congress rejected what would be Justice Scalia's main line of attack — that because the people can punish at the polls a president who abuses his powers, an independent counsel is unnecessary.

> President Nixon's illegal surveillance of the Democratic National Committee was aimed at preventing voters from making an informed choice in the 1972 election. The firing of Archibald Cox took place in Nixon's second term, so voters could hardly punish the president by voting him out of office. And while the threat of impeachment finally forced Nixon to resign, it was the work of the special prosecutors (Cox, and then his replacement, Leon Jaworski) that paved the way.

> The majority in the Supreme Court had no trouble rejecting Justice Scalia's arguments, which were palpably absurd in the wake of Watergate.[5]

---

5. *New York Times,* Feb. 5, 2018, A19.

I remain convinced that the majority in *Morrison* had the better of the argument, and as Professor Posner's opinion piece suggests, the majority's views appear to have withstood the test of time.

In *Boyle,* the father of the copilot of a U.S. Marine helicopter who had been killed in a crash during a training exercise sought damages under Virginia law from the allegedly negligent manufacturer of the helicopter. In a five-to-four decision, the Supreme Court created a new federal common law rule protecting the company from liability. The rule's only justification was the interest in minimizing federal procurement costs. In his dissent, Bill Brennan acknowledged that the Court would have been required to recognize the defense if it had been created by Congress. But "[t]he Court — unelected and unaccountable to the people — has unabashedly stepped into the breach to legislate a rule denying Lt. Boyle's family the compensation that state law assures them."[6]

In a separate dissent, I added a point that I often expressed:

> When judges are asked to embark on a lawmaking venture, I believe they should carefully consider whether they, or a legislative body, are better equipped to perform the task at hand. There are instances of so-called interstitial lawmaking that inevitably become part of the judicial process. But when we are asked to create an entirely new doctrine — to answer "questions of policy on which Congress has not spoken," — we have a special duty to identify the proper decision maker before trying to make the proper decision.[7]

Reflecting on our five-to-four decision in *Thompson,* it now seems incredible that our debate about whether it would violate the Constitution to execute a defendant who was only fifteen years old when he committed his crime occupies sixty-four pages in the U.S. Reports. I thought it clear that "the evolving standards of decency that mark the progress of a

---

6. 487 U.S., at 515–16.
7. *Id.,* at 531.

mature society" prohibited the imposition of the ultimate penalty on a juvenile.[8] But only three justices — Brennan, Marshall, and Blackmun — joined that view. Sandra O'Connor maintained that the national consensus did not support a blanket prohibition on juvenile capital punishment as a matter of constitutional law. Although Sandra's vote made a bare majority to vacate the particular capital sentence in *Thompson,* the Court would have to revisit the issue twice before conclusively forbidding the imposition of the death penalty on juveniles in 2005 in *Roper* v. *Simmons.*[9]

October Term 1988

Some Court watchers have occasionally assumed that differences between Nino Scalia's and my approach to the law reflected our differing biases, mine favoring recovery for injured plaintiffs with Nino favoring defendants. A five-to-four decision from early in the 1988 term belies any such assumption.

Pittston Coal Group v. *Sebben*[10] presented the question whether regulations promulgated by the secretary of labor to implement the Black Lung Benefits Reform Act of 1977 were invalid. The act required that miners' claims for benefits be assessed under "[c]riteria...not...more restrictive than the criteria applicable to a claim filed on June 30, 1973." In 1973 the relevant criteria were contained in regulations issued by the secretary of Health, Education and Welfare (HEW) pursuant to an earlier statute. Nino's majority opinion, joined by Bill Brennan, Thurgood Marshall, Harry Blackmun, and Tony Kennedy, read the older regulations issued by HEW to create a presumption of benefit eligibility for some miners who had worked for less than ten years. Nino's opinion therefore invalidated the newer regulations because, unlike in the 1973 rules, *no* miner was entitled to a presumption of eligibility unless he had worked at least ten years.

---

8. See *Trop* v. *Dulles,* 356 U.S. 86, 100–101 (1968).
9. 543 U.S. 551.
10. 488 U.S. 105 (1988).

I disagreed. I thought that the Secretary of Labor had reasonably construed the word "criteria" to include only medical criteria and not employment criteria. Moreover, I thought that the old regulations' presumption of eligibility for some miners who had worked for less than ten years was based on a scrivener's error. I began my twenty-eight-page dissent, which was joined by Chief Justice Rehnquist, Byron White, and Sandra O'Connor, with the following paragraph:

Pneumoconiosis is a serious respiratory disease that has afflicted hundreds of thousands of coal miners who have spent their entire working lives inhaling coal dust.... The severity of the disease is directly related to the duration of the miner's underground employment. Although pneumoconiosis may be present in its early stages in short-term miners (*i.e.,* miners with fewer than 10 years of coal-mine experience), it is seldom, if ever, disabling unless the employee has worked in the mines for well over 10 years. Not surprisingly, there is no evidence that any participant in the lawmaking process ever suggested that it would be reasonable to presume that short-term miners—even if afflicted with pneumoconiosis in its early stages — should be presumed to be totally disabled. In fact, the original draft of [the old regulation,] like the [final draft of the new regulation at issue in this case] unambiguously provided that the presumption of total disability for miners who satisfy the relevant medical criteria would not arise unless the miner had at least 10 years of coal-mine employment. The only basis for reaching the conclusion that the law now extends this presumption to short-term miners is an unexplained change in the HEW regulation, which was either a scrivener's error or a strikingly unique product of incompetent draftsmanship. Nonetheless, the Court today holds that Congress intended such short-term miners to receive the benefit of such an unreasonable presumption.[11]

---

11. *Id.,* at 123.

The details of our debate as to whether a scrivener's error had occurred are less significant than the fact that my work on the opinion reminded me so vividly of the incident during World War II when a garbled Japanese call sign gave rise to concern over the location of an enemy battleship. When judges are confronted with disputes about an agency's understanding of major congressional legislation, a careful study of relevant text is only a part of their search for the right answer.

Four other cases from the 1988 term bear mention because each was significantly modified by the 1991 Civil Rights Act. The Court acted in each case to curb the availability of relief for employment discrimination plaintiffs. But Congress's response reasserted its interest in vindicating the rights of those employees. In particular, I was gratified that in three of the four cases, Congress endorsed the position that I joined or expressed in dissent. In the fourth case, Congress adopted the view expressed in the plurality opinion — which I joined — but also added an important modification.

First, in *Ward's Cove Packing Company* v. *Atonio,*[12] a bare majority of the Court held that minority employees could not state a claim of employment discrimination simply by showing that nonwhites were underrepresented in certain jobs. Rather, employees needed to identify the *specific* employment practices that caused the underrepresentation. Then, the burden of production would shift to the employer to show a business justification for the challenged practice. I disagreed and authored a dissent that Bill Brennan, Thurgood, and Harry joined. We believed that the majority had underestimated the probative value of a racially stratified workplace, and had inappropriately redefined the employer's burden as one of production rather than persuasion.

Congress later endorsed our view. For one thing, the 1991 act permitted plaintiffs to challenge an entire decision-making process, rather than a single specific practice, if the elements of the process could not be

_____

12. 490 U.S. 642 (1989).

analytically differentiated. For another, the act provided that, if the employee successfully shifted the burden to the employer, the employer would carry the burden of production *and* of persuasion and would need to show that the challenged practice was both job-related and consistent with business necessity.

Second, in *Martin* v. *Wilks*,[13] the Court treated consent decrees that were put into place after black employees challenged discriminatory hiring and promotion practices at the Birmingham Fire Department. In another five-to-four decision, the majority ruled that white firefighters could challenge the consent decrees, which they alleged had resulted in the promotion of less qualified blacks at their expense. I again authored a dissent that Bill Brennan, Thurgood, and Harry joined. In my view, the scope of relief available to the white firefighters was limited: They could challenge the decrees as collusive, fraudulent, or transparently invalid, but they could not simply argue that "different relief would have been more appropriate than the relief that was actually granted."[14]

Again Congress later substantially limited the majority's rule and sided with the dissenters. The 1991 act provided that non-parties could not challenge consent decrees if they knew or should have known of the prior litigation, or if they were adequately represented by the original parties.

Patterson v. *McLean Credit Union*,[15] which I have already mentioned, was yet a third five-to-four decision. There, the majority held that an employee could not sue her employer for racial harassment during employment under Section 1981. The majority's view was that because Section 1981 prohibited discrimination only in the "mak[ing] and enforce[ment] [of] contracts," it did not protect employees from discrimination "after the contract relation has been established, including breach of the terms of the contract or imposition of discriminatory working conditions." I joined Bill Brennan's dissent, which explained our view that

---

13. 490 U.S. 755 (1989).
14. *Id.,* at 787.
15. 491 U.S. 164 (1989).

the majority needlessly limited the statute's reach and ignored powerful historical evidence about its goals.

Again Congress vindicated the dissenting view. The act redefined the phrase "make and enforce contracts" in Section 1981 to include "the making, performance, modification and termination of contracts, and the enjoyment of all benefits, privileges, terms, and conditions of the contractual relationship." Congress's change was obviously intended to ensure that Section 1981 protected employees from ongoing racial discrimination after the initiation of the employment contract.

Finally, in *Price Waterhouse* v. *Hopkins*,[16] Bill Brennan's plurality opinion, which I joined, elaborated the burden of proof in employment discrimination lawsuits. The opinion explained that, once the plaintiff proves that an unlawful consideration played a motivating part in the employer's personnel decision, the employer could escape liability entirely, but only by showing that it would have made the same decision even if it had not been motivated by that unlawful factor. Sandra O'Connor concurred, but believed that the plaintiff needed to show "direct evidence" that the unlawful consideration was a "substantial factor" in order to shift the burden of proof to the defendant.

Congress later codified the rule from the plurality opinion, providing that the plaintiff could shift the burden of proof by showing that the unlawful consideration was a motivating factor. But Congress also stipulated that the employer's proof that it would have made the same decision absent the unlawful factor was a defense to back pay and reinstatement, but not to liability per se. This meant that the plaintiff could still recover attorney's fees and obtain declaratory and injunctive relief, so long as he or she made the initial showing that the prohibited consideration was a motivating factor.

In *Rodriguez de Quijas* v. *Shearson/American Express, Inc.*,[17] a five-justice majority overturned an interpretation of a federal statute that had been

---

16. 490 U.S. 228 (1989).
17. 490 U.S. 477 (1989).

settled for over thirty-five years. In 1953, in *Wilko* v. *Swan*,[18] the majority had held, over Justice Frankfurter's dissent, that an agreement between securities brokers and buyers to arbitrate future controversies violated Section 14 of the Securities Act of 1933. In a dissenting opinion that I wrote as a circuit judge in 1973, I questioned whether *Wilko* gave an American party a defense to the enforcement of an international arbitration agreement but assumed that *Wilko* had been correctly decided. I ultimately concluded that *Wilko* did not apply to the particular facts of that case, and explained, "The dispute between these parties over the alleged shortage in defendant's inventory of European trademarks, a matter covered by contract warranties and subject to pre-closing verification, is the kind of commercial dispute for which arbitration is entirely appropriate.... I would require this representative of the American business community to honor its bargain."[19]

Tony Kennedy's majority opinion in *Rodriguez de Quijas* correctly noted that I had considered both the strengths and weaknesses of the *Wilko* decision in my Seventh Circuit dissent.[20] But I did not agree with the majority's decision in 1989 to overrule that well-established precedent. Instead, in my dissent, I wrote, "In the final analysis, a Justice's vote in a case like this depends more on his or her views about the respective law-making responsibilities of Congress and this Court than on conflicting policy interests. Judges who have confidence in their own ability to fashion public policy are less hesitant to change the law than those of us who are inclined to give wide latitude to the views of the voters' representatives on nonconstitutional matters."[21]

In *Pennsylvania* v. *Union Gas Co.*,[22] the Court confronted two important issues. Congress had recently amended federal environmental protection

---

18. 346 U.S. 427.
19. See *Alberto-Culver Company* v. *Scherk*, 484 F. 2d 611, 619–20 (CA7 1973).
20. See 490 U.S., at 480.
21. *Id.*, at 487.
22. 491 U.S. 1 (1989).

statutes to provide a cause of action for monetary damages against a state whose flood control efforts had negligently caused harm to a local property owner. The issues were, first, whether the text of the statutes clearly authorized such relief against a state, and second, whether the Constitution protected the states from such liability. The Court divided five to four on both issues. Bill Brennan's opinion, which I joined, held that the statute's plain language authorized suits against the states and that Congress had properly overridden the states' immunity by legislating pursuant to the Commerce Clause in this case. Nino Scalia provided the decisive vote to make the statutory holding the opinion of the Court, while Byron White — who wrote the dissent on that point — provided the fifth vote to uphold federal power under the Commerce Clause to impose damages liability on the states.

The case was a significant victory for those of us who believe the framers crafted a strong central government and who would limit the protection provided to the states by the Eleventh Amendment to that set forth in its text rather than treating the doctrine of sovereign immunity as though it had been embraced by that text. In particular, the majority on the constitutional holding recognized that Congress could authorize suits against states when acting pursuant to its constitutional powers other than the Fourteenth Amendment. I wrote separately to emphasize the distinction between the two Eleventh Amendments discussed in our cases — the first, correct and literal interpretation, and the second, the defense of sovereign immunity that had been effectively added to the text of the amendment. I pointed out that Congress has no power under the Constitution to violate the former but that it had plenary power to subject states to suit in federal court.

For reasons that I did not understand, instead of joining Bill Brennan's opinion explaining our constitutional holding, Byron White wrote a separate concurrence agreeing with the result but expressing doubt concerning the Court's reasoning. In my view, that choice weakened the precedential strength of the constitutional holding in *Union Gas* and made it vulnerable to being subsequently overruled. Indeed, several terms later, after Clarence Thomas replaced Thurgood Marshall, the Court was asked to reexamine *Union Gas*. In *Seminole Tribe of Florida* v. *Florida*,[23] the Court changed course and incorrectly endorsed the view that the Eleventh Amendment reflects a broader constitutional principle of sovereign immunity that protects states from virtually all suits in federal court. And as a practical matter, that expansive view of the Eleventh Amendment severely undermined Congress's power to authorize suits against the states by permitting such suits *only* under Section 5 of the Fourteenth Amendment.

On June 21, 1989, Tony Kennedy joined Bill Brennan's majority opinion in *Texas* v. *Johnson*,[24] the case holding that a demonstrator in Dallas had a constitutional right to burn the American flag during the Republican National Convention to express his opposition to President Reagan's policies. Over the years I have puzzled over the question whether his predecessor, Lewis Powell, would have agreed with that result because, on the one hand, he was an extremely patriotic veteran of World War II while, on the other hand, he supported a liberal reading of the First Amendment. In any event, his successor joined the majority "without reservation."[25] Indeed, he wrote a separate opinion stating that "sometimes we must make decisions we do not like." He concluded by stating that whether or not the demonstrator "could appreciate the enormity of the offense he gave, the fact remains that his acts were speech, in both the technical and the fundamental meaning of the Constitution. So I agree with the Court that he must go free."[26]

Of course, expressive conduct is often given the same constitutional protection as the use of words to express the same idea, but it is not entirely accurate to equate conduct that conveys a message with speech. It is also not true that all speech is constitutionally protected — fighting words and obscenity may be prohibited. In cases like *Johnson*, decisionmakers must exercise judgment in determining the outcome — typically

---

23. 517 U.S. 44, 46 (1996).
24. 491 U.S. 397 (1989).
25. *Id.*, at 420.
26. *Id.*, at 421.

weighing the interest in keeping the channels of communication open against the value of a countervailing concern such as preserving respect for a symbol. Even commercial symbols, like trademarks, have a value that merits protection against desecration.

But an interesting aspect of the flag-burning case is that its ultimate significance is not the practical effect of holding that burning the American flag is legal. For over the years it has become obvious that the interest in communicating messages by burning flags is minimal if not entirely non-existent, given the absence of any publicized examples of flag burning during the past thirty years. Instead, the case depended on the relative importance of two different symbols: the flag as a representation of patriotism; and the broad protection of free expression, as an ideal encouraging confidence in the individual's ability to say what he or she wishes. The outcome turned on the determination that the latter idea carried more weight, rather than on the need to preserve flag burning as a specific means of communication.

Thus the real importance of the majority's holding in *Texas* v. *Johnson* is as a symbol of every individual's freedom to oppose our government without fear of retaliation, rather than as a concrete protection against government interference with a particular way to exchange ideas. All of us can be proud of such a symbolic decision even while I continue to disagree with the majority's failure to recognize the importance of the symbolic value of the Texas law. As I concluded my dissent,

The Court is therefore quite wrong in blandly asserting that respondent "was prosecuted for his expression of dissatisfaction with the policies of this country, expression situated at the core of our First Amendment values." Respondent was prosecuted because of the method he chose to express his dissatisfaction with those policies. Had he chosen to spray-paint — or perhaps convey with a motion picture projector — his message of dissatisfaction on the façade of the Lincoln Memorial, there would be no question about the power of the Government to prohibit his means of expression.

The prohibition would be supported by the legitimate interest in preserving the quality of an important national asset. Though the asset at stake in this case is intangible, given its unique value, the same interest supports a prohibition on the desecration of the American Flag.

The ideas of liberty and equality have been an irresistible force in motivating leaders like Patrick Henry, Susan B. Anthony, and Abraham Lincoln, schoolteachers like Nathan Hale and Booker T. Washington, the Philippine Scouts who fought at Bataan, and the soldiers who scaled the bluff at Omaha Beach. If those ideas are worth fighting for — and our history demonstrates that they are — it cannot be true that the flag that uniquely symbolizes their power is not itself worthy of protection from unnecessary desecration.[27]

October Term 1989

In response to the Court's decision in *Texas* v. *Johnson,* Congress passed the Flag Protection Act of 1989 by a vote of 91–9 in the Senate and 371–43 in the House. Two groups of demonstrators who objected to that statute by burning flags in Seattle and on the steps of the Capitol were promptly indicted and successfully moved to dismiss the charges against them. The government's direct appeal to our Court resulted in a decision reaffirming the holding in the *Johnson* case. The four of us who had dissented in *Johnson* did so again, and I wrote,

The symbolic value of the American flag is not the same today as it was yesterday. Events during the last three decades have altered the country's image in the eyes of numerous Americans, and some now have difficulty understanding the message that the flag

---

27. 491 U.S., at 438–39.

conveyed to their parents and grandparents — whether born abroad and naturalized or native born. Moreover, the integrity of the symbol has been compromised by those leaders who seem to advocate compulsory worship of the flag even by individuals whom it offends, or who seem to manipulate the symbol of national purpose into a pretext for partisan disputes about meaner ends. And, as I have suggested, the residual value of the symbol after this Court's decision in *Texas* v. *Johnson* is surely not the same as it was a year ago.

Given all these considerations, plus the fact that the Court today is really doing nothing more than reconfirming what it has already decided, it might be appropriate to defer to the judgment of the majority and merely apply the doctrine of *stare decisis* to the case at hand. That action, however, would not honestly reflect my considered judgment concerning the relative importance of the conflicting interests that are at stake. I remain persuaded that the considerations identified in my opinion in *Texas* v. *Johnson* are of controlling importance in these cases as well.[28]

In *Austin* v. *Michigan Chamber of Commerce*,[29] the Court upheld the constitutionality of a Michigan statute that prohibited corporations from using their treasury funds to support or oppose any candidate for election to state office. In an opinion authored by Thurgood Marshall, we concluded that the statute ensured that expenditures reflect actual public support for the political ideas espoused by corporations. We also found that the unique state-conferred corporate structure that facilitated the amassing of large treasuries likewise warranted a limit on their expenditures.

Nino Scalia and Tony Kennedy wrote dissenting opinions that were

---

28. *United States* v. *Eichman*, 496 U.S. 310, 323–24 (1989).
29. 494 U.S. 652 (1990).

particularly significant because they were the first opinions written by any justice supporting the view that the Constitution affords corporations a right to spend unlimited sums of money to influence the outcome of political elections. Those dissenting opinions provided the basis for a differently constituted Court twenty years later to overrule the *Austin* case and, in the highly controversial *Citizens United* case, open the door for massive infusions of wealth in contested elections. My brief concurrence in *Austin* reminded the reader that the danger of either the fact or the appearance of quid pro quo relationships provided an adequate justification for state regulation of both corporate expenditures and contributions, and that "there is a vast difference between lobbying and debating public issues on the one hand, and political campaigns for election to public office on the other."[30]

In 1981, in *Widmar* v. *Vincent*,[31] the Court held that a state university that makes its facilities generally available to registered student groups — including groups that a state institution would not itself sponsor, such as the Young Socialist Alliance or the Young Democrats — could not refuse access to other groups desiring to use those facilities for religious worship and religious discussion. "Having created a forum generally open to student groups," the majority explained, the university could not exclude others on the basis of their religious speech.[32] In 1984, in the Equal Access to Justice Act, Congress extended the reasoning in *Widmar* to public high schools. In the October 1989 term, in *Board of Education of Westside Community Schools (Dist. 66)* v. *Mergens*,[33] the Court held that that statute prohibited a Nebraska high school from denying a student religious group permission to meet on school premises during non-instructional time.

Under the new statute, a high school's obligation to grant equal access to student groups existed if the school permitted one or more "noncur-

---

30. *Id.,* at 678.
31. 454 U.S. 263.
32. *Id.,* at 277.
33. 496 U.S. 226 (1990).

riculum related student groups" to meet on campus before or after classes. The term "noncurriculum related" was not defined in the statute, but, over my dissent, the Court interpreted it to mean any student group meeting that did not directly relate to the subject matter of any regularly offered course. I thought the term should be more narrowly confined to parallel the program that had prevailed at the university in *Widmar*. As I explained,

> I believe that the distinctions between Westside's program and the University of Missouri's program suggest what is the best understanding of the Act: An extracurricular student organization is "noncurriculum related" if it has as its purpose (or as part of its purpose) the advocacy of partisan theological, political, or ethical views. A school that admits at least one such club has apparently made the judgment that students are better off if the student community is permitted to, and perhaps even encouraged to, compete along ideological lines....

> Accordingly, as I would construe the Act, a high school could properly sponsor a French club, a chess club, or a scuba diving club simply because their activities are fully consistent with the school's curricular mission. It would not matter whether formal courses in any of those subjects — or in directly related subjects — were being offered as long as faculty encouragement of student participation in such groups would be consistent with both the school's obligation of neutrality and its legitimate pedagogical concerns. Nothing in *Widmar* implies that the existence of a French club, for example, would create a constitutional obligation to allow student members of the Ku Klux Klan or the Communist Party to have access to school facilities....

> Against all these arguments the Court interposes Noah Webster's famous dictionary. It is a massive tome but no match for the weight

the Court would put upon it. The Court relies heavily on the dictionary's definition of "curriculum." That word, of course, is not the Act's; moreover, the word "noncurriculum" is not in the dictionary. Neither Webster nor Congress has authorized us to assume that "noncurriculum" is a precise antonym of the word "curriculum." "Nonplus," for example, does not mean "minus" and it would be incorrect to assume that a "nonentity" is not an "entity" at all. Purely as a matter of defining a newly coined word, the term "noncurriculum" could fairly be construed to describe either the subjects that are "not a part of the current curriculum" or the subjects that "cannot properly be included in a public school curriculum." Either of those definitions is perfectly "sensible" because both describe subjects "that are not related to the body of courses offered by the school." When one considers the basic purpose of the Act, and its unquestioned linkage to our decision in *Widmar*, the latter definition surely is the more "sensible."[34]

By merging with a major competitor, American Stores Co. (American) more than doubled the number of supermarkets that it owned in California. It had notified the Federal Trade Commission and obtained its approval of the planned merger, but the state of California sued, claiming that the merger violated the federal antitrust laws and would harm consumers in sixty-two California cities. The district court granted a preliminary injunction preventing American from integrating the operations of the two companies; the Court of Appeals for the Ninth Circuit agreed that California had made an adequate showing of probable success on the merits, but held that the relief granted exceeded the district court's authority under Section 16 of the Clayton Act. In its view, the district court's order was the functional equivalent of divestiture which, although it would be authorized by Section 15 in an action brought by the government, was not authorized by Section 16 in an action brought by a

---

34. *Board of Education of Westside Community Schools*, 496 U.S., at 291.

non-federal litigant. We granted certiorari to review that important holding in *California* v. *American Stores Co.*[35]

In arguing that the district court's injunction was improper, American relied heavily on the legislative history of the Clayton Act, the statute that Congress had enacted in response to President Woodrow Wilson's address recommending that the antitrust laws be strengthened. Louis Brandeis had testified on behalf of the administration that "the right to change the status [of the combination], which is the right of dissolution, is a right which ought to be exercised only by the Government, although the right for full redress for grievances and protection against future wrongs is a right which every individual ought to enjoy…the Government ought to have the right, and the sole right, to determine whether the circumstances are such as to call for a dissolution of an alleged trust." In my opinion for a unanimous Court we rejected American's argument — not because of any disagreement with Brandeis's testimony — but rather because the argument mistakenly assumed that dissolution was no more severe a remedy than divestiture, when in fact dissolution "could be considerably more awesome."[36]

I wrote, "Once the historical importance of the distinction between dissolution and divestiture is understood, American's argument from the legislative history becomes singularly unpersuasive. The rejection of a proposed remedy that would terminate the corporate existence of American and appoint a receiver to supervise the disposition of its assets is surely not the equivalent of the rejection of a remedy that would merely rescind a purchase of stock or assets."[37]

The case was of particular interest to me, not only because of the absence of any debate over the relevance of the statute's legislative history, but more importantly because of the importance of treating the key witness's testimony with the respect that his entire career demanded.

---

35. 495 U.S. 271 (1990).
36. *Id.,* at 289.
37. *Id.,* at 292–93.

*   *   *

A Florida statute provided that the state and its agencies, including school boards, were subject to suit in state courts for tort claims "to the same extent as a private individual" — in other words, it waived a school board's defense of sovereign immunity. The Florida Supreme Court, however, held that that waiver did not apply to claims brought in state court under the federal Civil Rights Act, 42 U.S.C. § 1983. Thus, a former high school student's claim that his suspension by an assistant principal violated the federal constitution could not be heard in a Florida court. The case of *Howlett* v. *Rose*[38] presented us with the question whether the Florida courts could refuse to give the benefit of the state's waiver of the sovereign immunity defense to a plaintiff asserting a federal claim. After argument Bill Brennan, as the senior in a five-justice majority that had voted to require the state court to reject the defense, assigned the majority opinion to me.

My twenty-eight-page draft explained that federal law is enforceable in state courts because the Supremacy Clause in Article VI of the Constitution makes federal laws passed by Congress just as binding on the states and their agencies as are those passed by the state legislatures and "charges state courts with a coordinate responsibility to enforce that law according to their regular modes of procedure."[39] It followed that since the defense could not have been asserted if the action had been brought in federal court, the same rule must apply to cases brought in a Florida court. I remain proud of the fact that, despite the initial vote, the opinion was unanimous.

On the same day that I announced *Howlett,* I also announced another unanimous opinion in *Perpich* v. *Department of Defense,*[40] a case raising the question whether Congress may authorize the president to order members of the National Guard to active duty outside the country for purposes of training without either the consent of a state governor or the

---

38. 496 U.S. 356 (1990).
39. *Id.,* at 367.
40. 496 U.S. 334 (1990).

declaration of a national emergency. We preceded our affirmative answer to that question with a review of the history of the relative roles of the militia and the regular army.

Two conflicting themes that developed at the Constitutional Convention were repeated in debates about military policy during the century that followed. On the one hand, there was widespread fear that a national standing army posed an intolerable threat to individual liberty and to the sovereignty of the separate states, while, on the other hand, there was a recognition of the danger of relying on inadequately trained soldiers as the primary means of providing for the common defense. Thus Congress was authorized both to raise and support a national army and also to organize "the Militia." In the early years of the republic it did neither.

In 1792, less than a year after adopting the Second Amendment, Congress did pass a statute that sheds some light on its understanding of how the Second Amendment was expected to protect the "well-regulated Militia" mentioned in its preamble. The statute provided:

> That every citizen so enrolled and notified, shall, within six months thereafter, provide himself with a good musket or firelock, a sufficient bayonet and belt, two spare flints, and a knapsack, a pouch with a box therein to contain not less than twenty-four cartridges, suited to the bore of his musket or firelock, each cartridge to contain a proper quantity of powder and ball: or with a good rifle, knapsack, shot-pouch and powder-horn, twenty balls suited to the bore of his rifle, and a quarter of a pound of powder; and shall appear, so armed, accoutred and provided, when called out to exercise, or into service, except, that when called out on company days to exercise only, he may appear without a knapsack.[41]

That statute quite clearly identifies the type of weapon with which the members of a well-regulated Militia were being armed. Consistent with

---

41. 1 Stat. 271.

the text of the Second Amendment, it does not mention weapons of self-defense such as handguns.

In his First Annual Message to Congress in 1901, President Theodore Roosevelt declared that "[o]ur militia law is obsolete and worthless" and Congress began the process of transforming "the National Guard of the several States" into an effective fighting force. Originally the law contemplated that the services of the organized militia would be rendered only upon the soil of the United States or of its territories, but in 1908 an amendment expressly authorized service outside the United States. In 1916 Congress decided to "federalize" the National Guard, providing greater federal control and federal funding of the Guard, and requiring every guardsman to take a dual oath — to support the nation as well as the states — and to obey the president as well as the governor, and authorized the president to draft members of the Guard into federal service. When so drafted, members of the Guard were discharged from the militia and subject only to the rules and regulations governing the regular army. The president's exercise of that power during World War I was upheld by the Court, which specifically ruled that the federal power to raise armies was "not qualified or restricted by the provisions of the militia clause."[42] That draft virtually destroyed the guard as an effective organization because the statute did not provide for a restoration of the drafted members' prewar status as guardsmen.

In 1933, however, Congress amended the law to create two overlapping but distinct organizations — the National Guard of the various states and the National Guard of the United States. Those enlisted in the former simultaneously enlist in the latter, but unless and until ordered into active duty in the army they retain their status as members of separate guard units. An order into active duty makes them members of the army for, but only for, their period of duty in the army and relieves them of their status as members of a state guard for that period.

Until 1952 the statutory authority to order National Guard units to

---

42. See *Perpich,* 496 U.S., at 344.

active duty was limited to periods of national emergency. In that year Congress replaced the emergency requirement with a gubernatorial consent requirement, which was routinely granted until 1985 when the governor of California refused to consent to a training mission for 450 guard members in Honduras. That refusal, as well as a second by the governor of Maine, led to an amendment ending the governors' veto authority. In the *Perpich* case, we held that the gubernatorial consent requirement had not been mandated by the Militia Clauses, and therefore its repeal was not inconsistent with those clauses either.

At least four other important Court opinions were announced during what turned out to be Bill Brennan's last year as an active justice. He wrote the opinion for the Court in *Rutan* v. *Republican Party of Illinois*.[43] That case extended the rule of prior cases — that the First Amendment forbids government officials from discharging public employees solely for partisan reasons unless party affiliation is an appropriate qualification for the position involved — to encompass related patronage practices such as promotions, hiring, and transfers. The opinion prompted a strong dissent from Nino Scalia in which he argued that a long history of open and widespread use of a practice should immunize it from constitutional scrutiny. Having rebutted essentially the same argument as a circuit judge in *Illinois State Employees Union* v. *Lewis* almost eighteen years earlier, I was unable to resist writing a separate concurrence.

Bill Brennan also wrote the Court opinion upholding the Federal Communications Commission's policy of awarding preferences to minority owners in comparative licensing proceedings because the policy promoted program diversity.[44] As I emphasized in my concurring opinion, the Court squarely rejected the proposition that a governmental decision that rests on a racial classification is never permissible except as a remedy for a past wrong, and focused instead, as I had argued four years earlier in

---

43. 497 U.S. 62 (1990).
44. See *Metro Broadcasting, Inc.* v. *Federal Communications Commission*, 497 U.S. 547 (1990).

my dissent in *Wygant,* on whether the case fell within the narrow category of governmental decisions for which racial or ethnic heritage may provide a rational basis for differential treatment.

In *Cruzan v. Director, Missouri Department of Health,*[45] the Court confronted for the first time the question whether, and how, the Constitution protects the liberty of seriously ill patients to be free from life-sustaining treatment. Clear and convincing evidence had convinced the trial judge that Nancy Cruzan would never recover from a permanent vegetative state and that her parents were solely motivated by her best interests in seeking a court order allowing her to die. Nevertheless, a narrow majority of the Missouri Supreme Court reversed, and our Court affirmed in a five-to-four decision. The majority held that evidence supporting the view that Nancy would not have wanted to continue her life under the existing circumstances failed to meet a "clear and convincing" standard, which the state required.

In his dissenting opinion, Bill Brennan correctly noted that the imposition of that evidentiary standard could only be justified by a state interest in providing Nancy with treatment even when it had not been demonstrated that such treatment represented her choice. He wrote that Missouri had no power to disfavor Nancy's choice to discontinue treatment and could override her choice neither directly nor indirectly by imposing a heightened evidentiary standard on family members representing her interests.

In a separate dissent, I criticized the majority for relying on what was "tantamount to a waiver rationale: The dying patient's best interests are put to one side, and the entire inquiry is focused on her prior expressions of intent. An innocent person's constitutional right to be free from unwanted medical treatment is categorically limited to those patients who had the foresight to make an unambiguous statement of their wishes while competent. The Court's decision affords no protection to children, to young people who are victims of unexpected accidents or illnesses, or

---

45. 497 U.S. 261 (1990).

to the countless thousands of elderly persons who either fail to decide, or fail to explain, how they want to be treated if they should experience a [fate similar to Nancy Cruzan's]."[46]

After a quarter century of reflection about the case, my advanced age has merely confirmed the views I expressed in that dissent.

Hodgson v. *Minnesota*[47] was, I believe, the only case involving a challenge to the constitutionality of a state abortion statute in which I wrote the opinion for the Court. By a vote of five to four, we invalidated a state statute that required a doctor to give notice to both of the patient's parents before performing an abortion on a woman under eighteen years of age. The primary significance of the case is the fact that it was the first abortion-related case in which Sandra O'Connor provided the fifth vote in a majority that also included Bill Brennan, Thurgood Marshall, Harry Blackmun, and me.

---

46. *Id.,* at 339.
47. 497 U.S. 417 (1990).

26

The Souter Court

October Term 1990

On July 25, 1990, President George H. W. Bush appointed David H. Souter to fill the vacancy created by Bill Brennan's resignation. David was a former Rhodes Scholar and a graduate of the Harvard Law School. He had served as the attorney general of New Hampshire and as a member of the state supreme court, and had been a judge on the United States Court of Appeals for the First Circuit for less than a year when, with the strong support of Senator Warren Rudman of New Hampshire, President Bush selected him for our Court. I have two distinct memories of his televised testimony before the Senate Judiciary Committee. First, his modest, candid, and intelligent responses to the senators' questions convinced me that he would be an excellent colleague on the Court and that I would like to have him as a friend. Second, I was struck by the contrast between the first day of his hearings and the opening of mine. In my case, after a total of about ten or fifteen minutes of endorsements by Attorney General Ed Levi, the two Illinois senators, and the spokesman for the American Bar Association, I was sworn in and the senators' questioning began. At David's hearings, which, unlike mine, were televised, the entire morning and most of the afternoon were consumed by committee members' statements about how important the hearings were. The introduction of television obviously had an important impact on the hearing process.

David was overwhelmingly confirmed in the first week in October and took one of the two oaths required of a new justice at a ceremony at the White House early in that week and his second oath in a ceremony at the Court on Tuesday, October 9, 1990. Meanwhile, as the term began, Thurgood Marshall dissented from the denial of certiorari in over sixty capital cases pending at that time, stating in each that he would grant the writ and vacate the death sentence. In one, *Evans* v. *Muncy*,[1] in which Evans's death sentence had depended on a finding of his future dangerousness, Thurgood argued unsuccessfully that undisputed evidence of his help in preventing harm to twelve prison guards and two nurses who had been taken hostage during an attempted escape had revealed clear error in the jury's finding. The Court denied certiorari in that case, but it did grant review of a Florida case in which the trial judge had imposed the death sentence on one of the defendants notwithstanding the jury's contrary recommendation.[2] The Florida Supreme Court affirmed the sentence but five members of our Court reversed because the record did not indicate that either the trial judge or the appellate court had considered the nonstatutory mitigating evidence. The case is significant because it was the first in which Harry Blackmun assigned the Court opinion (to Sandra O'Connor) and because the five votes to reverse included David Souter.

David's first Court opinion in *Ford* v. *Georgia*[3] reviewed the constitutionality of a Georgia death sentence. The prosecution had used nine of its ten peremptory challenges to exclude blacks from the trial jury in a case charging that the black defendant had raped and murdered his white victim. David spoke for a unanimous court in rejecting Georgia's procedural objection to considering the merits of the defendant's claim. In these and other cases decided during his first term, David unquestionably

---

1. 498 U.S. 927 (1990).
2. *Parker* v. *Duggar*, 498 U.S. 308 (1991).
3. 498 U.S. 411 (1991).

established his qualifications for his new position. He also fulfilled my expectation that both Maryan and I would enjoy his friendship — a relationship fostered by his respect for the quality of her cooking. Of course, as was true of all of my colleagues, there were cases about which we seriously disagreed. Three of them merit special comment: *West Virginia University Hospitals, Inc.* v. *Casey;*[4] *Rust* v. *Sullivan;*[5] and *Payne* v. *Tennessee.*[6]

The question in *West Virginia University Hospitals* was whether a successful plaintiff could recover expert witness fees as part of the award of "a reasonable attorney's fee" authorized by the federal civil rights statute. Having found that a national accounting firm and three doctors who specialized in hospital finance had provided services essential to the plaintiff's success in the case, the district court approved an award of fees that included over $100,000 for their services. The Court of Appeals for the Third Circuit set aside that award except to the extent that it included the thirty-dollar-per-day amount expressly authorized for all witnesses. David Souter joined Justice Scalia's majority opinion affirming the court of appeals' reasoning that attorney's fees and expert fees are separate elements of litigation costs and that the statute authorized only the former.

In my dissent, I argued that under "either the broad view of costs typically assumed in the fee-shifting context or the broad view of 'a reasonable attorney's fee' articulated by this Court, expert witness fees are a proper component of an award under § 1988." After describing the background of the relevant amendment to the statute, I continued:

> This Court's determination today that petitioner must assume the cost of $104,133 in expert witness fees is at war with the congressional purpose of making the prevailing party whole....

---

4. 499 U.S. 83 (1991).
5. 500 U.S. 173 (1991).
6. 501 U.S. 808 (1991).

In recent years the Court has vacillated between a purely literal approach to the task of statutory interpretation and an approach that seeks guidance from historical context, legislative history, and prior cases identifying the purpose that motivated the legislation. Thus, for example, in *Christiansburg Garment Co.* v. *EEOC*, 434 U.S. 412 (1978), we rejected a "mechanical construction," *id.*, at 418, of the fee-shifting provision in § 706(k) of Title VII of the Civil Rights Act of 1964 that the prevailing defendant had urged upon us. Although the text of the statute drew no distinction between different kinds of "prevailing parties," we held that awards to prevailing plaintiffs are governed by a more liberal standard than awards to prevailing defendants. That holding rested entirely on our evaluation of the relevant congressional policy and found no support within the four corners of the statutory text. Nevertheless, the holding was unanimous and, to the best of my knowledge, evoked no adverse criticism or response in Congress.

On those occasions, however, when the Court has put on its thick grammarian's spectacles and ignored the available evidence of congressional purpose and the teaching of prior cases construing a statute, the congressional response has been dramatically different. It is no coincidence that the Court's literal reading of Title VII, which led to the conclusion that disparate treatment of pregnant and nonpregnant persons was not discrimination on the basis of sex, see *General Electric Co.* v. *Gilbert*, 429 U.S. 125 (1976), was repudiated by the 95th Congress; that its literal reading of the "continuous physical presence" requirement in § 244(a)(1) of the Immigration and Nationality Act, which led to the view that the statute did not permit even temporary or inadvertent absences from this country, see *INS* v. *Phinpathya*, 464 U.S. 183 (1984), was rebuffed by the 99th Congress; that its literal reading of the word "program" in Title IX of the Education Amendments of 1972, which led to the Court's gratuitous limit on the scope of the antidiscrimination provisions of Title IX, see *Grove City College* v. *Bell,* 465 U.S. 555 (1984), was rejected by the 100th Congress; or that its refusal to accept the teaching of earlier decisions in *Wards Cove Packing Co.* v. *Atonio,* 490 U.S. 642 (1989) (reformulating order of proof and weight of parties' burdens in disparate-impact cases), and *Patterson* v. *McLean Credit Union,* 491 U.S. 164 (1989) (limiting scope of 42 U.S.C. § 1981 to the making and enforcement of contracts), was overwhelmingly rejected by the 101st Congress, and its refusal to accept the widely held view of lower courts about the scope of fraud, see *McNally* v. *United States,* 483 U.S. 350 (1987) (limiting mail fraud to protection of property), was quickly corrected by the 100th Congress.

In the domain of statutory interpretation, Congress is the master. It obviously has the power to correct our mistakes, but we do the country a disservice when we needlessly ignore persuasive evidence of Congress' actual purpose and require it "to take the time to revisit the matter" and to restate its purpose in more precise English whenever its work product suffers from an omission or inadvertent error. As Judge Learned Hand explained, statutes are likely to be imprecise.

"All [legislators] have done is to write down certain words which they mean to apply generally to situations of that kind. To apply these literally may either pervert what was plainly their general meaning, or leave undisposed of what there is every reason to suppose they meant to provide for. Thus it is not enough for the judge just to use a dictionary. If he should do no more, he might come out with a result which every sensible man would recognize to be quite the opposite of what was really intended; which would contradict or leave unfulfilled its plain purpose." L. Hand, How Far Is a Judge Free in Rendering a Decision?, in The Spirit of Liberty 103, 106 (I. Dilliard ed. 1952).

The Court concludes its opinion with the suggestion that disagreement with its textual analysis could only be based on the dissenters' preference for a "better" statute. It overlooks the possibility that a different view may be more faithful to Congress' command. The fact that Congress has consistently provided for the inclusion of expert witness fees in fee-shifting statutes when it considered the matter is a weak reed on which to rest the conclusion that the omission of such a provision represents a deliberate decision to forbid such awards. Only time will tell whether the Court, with its literal reading of § 1988, has correctly interpreted the will of Congress with respect to the issue it has resolved today.[7]

Only a few months passed before Congress did express its will in Section 113 of the Civil Rights Act of 1991. It endorsed the reasoning in my dissent.

In *Rust* v. *Sullivan*,[8] David provided the critical fifth vote to uphold the constitutionality of the Department of Health and Human Services regulations limiting the ability of recipients of federal funds supporting family planning services to engage in abortion-related activities, including speech about abortion. The regulations did not merely prevent grantees from using federal funds to pay for abortions; instead, they prevented fund recipients from even discussing the possibility that an abortion might provide a permissible option for a pregnant person's medical condition. Because I was convinced that the Congress had not authorized the agency to censor the speech of either grant recipients or their employees, I thought that the regulations were plainly invalid; Harry Blackmun and Thurgood Marshall agreed but went further and concluded that if they did authorize such censorship they violated the First Amendment; Sandra O'Connor, the fourth dissenter, thought that the fact that the government's construction of the statute raised a serious constitutional issue

---

7. *West Virginia University Hospitals, Inc.*, 499 U.S., at 111–16.
8. 500 U.S. 173 (1991).

provided a sufficient reason for rejecting the regulation. I think David may have had some misgivings about his vote because he was the last to join the chief's majority opinion.

In addition to *Booth* v. *Maryland*,[9] which I discuss in earlier chapters, in *South Carolina* v. *Gathers*,[10] the Court held that "victim impact" evidence was inadmissible during the sentencing phase of a capital trial. Without expressing any opinion about the admissibility of that then new category of evidence in noncapital trials, those opinions relied on the reasoning that Potter Stewart, Lewis, and I had expressed in 1976 upholding the imposition of death sentences when "based on reason rather than emotion." On February 15, 1991 — after Tony Kennedy and David Souter had replaced the authors of *Booth* and *Gathers* — the Court granted certiorari in *Payne* v. *Tennessee*,[11] and requested the parties to brief and argue the question whether those cases should be overruled. Joined by Thurgood Marshall and Harry Blackmun, I dissented from that order, and after the argument of the case, and the issuance of four separate opinions supporting the anticipated overruling, Thurgood and I each wrote separate dissents that Harry joined.

Thurgood's dissent was the last opinion that he published. It was a powerful exposition of the importance of the doctrine of stare decisis, eloquently expressing his reaction to a decision explicable only as the product of a change in the Court's composition. His personal outrage about the decision was — as I remember it — at least as strong as and perhaps even stronger than his reaction to our earlier decision in the *Bakke* case. I felt the same way about the outcome, but was less concerned about stare decisis than about the impact of the decision on our capital punishment jurisprudence. The notion that the open-ended invitation to capital defendants to introduce any available mitigating evidence should justify allowing prosecutors to persuade jurors to vote for the death penalty based on evidence that shed no light on the blameworthiness of the

9. 482 U.S. 496 (1987).
10. 490 U.S. 805 (1989).
11. 501 U.S. 808 (1991).

defendant was so directly contrary to the reasoning that had persuaded Potter, Lewis, and me to vote to uphold the penalty in 1976 that I wrote separately to emphasize that point. The unfortunate decision in that case remains, in my judgment, one of the worst in the Court's history.

Later, in the summer of 1991, Maryan and I visited Oxford University to participate in the program for American judges sponsored by the Florida State University College of Law. A distinct memory from that visit is a conversation that I had with an Oxford faculty member who taught the course in evidence. He was bewildered by the reasoning of the majority in the *Payne* case overruling the earlier decisions making victim impact evidence inadmissible in capital cases.

Earlier that spring, on the morning of Saturday, April 20, 1991, Maryan and I drove from our apartment in Arlington, Virginia, to Camp David, Maryland, in response to George and Barbara Bush's invitation to the members of the Court. Any visit to that vacation residence is, of course, a special occasion, but our visit was especially memorable. We had both met our host and hostess at prior events, but never previously in such an informal setting. They made us both feel like old friends as they showed us the chapel, the golf course, the bowling alley, the swimming pool, and their living quarters. After sitting down for lunch, Barbara stood up and announced that she was about to observe a long-standing tradition pursuant to which any of their guests who happened to be enjoying a birthday was required to stand and address the group with remarks appropriate to the occasion. Although I did not regard that brief introduction as fair notice of what was expected of me, I was later assured by Maryan that I did not make a complete fool of myself.

On June 27, 1991, the last day of the 1990 term, the Court decided *Harmelin* v. *Michigan*,[12] a case that had been argued during the first week in November 1990. It presented the question whether a mandatory term of life

---

12. 501 U.S. 957 (1991).

imprisonment without the possibility of parole for the crime of possessing 672 grams of cocaine — an amount that would fit in the glove compartment of a car — violated the Eighth Amendment's ban on cruel and unusual punishment. The delay in announcing the decision was largely attributable to the fact that Nino Scalia, to whom Chief Justice Rehnquist had assigned the majority opinion, did not circulate his first draft until April. He took more time than usual to explain his novel theory that the Eighth Amendment does not prohibit disproportionately severe punishment, but instead is limited to banning only especially cruel methods of punishment. Although the Michigan attorney general's brief included a very short section arguing that the amendment does not apply to excessive punishments, it did not go to nearly the same lengths as did Nino in his thirty-page criticism of the proportionality principle. Thus, most of the reasoning in Nino's draft had been the result of his own research rather than the state's. The chief was the only member of the Court to endorse Nino's theory.

Tony Kennedy, writing for Sandra and David as well, later circulated a draft stating that whether or not Nino had correctly interpreted the intent of the framers of the Eighth Amendment, stare decisis counseled following eighty years of our earlier Eighth Amendment jurisprudence recognizing a proportionality principle. While that part of his opinion was dead right, he then went on to express what I still regard as the astounding view that the sentence imposed on the drug courier in the case before the Court was not excessive. Byron White's dissent convincingly exposed the flaws in both Nino's and Tony's reasoning. Again, however, I thought it appropriate to add a brief comment recalling Potter Stewart's opinion about capital cases:

> The death sentences that were at issue and invalidated in *Furman* were "cruel and unusual in the same way that being struck by lightning is cruel and unusual." ... In my opinion the imposition of a life sentence without possibility of parole on this petitioner is equally capricious. As Justice White has pointed out, under the Federal Sentencing Guidelines, with all relevant enhancements,

petitioner's sentence would barely exceed 10 years....In most States, the period of incarceration for a first offender like petitioner would be substantially shorter. No jurisdiction except Michigan has concluded that this offense belongs in a category where reform and rehabilitation are considered totally unattainable. Accordingly, the notion that this sentence satisfies any meaningful requirement of proportionality is itself both cruel and unusual.[13]

Nino retained his view of the Eighth Amendment for years to come. Notwithstanding his acknowledgment that stare decisis counseled in favor of accepting proportionality, he maintained that the principle could not be intelligently applied and for that reason never endorsed it.[14] But his view has been roundly criticized. For instance, John Stinneford, a professor at the University of Florida Levin College of Law, has undertaken an originalist inquiry into the purpose of the Eighth Amendment. He has concluded that Nino's own textual and historical arguments do not support his conclusion about the amendment's meaning. Rather, the early English and American versions of the amendment were expressly directed at excessive punishments, and the framers and early interpreters of the amendment understood it to encompass a proportionality principle. Thus, as Professor Stinneford put it, even accepting Nino's preferred analytical approach, "The Supreme Court's decision to engage in proportionality review under the Cruel and Unusual Punishments Clause is well-founded[.]"[15]

---

13. *Harmelin,* 501 U.S., at 1028–29.
14. See, e.g., *Ewing* v. *California,* 538 U.S. 11, 31 (2003) (Scalia, J., dissenting).
15. John Stinneford, "Rethinking Proportionality under the Cruel and Unusual Punishments Clause," *Va. L. Rev.* 97 (2011): 899.

27

The Thomas Court

October Term 1991

President Bush's nomination of Clarence Thomas to fill the vacancy created by Thurgood Marshall's resignation resulted in the most important change in the Court's jurisprudence that took place during my tenure. His Senate hearings focused more on whether there was something improper about his relationship with Anita Hill while she was employed at the Equal Employment Opportunity Commission during Clarence's chairmanship of that agency than his jurisprudence. I remain convinced that the parties' respective recollections about that issue were — and are — far less important than Clarence's views about the law, and more particularly about the Constitution.

I have long been impressed by Clarence's incredible life story, which is powerful evidence of his strong work ethic and equally strong intellect. He was born in a tiny coastal town in Georgia. He grew up speaking Gullah, a creole dialect. His father left his family when Clarence was only two. Raised by his grandparents, he attended Catholic school as a child and achieved remarkable success as a student. Having formed plans to become a priest in high school, he initially attended Immaculate Conception Seminary, but he left soon after Martin Luther King Jr.'s assassination. He later wrote in his memoir that he had grown disillusioned with the church for not doing enough to combat racism.

After leaving seminary, Clarence graduated in 1971 from Holy Cross College with an AB cum laude in English literature, and went on to make a fine record at Yale Law School. He began his career in the office of John Danforth, then attorney general of Missouri, until 1977. He became a lawyer for the Monsanto Chemical Company, but left in 1980 to work as a legislative assistant to then senator Danforth. In 1981, he was appointed by President Reagan to serve as the assistant secretary for civil rights in the Department of Education. Less than one year later, President Reagan named him the chairman of the EEOC.

In 1990, President George H. W. Bush appointed Clarence to the Court of Appeals for the D.C. Circuit. His nomination to that court, like his later nomination to the Supreme Court, was strongly supported by Senator Danforth. More importantly, Nino Scalia, whose former colleagues had served with Clarence on the D.C. Circuit, vouched for his judicial qualifications even though Clarence and Nino had not met each other before he joined our Court.

He was first sworn in as a justice at a ceremony at the White House on October 18, 1991. Because Nan Rehnquist had just passed away, Byron White rather than the chief justice administered that oath, but five days later Bill Rehnquist swore him in again. I first met him shortly before he was sworn in for a third time at a public ceremony at the Court on November 1, 1991. He had a deep voice, a contagious laugh, and a personality that promptly led to the formation of a friendship that has persisted ever since, despite our profound disagreements about legal issues. The fact that he was a Dallas Cowboys fan — based largely on his admiration of "Bullet Bob" Hayes, the Olympic sprinter who became a star wide receiver and punt returner — while I preferred the Washington Redskins and their Mike Nelms — who, as I remember him, never called for a fair catch — did not preclude that friendship.

I wrote the dissent, joined by Byron White and Harry Blackmun, in the first important case decided during Clarence's first term. Had Bill

Brennan and Thurgood Marshall still been active justices when the case was decided, I am sure my views would have prevailed. The question in *Presley* v. *Etowah County Commission*[1] was whether, under Section 5 of the Voting Rights Act, the attorney general had to pre-clear changes in the decision-making powers of elected members of two Alabama county commissions that were made on the eve of and just after the election of their first black members. The majority held that the statute required pre-clearance only for changes in the voting process itself. I was convinced that the lower federal courts and the attorney general had correctly concluded that transfers of decision-making powers — especially when made in response to the unprecedented election of a black candidate — had the same potential for discrimination against minority voters as changes in electoral rules.

A short time later, Clarence wrote an important dissent, joined by Nino Scalia, expressing his view that the Eighth Amendment's prohibition against cruel and unusual punishment had not been violated by prison guards' deliberate beating of an inmate who had not suffered any permanent injury.[2] The evidence showed that when Hudson, the prisoner, argued with a guard, the guard placed him in shackles and punched him in the mouth, eyes, chest, and stomach while another guard kicked and punched him from behind and their supervisor admonished them "not to have too much fun." As a result, Hudson suffered minor bruises and swelling of his face, mouth, and lip, and cracked his dental plate. In an action in which he alleged that the guards' conduct violated the Eighth Amendment, the lower court found that the guards had used force when it was not necessary and awarded Hudson eight hundred dollars in damages.

The Court of Appeals for the Fifth Circuit agreed that the use of force was excessive and unreasonable and occasioned unnecessary and wanton infliction of pain, but it reversed because Hudson's injuries were "minor"

1. 502 U.S. 491 (1992).
2. *Hudson* v. *McMillian,* 503 U.S. 1 (1992).

and required no medical attention. Sandra, writing for seven justices, recognized a distinction between two different types of Eighth Amendment claims: those challenging conditions of confinement, such as deliberate indifference to a prisoner's medical needs, in which only serious harms are actionable; and those in which guards are accused of using excessive force. We held that "[w]hen prison officials maliciously and sadistically use force to cause harm, contemporary standards of decency are always violated."[3]

Though Clarence Thomas assumed that Hudson might have had a claim under state law, and perhaps even under the Due Process Clause of the Fourteenth Amendment, he wrote a twelve-page dissent arguing that a prisoner seeking to establish that he has been subjected to cruel and unusual punishment must always show that he has suffered a serious injury. Nino Scalia joined that opinion. In later years, those two justices continued to construe that provision of the Constitution more narrowly than their colleagues.

On the day after we decided *Hudson,* I announced two unanimous opinions. In the first we rejected a claim Oklahoma filed against Arkansas.[4] In the second, we held that substantive due process did not impose an independent federal obligation upon municipalities to provide minimum levels of safety in the workplace and that a city's alleged failure to train or warn its employees was not arbitrary in a constitutional sense.[5]

In a capital case decided in March, Clarence wrote a lone dissent from the Court's decision to set aside the death sentence of David Dawson because the prosecutor had introduced evidence that he was a member of the Aryan Brotherhood.[6] In the Court's view, since both Dawson and his victim were white, mere membership in a racist organization was not relevant to the jury's sentencing decision. Just as the majority during the

---

3. *Id.,* at 9.
4. *Arkansas* v. *Oklahoma,* 503 U.S. 91 (1992).
5. *Collins* v. *City of Harker Heights,* 503 U.S. 115 (1992).
6. *Dawson* v. *Delaware,* 503 U.S. 159 (1991).

previous term had approved the use of victim impact evidence, in part in response to our cases allowing the defendant in a capital case to introduce an unlimited amount of mitigating evidence, Clarence contended that prohibiting this evidence would impose a double standard on prosecutors. Clarence also explained that, because defense counsel can introduce a broad range of mitigating evidence and "assume…that a jury understands the nature of a church choir, a softball team, or the Boy Scouts, so too may a prosecutor assume when rebutting this evidence that a jury knows the nature of a prison gang."[7] Moreover, the racist character of the gang tended to rebut Dawson's evidence of good character.

In another capital case, decided in April without the benefit of briefs addressing the merits or oral argument, the Court vacated a stay of execution entered by a California district judge and affirmed by the Court of Appeals for the Ninth Circuit. Harry Blackmun and I dissented.[8] The petitioner, who had been sentenced to death in California ten years earlier, had filed a petition claiming that his scheduled execution by exposure to cyanide gas would violate the Eighth Amendment. That method of execution had been authorized by a California statute enacted in 1937, but in the ensuing fifty-five years, state after state had abandoned it as inhumane and torturous. By 1992 only three states continued to mandate execution by gas. Dozens of expert statements in the record explained that that method of execution was extremely and unnecessarily painful. Based on those facts, the district court had granted a stay of execution in short order on April 18, 1992. A divided Ninth Circuit panel vacated that stay close to midnight the next day — Easter Sunday. In response, eleven judges of the Ninth Circuit quickly called for an en banc hearing. When the panel refused to order a stay so that the en banc case could be heard before the petitioner's execution, ten judges signed an order themselves staying the execution.

The Supreme Court responded by vacating that stay. Seven members

---

7. *Id.*, at 171.
8. *Gomez v. United States District Court for the Northern District of California,* 503 U.S. 653 (1992).

of the Supreme Court joined a three-paragraph unsigned order vacating that stay because the "claim could have been brought more than a decade ago" and there was "no good reason for this abusive delay, which has been compounded by last-minute attempts to manipulate the judicial process."[9] The basis for the Court's action was the fact that the defendant had filed four prior federal habeas petitions and had failed to explain why he had not previously relied on the Eighth Amendment. In my dissent, which Harry Blackmun joined, I correctly pointed out that "if execution by cyanide gas is in fact unconstitutional, then the State lacks the *power* to impose such punishment. Harris' delay, even if unjustified, cannot endow the State with authority to violate the Constitution."[10] The Court's precipitous action in this case is difficult to understand or to defend.

A final wrinkle in the case was that, in the early morning hours of Tuesday, April 21, word reached California that the Supreme Court had vacated the stay. The petitioner's lawyers phoned Ninth Circuit Judge Harry Pregerson to make one last request for a stay. Judge Pregerson was not aware of the Supreme Court's reasoning, but knew that the original Ninth Circuit panel had denied relief at least in part because the petitioner's claims should have been brought in state court. Judge Pregerson thus responded to the Supreme Court's order by granting a twenty-four-hour stay for the petitioner to pursue his claim in state court. The Supreme Court responded within two hours with a final order: "No further stays of Robert Alton Harris' execution shall be entered by the federal courts except upon order of this Court."[11] The petitioner was executed early that same morning.

The treatment of the case was severely criticized in law review commentary. Professors Evan Caminker and Erwin Chemerinsky described the series of judicial opinions attending these last appeals as "shocking."[12] Their article bemoaned the prioritization of the state's schedule at the

---

9. *Id.,* at 654.
10. *Id.,* at 659.
11. *Vazquez* v. *Harris,* 112 S. Ct. 1713, 1714 (1992).
12. "The Lawless Execution of Robert Alton Harris," *Yale L. J.* 102 (1992): 225.

expense of hearing the petitioner's claim on the merits. The authors wrote, "Starkly put, judges who have grown impatient with repeated delays prior to executions were determined that Robert Harris be executed on schedule.... We firmly believe, however, that persons across the ideological spectrum should be troubled that the Court's desire to expedite the process of death — perhaps rooted in legitimate concerns about abuse in specific cases — has now accrued a life of its own."[13]

Judge Stephen Reinhardt of the Ninth Circuit wrote an essay on the case that same week that struck a similar tone, describing the case as "ugly, cruel, injudicious" and "a nightmare."[14] According to Judge Reinhardt, the case demonstrated two points. The first was that the Court's concerns over federalism and procedural conformity were trumping its substantive interest in preserving individual liberties. The second, perhaps more disturbing, was that the judicial system was — at least in that case — "not functionally equipped" to handle the administration of the death penalty.[15] In making this point, Judge Reinhardt emphasized the scattered nature of the judicial system's processing of the petitioner's final appeal. He concluded with the obvious premise that "we must adjudicate fairly, judiciously, and expeditiously, *all* [last-minute death penalty] claims which raise substantial and legitimate questions."[16]

In *Burson* v. *Freeman*,[17] the Court upheld the constitutionality of a Tennessee statute creating election-day "campaign-free-zones" around polling places. The statute not only prohibited speech or the display or distribution of any materials soliciting votes inside polling places, but also imposed the same prohibition in outside adjoining areas, originally encompassing one-hundred-foot zones, but later amended to cover three-hundred-foot zones in twelve of the state's ninety-five counties. The

---

13. *Id.*, at 252–53.
14. "The Supreme Court, the Death Penalty, and the Harris Case," *Yale L. J.* 102 (1992): 205, 205.
15. *Id.*, at 207.
16. *Id.*, at 222.
17. 504 U.S. 191 (1992).

prohibition served two quite different functions — it protected orderly access to the polls and prevented last-minute campaigning. In our dissent, Sandra O'Connor, David Souter, and I framed the issue as whether the means that the state had chosen to achieve its valid interest in ensuring access to the polls did not unnecessarily hinder last-minute campaigning. We were convinced that application of traditional strict scrutiny analysis would clearly demonstrate that the large areas defined in the statute were not necessary. The majority nevertheless held, based largely on the long and widespread approval of such zones, that tradition rather than straightforward application of First Amendment rules should prevail. Nino Scalia wrote an interesting brief opinion in which he explained that the traditions advanced by the plurality to justify the curtailment of political speech, although not sufficient to survive "exacting scrutiny," were at least reasonable and not viewpoint discriminatory. The case is often cited in debates about whether the Court has appropriately valued the First Amendment's protection of political campaign speech.

On April 22, 1992, the Court heard argument in *Planned Parenthood of Southeastern Pa. v. Casey*,[18] the most important abortion case that the Court has decided since *Roe v. Wade*. The case involved a challenge to five provisions of the Pennsylvania Abortion Control Act, all of which had been held invalid by the district court. The act required that a woman seeking an abortion give her informed consent prior to the abortion procedure; that she be provided with certain information at least twenty-four hours before the abortion is performed; that she obtain the informed consent of at least one parent if she is a minor; and that she sign a statement indicating that she has notified her husband, if she is married. The act also imposed certain reporting requirements on facilities that provide abortion services. The Court of Appeals for the Third Circuit had reversed four of those rulings but affirmed the invalidation of the spousal notice requirement. We granted both the plaintiffs' and the state's

---

18. 505 U.S. 833 (1992).

petitions for certiorari. As he had in earlier abortion-related litigation, the solicitor general supported the defendant's argument that *Roe* v. *Wade* should be overruled.

After oral argument, everyone except Harry Blackmun and me agreed that the Third Circuit had correctly upheld all of the challenged provisions except the requirement that a married pregnant woman certify that she had notified her husband of her intent to obtain an abortion before the procedure could be performed. Harry and I both assumed that the result would be explained in an opinion overruling *Roe* v. *Wade,* and Chief Justice Rehnquist circulated a draft opinion for the Court on May 27, 1992, that met our expectation — it did not expressly overrule *Roe,* but like his proposed opinion in the *Webster* case three years earlier, it effectively repudiated its central holding. Much to our surprise, however, on June 3, 1992, Sandra O'Connor, Tony Kennedy, and David Souter circulated a draft opinion "concurring in the judgment in part and dissenting in part," which supported an affirmance of the Third Circuit's judgment, but also contained a long and persuasive explanation of why "the essential holding of *Roe* v. *Wade* once again should be endorsed, continued and reaffirmed." Their opinion described that holding as containing these three parts:

> First is recognition of the right of the woman to choose to have an abortion before viability and to obtain it without undue interference from the State. Before viability the State's interests are not strong enough to support a prohibition of abortion or the imposition of substantial obstacles to the woman's effective right to elect the procedure.

> Second is a confirmation of the State's power to restrict abortions after fetal viability, if the law contains exceptions for pregnancies which endanger a woman's life or health. And third is the principle that the State has legitimate interests from the outset of the pregnancy in promoting the health of the woman and the life of the fetus that may become a child.

As soon as I finished reading their draft I responded with a letter to the three authors congratulating them on a fine piece of work, asking them whether they would be "interested in a partial join by a non-author" and identifying several parts of their opinion that I believed I could join.

After they indicated that they would welcome suggestions, I did make several, most importantly to postpone their criticism of certain earlier cases, "thereby making it possible for Harry and me to join Parts I and II, and (if you will consider a couple of relatively minor suggestions) Part III as well. In my view, an opinion that begins as an opinion of the Court and continues to speak for the Court for 25 pages would be far more powerful than one that starts out as a plurality opinion and shifts back and forth between a Court opinion and a plurality opinion." They adopted most of my suggestions.

What then became a Court opinion correctly identified "liberty" as the source of the woman's right to choose whether to have an abortion and as the primary value that the opinion protected by defending the ongoing vitality of *Roe*. As the joint authors famously wrote, "Liberty finds no refuge in a jurisprudence of doubt."[19] I thought it notable that the sections of the opinion joined by a majority of the Court did not mention "privacy."

The opinion also contains a thorough and persuasive discussion of the importance of adhering to the doctrine of stare decisis. I joined that discussion without reservation even though it did not provide even an arguable justification for the decision during the previous term in *Payne*, which all three of *Casey*'s authors had joined, to overrule two earlier cases — *Booth* and *Gathers* — in order to approve the use of victim impact statements in capital cases.

It was also in 1992 that the Northwestern Law School established a professorship in my name. That action was especially gratifying because it was financed by my classmates.

---

19. 505 U.S., at 844.

October Term 1992

On October 6, 1992, we heard the reargument in *Bray* v. *Alexandria Women's Health Clinic*,[20] a case that four justices (Rehnquist, White, Scalia, and Kennedy) had voted to grant in February 1991 while Thurgood Marshall was still a member of the Court, and which was argued for the first time in October of 1991 after Clarence Thomas had replaced him. It is obvious that the outcome of the case is attributable to Clarence's replacement of Thurgood. And I think it appropriate to explain its importance by quoting the following passages from the beginning of my dissent, which Harry Blackmun, Sandra O'Connor, and David Souter joined:

> After the Civil War, Congress enacted legislation imposing on the Federal Judiciary the responsibility to remedy both abuses of power by persons acting under color of state law and lawless conduct that state courts are neither fully competent, nor always certain, to prevent. The Ku Klux Act of 1871, 17 Stat. 13, was a response to the massive, organized lawlessness that infected our Southern States during the post-Civil War era. When a question concerning this statute's coverage arises, it is appropriate to consider whether the controversy has a purely local character or the kind of federal dimension that gave rise to the legislation....

> It is unfortunate that the Court has analyzed this case as though it presented an abstract question of logical deduction rather than a question concerning the exercise and allocation of power in our federal system of government. The Court ignores the obvious (and entirely constitutional) congressional intent behind [Section 2 of the Ku Klux Act now codified at 42 U.S.C. § 1985(3)] to protect this Nation's citizens from what amounts to the theft of their constitutional rights by organized and violent mobs across the country....

---

20. 506 U.S. 263 (1993).

To achieve their goals, the individual petitioners have agreed and combined with one another and with defendant Operation Rescue to organize, coordinate and participate in "rescue" demonstrations at abortion clinics in various parts of the country, including the Washington metropolitan area. The purpose of these "rescue" demonstrations is to disrupt operations at the target clinic and indeed ultimately to cause the clinic to cease operations entirely.

Rescue operations effectively hinder and prevent the constituted authorities of the targeted community from providing local citizens with adequate protection. The lack of advance warning of petitioners' activities, combined with limited police department resources, makes it difficult for the police to prevent petitioners' ambush by "rescue" from closing a clinic for many hours at a time. The trial record is replete with examples of petitioners overwhelming local law enforcement officials by sheer force of numbers....

To summarize briefly, the evidence establishes that petitioners engaged in a nationwide conspiracy; to achieve their goal they repeatedly occupied public streets and trespassed on the premises of private citizens in order to prevent or hinder the constituted authorities from protecting access to abortion clinics by women, a substantial number of whom traveled in interstate commerce to reach the destinations blockaded by petitioners. The case involves no ordinary trespass, nor anything remotely resembling the peaceful picketing of a local retailer. It presents a striking contemporary example of the kind of zealous, politically motivated, lawless conduct that led to the enactment of the Ku Klux Act in 1871 and gave it its name.[21]

---

21. *Id.,* at 307–13 (footnotes and internal quotation marks omitted).

In his opinion for the Court explaining why so many lower courts had misconstrued Section 1985(3), Nino Scalia reasoned that the record did not contain proof of the kind of "racial, or otherwise class-based, invidiously discriminatory animus" that the statute required. The goal of preventing abortion did not "remotely qualify for such harsh criticism, and for such derogatory association with racism.... Congress itself has, with our approval, discriminated against abortion in its provision of financial support for medical procedures.... This is not the stuff of which a § 1985(3) 'invidiously discriminatory animus' is created."[22]

In responding to the Court in her dissent, Sandra O'Connor noted that the Court's prior approach to Reconstruction-era statutes had been to accord them "a sweep as broad as their language," whereas it was now doing "just the opposite, precluding application of the statute to a situation that its language clearly covers." She specifically objected to reliance on an "element" of the cause of action that did not appear in the text of the statute. But she also thought it clear, like the seven courts of appeals to have addressed the question, that "at the very least" the class of "women" falls within the protection of the statute. "If women are a protected class, and I think they are, then the statute must reach conspiracies whose motivation is directly related to characteristics unique to that class."[23]

I continue to profoundly disagree with the Court's holding in *Bray*.

After their victory in the 1992 election and before their inauguration, Bill Clinton and Al Gore made a courtesy visit to the Court. They were both likeable men. After appropriate greetings, informal conversations, and a variety of photo opportunities consuming about thirty minutes, they departed, exiting the Court by walking through the Great Hall on the main floor. Many Court employees had gathered to see the visitors. The most memorable aspect of that visit was the time that the new president spent shaking hands and greeting the many members of the

22. *Id.*, at 274.
23. *Id.*, at 350.

Court's workforce. He obviously enjoyed — as all of them did as well — meeting and talking to new acquaintances.

I was reminded of that occasion about a year later when visiting the White House and waiting about twenty minutes for Clinton's arrival to announce his presentation of Presidential Medals of Honor to Bill Brennan and Thurgood Marshall (posthumously). He was not known for his promptness.

At the time of his death, John Emmett Smith was a carpenter for a construction company under contract with the National Science Foundation, an agency of the United States. He was working at McMurdo Station on Ross Island, Antarctica. When he and two companions were returning to the station after a long hike, they took a shortcut, departing from the marked route, and two of them fell into a crevasse and suffered fatal injuries. Smith's widow brought a wrongful death action against the United States in federal district court in Oregon, where she resided, alleging that the government was negligent in failing to provide adequate warnings of the dangers posed by crevasses in areas beyond the marked paths.

The plaintiff alleged that her suit was authorized by the Federal Tort Claims Act, which waives the federal government's sovereign immunity from liability for torts committed by its agents. The government argued that the claim was barred by an exception to the statute precluding the exercise of jurisdiction over "[a]ny claim arising in a foreign country." The district court dismissed the action and the Court of Appeals for the Ninth Circuit affirmed. Because another court of appeals had concluded that Antarctica was not a "foreign country" within the meaning of the statute, we granted certiorari to resolve the conflict. Writing for a majority of eight justices, Bill Rehnquist affirmed.[24] I dissented.

I agreed with the plaintiff's argument that the purpose of the foreign country exception was to insulate the United States from tort liability imposed pursuant to foreign law. That purpose simply did not apply to an

---

24. *Smith* v. *United States,* 507 U.S. 197 (1993).

area where there was no sovereign government. It was undisputed that Smith's death occurred in a sovereignless area, and I could see no reason why the broad waiver of sovereign immunity in the FTCA should not apply to Antarctica. After all, Congress had expressly waived its sovereign immunity for accidents on the high seas, and the "foreign country" exception surely would not have applied to tortious conduct in outer space. I concluded my dissent by noting:

> The international community includes sovereignless places but no places where there is no rule of law. Majestic legislation like the Federal Tort Claims Act should be read with the vision of the judge, enlightened by an interest in justice, not through the opaque green eyeshade of the cloistered bookkeeper. As President Lincoln observed in his first State of the Union message: "It is as much the duty of Government to render prompt justice against itself, in favor of citizens, as it is to administer the same between private individuals."[25]

Section 5 of the Voting Rights Act of 1965 required jurisdictions subject to its provisions (because of a history of discrimination against minority voters) to obtain the prior approval of either the Attorney General of the United States or the Federal District Court for the District of Columbia of any changes in their voting procedures. Following the 1990 census, North Carolina became entitled to an additional seat in the House of Representatives. The attorney general objected to the state's reapportionment plan because it included only one majority-black district even though its voting population was approximately 20 percent black. The state responded to the objection by enacting a revised plan that included a second majority black district. The new district had an extremely bizarre shape — it was about 160 miles long and wound in snakelike fashion through ten different counties gobbling up enough black neighborhoods

---

25. *Id.*, at 216–17.

to give blacks a clear majority of the voting age population in the new district. The attorney general approved the plan, but in *Shaw* v. *Reno,* five white voters challenged its constitutionality on the ground that it created a "racial gerrymander" that violated the Equal Protection Clause.

The three-judge district court, by a two-to-one vote, dismissed their suit. The majority held that a redistricting plan does not violate white voters' rights unless the plan was "adopted with the purpose and effect of discriminating against white voters on account of their race." Favoring minority voters and complying with the Voting Rights Act did not satisfy that test. The third judge, however, would only have permitted race-based districting if the state used traditional districting principles, such as compactness and contiguity, in drawing boundaries. Sandra O'Connor, joined by the chief, Nino Scalia, Tony Kennedy, and Clarence Thomas, endorsed the dissenter's approach. "What appellants object to is redistricting legislation that is so extremely irregular on its face that it rationally can be viewed only as an effort to segregate the races for purposes of voting, without regard for traditional districting principles and without sufficiently compelling justification."[26]

Later in Sandra's opinion she explained that "[w]hen a district obviously is created solely to effectuate the perceived common interests of one racial group, elected officials are more likely to believe that their primary obligation is to represent only the members of that group rather than their constituency as a whole."[27] What I still do not understand about that reasoning, however, is why bizarre shapes unrelated to any traditional districting principles enhance that risk any more than a frank acknowledgment of a remedial purpose achieved by drawing lines that favor the election of minority candidates. Indeed, bizarre shapes are relevant because they provide evidence of either a partisan or a racial purpose, but their existence does not make the purpose any more or less desirable than a frank statement by the body responsible for the line-drawing.

---

26. *Shaw* v. *Reno,* 509 U.S. 630, 642 (1993).
27. *Id.,* at 648.

While *Shaw* v. *Reno* is important for condemning a bizarrely shaped district as a species of gerrymander, the Court still has not expressly acknowledged that those shapes are equally probative as establishing political gerrymanders. The districts at issue in *Shaw* should have been upheld because they had the virtue of remedying past injustice. Bizarre districts today identify political gerrymanders that improperly create or preserve powerful political parties or actors.

Late in the spring, Byron White told me that he had decided to retire at the end of the term. That was especially disappointing news to me because what had begun as a warm friendship when I first joined the Court had become even more so during the ensuing years. We were both honorary members of the Washington Golf and Country Club in Arlington, Virginia, and in recent years had played golf together as a twosome on frequent occasions. The quality of his golf did not equal his incomparable skill on either the football field or the basketball court, but he enjoyed the game immensely, frequently practicing putting in his chambers. When we first met in Court on Monday mornings, he often asked me, "How many pars did you get over the weekend?" That was a diplomatic way of asking a question that could be honestly answered without too much embarrassment. While we often disagreed about legal issues, I always respected his views because they were the product of his own independent thinking and he was uncommonly intelligent.

28

The Ginsburg Court

October Term 1993

President Bill Clinton appointed Ruth Bader Ginsburg to fill Byron White's seat on the Supreme Court. She was obviously well qualified for the job, having been a tenured professor on the faculty of the Columbia Law School (and the first woman with that distinction), a successful advocate in cases establishing constitutional protections for women, and a respected judge on the Court of Appeals for the D.C. Circuit. Although best known for her role in opposing gender-based discrimination, her testimony before the Senate Judiciary Committee included her recollection of anti-Semitism during her younger years.

She testified: "I am…a first generation American on my father's side, barely second generation on my mother's. Neither of my parents had the means to attend college, but both taught me to love learning, to care about people, and to work hard for whatever I wanted or believed in. Their parents had the foresight to leave the old country, where Jewish ancestry and faith meant exposure to pogroms and denigration of one's human worth." In response to a question by Senator Kennedy about whether her pioneering work with gender discrimination would sensitize her to racial discrimination, she stated: "Senator Kennedy, I am alert to discrimination. I grew up during World War II in a Jewish family. I have memories as a child, even before the war, of being in a car with my parents and passing a place in [Pennsylvania], a resort with a sign out in front that read: 'No dogs or Jews allowed.' Signs of that kind existed in this country during my childhood. One couldn't help but be sensitive to discrimination living as a Jew in America at the time of World War II."

Ruth often commented on the fact that she was an appropriate successor to Byron White because he had voted in her favor in all of her arguments in our Court. I had agreed with her in both of the cases that she argued while I was on the Court, but in her victory in *Califano* v. *Sanders*,[1] which was decided by a five-to-four vote, I wrote a separate concurrence because I thought males rather than females were the victims of the discriminatory rule. The case involved the constitutionality of the provision in the Federal Old-Age Survivors and Disability Insurance Benefits program that required a widower, but not a widow, to prove that he was receiving at least one-half of his support from his deceased spouse. Unlike Bill Brennan, I thought the rule discriminated against the class of male survivors who, unlike female survivors, had to prove dependency on their deceased spouses; Bill reasoned that the victims of the discrimination were the female taxpayers whose surviving spouses received no benefits unless they were dependent on their deceased spouses. Perhaps both of us were right.

Early in Ruth's first term on the Court we considered the definition of a "hostile work environment" under Title VII of the Civil Rights Act of 1964.[2] Teresa Harris, a female manager at an equipment rental company, was the target of unwanted sexual innuendoes by the company's president. In front of others, he had suggested that they go to the Holiday Inn to negotiate an increase in her salary; he had also referred to her as a "dumb ass woman." In mid-August 1987 she complained to the president about his conduct; he apologized and promised to stop, but in early

---

1. 430 U.S. 99 (1977).
2. See *Harris* v. *Forklift Systems, Inc.*, 510 U.S. 17 (1993).

September, in response to her successful negotiation with a customer, he asked if she had promised "the guy some sex on Saturday night." On October 1, Harris collected her paycheck and quit. She sued the company, claiming that the president's conduct had created an abusive work environment for her because of her gender. The district court, while agreeing that a reasonable woman would have been offended by the president's conduct, concluded that he had not created "a work environment so poisoned as to be intimidating or abusive to Harris."

Sandra O'Connor, writing for a unanimous Court, concluded that a violation of the statute did not require that the plaintiff suffer tangible injury. The case was remanded to enable the lower courts to decide whether Harris's work environment "would reasonably be perceived, and is perceived, as hostile or abusive," without any "need for it also to be psychologically injurious." Ruth added a concurring opinion noting that the critical issue under the statute was "whether members of one sex are exposed to disadvantageous terms of employment to which members of the opposite sex are not exposed." The plaintiff should prevail if a reasonable person subjected to the discriminatory conduct would find, as Harris did, that the harassment so altered working conditions as to make it more difficult for her to do her job.

During Ruth's first term, a narrow majority of the Court took an important step in reducing the federal protection Section 10(b) of the Securities Exchange Act of 1934 provides investors. Over my dissent, joined by Harry Blackmun, David Souter, and Ruth, the majority rejected the consensus of court of appeals decisions that had developed during the preceding half century imposing liability on aiders and abettors of violators of the statute.[3] In doing so, it relied on its recently developed approach to the question whether federal courts should provide a remedy for violations of federal statutes that did not expressly authorize such a remedy. That is, the

---

3. See *Central Bank of Denver, N. A.* v. *First Interstate Bank of Denver, N. A.*, 511 U.S. 164 (1994).

Court acknowledged that Section 10(b) created an implied right of action against persons who violate the section. But then, rather than relying on the character of Section 10(b), it looked to express private causes of action in the statute to decide whether the implied actions under Section 10(b) covered aiding and abetting liability. The Court explained, "From the fact that Congress did not attach private aiding and abetting liability to any of the express causes of action in the securities Acts, we can infer that Congress likely would not have attached aiding and abetting liability to § 10(b) had it provided a private § 10(b) cause of action."[4]

I disagreed, writing,

> In *hundreds* of judicial and administrative proceedings in every Circuit in the federal system, the courts and the SEC have concluded that aiders and abettors are subject to liability under § 10(b) and Rule 10b-5.... The early aiding and abetting decisions relied upon principles borrowed from tort law; in those cases, judges closer to the times and climate of the 73d Congress than we concluded that holding aiders and abettors liable was consonant with the Exchange Act's purpose to strengthen the antifraud remedies of the common law....

> Our approach to implied causes of action, as to other matters of statutory construction, has changed markedly since the Exchange Act's passage in 1934. At that time, and indeed until quite recently, courts regularly assumed, in accord with the traditional common law presumption, that a statute enacted for the benefit of a particular class conferred on members of that class the right to sue violators of that statute. Moreover, shortly before the Exchange Act was passed, this Court instructed that such "remedial" legislation should receive "a broader and more liberal interpretation than that to be drawn from mere dictionary definitions of the words

---

4. *Id.*, at 179.

employed by Congress." There is a risk of anachronistic error in applying our current approach to a statute enacted when courts commonly read statutes of this kind broadly to accord with their remedial purposes and regularly approved rights to sue despite statutory silence.[5]

Although I vividly remember my strong and adverse reaction to the Court's aggressive role in curtailing the coverage of the securities laws in *Central Bank* and a few other similar cases, it was not until after I retired that I learned — or any scholar mentioned — the fact that I had "authored more securities law opinions than any justice in the history of the Supreme Court."[6] As it turns out, I also wrote more dissenting opinions in the securities area than any other justice.[7]

As I have already noted in previous chapters, for years there has been a difference of opinion among members of the Court over whether the Due Process Clause of the Fourteenth Amendment merely provides procedural protections for deprivations of life, liberty, and property or whether it also guarantees some undefined substantive rights, such as the right to choose whether to have an abortion.

In *Albright* v. *Oliver*,[8] we were confronted with the question whether the Due Process Clause protects a right to be free from criminal prosecution without probable cause.

The state of Illinois initiated a prosecution against Kevin Albright for selling a substance that looked like an illegal drug. After learning of the charge, Albright surrendered to the police and was released on bail. The trial court later dismissed the action on the ground that the charge did not state an offense under state law, whereupon Albright filed suit against

---

5. 511 U.S., at 192–96 (Stevens, J., dissenting) (citation omitted).
6. See Lyman Johnson and Jason A. Cantone, "Justice Stevens and Securities Law," *J. L. Econ. & Pol'y* 12 (2016): 77, 78.
7. *Id.,* at 79.
8. 510 U.S. 266 (1994).

the arresting officer, alleging that the arrest had deprived him of substantive due process. The district court dismissed the case and the Court of Appeals for the Seventh Circuit affirmed, holding that a state prosecution without probable cause is a constitutional tort only if it results in imprisonment, loss of employment, or some other "palpable consequence." Over my dissent that only Harry Blackmun joined, seven members of the majority agreed with the Seventh Circuit. Their conclusion was supported by four different opinions, none of which endorsed the Seventh Circuit's reasoning or was supported by a court majority. The case is interesting because it illustrates how a rather simple issue can generate a variety of responses that leave a novel and interesting question unanswered.

My view of the case was quite straightforward. The Fifth Amendment prohibits a federal felony prosecution unless it is preceded by a grand jury indictment. In *Hurtado* v. *California*,[9] the Court had held that the Due Process Clause did not compel a state to use the grand jury procedure before filing criminal charges, but it had noted that the substance of that guarantee was protected by California's requirement that a magistrate must certify "to the probable guilt of the defendant." I thought it clear that Illinois, like California, could not dispense with the grand jury procedure unless the substance of the probable-cause requirement was adequately protected. And, accepting the allegations of the complaint as true, it was clear that the officer attesting to the charges against Albright knew, or should have known, that he did not have probable cause to accuse Albright of a crime. The injury to Albright's reputation may not have been as substantial as any of the consequences that the Seventh Circuit required as a predicate for his claim, but no one on our Court relied on the absence of more serious harm as the basis for rejecting the claim. Instead, without answering the question whether a frivolous prosecution is itself prohibited by the Constitution, four different opinions merely refused to allow recovery based on a substantive due process theory.

---

9. 110 U.S. 516 (1884).

In his opinion affirming the dismissal of the complaint, Chief Justice Rehnquist reasoned that because the Fourth Amendment was the provision of the Bill of Rights that was most relevant to claims of deprivations of liberty incident to an arrest, Albright's reliance on a substantive due process rationale required dismissal of his complaint without considering whether he might have prevailed on a Fourth Amendment theory. Nino Scalia joined the chief's opinion but wrote separately to express the view that procedural guarantees relating to the period before and during a state criminal trial should not be supplemented through the device of substantive due process to provide any protection not already recognized in earlier cases. In my view, his reasoning should have prevented him from providing the fifth vote supporting the decision many years later relying on a substantive due process rationale for applying the Second Amendment's protection of the right to bear arms to states as well as the federal government in *McDonald* v. *City of Chicago*.[10]

Ruth Ginsburg also joined the chief's opinion but wrote separately to explain more particularly why she thought it appropriate to view the case "through a Fourth Amendment lens." She noted that Albright had invoked the Fourth Amendment as a basis for his claim (although he had not included that theory in his petition for certiorari). She speculated that Albright had subordinated his invocation of the Fourth Amendment, and pressed instead a substantive due process right to be free from prosecution without probable cause, for two incorrect strategic reasons: that the court might have doubted that his voluntary surrender to the police constituted a "seizure"; and that he mistakenly feared that the applicable two-year statute of limitations had run out because his seizure had terminated before the complaint was dismissed. Having thus made it pretty clear that she found merit in the Fourth Amendment claim, Ruth concluded that the "principle of party presentation cautions decision makers against asserting it for him" and resisted the opportunity "to break new ground" in the field of substantive due process.

---

10. 561 U.S. 742, 791 (2010).

Tony Kennedy, joined by Clarence Thomas, concurred in the judgment without joining Chief Justice Rehnquist's opinion. He agreed that an alleged arrest without probable cause should be analyzed under the Fourth Amendment without reference to substantive due process but regarded Albright's claim as based on the malicious initiation of a baseless prosecution. He noted that the Constitution does not include any standard for the initiation of criminal proceedings. Moreover, the fact that a person's interest in freedom from malicious prosecution is protected by state tort law eliminated the need for a federal remedy. (Albright's attempt to invoke that state law remedy had been barred by the statute of limitations.) If a state did not provide a remedy for malicious prosecution, Tony apparently would have endorsed Albright's reliance on substantive due process.

David Souter agreed with the judgment that Albright had not justified the recognition of a substantive due process violation, but did so because all of the harms Albright alleged were products of his arrest rather than attributable just to the baseless prosecution itself. The Fourth Amendment would have provided an adequate remedy for those harms (if Albright had relied on it). Thus, even though there might be exceptional cases in which some harm occurs in the interim between the filing of baseless charges and the defendant's arrest, the Court did not have to decide whether substantive due process protected against that harm when such a case was not before it.

Early in the term, Ruth wrote for the majority in a case involving the federal requirement that banks must file a report with the secretary of the treasury whenever they are involved in a cash transaction involving more than $10,000.[11] Waldemar Ratzlaf, the defendant in the case, arrived at a Nevada casino with a shopping bag full of cash, stating that he wanted to pay a $160,000 gambling debt without creating any written report of the payment. When the casino vice president told him that he could not accept a cash payment of over $10,000 without filing a report, Ratzlaf, his wife, and

---

11. *Ratzlaf* v. *United States,* 510 U.S. 135 (1994).

a casino employee visited several banks in the area, purchasing separate cashier's checks for $9,500 each, and used them to pay off his debt; he later bought several more cashier's checks in amounts less than $10,000.

The question in the case was whether, in order to obtain a conviction for violating the reporting requirement, the government had to prove not just that the defendant knew of the banks' duty, but also that he knew that his own conduct was unlawful. Ruth's opinion for the narrow majority that included Nino Scalia, Tony Kennedy, David Souter, and me, concluded that the word "wilfully" in the statute would have been unnecessary had it not been intended to refer to the defendant. Harry Blackmun, writing in dissent for Chief Justice Rehnquist, Sandra O'Connor, and Clarence Thomas, thought the word "wilfully" merely required that the defendant knew what he was doing without necessarily encompassing his knowledge that he was acting unlawfully.

On Thursday, December 23, 1993, I ruled on an application to stay an injunction that had been filed the preceding evening with me in my capacity as circuit justice for the Sixth Circuit. The injunction required government officials in Columbus, Ohio, to allow the Ku Klux Klan to erect a large Latin cross in front of the Ohio statehouse. While, unlike many of my colleagues, I strongly agreed with the applicants' argument that government has no business endorsing religious messages in displays on public property (four years earlier, I had written an opinion expressing my disapproval of the placement of the menorah and the crèche on the city-county building in Pittsburgh), I denied the application. The cross was already in place and was scheduled to be removed the next day. Moreover, the case was unique because the district court had found that the local government had effectively disassociated itself from any messages that might reasonably be communicated by the Klan's display of the cross. Had I granted the stay application, the time required to resolve the dispute that would inevitably have followed the Klan's request for reconsideration by the full Court would not have been justified no matter how the case would have been resolved.

*   *   *

Toward the end of the 1993 term, Harry Blackmun announced his intention to step down from the Court at the close of the term. President Clinton held a press conference on the morning of April 6, 1994, in the
Roosevelt Room at the White House. He praised Harry as a "steady and
strong hand" who "struck the right balance" in areas of civil liberties,
criminal law, and separation of powers, as in the *United States* v. *Nixon*
case.[12] Perhaps unsurprisingly, the reporters who were gathered took the
opportunity to ask Justice Blackmun about his decision in *Roe* v. *Wade*,
upon which he reflected, "[P]eople forget that it was a 7–2 decision. They
always typify it as a Blackmun opinion. But I'll say what I've said many
times publicly: I think it was right in 1973, and I think it was right today.
It's a step that had to be taken as we go down the road toward the full
emancipation of women."

---

12. 418 U.S. 683 (1974).

29

The Breyer Court

October Term 1994

The Senate confirmed President Clinton's nomination of Steve Breyer to the Supreme Court by a vote of 87–9. I had known Steve and his wife, Joanna, as friends since the summer of 1976 when we were both members of the faculty during a seminar for young foreign lawyers held in Salzburg, Austria. Steve and I shared an interest in antitrust law, a subject that he then taught at Harvard Law School, and Joanna and I shared an interest in tennis, a game at which she excelled. During the intervening years he had enhanced his already enviable reputation as a scholar by serving as the Chief Counsel of the Judiciary Committee of the Senate, and as a judge on the United States Court of Appeals for the First Circuit in Boston. While occupying that position he had supervised the construction of a new courthouse and served as a member of the federal commission that drafted the guidelines that apply to most sentencing decisions in federal criminal cases. He was — and still is — superbly well qualified to serve as a member of the Supreme Court.

His appointment — or perhaps more precisely Harry's resignation — had an important impact on my role on the Court, for beginning in the 1994 term and continuing until I resigned in 2010, I served as the senior associate justice on the Court. This seniority meant that I acted as the chief when he was ill or otherwise absent, and that I had the responsibility for assigning opinions of the Court whenever the chief was in dissent and I was in the majority. That happened four times during our first argument session in October 1994.

In *Hess* v. *Port Authority Trans-Hudson Corporation*,[1] a narrow majority held that a bistate entity created by New York, New Jersey, and the federal government was not entitled to the states' Eleventh Amendment immunity from suit in a federal court. I assigned the Court opinion to Ruth Ginsburg. Even though her flawless opinion effectively responded to Sandra O'Connor's dissent, I added a brief comment to highlight a consideration that affected my votes in all Eleventh Amendment cases:

> Most of this Court's Eleventh Amendment jurisprudence is the product of judge-made law unsupported by the text of the Constitution.... The doctrine of sovereign immunity has long been the target of scholarly criticism. And rightly so, for throughout the doctrine's history, it has clashed with the just principle that there should be a remedy for every wrong.

> Sovereign immunity inevitably places a lesser value on administering justice to the individual than on giving government a license to act arbitrarily.... In my view, when confronted with the question whether a judge-made doctrine of this character should be extended or contained, it is entirely appropriate to give controlling weight to the Founders' purpose [as expressed in the Preamble to the Constitution] to "establish Justice."[2]

Another five-to-four decision, *Tome* v. *United States*,[3] addressed whether the Federal Rules of Evidence permitted prosecutors to use a

---

1. 513 U.S. 30 (1994).
2. *Id.*, at 53–55.
3. 513 U.S. 150 (1995).

child's prior out-of-court statements, made after her motive to fabricate evidence had arisen, to rebut any charge of improper motive in her testimony. The trial court had admitted the evidence, but, in an opinion that I assigned to Tony Kennedy, we held that the evidence should have been excluded. My reason for making that assignment reflected my judgment that Tony's experience as a trial lawyer would enhance his ability to discuss the issue.

In a third case argued in October 1984, *O'Neal* v. *McAninch*,[4] in which the chief justice was one of only three dissenters, I was able to choose Steve Breyer from the remaining six justices to author the Court opinion. The question in the case was whether a district judge should treat an erroneous jury instruction in a murder case as harmless or prejudicial when he was in grave doubt — that is, "in virtual equipoise" — concerning the impact of the error.[5] I was happy with my choice because Steve's opinion explaining our ruling in the defendant's favor relied so heavily on the discussion of harmless error in *Kotteakos* v. *United States;*[6] *Kotteakos,* the leading case discussing the harmless error issue, was written by my former boss, Wiley Rutledge, the year before I served as his law clerk.

Fourth, I assigned the Court opinion in *Schlup* v. *Delo*[7] to myself. A Missouri prisoner under sentence of death for cooperating with two other white prisoners in the murder of a black inmate filed a second habeas corpus petition claiming that his trial lawyer had been ineffective because he had failed to interview witnesses who would have supported his alibi that he was en route to the dining area when the fatal attack occurred. He claimed that this constitutional error in his trial had deprived the jury of evidence that would have established his innocence. An earlier decision of the Court had held that a district court should not entertain a second petition for habeas relief unless the defendant could

---

4. 513 U.S. 432 (1995).
5. *Id.,* at 434.
6. 328 U.S. 750 (1946).
7. 513 U.S. 298 (1995).

show by clear and convincing evidence that but for the constitutional error no reasonable juror would have found him guilty. The question presented to us in the *Schlup* case was whether that standard provided adequate protection against the risk of miscarriage of justice that would result from the execution of a person who was actually innocent. By a vote of five-to-four we held that a less strict standard — that the error had "probably resulted" in an erroneous conviction — should have been applied.

The case is particularly memorable because Schlup's new lawyers were successful in proving that he was just arriving in the dining area of the prison when the murder occurred and thus had been misidentified by a guard who witnessed the killing from a distance; he was in fact innocent of the crime for which he had been sentenced to death. Moreover, a dramatic description of the case later written by his lawyer, Sean D. O'Brien, explained how close Schlup had come to being executed before our Court decided to hear his case. In a meeting with the mother of the victim on the day before a stay of execution was due to expire, Schlup's lawyers identified several of their alibi witnesses, including some that she recognized as friends of her deceased son, and persuaded her to call the Missouri governor's office to explain why she was convinced of his innocence. As I later learned, one of those lawyers, Jim Liebman, is a former law clerk of mine and the author of *The Wrong Carlos,* a convincing book about another innocent defendant who was not only erroneously convicted of murder by the state of Texas, but also was actually executed for the crime that he almost certainly did not commit. As I note elsewhere in this book, cases like these have convinced me that we should abolish the death penalty to avoid the risk of such unacceptable miscarriages of justice.

The Court's eight-to-one decision in *Harris* v. *Alabama,*[8] which upheld a death sentence ordered by a trial judge despite the jury's recommendation of life imprisonment, illustrates another reason for abolishing this form of punishment. As I wrote in my dissent: "Not surprisingly, given the political pressures they face, judges are far more likely than

---

8. 513 U.S. 504 (1995).

juries to impose the death penalty. This has long been the case, and the recent experience of judicial overrides confirms it. Alabama judges have vetoed only five jury recommendations of death, but they have condemned 47 defendants whom juries would have spared.... Death sentences imposed by judges over contrary jury verdicts do more than countermand the community's judgment: They express contempt for that judgment.... Overrides also sacrifice the legitimacy of jury verdicts, at potentially great cost. Whereas the public presumes that a death sentence imposed by a jury reflects the community's judgment that death is the appropriate response to the defendant's crime, the same presumption does not attach to a lone government official's decree. Indeed, government-sanctioned executions unsupported by judgments of a fair cross section of the citizenry may undermine respect for the value of human life itself and unwittingly increase tolerance of killing."[9] *Harris* has been eroded somewhat with time, as the Court's more recent cases establish that a jury must find all of the facts necessary to sentence a defendant to death. But it remains true that a judge can still impose a death sentence notwithstanding the jury's contrary recommendation.

One case decided early in the term was *Federal Election Commission* v. *NRA Political Victory Fund*.[10] The Federal Election Commission filed a petition for certiorari in a civil action seeking to enforce the Federal Election Campaign Act (FECA). The United States, however, filed a brief contending that the operative statutory regime did not permit the FEC to file such a certiorari petition without authorization from the solicitor general. The Court agreed.

I was the lone dissenter. I thought the majority's reading of the statutory text was too narrow. In my opinion I also emphasized the historic context in which Congress adopted the statute empowering the FEC to appeal FECA enforcement actions. As I explained: "Section 437d(a)(6)

9. *Id.*, at 522–23.
10. 513 U.S. 88 (1994).

was passed as part of the Federal Election Campaign Act Amendments of 1974. The 1974 amendments represented a response by Congress to perceived abuses arising out of the 1972 Presidential election campaign and culminating in the resignation of President Nixon. Indeed, the legislative history reveals Congress's belief that '[p]robably the most significant reform that could emerge from the Watergate scandal is the creation of an independent nonpartisan agency to supervise the enforcement of the laws relating to the conduct of elections.'"[11] Moreover, "[o]ne of the most dramatic events of the entire Watergate scandal was the firing of special prosecutor Archibald Cox," which was carried out by the solicitor general after both the attorney general and the deputy attorney general refused and instead resigned. This incident — and the public outrage that it incited — made it highly unlikely that Congress, in enacting the FECA amendments less than one year later, intended to make the FEC dependent for its Supreme Court litigation on the approval of the solicitor general.

In 1989, Congress enacted a law that broadly prohibited federal employees from accepting honoraria — defined as any compensation for making speeches or writing articles. The prohibition applied even when neither the subject of the speech or article nor the person or group paying for it had any connection with the employee's official duties. In a class action maintained by two unions and several career civil servants employed by executive agencies, the district court and the Court of Appeals for the D.C. Circuit held the statute unconstitutional and we granted certiorari to review that decision. Because Chief Justice Rehnquist (joined by Nino Scalia and Clarence Thomas) thought that the statute was valid, I was able to assign the majority opinion affirming the D.C. Circuit to myself.[12]

In that opinion, I noted that federal employees who write for publication in their spare time have made significant contributions to the marketplace of ideas. They include literary giants like Nathaniel Hawthorne

---

11. *Id.*, at 102.
12. *United States* v. *National Treasury Employees Union*, 513 U.S. 454 (1995).

and Herman Melville, who were employed by the Customs Service; Walt Whitman, who worked for the Departments of Justice and Interior; and Bret Harte, an employee of the United States Mint. The respondents in the case before us described past activities for which the new law prohibited them from being compensated: a postal worker in Virginia had given lectures on the Quaker religion for which he received small payments that supplemented his income; an aerospace engineer had lectured on black history for a fee of one hundred dollars per lecture; a microbiologist at the Food and Drug Administration had earned almost $3,000 per year reviewing dance performances; and a tax examiner had received comparable pay for articles about the environment.

The honoraria ban was enacted in response to the practices of a small group of lawmakers. Such officials often receive invitations to talk about subjects related to their official duties, while invitations to rank-and-file employees usually depend only on the market value of their messages. Thus the principal burden of the statute was imposed on the vast group of employees — some 1.7 million individuals — whose conduct had nothing to do with its enactment. The dissenters thought that we had underestimated the ability of lower level employees to confer improper benefits on potential donors of honoraria and that we should have deferred to Congress's judgment about the need for reform. In the majority opinion, I recognized the obligation to defer to considered congressional judgments, but wrote that "on the record of this case we must attach greater weight to the powerful and realistic presumption that the federal work force consists of dedicated and honorable civil servants." I am not aware of any attempt by Congress to reenact the ban on honoraria.

Ruth Ginsburg made two important and valid points in her dissenting opinion in *Arizona* v. *Evans*,[13] which I joined. In that case, an Arizona state police officer had pulled over a car as part of a routine traffic stop and then learned from a computer search that the driver had an outstanding

---

13. 514 U.S. 1 (1995).

arrest warrant. After the driver was placed under arrest he dropped a marijuana cigarette, and the officer later discovered a bag of marijuana in the
car. Because of a computer error, however, the computer record indicating
that the driver had an outstanding arrest warrant was incorrect. And
because in fact no arrest warrant existed, the search was not authorized
and the Arizona Supreme Court held that evidence should be suppressed.

There was ambiguity in the Arizona Supreme Court's opinion on the
question whether its ruling was based on state or federal law. Applying its
reasoning in *Michigan* v. *Long*[14] — a decision from which I had dissented —
the Court accepted jurisdiction of the case by presuming that in the absence
of a clear statement in the state court's opinion that its ruling was based on
its understanding of state law, a federal court should assume that the state
court thought it was bound by federal law. In her dissent, Ruth noted that
the *Long* presumption impeded the state courts' ability to serve as laborato-
ries for testing solutions to novel legal problems. "Specifically, the Arizona
Supreme Court saw the growing use of computerized records in law enforcement as a development presenting new dangers to individualized liberty;
excluding evidence seized as a result of incorrect computer data, the Arizona
court anticipated, would reduce the incidence of uncorrected errors."[15]

The majority of our Court, however, narrowly construed the purpose
of the exclusionary rule as directed at deterrence of police misconduct,
and therefore reversed the decision of the Arizona court. (I also wrote
separately to explain my view that the exclusionary rule has a broader
purpose to protect the fundamental rights of citizens against the indig-
nity of unreasonable searches and seizures.) The following portion of a
footnote in Ruth's opinion adequately responded to the majority's ruling
on the merits: "That the mistake may have been made by a clerical worker
does not alter the conclusion that application of the exclusionary rule has
deterrent value. Just as the risk of *respondeat superior* liability encourages
employers to supervise their employees' conduct, so the risk of exclusion

---

14. 463 U.S. 1032, 1062 (1983).
15. 514 U.S., at 25.

of evidence encourages policymakers and systems managers to monitor the performance of the systems they install and the personnel employed to operate those systems. In the words of the trial court, the mistake in Evans' case was 'perhaps the negligence of the Justice Court, or the negligence of the Sheriff's office. But it is still the negligence of the State.' "[16]

In *McIntyre* v. *Ohio Elections Comm'n,*[17] by a vote of seven to two, the Court held that an Ohio regulation of the electoral process that prohibited the distribution of anonymous pamphlets urging voters to vote against a proposed school tax levy was unconstitutional. Because Chief Justice Rehnquist was one of the two dissenters — he joined Nino Scalia's dissent — I was able to assign myself the majority opinion, in which I began by noting that at least in the field of ordinary literature the interest in allowing anonymous works to enter the marketplace of ideas unquestionably outweighs any public interest in requiring identity of the author as a condition of entry. In a footnote I referred to Mark Twain and O. Henry, and to the numerous pseudonyms that Benjamin Franklin had used, and suggested that even the name William Shakespeare may have been used to conceal the name of the true author of the plays attributed to him.

Ohio argued that its disclosure requirement was justified by its interest in preventing fraudulent and libelous statements and its interest in providing the electorate with relevant information. But the prohibition broadly applied to documents that were not even arguably libelous or fraudulent, and the author's identity is merely one of a host of facts that an author may or may not decide to include in her writing. We noted that a state's enforcement interest might justify a more limited identification requirement, but not the broad prohibition of leafletting at issue in the case.

In his dissent, Nino primarily disagreed with Clarence's view — expressed in a separate concurrence — that the phrase "freedom of speech, or of the press," as originally understood, protected anonymous political

---

16. *Id.,* at 29n5.
17. 514 U.S. 334 (1995).

leafletting. Unlike Clarence (and the rest of us), he thought it did not. In addition, if he were guided exclusively by our case law, he would have asked "whether protection of the election process justifies limitations upon speech that cannot constitutionally be imposed generally." He thought that our "cases plainly answer that question in the affirmative — indeed, they suggest that no justification for regulation is more compelling than protection of the electoral process."[18]

In recent years I have often reflected on how directly that comment supports Byron White's dissent in *Buckley* v. *Valeo,*[19] that protecting the electoral process provides ample support for a rule limiting expenditures during political campaigns.

Later in the term the chief justice announced an opinion that dramatically limited the power of Congress to regulate the possession of handguns.[20] The opinion invalidated the Gun-Free School Zones Act of 1990, which made it a federal offense "for any individual knowingly to possess a firearm at a place that the individual knows, or has reasonable cause to believe, is a school zone."

The chief's opinion observed that Congress may regulate activities that "substantially affect" interstate commerce. But it then concluded, "The possession of a gun in a local school zone is in no sense an economic activity that might, through repetition elsewhere, substantially affect any sort of interstate commerce. Respondent was a local student at a local school; there is no indication that he had recently moved in interstate commerce, and there is no requirement that his possession of the firearm have any concrete tie to interstate commerce."[21] The opinion further explained that acceptance of the government's argument that possession of firearms in school affected the functioning of the national economy would erase any "distinction between what is truly national and what is truly local."[22]

---

18. *Id.,* at 379.
19. 424 U.S. 1 (1976).
20. *United States* v. *Lopez,* 514 U.S. 549 (1995).
21. *Id.,* at 567.
22. *Id.,* at 568.

The difference between the chief justice's tentative and unpersuasive opinion and Steve Breyer's thorough and convincing description of the impact of handguns on the quality of high school education in America could not be more dramatic. One brief excerpt from Steve's thirty-page dissent illustrates my point:

[R]eports, hearings, and other readily available literature make clear that the problem of guns in and around schools is widespread and extremely serious. These materials report, for example, that four percent of American high school students (and six percent of inner-city high school students) carry a gun to school at least occasionally; that 12 percent of urban high school students have had guns fired at them; that 20 percent of those students have been threatened with guns; and that, in any 6-month period, several hundred thousand schoolchildren are victims of violent crimes in or near their schools. And, they report that this widespread violence in schools throughout the Nation significantly interferes with the quality of education in those schools.... Having found that guns in schools significantly undermine the quality of education in our Nation's classrooms, Congress could also have found, given the effect of education upon interstate and foreign commerce, that gun-related violence in and around schools is a commercial, as well as a human, problem.[23]

In a concurring opinion Clarence Thomas advocated a reexamination of cases that had upheld legislation that had a "substantial effect" on interstate commerce, noting that those cases lent support to Stephen Breyer's dissent. He thought it clear that Congress had no more power to regulate mere gun possession than to regulate marriage or cruelty to animals; he clearly did not foresee the later cases upholding such statutes.

While I joined both Steve's and David's dissents, I added a few sentences of my own: "Guns are both articles of commerce and articles that

---

23. *Id.*, at 619–20.

can be used to restrain commerce. Their possession is the consequence, either directly or indirectly, of commercial activity. In my judgment, Congress's power to regulate commerce in firearms includes the power to prohibit possession of guns at any location because of their potentially harmful use; it also necessarily follows that Congress may also prohibit their possession in particular markets. The market for the possession of handguns by school-age children is, distressingly, substantial. Whether or not the national interest in eliminating that market would have justified federal legislation in 1789, it surely does today."[24]

October Term 1995

Early in the 1995 term, Ruth Ginsburg wrote an opinion explaining our unanimous decision to reverse a Seventh Circuit case that had held that a 1987 statute enacted to improve the nation's check payment system, which clearly authorized jurisdiction in suits between banks and their customers, did not also authorize suits between two banks.[25] Ruth Ginsburg neutralized the argument that the two different kinds of suits were authorized by two different sections of the statute — a point that the Seventh Circuit used to support its erroneous conclusion — by including a two-page discussion of legislative history. While Nino Scalia agreed with most of the reasoning in her opinion, he did not join the portion discussing legislative history, stating that the "law *is* what the law *says,* and we should content ourselves with reading it rather than psychoanalyzing those who enacted it."[26] His opinion not only argued that the use of legislative history was both unnecessary and unwise, but also that it violated his view that the legislative power vested in Congress is "nondelegable." His separate writing prompted a response from me (with which Stephen Breyer agreed). I explained, among other points, the utility of the legislative history in that particular opinion: "Thus, the net result of the inquiry

---

24. 514 U.S., at 602–3.
25. *Bank One Chicago, N. A.* v. *Midwest Bank & Trust Co.,* 516 U.S. 264 (1996).
26. *Id.,* at 279.

into drafting history is to find the answer to an otherwise puzzling aspect of the statutory text."[27]

Tina Bennis and her husband were joint owners of a car that he used to commute to and from his job. One evening while he was on the way home, a prostitute joined him in the car, where they engaged in sexual activity that was observed by the Detroit police. In addition to punishing him for his crime, the state treated the car as a public nuisance and forfeited it without allowing Tina any credit for her interest in it despite the fact that she had no knowledge of its unlawful use. The state appellate court held the action unconstitutional, but the Michigan Supreme Court reversed. Bill Rehnquist wrote the opinion for the five justices on our Court who affirmed; I dissented.[28] It seemed to me that Tina's complete lack of culpability — indeed, in a sense she was a victim of her husband's wrongdoing — made it outrageous to penalize her for his crime. While I was not prepared to draw a bright line that would separate all the permissible and impermissible forfeitures of property of innocent owners, I was convinced (and still am) that the blatant unfairness of the seizure of Tina's interest in her car placed it on the unconstitutional side of the line.[29]

In *Seminole Tribe of Fla.* v. *Florida*,[30] by a five-to-four vote, the Court held that Congress did not have the constitutional power to authorize an Indian tribe to sue a state to compel performance of a duty to negotiate in good faith toward the formation of a compact regulating gambling on a reservation. What had started as a common law doctrine of sovereign immunity had become a constitutional rule protecting states from suits by citizens of other states, even those suits expressly authorized by Congress. Whereas Congress had previously authorized a variety of kinds of lawsuits against state agencies, such as actions for patent infringement or

---

27. *Id.*, at 277.
28. *Bennis* v. *Michigan,* 516 U.S. 442 (1996).
29. *Id.*, at 472.
30. 517 U.S. 44 (1996).

trademark infringement, the case invalidating the Indian Regulatory Act made an unprecedented withdrawal of federal power to regulate state activities. Both David Souter, joined by Ruth Ginsburg and Stephen Breyer, and I wrote dissents objecting at length to the Court's dramatic change in settled law. In my view the Court's decision in *Seminole Tribe* is one of the most objectionable cases that the Court decided during my tenure as a justice, both in its reasoning and in the impact of its holding on the efficient functioning of our national government.

In 1956 the Rhode Island legislature enacted two separate prohibitions against advertising the retail price of alcoholic beverages — the first applied to liquor dealers and the second applied to the press. Concluding that the laws promoted temperance, the state supreme court upheld them. Thirty years later a case reached our Court again challenging those two laws.[31] We recognized that they might indeed serve their purpose of lessening the demand for liquor, but our entire Court held that the First Amendment did not allow a state to outlaw speech as a means of curtailing consumption of a harmful product. We also rejected an argument that the Twenty-First Amendment, which had repealed the Eighteenth Amendment's prohibition of the sale of alcoholic beverages, had somehow provided a justification for the state's rules limiting the quantity of alcoholic beverages in the Rhode Island market. I wrote the principal opinion in the case, but Nino Scalia, Clarence Thomas, and Sandra O'Connor each wrote separately.

The national distributor of BMW cars decided not to advise its dealers, and hence their customers, of predelivery damage to new cars when the cost of repair amounted to less than 3 percent of the car's suggested retail price. Dr. Ira Gore purchased a BMW sedan for $40,750.88; after driving it for nine months without noticing any flaws in its appearance, he took the car to a detailer who detected evidence that it had been repainted. Convinced that he had been cheated, Gore brought suit against BMW of North America

---

31. *44 Liquormart, Inc.* v. *Rhode Island,* 517 U.S. 484 (1996).

alleging that the failure to disclose the car's repainting constituted fraud and sought recovery of compensatory and punitive damages.

At trial BMW acknowledged its policy of not disclosing repairs that cost less than 3 percent of a car's suggested retail price. Because the cost of repainting Gore's car amounted to only $601.37 — or about 1.5 percent of its price — the repair was not disclosed to either the dealer or Gore. To prove his actual damages of $4,000, Gore relied on testimony estimating that the value of the repainted car was about 10 percent less than he had paid for it. To support his claim for punitive damages, Gore introduced evidence that BMW had sold 983 refinished cars as new, without disclosing that they had been repainted. Using an actual damage estimate of $4,000 per car, the plaintiff then argued that he should receive a punitive damages award of $4,000 per vehicle.

The jury found BMW liable for compensatory damages of $4,000 and punitive damages of $4 million, based on a finding that the nondisclosure policy constituted "gross, oppressive or malicious" fraud. BMW filed a motion to set aside the punitive damages award, arguing that its nondisclosure policy was lawful in twenty-five states and therefore could not provide the basis for punitive damages. The trial court denied the motion, but the state supreme court reduced the award to $2 million because it was erroneously based partly on conduct that had occurred outside Alabama. We granted certiorari to decide whether the award was excessive — whether it deprived BMW of property without due process of law.[32]

We disagreed about the outcome. A majority of us agreed that Alabama had not given BMW adequate notice that it might be punished so severely for its nondisclosure policy. In my opinion for the Court I examined the degree of reprehensibility of BMW's conduct, the ratio of the amount of the award to the actual harm suffered by the plaintiff, and the sanctions that the state imposed for comparable misconduct (for example, the maximum civil penalty authorized by the Alabama legislature for a violation of its Deceptive Trade Practices Act was $2,000). All three approaches supported the conclusion that the award was grossly excessive. In a concurring

---

32. *BMW of North America* v. *Gore*, 517 U.S. 559 (1996).

opinion, Steve Breyer pointed out how the absence of any guidance in the trial judge's instructions invited the jury to impose an unreasonable sanction on BMW. In separate dissents, Nino Scalia joined by Clarence Thomas and Ruth Ginsburg joined by the chief justice would have allowed the jury's verdict to stand, arguing that our Court had no constitutional authority to review the amount of a state court's award of punitive damages. Nino's position was consistent with his skeptical view of the whole notion that the Due Process Clause imposes substantive limits on state power.

Before 1992, Denver, Aspen, Boulder, and other Colorado cities had adopted ordinances that protected homosexuals from employment, housing, and other forms of discrimination. In that year Colorado adopted an amendment to its state constitution repealing those ordinances to the extent that they prohibited discrimination on the basis of "homosexual, lesbian or bisexual orientation, conduct, practices, or relationships." In addition to repealing existing laws, the amendment prohibited all future legislative, executive, or judicial action designed to protect gays and lesbians from discrimination. A Colorado trial court enjoined enforcement of the amendment and the Colorado Supreme Court affirmed. We granted the state's petition for certiorari and, after argument, affirmed by a six-to-three vote.[33] Because the chief was one of the dissenters, I was responsible for assigning the majority opinion and chose Tony Kennedy because he was so firmly convinced about the outcome.

Nino's dissent was more persuasive then than it would be later because Byron White's opinion in *Bowers* v. *Hardwick*[34] — which held that a state could punish sodomy as a crime — had not yet been overruled. In his opinion for the Court, Tony simply ignored that case even though there is admittedly some tension between a holding that permits a state to punish conduct as a crime while prohibiting it from taking any adverse action against a person who engages in the controversial conduct.

---

33. *Romer* v. *Evans*, 517 U.S. 620 (1996).
34. 478 U.S. 186 (1986).

*   *   *

Following the 1990 census disclosing that its increase in population entitled Texas to three additional congressional seats, the Texas legislature promulgated a new plan that included three new seats. To comply with the Voting Rights Act of 1965, the new plan intentionally included two-majority black districts and one new Hispanic district. Despite that permissive motivation, the Court upheld a challenge to the three new districts.[35] The majority held that districts should be judged by "strict scrutiny" where the redistricting legislation at issue is "so extremely irregular on its face that it rationally can be viewed only as an effort to segregate the races for purposes of voting, without regard for traditional districting principles," or where "race for its own sake, and not other districting principles, was the legislature's dominant and controlling rationale in drawing its district lines."[36] The Court relied on the bizarre shape of the district to conclude that race was the predominant factor motivating the legislature's redistricting and that strict scrutiny was therefore warranted. Since the purpose of drawing the new districts was admittedly to comply with the Voting Rights Act, there really was no need to rely on their bizarre shapes to demonstrate the part that race played in their design. I dissented, explaining that the Court erred under its precedents in applying strict scrutiny and that each challenged district could survive strict scrutiny in any event because the districts considered race only to the extent necessary to comply with the state's responsibilities under the Voting Rights Act. How a state's decision to provide better representation of minority groups in the legislature can be treated as a violation of the Equal Protection Clause remains one of the most puzzling questions that I confronted during my tenure on the Court.

In two Court opinions announced on June 28, 1996, by Sandra O'Connor and Tony Kennedy, respectively — *Board of Commissioners,*

---

35. *Bush* v. *Vera,* 517 U.S. 952 (1996).
36. *Id.,* at 958.

Wabaunsee County v. *Umbehr*,[37] and *O'Hare Truck Service, Inc.* v. *City of Northlake*[38] — the Court held that local governments could not terminate contracts for trash hauling or towing services in retaliation for the contractor's exercise of his free speech. Both opinions applied the rules developed in earlier cases prohibiting patronage practices in public employment, from which Lewis Powell and Nino Scalia had dissented.[39]

In his dissent in the two 1996 cases, Nino Scalia, joined by Clarence Thomas, relied on an argument that he advanced in other contexts as well:

> [W]hen a practice not expressly prohibited by the text of the Bill of Rights bears the endorsement of a long tradition of open, widespread, and unchallenged use that dates back to the beginning of the Republic, we have no proper basis for striking it down. Such a venerable and accepted tradition is not to be laid on the examining table and scrutinized for its conformity to some abstract principle of First Amendment adjudication devised by this Court. To the contrary, such traditions are themselves the stuff out of which the Court's principles are to be formed. They are, in these uncertain areas, the very points of reference by which the legitimacy of *other* practices is to be figured out. When it appears that the latest "rule," or "three-part test," or "balancing test" devised by the Court has placed us on a collision course with such a landmark practice, it is the former that must be recalculated by us, and not the latter that must be abandoned by our citizens.[40]

That argument for preserving patronage practices at one time would have supported the preservation of slavery and remains the only arguable justification for partisan gerrymandering.

---

37. 518 U.S. 668.
38. 518 U.S. 712.
39. See *Elrod* v. *Burns,* 427 U.S. 347, 376 (1976) (Powell, J., dissenting); *Branti* v. *Finkel,* 445 U.S. 507, 521 (1980) (Powell, J., dissenting); *Rutan* v. *Republican Party of Illinois,* 497 U.S. 62, 92 (1990) (Scalia, J., dissenting).
40. 518 U.S., at 687–688, quoting *Rutan,* 497 U.S., at 95–96.

October Term 1996

Before I joined the Court in 1975, when considering whether a statute violated the Free Exercise Clause of the First Amendment, the Court had asked two questions: (1) whether the law imposed a substantial burden on a religious practice, and (2) if so, whether the burden was justified by a compelling state interest.[41] In cases decided in 1982 and 1987, while I concurred in judgments applying that test, I objected to the test itself because it imposed too high a burden on the government when defending neutral laws of general applicability.[42] In 1990, I joined Nino Scalia's opinion for the Court in *Employment Division, Department of Human Resources of Oregon v. Smith*,[43] a case holding that Oregon could enforce its law prohibiting the use of the drug peyote by denying unemployment compensation to two Native Americans who used the drug for religious purposes. His opinion expressly refused to apply the *Sherbert v. Verner* test to a neutral law of general applicability. It was an extremely controversial decision that led to the enactment by Congress of the Religious Freedom Restoration Act of 1993 (RFRA). By enacting that statute, Congress intended to overrule Nino's opinion and reinstate the test set forth in *Sherbert*.

The constitutionality of RFRA was at issue in *City of Boerne v. Flores*,[44] a case decided during the last week of the 1996 term. P. F. Flores, the archbishop of San Diego, had been denied his application for a permit to enlarge a church that was a historic landmark, and he relied on RFRA to challenge that denial. The district court had dismissed his complaint, reasoning that Congress had exceeded its enforcement power under Section 5 of the Fourteenth Amendment; the Court of Appeals for the Ninth Circuit had reversed; and we in turn reversed the Ninth Circuit. In an opinion written by Tony Kennedy and joined by Chief Justice Rehnquist,

---

41. *Sherbert* v. *Verner,* 374 U.S. 398 (1963).
42. See *United States* v. *Lee,* 455 U.S. 252, 261 (1982), and *Hobbie* v. *Unemployment Appeals Commission of Fla.,* 480 U.S. 136, 148 (1987).
43. 494 U.S. 872.
44. 521 U.S. 507 (1997).

Clarence Thomas, Ruth Ginsburg, me, and (in pertinent part) Nino Scalia, we held that Congress did not have the power to change our construction of the Constitution by enacting RFRA. I wrote a brief concurring statement noting that RFRA had purported to give the owner of a historic landmark a statutory entitlement to an exemption from a generally applicable, neutral civil law that no atheist or agnostic would possess, and thus was a governmental preference for religion forbidden by the First Amendment. I also joined Nino Scalia's more complete and more persuasive concurring opinion defending his earlier reasoning in *Smith*.

In *Washington* v. *Glucksberg*[45] and *Vacco* v. *Quill*,[46] Chief Justice Rehnquist wrote opinions rejecting constitutional challenges to Washington and New York statutes making it a crime to knowingly cause or aid another person to commit suicide. The challengers in the former case relied on the Due Process Clause and in the latter they relied on the Equal Protection Clause. While the chief rejected the substantive due process argument in *Glucksberg*, his opinion sets forth a particularly lucid description of the doctrine. He carefully distinguished between the right to direct the removal of life-sustaining medical treatment that might hasten death — a right that had been acknowledged in *Cruzan* v. *Director, Missouri Department of Health*[47] — and the claimed right to assistance in committing suicide. He noted that the latter had never been recognized, but the common law rule that made forced medication a battery supported a long legal tradition protecting a patient's decision to refuse unwanted medical treatment.

The Telecommunications Act of 1996 was enacted to reduce regulation and encourage the rapid deployment of new telecommunications technologies. The major provisions of the statute were designed to promote competition in the local telephone service market, the multichannel

45. 521 U.S. 702 (1997).
46. 521 U.S. 793 (1997).
47. 497 U.S. 261 (1990).

television market, and the market for over-the-air broadcasting. The act includes seven titles, six of which are the product of extensive committee hearings and the subject of discussion in reports prepared by House and Senate committees. Title V, however — known as the "Communications Decency Act of 1996" — contains provisions that were added either in executive committee or by floor amendments after the hearings were concluded. The American Civil Liberties Union challenged the constitutionality of two provisions in Title V — known informally as the "indecent transmission" provision and the "patently offensive display" provision — in *Reno* v. *American Civil Liberties Union*.[48]

The first challenged provision prohibited the knowing transmission of obscene or indecent messages to any recipient under eighteen years of age. The second prohibited the knowing sending or displaying of patently offensive messages in a manner that is available to a person under eighteen years of age. My opinion for the Court holding those provisions unconstitutional — largely because of the difficulty of identifying the age of listeners to mass transmissions of messages — is less significant and less interesting than its description of the origin and dramatic growth of the international network of interconnected computers now known as the internet.

What began in 1969 as a military program called ARPANET, which was designed to enable the military, defense contractors, and universities conducting defense-related research to communicate with one another by redundant channels even if some portions of the network were damaged in a war, provided the example for the development of a number of civilian networks that soon enabled millions of people to communicate with one another and to access vast amounts of information from around the world. The number of computers that stored information and relayed communications increased from about 300 in 1981 to approximately 9.4 million by the time of the underlying trial in 1996. About 40 million people used the internet at the time of trial — a number that was expected to mushroom to 200 million by 1999.

---

48. 521 U.S. 844 (1997).

In our Court, in addition to emphasizing its interest in protecting children from exposure to indecent speech and images, the government made the "singularly unpersuasive" argument that upholding the constitutionality of the statute would foster the growth of the internet because the unregulated availability of indecent material was driving countless citizens away from the medium to protect their children. The dramatic expansion of the new marketplace of ideas contradicted the factual basis for that contention. Moreover, as a matter of constitutional tradition, we presumed in the absence of evidence to the contrary "that governmental regulation of the content of speech is more likely to interfere with the free exchange of ideas than to encourage it. The interest in encouraging freedom of expression in a democratic society outweighs any theoretical but unproven benefit of censorship."[49]

On May 6, 1994, Paula Jones, who then resided in California but was a former resident of Arkansas, filed suit against William Clinton, who was then the president of the United States, alleging that he had made sexual advances toward her when she was an employee of the State of Arkansas and he was the governor of the state. The federal district judge granted the president's request to postpone the trial until after he was out of office, but the court of appeals reversed, and the president persuaded us to grant review. We unanimously affirmed, holding that the Constitution did not grant the president immunity from liability for any wrongful conduct that may have occurred before he became president.

Clinton's strongest argument was that this case—as well as the additional cases that would predictably be filed if we allowed this one to proceed—would impose an unacceptable burden on the president. Time has vindicated our judgment that it was "unlikely that a deluge of such litigation will ever engulf the Presidency."[50]

---

49. *Id.,* at 885.
50. *Clinton v. Jones,* 520 U. S. 681, 702 (1997).

*　　*　　*

The 1993 Brady Handgun Violence Protection Act was Congress's ultimate response to the attempted assassination of President Ronald Reagan and the serious wounding of his press secretary Jim Brady in 1981. Their assailant, John Hinckley, had been found not guilty by reason of insanity. The new statute amended the federal scheme governing the distribution of firearms by establishing a national instant background check to prevent felons and the mentally ill from buying guns. The act authorized $200 million in federal grants to the states to compensate them for their assistance in developing the new system. It required firearms dealers to give advance notice of prospective sales to the local chief law enforcement officer who was then required to make a reasonable effort to determine whether the proposed sale would be lawful. An amicus brief filed by groups representing many thousands of police officers, including major police unions, indicated that the vast majority of police officers and police organizations strongly supported the new statute and thought the burden imposed on local officials was minimal. Nevertheless, two chief law enforcement officers — Jay Printz, for Ravalli County, Montana, and Richard Mack, for Graham County, Arizona — brought test cases challenging the constitutionality of the provision imposing a federal duty on them. Despite what I regard as overwhelmingly persuasive legal and practical arguments for upholding the statute, Printz and Mack ultimately prevailed.[51] Nino Scalia wrote the opinion for the five-justice majority while Steve Breyer and I wrote dissenting opinions. I still find it difficult to believe that we failed to obtain a majority in that case.

As I described in my book *Six Amendments,* the ensuing limitations on the federal government's ability to execute background checks of prospective gun purchasers may have been a factor in at least a few of the numerous incidents of gun violence that have beset this country since the *Printz* case. As a more general matter, the inability of the federal government to obtain the aid of the states may have substantial implications in

---

51. *Printz* v. *United States,* 521 U.S. 898 (1997).

times of national emergency. My primary concern is not with the courts' power to facilitate these federal-state interactions but with the imperative for judicial deference to the legislature's policy judgments that collaboration is appropriate. As I asked in my dissent in *Printz:* "If the Constitution empowers Congress and the President to make an appropriate response, is there anything in the Tenth Amendment, in historical understanding and practice, in the structure of the Constitution, or in the jurisprudence of this Court, that forbids the enlistment of state officers to make that response effective? More narrowly, what basis is there in any of those sources for concluding that it is the Members of this Court, rather than the elected representatives of the people, who should determine whether the Constitution contains the unwritten rule that the Court announces today? Perhaps today's majority would suggest that no...emergency is presented by the facts of these cases. But such a suggestion is itself an expression of a policy judgment. And Congress' view of the matter is quite different from that implied by the Court today."[52]

October Term 1997

In *Oncale* v. *Sundowner Offshore Services, Inc.,*[53] Nino Scalia wrote an opinion for a unanimous Court resolving the conflict among the courts of appeals on the question whether workplace harassment violates the federal statute prohibiting employment "discrimination...because of...sex" when the harasser and the harassed employee are of the same sex. The statute's language provided no justification for eliminating a class of harassment claims even though some courts had observed that "male-on-male sexual harassment in the workplace was assuredly not the principal evil Congress was concerned with when it enacted Title VII."[54] But, in a much quoted statement, Nino Scalia responded,

---

52. *Id.,* at 940 (internal quotation marks and alteration omitted).
53. 523 U.S. 75 (1998).
54. *Id.,* at 79.

"Statutory prohibitions often go beyond the principal evil to cover reasonably comparable evils, and it is ultimately the provisions of our laws rather than the principal concerns of our legislators by which we are governed."[55]

A few days later Nino Scalia published a twenty-three-page dissent, which David Souter, Ruth Ginsburg, and I joined, in a case holding that an alien who had once been deported and had returned to the United States without permission could be sentenced to prison for as long as twenty years, even though the statutory provision describing the crime charged in the indictment (8 U.S.C. § 1326[a]) authorized a maximum punishment of no more than two years of imprisonment.[56] The Court treated subsection (b) (2) of Section 1326, which authorized a prison term of up to twenty years for any alien described in Section 1326(a) if that person's initial deportation had been for "commission of an aggravated felony," as a penalty provision that simply authorized an increased penalty, rather than as a separate substantive crime. The Court's treatment of the earlier deportation as a mere sentencing enhancement meant that it was unnecessary to prove the fact of the prior aggravated-felony conviction in the proceedings before the jury or to mention it in the indictment. As Nino Scalia argued in his dissent, it therefore, quite unacceptably, contravened a defendant's right to have all facts necessary to support the sentence be charged in the indictment and found beyond a reasonable doubt by the jury. The debate between the justices in *Almendarez-Torres* over the question whether legislatures could limit a defendant's right to a jury trial by treating provisions authorizing enhanced sentences as mere "sentencing factors" was not resolved until after I retired from the Court. In *Alleyne* v. *United States*,[57] the Court held that facts that increase a defendant's mandatory minimum sentence must be submitted to the jury and found beyond a reasonable doubt. In a footnote, however, the Court approved a continuing exception to that rule:

---

55. *Ibid.*
56. *Almendarez-Torres* v. *United States,* 523 U.S. 224 (1998).
57. 570 U.S. 99 (2013).

Under *Almendarez-Torres,* the fact of a prior conviction still does not need to be found by the jury in order to enhance a sentence.

On April 14, 1998, the date that Virginia had scheduled the execution of Angel Francisco Breard, a citizen of Paraguay who had been convicted of murder, our Court issued an unsigned per curiam opinion denying applications for a stay of execution filed by the defendant and Paraguayan officials.[58] The applicants correctly alleged that Virginia had violated the Vienna Convention on Consular Relations by failing to advise Breard that he had a right to notify the Paraguayan consulate of his arrest. The per curiam opinion explained why there were procedural obstacles to considering the stay applications even if the treaty violation might otherwise have merited relief. Ruth Ginsburg, Steve Breyer, and I each wrote brief dissents. Among the points that Steve and I both made was that Virginia had scheduled the execution on a date over a month before the expiration of the ninety-day period that our rules allowed for the defendant to file his petition for certiorari from the lower court's decision denying his first application for habeas corpus relief. I concluded my dissent with this point:

> There is no compelling reason for refusing to follow the procedures that we have adopted for the orderly disposition of noncapital cases. Indeed, the international aspects of this case provide an additional reason for adhering to our established Rules and procedures. I would therefore grant the applications for a stay, and I respectfully dissent from the decision to act hastily rather than with the deliberation that is appropriate in a case of this character.[59]

Chief Justice Rehnquist assigned to me the task of writing the opinion for the Court in *Miller* v. *Albright;*[60] in the end, however, only he joined

---

58. *Breard* v. *Greene,* 523 U.S. 371 (1998).
59. *Id.,* at 380.
60. 523 U.S. 420 (1998).

my draft. The case raised the question whether the petitioner, who was born on June 20, 1970, in the Philippines, was an American citizen. Her birth certificate identified her mother as a Filipino national and described her birth as "illegitimate"; spaces on the form referring to the name and nationality of the father were blank. She grew up and received her high school and college education in the Philippines. At least until after her twenty-first birthday, she never lived in the United States.

Petitioner's father, Charlie Miller, was an American citizen residing in Texas who was stationed in the Philippines at the time of petitioner's conception but apparently had returned to the United States before petitioner was born. In 1992 he filed a petition in a Texas court, which entered a decree providing that Miller's biological relationship with petitioner created the same parent-child relationship as if the child had been born during marriage. Petitioner then filed an application for citizenship that was denied because she had not been legitimated before reaching the age of eighteen. Section 309(a)(4) of the Immigration and Nationality Act distinguished between the child of a citizen mother and alien father, whose citizenship was established at birth; and the child of a citizen father and alien mother, whose citizenship was not established until the father or the child took certain affirmative steps to confirm their relationship (including legitimation before the child turned 18). Thereafter petitioner and her father sued the secretary of state, arguing that the statute violated their constitutional right to equal treatment.

The district court in Texas dismissed the father's case on the ground that he had no standing, and then, because his daughter did not live in Texas, transferred her case to the District of Columbia where the defendant, Secretary of State Albright, resided. Both the district court and the Court of Appeals for the D.C. Circuit denied relief.

In my affirming opinion for the Court I explained that the interest in "ensuring reliable proof of a biological relationship between the potential citizen and its citizen parent" was a sufficiently important and relevant justification for treating the two classes differently. "The blood relationship to the birth mother is immediately obvious and is typically established by hospital records and birth certificates; the relationship to the unmarried father may often be undisclosed and unrecorded in any contemporary public record. Thus, the requirement that the father make a timely written acknowledgement under oath, or that the child obtain a court adjudication of paternity, produces the rough equivalent of the documentation that is already available to evidence the blood relationship between the mother and child."[61]

Sandra O'Connor, in a separate opinion joined by Tony Kennedy, concluded that petitioner did not have standing to challenge the statute's differential treatment between fathers and mothers, because the citizen father had been dismissed from the suit and the statute did not discriminate against petitioner herself based on gender. Thus, petitioner could only challenge the statute's discrimination between illegitimate children of citizen fathers and those of citizen mothers. Although Sandra did not think my opinion would support a rule that discriminated against the plaintiff because of her gender, it did provide a rational basis for treating her differently from an illegitimate male. Nino Scalia, joined by Clarence Thomas, also concurred in the result, but on the ground that regardless of the merits of her claim, the petitioner could not prevail because federal courts have no power to confer citizenship on a basis not prescribed by Congress.

David Souter, Ruth Ginsburg, and Stephen Breyer dissented for reasons stated in opinions written by Ruth and Stephen. Ruth's opinion described a history of rules pertaining to the acquisition of citizenship for children born abroad that revealed that most of our laws dealing with the transmission of citizenship from parent to child discriminated adversely against citizen mothers rather than citizen fathers. Steve's opinion focused more directly on the facts of the case, emphasizing that the statute required a citizen father to agree to provide financial support for the child until he or she reached the age of eighteen, whereas no similar burden was imposed on the citizen mother. Congress's assumption of a far greater probability that the mother would have custody of the child

---

61. 523 U.S., at 436.

presumably explained why Congress thought it unnecessary to require the mother to make a similar undertaking.

Reflection about the basic problem presented by the case leaves me puzzled about an issue that is not mentioned in any of our lengthy opinions. We all agreed that citizenship may only be acquired at birth or by naturalization (which of course was not an option in this case, in which it was undisputed that the petitioner had become an American citizen when she was born if either of her parents was then a citizen). We also all agreed that the record contained credible and undisputed evidence that she was the child of an American father. My opinion contained an acceptable explanation for a gender-based distinction between the testimony of fathers and mothers of children born out of wedlock. But it nevertheless failed to explain why we refused to recognize that Lorelyn Miller was in fact an American citizen.

In 1834 the states of New York and New Jersey entered into a compact providing that Ellis Island, then only three acres in size and located on New Jersey's side of its common boundary with New York in New York Harbor, was a part of New York. After 1891, when the United States decided to use the Island to receive immigrants coming to the states, the federal government began placing fill around the island, and over the next forty-two years that fill added over twenty-four acres to the original tiny island. In 1993 New Jersey filed an original action in our Court asking us to hold that the filled land added to the island was a part of New Jersey and only the original three-acre portion of the island belonged to New York. David Souter, joined by Chief Justice Rehnquist, Sandra O'Connor, Tony Kennedy, Ruth Ginsburg, and Steve Breyer, wrote a scholarly opinion ruling for New Jersey.[62] Steve, joined by Ruth, wrote a brief concurring opinion noting that many of us have parents or grandparents who had landed as immigrants at "Ellis Island, New York" and acknowledging that when the case was argued he had assumed that history would support his belief that Ellis Island was part of New York. The

---

62. See *New Jersey v. New York*, 523 U.S. 767 (1998).

evidence discussed in detail in Souter's forty-five-page opinion, however, convinced him that the filled portions of Ellis Island belonged to New Jersey.

In my dissent I noted that all interested parties had shared a belief for over sixty years that the filled portions as well as the original three acres of Ellis Island were part of New York. I therefore thought New York had acquired the power to govern the entire island under the property doctrine of prescription, which applies when a claimant takes action to acquire ownership and the owner fails to protest. I wrote:

> With all respect, I am persuaded that the Court's contrary conclusion rests on a hypertechnical focus on detail that overlooked the significance of the record as a whole. What I believe was apparent to virtually everyone in New York and New Jersey, as well as to the millions of immigrants who entered our melting pot through the Ellis Island Gateway during the early part of this century, is somehow obscured in a voluminous trial record. The implausibility of the Court's conclusion is underscored by the strange boundary lines that it has decreed.

> Instead of the entire Island constituting an enclave within the borders of New Jersey, now New York's share of the Island is an enclave within New Jersey's share of the Island. The new state line intersects three buildings — the Main Building, the Baggage and Dormitory Building, and the Boathouse Building. Thin strips of New Jersey's sovereign territory separate New York from the ferry slip where boats operated by the City of New York have been delivering millions of visitors annually. By ending New York's sovereignty over a large portion of the ferry slip in front of the Main Building, well short of the slip's seawall, the decree denies New York access to, and control over, the area of land most intimately and functionally connected to the operation of the Main Building. The Master correctly stated that this result is "neither just nor fair to New York."

In my opinion it is not only the bizarre boundary that is unfair to New York. It is the failure to draw the commonsense inference that neither state could have contemplated such a bizarre division of the Island during the prescriptive period that lasted over 60 years. During that entire period both States most certainly treated Ellis Island as part of a single State. Unquestionably, that State was New York.[63]

Nino Scalia agreed with my conclusion, though he did not think the property doctrine of prescription was the applicable rationale. Instead, he believed that, although the 1834 compact was ambiguous as to the status of the filled island, its meaning was revealed by the later conduct of the parties in treating the island as part of New York.

Under the Railway Labor Act, employees of a common carrier who are not members of the established union may be charged an "agency fee," consisting of their fair share of union expenditures related to collective bargaining. The fee is designed to mitigate the problem of free riders who benefit from the union's representative function but avoid contributing to it.

A similar rule applies to public employees and unions. In *Chicago Teachers Union* v. *Hudson*,[64] I wrote a unanimous opinion, elaborating that rule by holding that the First Amendment requires unions and employers to provide procedural protections for nonunion employees who object to the calculation of the agency fee. Employees must receive sufficient information to gauge the propriety of the fee; objectors must have "a reasonably prompt opportunity to challenge the amount of the fee before an impartial decisionmaker"; and any amount of the fee reasonably contested must be held in escrow while the challenge is pending.[65]

In *Air Line Pilots Association* v. *Miller*,[66] the Court assumed that the procedural requirements articulated in *Hudson* applied equally to union

---

63. 523 U.S., at 828–29.
64. 475 U.S. 292 (1986).
65. *Id.*, at 303, 306, 310.
66. 523 U.S. 866 (1998).

relations governed by the Railway Labor Act. Some pilots had objected to the agency fee being charged by the Air Line Pilots Association Union, and had challenged the amount in federal court. An overlapping set of objecting pilots also filed complaints about the fee calculation with the union directly, which the union referred to arbitration pursuant to its own internal policies. After the arbitrator issued his decision (which sustained the agency fee in substantial part), the union moved for summary judgment in the federal court action, which the district court granted, although the D.C. Circuit reversed.

We granted certiorari to address whether an employee who objects to the agency fee must exhaust a union-provided arbitration process before bringing a challenge in federal court. A majority of the Court held that the objectors could turn immediately to the courts, explaining that the nonmember employees had never consented to arbitration and defending the validity of their countervailing election of federal court as the forum in which to bring their challenge.

Stephen Breyer wrote a dissent, which only I joined. Under our view, initial nonbinding arbitration was surely a permissible way to satisfy the requirements of *Hudson,* which said simply that the objectors must have a "prompt" way to challenge the fee "before an impartial decisionmaker."[67] As a practical matter, arbitration would lower the union's costs for resolving fee disputes, would not prejudice the objecting employees' interests (especially because their disputed fees would remain in escrow during the pendency of arbitration), and could even help reduce the burden on the courts if the arbitration yielded a satisfactory result for the parties. The dissent explained that the majority was too easily swayed by the fact that the objecting employees had not expressly consented to the arbitration procedure. That should not have been determinative; instead, the key point was that an "arbitration first" rule was a satisfactory means of implementing the mandate established in *Hudson.*

---

67. See *Hudson,* 475 U.S., at 306.

*   *   *

Title IX of the Education Amendments of 1972 provides, "No person in the United States shall, on the basis of sex, be excluded from participation in, be denied the benefits of, or be subjected to discrimination under any education program or activity receiving Federal financial assistance." The statute does not, however, expressly authorize a private right of action by a person injured by a violation of the provision. Nevertheless, in an opinion that I authored in 1979, we held that the legislative history of Title IX indicated that Congress intended to authorize a private remedy for a person excluded from participating in a federally funded program on the basis of sex.[68] In a later case in which Byron White, who had dissented in that case, wrote the opinion for the Court, we held that monetary damages are available in such an action.[69] But then, in a five-to-four decision in 1998, the Court held that a high school student could not recover damages from her school for sexual abuse by a teacher because no official with authority to take corrective action had actual notice of the teacher's misconduct.[70]

The majority's holding was inconsistent with the government's interpretation of Title IX, which simply adhered to a well-settled rule of agency law. As I argued in my dissent, "The reason why the common law [of agency] imposes liability on the principal in such circumstances is the same as the reason why Congress included the prohibition against discrimination on the basis of sex in Title IX: to induce school boards to adopt and enforce practices that will minimize the danger that students will be exposed to such odious behavior. The rule that the Court has crafted creates the opposite incentive."[71]

I was in the majority in another five-to-four decision, and had the opportunity to assign a Court opinion to Clarence Thomas. The case involved Hosep Bajakajian, who attempted to leave the country without reporting,

---

68. *Cannon* v. *University of Chicago,* 441 U.S. 677 (1979).
69. *Franklin* v. *Gwinnett County Public Schools,* 503 U.S. 60 (1992).
70. *Gebser* v. *Lago Vista Independent School Dist.,* 524 U.S. 274 (1998).
71. *Id.,* at 300.

as required by federal law, that he was transporting more than $10,000 in currency. Federal law also provides that a person convicted of violating this reporting requirement shall forfeit the unreported cash to the government. The case raised the novel question whether the forfeiture of $357,144 was an excessive fine prohibited by the Eighth Amendment.[72]

After a bench trial, the district court found that Bajakajian was transporting the funds for the purpose of paying a lawful debt and that the unreported funds were not connected to any other crime. He failed to make the required report because of fear stemming from "cultural differences"; he had grown up as a member of the Armenian minority in Syria and had developed a "distrust for the Government."[73] Although the judge noted that the statute mandated a forfeiture of the entire $357,144, he concluded that such forfeiture would be "extraordinarily harsh" and therefore violate the constitutional ban on excessive fines.[74] The Court of Appeals for the Ninth Circuit affirmed and our Court granted the government's petition for certiorari.

Clarence wrote a straightforward opinion concluding that the forfeiture clearly qualified as punishment and that it was excessive. Tony Kennedy, writing for the four dissenters, authored the first opinion of any of the thirteen judges reviewing the case concluding that the forfeiture was not excessive. He emphasized the fact that the respondent had repeatedly lied about the concealed funds, and that the decision created a precedent that would enable drug traffickers and money launderers to avoid appropriate punishment for their crimes.

The Line Item Veto Act became effective on January 1, 1997. The act gave the president the authority to cancel certain spending and tax benefit measures after he signed them into law. During the 1997 term, the Court reviewed an initial challenge to the act, but did not reach the question of its validity. The day after the act's passage, six members of Congress who had voted against it brought suit challenging its constitutionality. The district

---

72. *United States* v. *Bajakajian,* 524 U.S. 321 (1998).
73. *Id.,* at 326.
74. *Ibid.*

court accepted the challenge, but on direct appeal we determined that the plaintiffs had not alleged a sufficiently concrete injury to establish standing and therefore reversed.[75] I dissented because I thought the statute established a procedure for the enactment of laws that were "truncated versions" of bills passed by Congress and signed by the president; if it were valid, the act deprived every member of Congress of the right to vote for or against the truncated measures that would become law.[76] I thought it clear that the deprivation of the right of members of Congress to vote on the final text of federal laws, which is guaranteed by the text of the Constitution, not only sufficed to establish their standing, but also led to the conclusion that the act was invalid.

Less than two months after our decision on standing, President Clinton exercised his line-item veto authority by canceling one provision in the Balanced Budget Act of 1997 and two provisions in the Taxpayer Relief Act of 1997. The provision of the Balanced Budget Act had permitted New York to retain the benefit of a large tax settlement with the federal government, and the provisions of the Taxpayer Relief Act had permitted food refiners and processors to defer the recognition of any capital gains if they sold their stock to eligible farmers' cooperatives. New York clearly had standing to object to the cancellation of an extremely large contingent liability, but the government argued that the statute, which used the word "individual" rather than "person" to identify a litigant authorized to file a direct appeal in our Court, did not include New York. As to the change to the Taxpayer Relief Act, the government argued that the loss of a possible tax benefit to purchasers of facilities from cooperatives was too speculative to confer standing on the sellers. Over Nino Scalia's dissent, we rejected both of those arguments and, without expressing any opinion about the wisdom of the cancellation procedures authorized by the Line Item Veto Act, held that they violated Article I, Section 7 of the Constitution.[77]

In my opinion for the Court, I repeated what I had said in my earlier

75. *Raines* v. *Byrd,* 521 U.S. 811 (1997).
76. *Id.,* at 835.
77. *Clinton* v. *City of New York,* 524 U.S. 417 (1998).

dissent. "In both legal and practical effect, the President has amended two Acts of Congress by repealing a portion of each."[78]

I went on to explain why I thought this action violated our constitutional structure:

> There is no provision in the Constitution that authorizes the President to enact, to amend, or to repeal statutes.... There are powerful reasons for construing constitutional silence on this profoundly important issue as equivalent to an express prohibition. The procedures governing the enactment of statutes set forth in the text of Article I were the product of the great debates and compromises that produced the Constitution itself. Familiar historical materials provide abundant support for the conclusion that the power to enact statutes may only "be exercised in accord with a single, finely wrought and exhaustively considered, procedure." *INS* v. *Chadha*, 462 U.S. 919, 951 (1983). Our first President understood the text of the Presentment Clause as requiring that he either "approve the parts of a Bill, or reject it in toto." What has emerged in these cases from the President's exercise of his statutory cancellation powers, however, are truncated versions of two Bills that passed both Houses of Congress. They are not the product of the "finely wrought" procedure that the Framers designed.[79]

Over the years I have frequently bragged about the quality of my law clerks. I am convinced that I have had better success in selecting clerks than any of my colleagues. They are not only especially good lawyers, but, even more importantly, they are uniformly nice people who are enjoyable company in good times and bad. Characteristically, in 1997, under the leadership of Skip Paul, Doug Winthrop, and Larry Marshall, my clerks created the John Paul Stevens Fellowship Foundation to finance awards

---

78. *Id.,* at 438.
79. *Id.,* at 439–40.

that support law students who spend their summer working in unpaid public interest internships. The awards not only finance the scholars' summer work but also have a positive effect on their later career choices. The program started at Northwestern and almost immediately expanded to include the law schools at Santa Clara and Stanford; many other leading law schools in the country now also participate.

October Term 1998

On December 19, 1998, for only the second time in history, the House of Representatives voted to impeach the president of the United States. As required by Article I, Section 3 of the Constitution, Chief Justice Rehnquist presided over the Senate's impeachment trial of Bill Clinton. Other than adding to the chief's workload, those proceedings did not affect our work at the Court. Based on my memory of conversations with him at the time, which included comments on some of the senators' obvious lack of trial experience and the fact that he did not have any difficult issues to resolve, I think he enjoyed his role. As was true of his conduct during oral arguments in our Court, he was a good presiding officer. Perhaps because political considerations had a greater impact on the senators' votes than the merits of specific charges, the Republican prosecutors fell far short of obtaining the necessary two-thirds vote required to convict.

Also early in the October 1998 term, Nino Scalia and I wrote opposing opinions in a case presenting the question whether a then recent amendment to the federal statute prohibiting carjacking "with the intent to cause death or serious bodily harm" required the government to prove that the defendant had an unconditional intent to kill or harm in all events, or whether it merely required proof of an intent to kill or harm if necessary to effect a carjacking.[80] The Court decided that the conditional intent was sufficient, stating, "[T]he question is whether a person who points a gun at a driver, having decided to pull the trigger if

---

80. *Holloway* v. *United States,* 526 U.S. 1, 3 (1999).

the driver does not comply with a demand for the car keys, possesses the intent, at that moment, to seriously harm the driver. In our view, the answer to that question does not depend on whether the driver immediately hands over the keys or what the offender decides to do after he gains control of the car. At the relevant moment, the offender plainly does have the forbidden intent."[81]

The dissenter thought the plain text of the statute required proof of an unconditional intent to kill or harm the driver even if he complied with the offender's demand. Alternatively, the dissenter argued that even if the text was not clear, the rule of lenity required the Court to accept the defendant's construction of an ambiguous criminal statute. The majority rejected that argument in a footnote confining the rule of lenity to cases of true ambiguity.[82] I authored the pro-prosecution opinion for the Court, and Nino wrote the defendant-friendly dissent.

California is not only one of the largest, most populated, and most beautiful states in the nation; it is also one of the most generous. Like all other states, California has participated in several welfare programs authorized by the Social Security Act and partially funded by the federal government. Its programs, however, traditionally provide a higher level of benefits and serve more needy citizens than those of most other states. In 1992 California's monthly cash benefit for a mother and child was $456 a month whereas in the neighboring state of Arizona it was only $275. In that year the state of California enacted an amendment to its welfare code limiting benefits for new residents for their first year of residence to the amount that they would have received in the state of their prior residence.

Three mothers who had recently moved to California from Louisiana, Oklahoma, and Colorado to live with relatives to escape family abuse challenged the constitutionality of the California statute. The former

---

81. *Id.*, at 6–7.
82. See *id.*, at 12n14.

residents of Louisiana and Oklahoma, each of whom had two children, would receive $190 and $341 respectively for a family of three even though the full California grant was $641; the former resident of Colorado, who had just one child, received $280 a month as opposed to the full California grant of $504 for a family of two. District Judge David Levi upheld the challenge, the Court of Appeals for the Ninth Circuit affirmed, and we granted the state's petition for certiorari. Amendments to the law prevented us from deciding the issue in that case, but another case presenting the same issue and decided by the same judge arose in the 1998 term, and we upheld the ruling of the lower courts.[83]

In my opinion for the Court I relied on the "right to travel" which, as discussed in our earlier cases, embraced at least three different components. It protected the right of a citizen of one state to enter and to leave another state, the right to be treated as a welcome visitor rather than an unfriendly alien when temporarily present in another state, and, for those travelers who elect to become permanent residents, the right to be treated like other citizens of that state. It was the third component of the right to travel that was at issue in *Saenz*. That component had always been protected by the Privileges or Immunities Clause of the Fourteenth Amendment.

The state's discriminatory scheme could be understood in the following way: The favored class of beneficiaries included all eligible citizens who had resided in California for at least a year, plus those new arrivals who last resided in either another country or a state with more generous welfare benefits than California. Within the broad category of new arrivals who were treated less favorably, there were many smaller classes, as each individual's benefits were determined by the law of the state from whence they came. To justify its discrimination, the state really had to explain not only why it was sound fiscal policy to discriminate against the entire class of new arrivals but also why it was permissible to apply such a variety of rules within that class.

---

83. *Saenz* v. *Roe,* 526 U.S. 489 (1999).

JUSTICE JOHN PAUL STEVENS

Disavowing any desire to fence out the indigent, California simply argued that its multi-tiered scheme was justified by its saving about $10.9 million a year, which equated to about seventy-two cents per month for every beneficiary. We did not evaluate the strength of that justification, but rejected it as foreclosed by the language in the Citizenship Clause of the Fourteenth Amendment, which states: "All persons born or naturalized in the United States, and subject to the jurisdiction thereof, are citizens of the United States and of the state wherein they reside." The Court had already recognized that the Clause "does not provide for, and does not allow for degrees of citizenship based on length of residence."[84] It was equally clear to us that the Citizenship Clause would "not tolerate a hierarchy of 45 subclasses of similarly situated citizens based on the location of their prior residence."[85] The bottom line was that the state's legitimate interest in saving money did not justify a decision to discriminate among equally eligible citizens.

In his dissent, joined by Clarence Thomas, the chief justice argued that the state's need to ensure that only persons who establish a bona fide residence receive the benefits provided to current residents — which justified imposing a one-year residence requirement on the college students' eligibility for in-state tuition rates at state universities, or on married couples' eligibility for a divorce — should also justify a durational residence requirement for welfare benefits. In my opinion for the Court, however, I had rebutted that argument:

> It is undisputed that respondents and the members of the class they represent are citizens of California and that their need for welfare benefits is unrelated to the length of time that they have resided in California. We thus have no occasion to consider what weight might be given to a citizen's length of residence if the bona fides of her claim to state citizenship were questioned. Moreover, because whatever

---

84. 526 U.S., at 506, quoting *Zobel* v. *Williams,* 457 U.S. 55, 69 (1982).
85. *Id.,* at 506–7.

benefits they receive will be consumed in California, there is no danger that recognition of their claim will encourage citizens of other States to establish residency for just long enough to acquire some readily portable benefit, such as a divorce or college education, that will be enjoyed after they return to their original domicile.[86]

In 1992 the Attorney General of the United States approved "Operation Gunsmoke," a special national fugitive apprehension program in which U.S. Marshals worked with state and local police to apprehend dangerous criminals. The operation concentrated on armed individuals who were wanted for serious violent offenses, and it ultimately led to over 3,000 arrests in forty metropolitan areas. One individual targeted by the program was Dominic Wilson, the son of Charles and Geraldine Wilson, residents of Rockville, Maryland. Three warrants for the son listed his parents' home as his address.

In the early morning hours of April 16, 1992, a Gunsmoke team of U.S. Marshals and Montgomery County police officers assembled to execute the warrants. The marshals had invited a *Washington Post* reporter and a photographer to accompany them as a part of a "ride-along" program that the Marshals Service had developed to promote a better understanding of their work. They arrived and entered the parents' home while they were still in bed. Dominic was not present so they were unable to execute the warrants. They did, however, have a skirmish with his father that was witnessed and photographed by *Post* employees. The newspaper did not publish any of the pictures taken by its employee.

The Wilsons sued both the state officers and the federal marshals, seeking damages for law enforcement having invited the *Washington Post* employees to invade the privacy of their home. Their case raised two issues: whether the "media ride-along" violated the Fourth Amendment; and if so, whether they could recover damages from the officers. The answer to the first question was easy. We unanimously agreed that the "centuries-old principle of respect for the privacy of the home" provided

---

86. *Id.*, at 489, 505.

the correct answer: "[I]t is a violation of the Fourth Amendment for police to bring members of the media or other third parties into a home during the execution of a warrant when the presence of the third parties in the home was not in aid of execution of the warrant."[87]

The answer to the second question was less clear because a plaintiff may not recover damages from a public officer's violation of a constitutional right unless the right was clearly established at the time of the violation, and we had not previously decided any cases involving media ride-alongs. In his opinion for the Court, the chief concluded that the issue was sufficiently doubtful to support a holding that the officers were entitled to qualified immunity, especially since agency booklets describing ride-alongs did not caution against allowing press representatives to enter private homes. Eight members of the Court joined his entire opinion, but I dissented from his discussion of qualified immunity. I concluded my dissent with these two paragraphs:

> The most disturbing aspect of the Court's ruling on the qualified immunity issue is its reliance on a document discussing "ride-alongs" apparently prepared by an employee in the public relations office of the United States Marshals Service. The text of the document, portions of which are set out in an appendix, makes it quite clear that its author was not a lawyer, but rather a person concerned with developing the proper public image of the Service, with a special interest in creating a favorable impression with the Congress. Although the document occupies 14 pages in the joint appendix and suggests handing out free Marshals Service T-shirts and caps to "grease the skids," it contains no discussion of the conditions which must be satisfied before a news-person may be authorized to enter private property during the execution of a warrant. App. 12. There are guidelines about how officers should act and speak in front of the camera, and the document does indicate that "the camera" should not enter a private home until a "signal" is given.

---

87. *Wilson* v. *Layne,* 526 U.S. 603, 610, 614 (1999).

Id., at 7. It does not, however, purport to give any guidance to the marshals regarding when such a signal should be given, whether it should ever be given without the consent of the homeowner, or indeed on how to carry out any part of their law enforcement mission. The notion that any member of that well-trained cadre of professionals would rely on such a document for guidance in the performance of dangerous law enforcement assignments is too far-fetched to merit serious consideration.

The defense of qualified immunity exists to protect reasonable officers from personal liability for official actions later found to be in violation of constitutional rights that were not clearly established. The conduct in this case, as the Court itself reminds us, contravened the Fourth Amendment's core protection of the home. In shielding this conduct as if it implicated only the unsettled margins of our jurisprudence, the Court today authorized one free violation of the well-established rule it reaffirms.[88]

After extensive hearings conducted in 1992, the Chicago City Council enacted the Gang Concentration Ordinance, which prohibited "criminal street gang members" from "loitering" with one another or with other persons in any public place. In *Chicago* v. *Morales,*[89] we granted the city's petition for certiorari to decide whether the Illinois Supreme Court had correctly held that the ordinance violated the Due Process Clause of the Fourteenth Amendment.

The ordinance created a criminal offense that included four elements: First, a police officer must reasonably believe that one of two or more persons present in a "public place" is a "criminal street gang member"; second, the persons must be "loitering," which the ordinance defined as "remaining in any one place with no apparent purpose"; third, the officer

88. *Id.,* at 624–25.
89. 527 U.S. 41 (1999).

must then order all of the persons present to disperse themselves from the area; and fourth, a person must disobey the order. During three years of enforcement the police issued over 89,000 dispersal orders and arrested over 42,000 people for violating the ordinance. In the ensuing enforcement proceedings, only two trial judges had upheld the ordinance, while eleven others ruled that it was invalid. One of those eleven judges explained that it failed "to notify individuals what conduct is prohibited, and it encourages arbitrary and capricious enforcement by police."[90]

The state courts both agreed that the ordinance was unconstitutional. The city, represented by its corporation counsel, Larry Rosenthal, one of my former law clerks, then sought review in our Court. His petition for certiorari asked us to review two questions: (1) Whether a loitering ordinance authorizing the arrest of persons who have disobeyed a police order to move on, given when an officer has reasonable cause to believe a group of loiterers contains a member of a street gang, is impermissibly vague in violation of due process guarantees; (2) whether, despite legislative findings about the deleterious effects of loitering by criminal street gangs, an ordinance that requires a group of loiterers containing criminal street gang members to obey a police order to move on violates substantive due process guarantees.

The obvious importance of the case led my law clerk Ben Powell to write an eleven-page memorandum recommending that I vote to grant the petition. Despite the persuasive arguments in that memo and in Larry's petition, I was one of the five justices who voted to deny. The chief justice and Nino Scalia, Sandra O'Connor, and Clarence Thomas, however, voted to grant the petition. After argument, three of those justices — the chief, Nino, and Clarence — voted to uphold the ordinance. Sandra, however, joined the rest of us in concluding that the ordinance was unconstitutionally vague. With the chief in dissent, I assigned the majority opinion to myself.

David and Ruth joined all six parts of my draft, but Sandra, Tony, and

90. *Id.*, at 49–50.

Stephen each wrote separate concurrences and did not join the two parts of my opinion discussing the fact that the freedom to loiter for innocent purposes is part of the "liberty" protected by the Due Process Clause. The dissenters interpreted that discussion as equivalent to a holding that the ordinance was invalid on substantive due process grounds.[91] In fact, it was merely part of my explanation for approving a facial challenge to the law and concluding that the entire ordinance failed to give the ordinary citizen adequate notice of what is forbidden and what is permitted. In particular, I noted the ordinance's lack of clarity about what a loiterer was required to do in order to comply. I asked: "After such an order [from the police, requiring dispersal] issues, how long must the loiterers remain apart? How far must they move? If each loiterer walks around the block and they meet again at the same location, are they subject to arrest or merely to being ordered to disperse again?"[92] I explained: "Lack of clarity in the description of the loiterer's duty to obey a dispersal order... buttress[es] our conclusion that the entire ordinance fails to give the ordinary citizen adequate notice of what is forbidden and what is permitted."[93]

In Part V of my opinion, which all of the justices who voted to affirm joined, I stated in express terms that the "broad sweep of the ordinance also violates 'the requirement that a legislature establish minimum guidelines to govern law enforcement.' "[94]

In their concurring opinions, Sandra, Tony, and Stephen pointed out that the constitutionality of the ordinance might have been saved if the Illinois Supreme Court had construed its text more narrowly but, as Steve concluded, "*this* ordinance... cannot be constitutionally applied to anyone."[95]

Nino and Clarence filed dissenting opinions. Clarence's writing, joined by both Nino and the chief, concludes with this paragraph:

---

91. See, e.g., 527 U.S., at 85–86 (Scalia, J., dissenting).
92. *Id.*, at 59.
93. *Ibid.*
94. *Id.*, at 60.
95. *Id.*, at 73.

Today, the Court focuses extensively on the "rights" of gang members and their companions. It can safely do so — the people who will have to live with the consequences of today's opinion do not live in our neighborhoods. Rather, the people who will suffer from our lofty pronouncements are people like Ms. Susan Mary Jackson; people who have seen their neighborhoods literally destroyed by gangs and violence and drugs. They are good, decent people who must struggle to overcome their desperate situation, against all odds, in order to raise their families, earn a living, and remain good citizens. As one resident described: "There is only about maybe one or two percent of the people in the city causing these problems maybe, but it's keeping 98 percent of us in our houses and off the streets and afraid to shop." By focusing exclusively on the imagined "rights" of the two percent, the Court today has denied our most vulnerable citizens the very thing that JUSTICE STEVENS elevates above all else — the "freedom of movement." And that is a shame. I respectfully dissent.[96]

The two petitioners in *Sutton* v. *United Air Lines, Inc.,*[97] were twin sisters presumably qualified to serve as commercial airline pilots who were denied employment because they needed to wear eyeglasses or contact lenses when flying. They claimed that United's policy violated the Americans with Disabilities Act of 1990 (ADA). Their case presented the question whether a disability determination under the ADA must be made with reference to measures that mitigate the individual's impairment. Without their glasses the Sutton twins were unquestionably disabled.

Each of the three executive agencies charged with implementing the ADA had consistently interpreted it as mandating that the presence of disability turns on an individual's uncorrected state. Eight of the nine federal courts of appeals to address the issue had reached the same

---

96. *Id.,* at 114–15 (internal citations omitted).
97. 527 U.S. 471 (1999).

conclusion. The legislative history discussed in the dissenting opinions that Steve Breyer and I wrote provided abundant support for that result. Nevertheless both Sandra's opinion for the Court and Ruth's brief concurrence concluded that a contrary result was compelled by the fact that Congress had made a finding that "some 43,000,000 Americans have one or more physical or mental disabilities, and this number is increasing as the population as a whole is growing older."[98] "Had Congress intended to include all persons with corrected physical limitations among those covered by the Act, it undoubtedly would have cited a much higher number of disabled persons in the findings."[99]

Our dissents analogized, however, to the *Oncale* case decided during the preceding term, in which the Court held that Title VII covered claims of same-sex sexual harassment. There, as in *Sutton,* I thought the governing principle was that "statutory prohibitions often go beyond the principal evil that concerned the enacting Congress to cover comparable evils, and it is ultimately the provisions of our laws rather than the principal concerns of our legislators by which we are governed."[100] On that basis, my conclusion seemed quite defensible: "So long as an employer makes a decision based on an impairment that is substantially limiting, it matters not under the structure of the Act whether the impairment is widely shared or so rare that it is seriously misunderstood."[101]

As I noted in an earlier chapter, apart from the five cases involving the constitutionality of the death penalty, the most important case decided in my first term was *National League of Cities* v. *Usery.*[102] In that five-to-four decision, the Court held unconstitutional an amendment to the Fair Labor Standards Act (FLSA) that subjected state employees to the FLSA's coverage. A few years later, Harry Blackmun changed his

98. *Id.,* at 485.
99. *Id.,* at 487.
100. *Id.,* at 505–6.
101. *Id.,* at 507.
102. 426 U.S. 833 (1976).

mind, and in *Garcia* v. *San Antonio Metropolitan Transit Authority*[103] the Court overruled *National League of Cities.* The issue in both cases was the constitutionality of the FLSA amendment; in neither did any justice question the plaintiffs' right to sue the state agency to enforce the statute.

In 1999, however, in *Alden* v. *Maine,*[104] the Court announced one of the most profound changes in the law in the Court's history, holding that the doctrine of sovereign immunity barred an action brought against the state of Maine by a group of its probation officers to recover certain compensation mandated by the overtime provisions of the FLSA. By a five-to-four vote in what I still regard as one of the least wise decisions in our history, the Court found that a sovereign state could claim immunity from federal law.

Tony Kennedy authored the majority opinion; David Souter wrote the dissent. David not only repeated much of the debate from *Chisholm* v. *Georgia,*[105] but also discussed the various interpretations of the Eleventh Amendment that the Court had endorsed over the years (interpretations most often at odds with the amendment's plain text), the anomaly of assuming that the framers embraced a doctrine of sovereign immunity in a democratic society, and the lack of either scholarly support or wise reasoning for the position the Court has endorsed. David concluded his dissent with the following paragraph:

> The Court has swung back and forth with regrettable disruption on the enforceability of the FLSA against the States, but if the present majority had a defensible position one could at least accept its decision with an expectation of stability ahead. As it is, any such expectation would be naïve. The resemblance of today's state sovereign immunity to the *Lochner* era's industrial due process is striking. The Court began this century by imputing immutable

---

103. 469 U.S. 528, 557 (1985).
104. 527 U.S. 706.
105. 2 Dall. 419 (1793).

constitutional status to a conception of economic self-reliance that was never true to industrial life and grew insistently fictional with the years, and the Court has chosen to close the century by conferring like status on a conception of state sovereign immunity that is true neither to history nor to the structure of the Constitution. I expect the Court's late essay into immunity doctrine will prove the equal of its earlier experiment in laissez-faire, the one being as unrealistic as the other, as indefensible, and probably as flecting.[106]

October Term 1999

Early in the 1999 term, the Court issued an opinion applying *Alden* to three sets of Florida state employees seeking recovery for alleged violations of the Age Discrimination Act.[107] Answering two questions, the majority first held that Congress clearly intended to abrogate the states' sovereign immunity, but then, despite our contrary holding seventeen years earlier in *EEOC* v. *Wyoming*,[108] concluded that neither the Commerce Clause nor Section 1 of the Fourteenth Amendment gave Congress the power to do so. Writing on behalf of the four dissenters, I argued that the Court was incorrectly treating the judiciary as the primary guardian of state interests, rather than the Congress, in which all states are represented. I wrote,

> The application of the ancient judge-made doctrine of sovereign immunity in cases like these is supposedly justified as a freestanding limit on congressional authority, a limit necessary to protect States' dignity and respect from impairment by the National Government. The Framers did not, however, select the Judicial Branch as the constitutional guardian of those state interests. Rather, the Framers designed important structural safeguards to ensure that

---

106. 527 U.S., at 814.
107. See *Kimel* v. *Florida Bd. of Regents*, 528 U.S. 62 (2000).
108. 460 U.S. 226 (1983).

when the National Government enacted substantive law (and provided for its enforcement), the normal operation of the legislative process itself would adequately defend state interests from undue infringement.

It is the Framers' compromise giving each State equal representation in the Senate that provides the principal structural protection for the sovereignty of the several States. The composition of the Senate was originally determined by the legislatures of the States, which would guarantee that their interests could not be ignored by Congress. The Framers also directed that the House be composed of Representatives selected by voters in the several States, the consequence of which is that the States are the strategic yardsticks for the measurement of interest and opinion, the special centers of political activity, the separate geographical determinants of national as well as local politics.

Whenever Congress passes a statute, it does so against the background of state law already in place; the propriety of taking national action is thus measured by the metric of the existing state norms that Congress seeks to supplement or supplant. The persuasiveness of any justification for overcoming legislative inertia and taking national action, either creating new federal obligations or providing for their enforcement, must necessarily be judged in reference to state interests, as expressed in existing state law. The precise scope of federal laws, of course, can be shaped with nuanced attention to state interests. The Congress also has the authority to grant or withhold jurisdiction in lower federal courts. The burden of being haled into a federal forum for the enforcement of federal law, thus, can be expanded or contracted as Congress deems proper, which decision, like all other legislative acts, necessarily contemplates state interests. Thus, Congress can use its broad range of flexible legislative tools to approach the delicate issue of how to balance local and national interests in the most responsive and careful manner. It is quite evident, therefore, that the Framers did not view this Court as the ultimate guardian of the States' interest in protecting their own sovereignty from impairment of burdensome federal laws.[109]

In *Nixon* v. *Shrink Missouri Government PAC*,[110] the Court, relying on its 1976 decision in *Buckley* v. *Valeo,* upheld the constitutionality of a Missouri statute imposing limits on contributions to political candidates. Chief Justice Rehnquist, who was in the majority, assigned the Court opinion to David Souter, who rejected the plaintiffs' argument that intervening decisions had increased the state's burden of justifying such a law, and also rejected the argument from Clarence Thomas, Nino Scalia, and Tony Kennedy that we should overrule *Buckley.* I wrote a concurring opinion responding to the three dissenters in which I made "one simple point. Money is property; it is not speech."[111]

While our Constitution and our heritage properly protect the individual's interest in making decisions about the use of his or her own property, governmental regulations of such decisions are better viewed as possible deprivations of liberty or property protected by the doctrine of substantive due process than as abridgments of speech. The dissenters' treatment of campaign contributions and expenditures as a form of speech misleadingly enhanced the appeal of their arguments. It is perhaps notable that even Chief Justice Rehnquist was unpersuaded by the *Nixon* dissenters.

The federal law by which Hawaii was admitted to the Union and the terms of that state's constitution charge the Office of Hawaiian Affairs (OHA) with managing vast acres of land held in trust for the descendants of the Polynesians who occupied the Hawaiian Islands before the arrival

---

109. *Kimel,* 528 U.S., at 93–95 (citations and internal quotation marks omitted).
110. 528 U.S. 377 (2000).
111. *Id.,* at 398.

of Captain Cook in 1778. OHA is responsible for programs providing special benefits for the Islands' indigenous people, intended to compensate for past wrongs to their ancestors and to preserve the indigenous culture that existed for centuries before Cook's arrival. The state's constitution provides that only "native Hawaiians" — descendants of people inhabiting the Hawaiian Islands in 1778 — are eligible to vote for the nine trustees of OHA.

In *Rice* v. *Cayetano*,[112] a citizen of Hawaii who did not qualify as a "native Hawaiian" challenged that qualification on the right to vote for OHA trustees under the Fourteenth and Fifteenth Amendments. The lower federal courts rejected the challenge. John Roberts, who later became the chief justice, argued in favor of affirmance in our Court, and Ted Olson, an equally effective and successful advocate, made the opposing argument and ultimately persuaded the Court to reverse. Both Tony Kennedy and Stephen Breyer wrote opinions supporting that result. Only Ruth and I wrote opinions supporting what I still regard as a permissible race-based voting qualification. The opinions are of historical interest and serve to remind us that laws providing special benefits to minority races are often difficult to defend.

Originally enacted in 1863, the False Claims Act (FCA) imposes civil liability on "any person" who seeks payment from the federal government of any false or fraudulent claim,[113] and it typically does so through a *qui tam* action in which an individual with knowledge of the false or fraudulent claim brings an action on the government's behalf.

The question in *Vermont Agency of Natural Resources* v. *United States ex rel. Stevens*[114] was whether the state of Vermont could be made a defendant in a *qui tam* action. The district court and the Court of Appeals for the Second Circuit both held that it could, but our Court, over my dissent joined by David Souter, held that a state was not a "person" subject to

---

112. 528 U.S. 495 (2000).
113. 31 U.S.C. § 3279(a).
114. 529 U.S. 765 (2000).

qui tam liability. In my judgment, the majority's holding was yet another product of the Court's recent and increasingly numerous decisions cloaking the states with an increasingly protective mantle of sovereign immunity. It also seemed to me that the majority had incorrectly relied on the presumption that the word "person" should not be construed to include a sovereign. The doctrinal origins of that presumption supported my conclusion that the presumption should only apply to the "enacting sovereign," which, in the case of the FCA, was the federal government.

In *Santa Fe Independent School Dist.* v. *Doe,*[115] Chief Justice Rehnquist and I reacted quite differently to some students and their parents objecting to organized prayer at high school football games.

Prior to 1995, Santa Fe High School had a practice of having a student council chaplain deliver a prayer over the public address system before each home varsity game. Mormon and Catholic students, alumni, and parents filed suit in a federal district court in Texas challenging the practice. While the suit was pending, the school district modified its policy by authorizing two student elections, the first to determine whether "invocations" should be delivered at football games and the second to select the person to deliver them. After the students had decided to continue their prayers and had selected their spokesperson, the district court entered an order limiting the content of their messages. The Court of Appeals for the Fifth Circuit held that, even as modified by the district court, the football prayer policy was invalid. The Court granted cert and, after argument, Sandra, Tony, David, Ruth, Steve, and I voted to affirm; I assigned the majority opinion to myself.

Among the school's defenses of its policies was the claim that prayer served the legitimate purpose of "solemnizing" the event. I found that argument puzzling because I did not regard solemnity as an important characteristic of high school football games. In the first draft of my opinion for the Court, I included these two sentences:

---

115. 530 U.S. 290 (2000).

Apart from the pre-game ceremony itself—which in other athletic contests is traditionally "solemnized" by our National Anthem— solemnity is not a normal characteristic of competitive sporting events. It is true, of course, that things can become pretty solemn for the student body if its team loses game after game, but the Santa Fe policy mandates pre-game solemnity for the entire season no matter how exhilarating the team's winning streak might become for the fans.

In a footnote to those two sentences, I added,

For example, solemnity was the proper mood during Northwestern University's 1944 unsuccessful football season (1–7–1), but in 1948 the fans' prayers were answered when the team qualified to play in the Rose Bowl. The crowd was anything but solemn as "[c]onservative Northwestern...literally stood on its head in a 24-hour Rose Bowl celebration. The festivities were marked by parades, a student "strike," pep rallies, a dance, open houses [and] no classes....More than 3,000 students paraded through Evanston [following] the NU marching band...[and] almost 500 interrupted noon business in the Chicago loop...[by conducting] a snake dance through Marshall Field's. Herb Hart, *Pep Bursts Out All Day,* Daily Northwestern. Nov. 13, 1948, at 1.

Ruth Ginsburg objected to including that footnote in our opinion, correctly noting that the fact that the school policy was intended to solemnize the football games did not necessarily suggest an intent to encourage prayer, and, more importantly, that the footnote might be offensive to "millions of people" who could be expected to have strong emotional reactions hostile to our decision. Ruth's letter was a wise reminder of the importance of showing respect for the views of losing litigants. I, of course, deleted the footnote from the draft.

*   *   *

James Dale entered Scouting when he was eight years old, became an Eagle Scout ten years later, and was approved for a position as assistant scoutmaster about when he entered college. He then first acknowledged to himself and others that he was gay and received publicity as an officer of the Lesbian-Gay Alliance. As a result, the Boy Scouts revoked his adult membership, explaining that they specifically forbid membership to homosexuals. He sued, claiming that his ouster violated New Jersey's public accommodations statute, which prohibits discrimination on the basis of sexual orientation, and both state appellate courts ruled in his favor. Our Court granted the Scouts' petition for cert and by a five-to-four vote reversed.[116] Sandra, Nino, Tony, and Clarence joined Chief Justice Rehnquist's majority opinion; my three other colleagues joined my dissent.

Although some of the Scouts' leaders strongly opposed allowing homosexuals to occupy positions of leadership in their organization, there was little to no evidence that the organization had engaged in vigorous public advocacy for that position, which undermined their claim that complying with the state's antidiscrimination statute imposed a serious burden on the organization's goals. I thought it especially critical that Boy Scouts of America had not "adopt[ed] any clear position on homosexuality," and I criticized the majority's willingness to give near-absolute "deference to an association's assertions regarding the nature of its expression" and regarding "what would impair its expression."[117] At the time I found it difficult to accept the majority's decision; in light of fairly prompt reactions — including the Scouts' own change of policy — the decision seems particularly anachronistic.

The wise words of Justice Louis Brandeis that I quoted at the outset of my dissent are worthy of repetition:

---

116. *Boy Scouts of America* v. *Dale*, 530 U.S. 640 (2000).
117. 530 U.S., at 685–86 (Stevens, J., dissenting).

"To stay experimentation in things social and economic is a grave responsibility. Denial of the right to experiment may be fraught with serious consequences to the Nation. It is one of the happy incidents of the federal system that a single courageous State may, if its citizens choose, serve as a laboratory; and try novel social and economic experiments without risk to the rest of the country. This Court has the power to prevent an experiment. We may strike down the statute which embodies it on the ground that, in our opinion, the measure is arbitrary, capricious or unreasonable. We have power to do this, because the due process clause has been held by the Court applicable to matters of substantive law as well as to matters of procedure. But in the exercise of this high power, we must be ever on our guard, lest we erect our prejudices into legal principles. If we would guide by the light of reason, we must let our minds be bold."[118]

In 1993 Colorado enacted a statute regulating speech-related conduct within one hundred feet of the entrance to a health care facility. In that area it was made unlawful to "knowingly approach" within eight feet of another person, without that person's consent, "for the purpose of passing a leaflet or handbill to, displaying a sign to, or engaging in oral protest, education, or counseling with such other person."[119] The statute prohibited speakers from approaching unwilling listeners but did not require a standing speaker to move away from anyone passing by. Nor did it place any limit on the content of any message that anyone wished to communicate to anyone else. The Colorado Supreme Court upheld the validity of the statute, and we granted certiorari.

While Nino Scalia, Tony Kennedy, and Clarence Thomas voted in favor of invalidating the statute as a violation of the First Amendment rights of individuals who provided "sidewalk counseling" to women entering abortion clinics, the chief justice voted with the majority to uphold the statute. He

---

118. *Id.,* at 664, quoting *New State Ice Co.* v. *Liebmann,* 285 U.S. 262, 311 (1932) (dissenting opinion).
119. *Hill* v. *Colorado,* 530 U.S. 703, 707 (2000).

assigned the Court opinion to me and joined my draft, despite the dissenters' particularly strong criticism of the portions of my draft suggesting that some weight should be given to the patients' interest in avoiding hostile comments by counselors suggesting that they were about to commit murder.

Nino Scalia, Clarence Thomas, David Souter, and Ruth Ginsburg joined what may well be the most significant majority opinion I authored as a justice: *Apprendi* v. *New Jersey*.[120] The defendant pleaded guilty to possession of a fire- arm for an unlawful purpose, an offense punishable by imprisonment for five to ten years. A separate statute, described as a "hate crime" law, provided for a longer term of imprisonment — "between 10 and 20 years" — if the sentenc- ing judge found by a preponderance of the evidence that in committing his crime the defendant acted with a purpose to intimidate an individual because of his race. Even though the indictment did not mention the hate crime law, the judge made such a finding based on that standard and imposed a twelve- year sentence. The New Jersey courts rejected Apprendi's argument that a fac- tual determination that increases the range of permissible sentencing must be made by a jury and supported by proof beyond a reasonable doubt.

The New Jersey courts, and the four dissenters on our Court, relied on Bill Rehnquist's 1986 opinion in *McMillan* v. *Pennsylvania*[121] to find that the state legislature's decision to make the defendant's racial motive a "sentencing factor" rather than an element of a crime eliminated the need for a jury decision supported by proof beyond a reasonable doubt. Bill Brennan, Thurgood Marshall, Harry Blackmun, and I had dissented in *McMillan,* which had coined the term "sentencing factor" to refer to a fact that was not found by a jury and did not have to be supported by proof beyond a reasonable doubt. While I would have preferred to over- rule that case then and there, Nino was unwilling to do so. I instead dis- tinguished *McMillan* on the ground that the "sentencing factor" in that case had only increased the defendant's minimum sentence, whereas the

---

120. 530 U.S. 466 (2000).
121. 477 U.S. 79 (1986).

fact found by the judge in *Apprendi* had increased the defendant's maximum sentence. In other words, the rule we announced in *Apprendi* required that any fact (other than a prior conviction) that increases the maximum punishment for a crime must be charged in an indictment, submitted to a jury, and proven beyond a reasonable doubt.

Although *Apprendi* pretty well put an end to "sentencing factors," *McMillan* was not formally overruled until after I retired from the Court in *Alleyne* v. *United States,* which held that "there is no basis in principle or logic to distinguish facts that raise the maximum from those that increase the minimum."[122]

Not long after *Apprendi* was decided, the Chicago Bar Association and the Chicago Bar Foundation began a series of annual luncheons at which they presented "John Paul Stevens Awards" to attorneys who best exemplify a commitment to integrity and public service in the practice of the law. My friends Bill Bauer and Abner Mikva, both of whom attended my surprise ninety-fourth-birthday party, were among the first recipients of that award. I never had any part in selecting award recipients, but I have attended about half of those luncheons, which were uniformly moving events.

October Term 2000

The outcome of the 2000 presidential election was determined by the results in Florida. Perhaps it would be more accurate to say that the outcome was determined by the misleading character of the "butterfly" ballot used in Palm Beach (and ten other counties in Florida), because post-election studies suggest that the number of accidental votes for Pat Buchanan in lieu of Al Gore in Palm Beach County exceeded George Bush's margin of victory in the entire state.[123] The state later took steps to

---

122. 570 U.S. 90, 116 (2013).
123. See, e.g., Brady et al., "Law and Data: The Butterfly Ballot Episode," *Political Science and Politics* 34 (2001): 59–69; Wand et al., "The Butterfly Did It," *American Political Science Review* 95 (2001): 4.

avoid the future use of such a misleading ballot.[124] But the 2000 election remains a matter of singular interest.

On November 8, the day after the votes were cast, the Florida Division of Elections reported that George W. Bush had won the election by a margin of only 1,784 more votes than his opponent, Albert Gore. Under the Florida Election Code, an automatic machine recount occurred, resulting in an even smaller margin of victory for Bush. Gore then exercised his statutory right to have the canvassing boards in four counties — Volusia, Palm Beach, Broward, and Dade — conduct manual recounts. Litigation in the Florida courts between the two political campaigns concerning the timing of those recounts ensued.

On November 14, a Florida trial court ruled that a seven-day deadline for the canvassing boards to submit their returns was mandatory, but that the Volusia board could amend its returns at a later date. The Florida court further held that the Florida secretary of state — a Republican — had discretion to decide whether to include the late amended returns in the state's totals. On the next day, the secretary rejected all four counties' requests for extended filing deadlines. The Gore campaign filed an emergency motion challenging the secretary's decision as arbitrary. When the Florida trial court denied the motion, the Gore campaign appealed to an intermediate appellate court, which certified the matter to the state supreme court. On Tuesday, November 21, that court entered an order enjoining the secretary from finally certifying the results of the election until after the recounts had been completed and resolving two questions of statutory construction in the Gore campaign's favor. It imposed a new deadline of November 26 at 5 p.m. for the completion of the recounts and return of ballot counts.

Despite the extraordinary closeness of the 2000 presidential election and the fact that litigation related to it was filed in both state and federal court within days of the election, my law clerks from that term — Andy Siegel, Anne Voigts, Eduardo Penalver, and Joe Thai — recalled that the

---

124. See, e.g., MacManus, "Voter Education," *U. Mich. J. L Reform* 36 (2003): 517.

case that would become *Bush* v. *Gore* snuck up on all of us because few inside or outside the building could have foreseen a potential role for the Court. The likelihood of Court intervention seemed so remote that though Andy had randomly drawn the assignment to follow these cases, he handed them off to Eduardo and Joe in order to leave town for Thanksgiving.

Even after the Florida Supreme Court handed down a major victory for the Gore campaign on November 21, my clerks and I still did not think the Court would become involved. My intuition at the time, which my clerks shared, was based on four overlapping factors. First, almost every issue the Florida Supreme Court decided involved interpretation of state law. And rightly so, as Article II of the Constitution assigns to the states the primary responsibility for determining the "manner" of selecting presidential electors. Second, to the extent there was a dispute over the rightful winner of Florida's electoral votes, relevant federal law clearly delegates the resolution of that dispute to Congress, not the Court. Third, the substance of the Florida Supreme Court's decision — which chose to err on the side of counting all discernible votes — was consistent with both the basic tenets of American democracy and the overwhelming majority of case law in other disputed federal elections. It was also consistent with how Florida courts had handled other election disputes, as Anne confirmed in a memo she prepared for me. Finally, it seemed implausible, particularly given these delineated points, that the Court would wager the vast amounts of its hard-earned institutional capital to wade into a bitter partisan dispute over the identity of the next president. The intuition my clerks and I shared that the Court would not become involved in the dispute was sound, but it proved to be, as my clerks later described it, shockingly wrong.

After the Florida Supreme Court handed down its decision on November 21, the Bush campaign promptly filed motions in our Court asking leave to file a petition for certiorari and for expedited consideration. It soon became apparent that the Court would indeed enter the fray, and my clerks made their way to the Court to assist me over the

Thanksgiving holiday. On Friday, November 24, we granted review, agreeing to hear argument on three questions. The two questions in the petition that we agreed to hear were whether the Florida Supreme Court, by effectively changing the state's electoral appointment procedures after election day, violated the Due Process Clause or 3 U.S.C. § 5 and whether the decision of that court changed the manner in which the state's electors are to be elected, in violation of the legislature's power to designate the manner for selection under Article II, Section 1, Clause 2 of the U.S. Constitution. We also ordered the parties to brief and argue this additional question: "What would be the consequences of this Court's finding that the decision of the Florida Supreme Court does not comply with 3 U.S.C. § 5?" We set the case for oral argument on Friday, December 1, 2000.

My clerks spent the better part of the week working together, often in conjunction with clerks to Steve Breyer and Ruth Ginsburg, on a substantial opinion challenging the wisdom and authority behind the Court's intervention. As oral argument drew closer, they became more and more convinced that they were working on the lead dissent in what would be a five-to-four case.

At the argument, Ted Olson ably represented the Bush campaign, arguing that the Florida court had unfairly changed the law after the election was over. Harvard professor Larry Tribe, the well-respected constitutional law scholar, represented the Gore campaign and unfortunately got bogged down in a colloquy with the chief justice about *McPherson* v. *Blacker*,[125] which contains some language identifying the state legislature rather than its supreme court as the source of the state's power to decide how to select its presidential electors. Neither the parties' briefs nor the oral arguments were focused on the possible failure of the Florida court's edict to comply with the federal statute or any possible violation of the Equal Protection Clause.

At our conference after argument, we really did not decide anything.

---

125. 146 U.S. 1 (1892).

The chief drafted an opinion reciting the history of the case and stating that we were unclear as to whether the Florida Supreme Court had seen its state constitution as circumscribing the legislature's authority under the federal Constitution and as to the consideration the Florida court accorded to 3 U.S.C. § 5. Most of the rest of us made suggestions to his draft, which, for the most part, he accepted. In my letter joining his draft, I wrote, "You have steered us through turbulent waters with real skill and characteristic fair-minded leadership." Our opinion was announced on Monday, December 4, 2000.

My clerks recall that my assumption that the Court had dodged a bullet was echoed throughout the building and in the national press. After the Court's decision issued on December 4, I commended my clerks for their work on the draft dissent and, perhaps tempting fate, commented to them that my only regret was that their fine work would not see the light of day.

On Friday, December 8, 2000, there was a dramatic development — the Supreme Court of Florida issued a seventy-page opinion ordering manual recounts of all votes in counties where so-called undervotes had not yet been counted. The court explained that there was no doubt that the failure to tabulate by hand some 9,000 votes in Miami-Dade County, on which the voting machines had failed to register a vote for president, included a sufficient number of legal votes — that is, votes for which there was a "clear indication of the intent of the voter"[126] — to place the results of the election in doubt. The court ordered the recount to begin at once. The Bush campaign responded by filing a combined application for a stay and petition for certiorari in our Court.

Late in the afternoon on December 8, after our regular conference had ended, I was preparing to take Maryan, as well as my grandchildren Hannah and Haley and their parents, to the annual Christmas party at the National Gallery of Art. Chief Justice Rehnquist called me at home to tell me that he had scheduled a conference the following morning to

126. Fla. Stat. § 101.5614.

discuss the stay application. I told him that Maryan and I had plane reservations for a flight to Florida the following morning, and because it was so clear that the stay application lacked merit — given the absence of any basis for claiming irreparable injury — there seemed to be no need for my attendance. He responded that Nino Scalia thought the matter was sufficiently important for consideration by the full Court in conference and urged me to attend, which I agreed to do. At the party that evening, I bumped into Steve Breyer, we had a brief discussion about the matter, and I learned that he also thought that the Saturday conference was unnecessary for the same reason as I did.

The most memorable aspect of the conference at the Court the next morning was the almost complete absence of any discussion of the merits of the case. We did little more than vote to grant the stay by a five-to-four margin, vote to grant review of the merits, order the filing of briefs by both sides by Monday, and set the case for argument on Monday morning. The chief granted my request for a brief delay to write a dissent from the order granting the stay and for Nino's request for an additional delay to respond to that dissent.

David, Ruth, and Steve all joined the short dissent that I drafted and circulated in the next few minutes. I began by pointing out that by granting the stay the Court was violating three settled rules of judicial restraint: our respect for state court decisions on questions of state law; our cautious approach to questions of federal law whose resolution is largely committed to another branch of the federal government; and our reluctance to answer federal constitutional questions that had not been fairly presented to the court whose judgment was being reviewed. I then pointed out that "[c]ounting every legally cast vote cannot constitute irreparable harm. On the other hand, there is a danger that a stay may cause irreparable harm to respondents — and, more importantly, the public at large.... Preventing the recount from being completed will inevitably cast a cloud on the legitimacy of the election."[127] In the third paragraph, I

---

127. *Bush* v. *Gore,* 531 U.S. 1046, 1047–48 (2000).

cited the Florida statutory provisions relating to damaged and defective ballots requiring that no vote should be declared invalid "if there is a clear indication of the intent of the voter." The Florida Supreme Court had heeded that legislative command by interpreting that standard to apply to "undervote" ballots. I closed my dissent by referring to the "fundamental matter" that "the Florida court's ruling reflects the basic principle, inherent in our Constitution and our democracy, that every legal vote should be counted."[128] Finally, I cited my 1970 dissent as a circuit judge in *Roudebush* v. *Hartke*[129] and the Supreme Court's subsequent endorsement of my position.[130] I thought — and still think — recounts should be presumed to be more, rather than less, reliable than the original tally of votes.

In his "brief response" to my dissent, Nino stated that my comment on the issue of irreparable harm had misstated the issue, because the question was not whether counting legal votes could constitute harm but "whether the votes that have been ordered to be counted are, under a reasonable interpretation of Florida law, 'legally cast vote[s].'"[131] That statement, however, was simply an incorrect reading of the Florida court's opinion, which plainly required a determination that a ballot identified the intent of the voter before it should be counted, and also made it abundantly clear that under Florida law the test of whether a ballot was a legal vote depended on there being unambiguous evidence of the voter's intent. Nevertheless, Nino's opinion went on: "Count first, and rule upon legality afterwards, is not a recipe for producing election results that have the public acceptance democratic stability requires."[132] (Of course, Nino's description might have been accurate if the recount had been ordered without announcing the "intent of the voter" standard.)

He then referred to "another issue" in the case as "the propriety,

---

128. *Id.*, at 1048.
129. 321 F. Supp. 1370, 1378–79 (S.D. Ind. 1970).
130. See 405 U.S. 15 (1972).
131. 531 U.S., at 1046–47.
132. *Id.*, at 1047.

indeed the constitutionality, of letting the standard for determination of voters' intent — dimpled chads, hanging chads, etc. — vary from county to county, as the Florida Supreme Court opinion, as interpreted by the Circuit Court, permits."[133] The Florida Supreme Court opinion itself, however, did not contain a single word suggesting that the standard should vary from county to county, and, even if it did, there is no basis for assuming that allowing different counties to use different voting machines or counting procedures of differing reliability would raise any constitutional issue. Unless there was some evidence that the voters in one party or the other were more apt to cast ballots with dimpled chads or hanging chads than the other, such possible differences among counties would not raise a constitutional issue.

Nino ended his concurrence by arguing that permitting the count to proceed on an erroneous basis "will prevent an accurate recount from being conducted on a proper basis later, since it is generally agreed that each manual recount produces a degradation of the ballots, which renders a subsequent recount inaccurate."[134] But the Court had come to the opposite conclusion in 1972 in *Roudebush*.[135] One of the most remarkable features of the majority's disposition of this entire litigation is the fact that its only written statement of reasons for staying the recount at all is set forth in Nino's hastily drafted response to my dissent from the order granting the stay.

As everyone in the Court prepared for oral argument, my clerks again began working on an anticipated draft dissent with me, hoping that it would share the same fate as its predecessor. Yet they sensed that would not be the case and that instead its publication would be both inevitable and imminent.

At the oral argument on Monday morning, Olson again represented

133. *Ibid.*
134. *Ibid.*
135. 405 U.S., at 25–26 (explaining that a recount did not prevent a subsequent independent recount).

the Bush campaign, and Joseph Klock, the Florida attorney general, again represented the Florida secretary of state. David Boies, an excellent trial lawyer from New York who had apparently been the senior counsel for Gore during the trial proceedings, replaced Tribe as the advocate for the Gore campaign.

My most vivid memory of Klock's argument is the fact that immediately after addressing me as "Justice Brennan," David Souter had to correct him for addressing him as "Justice Breyer." He argued that the Supreme Court of Florida had used the "intent of the voter" standard incorrectly because the statute applying that standard was designed for the limited situation involving a problem with a voting mechanism, as opposed to voter error. He thought that only votes that complied with the instructions to make a complete hole in the ballot should be treated as legal votes. Otherwise, in his opinion, there would have to be an automatic recount in every close election. I did not find his disagreement with the Florida Supreme Court over issues of Florida law at all persuasive.

Boies began his argument by responding to the chief's questions about whether the Florida Supreme Court had, in effect, made new law that violated 3 U.S.C. § 5 and whether that federal statute would have been violated if the Florida legislature, instead of the Florida court, had extended the recount deadlines. Boies explained the difference between the state's protest statute, which contains a time limit, and its contest statute, which does not, and clarified that the Florida Supreme Court was focusing on the contest period rather than the protest period. David Souter then questioned Boies about whether "from the standpoint of the equal protection clause," each county could give its own interpretation of what "intent" means "so long as they are in good faith and with some reasonable basis [for] finding intent?" One of Boies's responses referred to Texas, where an attempt to clarify the intent standard had still "ended up with a catch-all provision that says look at the intent of the voter." A longer question followed, ending with the comment that the "objective rule varies, we are told, from county to county. Why shouldn't there be one objective rule for all counties and if there isn't, why isn't it an equal protection violation?"

Boies responded with an answer that was surprisingly different from what I am sure Tribe would have said. After denying that different standards were in fact being applied in different counties, he continued, "If you knew you had those two objective standards [for discerning the intent of the voter] and they were different, then you might have an equal protection problem." He finessed the issue by insisting that the same general standard, which required the counting of every undervote if the intent of the voter could be ascertained, would be applied by judicial review at the conclusion of the recount. But he failed to argue that even if different standards were employed in different counties, that difference would not violate the Equal Protection Clause unless it favored one political party over the other. There was a total absence of any such evidence. There was not even a claim that the members of either party were more likely than their opponents to cast ballots containing either dimpled chads or hanging chads.

In his reply, Olson continued to emphasize his point that Florida law had changed after the election was completed and that the standards for counting votes varied in different counties and were continuing to change. He did not, however, attempt to explain how an equal protection violation could have occurred without any facts demonstrating that differing standards somehow prejudiced the Bush campaign.

I have no recollection of any discussion of the equal protection issue at our conference, but I do remember both Clarence and the chief making the point that the Florida attorney general agreed with the view that only properly cast votes should be counted and that the Florida Supreme Court's reliance on an "intent of the voter" standard represented a change in the law — a point that was central to the separate concurring opinion that they later joined and which would have resulted in a reversal a few days earlier had Tony and Sandra agreed with them. Despite the fact that both David and Stephen had expressed the view that there was an equal protection issue in the background, their preferred solution involved directing the Florida Supreme Court to provide more detailed directions to governing the recount rather than allowing it to proceed under the more general standard. In any event the discussion of that issue was so perfunctory that I failed even to mention it in the dissent that I circulated shortly after the conference. (My clerks also recall that I made one last quixotic attempt to resolve the case with a brief per curiam opinion dismissing the Bush campaign's claims largely on jurisdictional grounds, but that the Court had gone too far to be pulled back.) Based on my report of the conference, my clerks assumed the Court would issue a five-to-four decision halting the recount largely based on the reasons provided in what later became the chief justice's concurring opinion.

My work largely done, I left for Florida on the morning of December 12 as I had originally planned to do after Thanksgiving. While en route, my clerks received a new draft opinion, largely drafted by Tony Kennedy and Sandra O'Connor, finding for the Bush campaign on equal protection grounds. My clerks were also told that five justices were on board for that opinion to be the opinion of the Court, and that the chief justice's original opinion would be issued as a concurrence, joined by Nino Scalia and Clarence Thomas. My clerks then had me paged at the airport to inform me of the development. I thanked them for informing me of the news, but told them I did not think it was much for them to worry about as my draft dissent had already dealt with the equal protection arguments.

Had I focused at conference on the equal protection argument that later turned out to provide the principal rationale for the per curiam opinion disposing of the merits, however, I surely would have mentioned a serious factual error with it as well as the total absence of precedent for it. The factual error is its misunderstanding of different versions of earlier rules that forbade the counting of dimpled chads while permitting hanging chads to be counted.

Ballots rejected by Florida's voting machines were either "overvotes" — ballots marked for more than one candidate for president — or "undervotes" — ballots not marked for any candidate in the manner specified in the voting instructions. As directed by the Florida Supreme Court, none of the overvotes were to be recounted, presumably because the probability of making an accurate identification of which of the

multiple candidates identified on the ballot was the voter's actual preference was too remote (and because no one had contested the overvotes
before the Florida court). There were four categories of "undervotes": (1)
ballots containing no marking identifying any candidate; (2) properly
marked ballots that were not counted because of a machine error; (3) ballots with "hanging chads," that is, partially dislodged chads opposite the
name of one candidate; (4) ballots with "dimpled chads," that is, those in
which the stylus had made a dent in the ballot opposite a candidate's
name but had failed to make any hole. The Florida Supreme Court's
instructions to election officials conducting the recount to use the "intent
of the voter" to decide whether or not to count an undervote obviously
would exclude all those in category (1) and include all those in categories
(2), (3), and (4).

In the Court's per curiam opinion, a critical paragraph makes the
mistake of treating two different descriptions of hanging chads as though
they represented two different categories of undervotes. It says, "And testimony at trial also revealed that at least one county changed its eval-
uative standards during the counting process. Palm Beach County, for
example, began the process with a 1990 guideline which precluded counting completely attached chads, switched to a rule that considered a vote
to be legal if any light could be seen through a chad, changed back to the
1990 rule, and then abandoned any pretense of a *per se* rule, only to have a
court order that the county consider dimpled chads legal."[136] Apparently
oblivious of the fact that the first three versions of the Palm Beach
County practice had all excluded dimpled chads and included hanging
chads, the opinion then incorrectly stated, "This is not a process with sufficient guarantees of equal treatment." In fact, the county's 1990 standard
was a reasonable means of discerning the intent of the voter. Any incon-
sistency was only the result of the court order to consider dimpled chads
legal, a different but also plausible standard for deciding which ballots
adequately conveyed the voter's intent.

---

136. *Bush* v. *Gore,* 531 U.S. 98, at 106–7 (2000).

The Court's failure to appreciate the Florida court's reliance on the "intent of the voter" as the controlling standard for the aborted recount sheds revelatory light on its flawed conclusion that the recount, if completed, would have violated the Equal Protection Clause. Had counties been permitted to follow the Florida Supreme Court's mandate and to consistently apply the "intent of the voter" standard, that would have eliminated the prior variations and avoided any factual basis for concluding that during the recount different counties would be applying different standards.

Even more significant than the Court's misunderstanding of how following the state supreme court's direction to use the "intent of the voter" standard would have eliminated the variation among counties was its implicit assumption that a variation among counties would have provided the basis for concluding that the recount might have violated the Equal Protection Clause. In fact there was a greater disparity between counties using optical scanning equipment and those using punch card ballots than there was among the counties that just used the punch card ballots, but no one suggested that that variation raised any constitutional problem. These variations in the electoral process could not have posed a problem under the Equal Protection Clause because of the complete lack of any evidence that the variations subjugated or disproportionately affected a protected class. Indeed, as I read the per curiam opinion, it both (a) faulted the court-ordered recount because it failed to announce sufficiently detailed standards to ensure internal consistency, and (b) simultaneously faulted the court for stating a single standard for governing the recount. The absence of a coherent rationale in the opinion probably explains why, during the succeeding years, the Court has never cited it as support for any legal proposition.

The case produced some dissenting opinions that are entitled to the highest respect. David Souter's one-paragraph response to the pages of argument devoted to 3 U.S.C. § 5 makes my point:

The 3 U.S.C. § 5 issue is not serious. That provision sets certain conditions for treating a State's certification of Presidential electors as conclusive in the event that a dispute over recognizing those electors must be resolved in the Congress under 3 U.S.C. § 15. Conclusiveness requires selection under a legal scheme in place before the election, with results determined at least six days before the date set for casting electoral votes. But no State is required to conform to § 5 if it cannot do that (for whatever reason); the sanction for failing to satisfy the conditions of § 5 is simply loss of what has been called its "safe harbor." And even that determination is to be made, if made anywhere, in the Congress.[137]

David also succinctly disposed of the majority's criticism of the Florida Supreme Court's failure to require a recount of the 170,000 overvotes — ballots containing votes for two or more presidential candidates — by pointing out that the court's determination that those ballots did not indicate what the voter intended was an entirely reasonable reading of the Florida statute. Even today, however, I remain puzzled by his apparent agreement with the majority's view that the Florida recount might have tolerated sufficient arbitrariness to violate the Equal Protection Clause unless the state supreme court crafted more precise standards to govern particular kinds of ballots, such as those with "hanging" or "dimpled" chads.

Ruth Ginsburg's dissent primarily responded to the chief justice's separate concurrence. She explained our settled practice of respecting state courts' interpretations of their laws as even more entrenched in the Supreme Court's jurisprudence than the federal courts' settled practice — following my oft-cited opinion in *Chevron* — of accepting federal administrative agencies' interpretations of ambiguous provisions in federal statutes. She also found no merit in the equal protection argument. She explained, "Ideally, perfection would be the appropriate standard for judging the recount. But we live in an imperfect world, one in which thousands of votes have not been counted. I cannot agree that the

---

137. *Bush,* 531 U.S., at 130 (Souter, J., dissenting).

recount adopted by the Florida court, flawed as it may be, would yield a result any less fair or precise than the certification that preceded that recount."[138]

In the longest of the four dissents, Stephen Breyer noted, "[I]n a system that allows counties to use different types of voting systems, voters already arrive at the polls with an unequal chance that their votes will be counted. I do not see how the fact that this results from counties' selection of different voting machines rather than a court order makes the outcome any more fair. Nor do I understand why the Florida Supreme Court's recount order, which helps to redress this inequity, must be entirely prohibited based on a deficiency that could easily be remedied."[139] (In Stephen's view, there was perhaps an equal protection problem with the opinion of the Florida Supreme Court, but a remand to that court could have remedied the deficiencies and nonetheless permitted a recount to go forward.) Stephen's opinion recounted some of the history — both of the original Constitution and of the statute enacted after the disputed election in 1876 — that supported allowing Congress rather than the Court to have the final say in controversies over presidential elections. He added, "And, above all, in this highly politicized matter, the appearance of a split decision runs the risk of undermining the public's confidence in the Court itself. That confidence is a public treasure. It has been built slowly over many years, some of which were marked by a Civil War and the tragedy of segregation. It is a vitally necessary ingredient of any successful effort to protect basic liberty and, indeed, the rule of law itself."[140]

In my dissent I emphasized the flaws in the majority's reasoning that most troubled me — the majority's second-guessing the Florida Supreme Court's interpretation of its own state's law. While each of the state-law issues might arguably have been resolved differently, the answers that that court provided were surely permissible; for example, whether two statutes that conflicted because one used the word "may" and the other used

---

138. *Id.,* at 143.
139. *Id.,* at 147.
140. *Id.,* at 157–58.

"shall" should have been construed by favoring the provision that gave the greater protection to votes that revealed the intent of the voter. I closed with this paragraph:

> What must underlie petitioners' entire federal assault on the Florida election procedures is an unstated lack of confidence in the impartiality and capacity of the state judges who would make the critical decisions if the vote count were to proceed. Otherwise, their position is wholly without merit. The endorsement of that position by the majority of this Court can only lend credence to the most cynical appraisal of the work of judges throughout the land. It is confidence in the men and women who administer the judicial system that is the true backbone of the rule of law. Time will one day heal the wound to that confidence that will be inflicted by today's decision. One thing, however, is certain. Although we may never know with complete certainty the identity of the winner of this year's Presidential election, the identity of the loser is perfectly clear. It is the Nation's confidence in the judge as an impartial guardian of the rule of law.[141]

My dissent was quite clear that I did not see any equal protection problem with the Florida Supreme Court's decision. Yet a proposed final draft of the per curiam opinion that was circulated prior to publication asserted that "[e]ight Justices of the Court agree" that the Florida recount posed an equal protection problem and that "the only disagreement" among them was the remedy. My clerks noted the glaring error in that the math did not add up: Both Ruth Ginsburg and I saw no equal protection problem with the recount. My clerks raised the error with the clerks working on the per curiam opinion, but they took the position that the tally was eight, not seven, for an equal protection violation because I had joined Stephen Breyer's dissent in full, unlike Ruth Ginsburg, who had explicitly withheld her join from a brief part of his opinion acknowledging that the recount "does

---

141. *Id.,* at 128–29.

implicate principles of fundamental fairness." My clerks pointed out that the passage of Stephen's opinion in question only acknowledged equal protection concerns but did not conclude there was a constitutional violation and, regardless, my draft dissent made clear that I did not think an equal protection claim was even colorable. The other clerks apparently refused to change the tally nonetheless. My clerks then called me and informed me of the disputed tally, and I agreed to change my join of Stephen's opinion to match Ruth's partial join as long as it would not upset him. My clerks confirmed with his that the change would be fine, and the change was made. Only then did the clerks drafting the per curiam agree to change the tally stated in that opinion. In any event, the attempt to show a supermajority on the equal protection question did little to hide the fact that the end result was a five-to-four decision to halt the recounting of votes in Florida.

The day after the decision, I called my clerks to commend them for the work they did in the case, and, sensing their despondency, advised them to put the case behind them. As much as I wish that the public confidence that the Court had earned a few years earlier when it ordered President Nixon to produce tapes containing evidence of his wrongdoing could be so easily restored, I remain of the view that the Court has not fully recovered from the damage it inflicted on itself in *Bush* v. *Gore*.

The five-justice majority in *Bush* v. *Gore* went on to narrowly construe the Clean Water Act (CWA) just a few days later in *Solid Waste Agency of Northern Cook County* v. *Army Corps of Engineers*.[142] Writing for the Court, the chief rejected the Army Corps of Engineers' expansive interpretation of the CWA as authorizing its regulation of an abandoned sand and gravel pit in northern Illinois that provided a habitat for migratory birds. The corps had construed its jurisdiction over "navigable waters," which the CWA defined as "the waters of the United States, including the territorial seas," to encompass intrastate waters used as habitat for migratory birds. Although the Court had previously held that the corps

---

142. 531 U.S. 159 (2001).

Throwing the first pitch before the game between the Cincinnati Reds and the Chicago Cubs in Wrigley Field, September 14, 2005.
Major League Baseball trademarks and copyrights are used with permission of Major League Baseball Properties, Inc.

Administering the oath to Chief Justice John Roberts on September 29, 2005, in the East Room at the White House with President George W. Bush and Mrs. Jane Roberts.
Christy Bowe, ImageCatcher News

Greeting President-elect Barack Obama during his visit to the Supreme Court on January 14, 2009.
Photograph by Steven Petteway, Collection of the Supreme Court of the United States

President-elect Barack Obama and Vice President–elect Joe Biden visit the Supreme Court on January 14, 2009. Pictured in the Justices' Conference Room (*left to right*): President-elect Obama, Chief Justice Roberts, me, Justice Ginsburg, Vice President–elect Biden, and Justices Souter and Kennedy.
Photograph by Steven Petteway, Collection of the Supreme Court of the United States

With Justices Ginsburg and Scalia, Chief Justice Roberts, and President-elect Barack Obama during his visit to the Supreme Court on January 14, 2009.
Photograph by Steven Petteway, Collection of the Supreme Court of the United States

Administering the oath of office to Vice President Joseph Biden at the Capitol, January 20, 2009.
Courtesy Barack Obama Presidential Library

Receiving the Presidential Medal of Freedom from President Obama on May 29, 2012.
Courtesy Barack Obama Presidential Library

Photo of William J. Cody ("Buffalo Bill") autographed to my father, Ernest J. Stevens.

With Judge Abner Mikva at my ninety-fourth-birthday brunch on April 27, 2014.
Photograph by Steven Petteway, Collection of the Supreme Court of the United States

Ken Manaster at my ninety-fourth birthday brunch on April 27, 2014.
Photograph by Steven Petteway, Collection of the Supreme Court of the United States

With Chief Justice John Roberts and Judge William Bauer at my ninety-fourth-birthday brunch on April 27, 2014.
Photograph by Steven Petteway, Collection of the Supreme Court of the United States

Justice Sandra Day O'Connor and Ginni Thomas at my farewell dinner at the Supreme Court on June 28, 2010.
Photograph by Steven Petteway, Collection of the Supreme Court of the United States

My farewell dinner at the Supreme Court on June 28, 2010 — a "bow tie" event. *Left to right:* Justices Stephen Breyer, Clarence Thomas, and Antonin Scalia, me, Chief Justice John Roberts, and Justices Anthony Kennedy, Samuel Alito, and David Souter.
Photograph by Steven Petteway, Collection of the Supreme Court of the United States

Harold Brett, *Justice Wiley B, Rutledge, Associate Justice* (1943–1949). Oil on canvas, 1947.
Collection of the Supreme Court of the United States

The judges of the Court of Appeals for the Seventh Circuit (1975). Seated (*left to right*): Judge Luther Swygert, Senior Judge John Hastings, Chief Judge Thomas Fairchild, Senior Judge Latham Castle, and Judge Walter J. Cummings. Standing (*left to right*): Judge Philip W. Tone, me, and Judges Wilbur Pell, Robert Sprecher, and William Bauer.
Used with Permission of the United States Court of Appeals for the Seventh Circuit

The Sotomayor Court. My last term as an active justice. Seated (*left to right*): Justice Anthony M. Kennedy, me, Chief Justice John G. Roberts Jr., and Justices Antonin Scalia and Clarence Thomas. Standing (*left to right*): Justices Samuel A. Alito Jr., Ruth Bader Ginsburg, Stephen G. Breyer, and Sonia Sotomayor, September 29, 2009.
Photograph by Steven Petteway, Collection of the Supreme Court of the United States

could regulate wetlands adjacent to navigable waters,[143] it refused to extend that holding to encompass the corps' ability to protect wetland areas under the corps' "Migratory Bird Rule."

The majority's analysis largely turned on the CWA's use of the phrase "navigable waters," which at first blush would seem to exclude the abandoned pit at issue in the case. Focusing on the CWA's legislative history, however, my dissent noted that Congress had fundamentally changed the nature of federal water regulation since its first enactments in this area in the nineteenth century — changes that demonstrated the majority's emphasis on "navigable waters" was misplaced. I pointed out that "[d]uring the middle of the 20th century, the goals of federal water regulation began to shift away from an exclusive focus on protecting navigability and toward a concern for preventing environmental degradation."[144] The climax of this shift occurred when Congress passed the CWA, which amended the existing Federal Water Pollution Control Act (FWCPA) "to establish a comprehensive long-range policy for the elimination of water pollution."[145] Although the CWA did not eliminate the phrase "navigable waters" from Congress's earlier enactments in this area, the statute clearly demonstrated an expansion from an earlier focus on the navigability of the nation's waterways to also protecting "the quality of our Nation's waters for esthetic, health, recreational, and environmental uses."[146] What is more, Congress expressly amended the definition of "navigable waters" from prior versions of the FWPCA to more broadly encompass all "waters of the United States."[147] Based on this history, which my dissent covered in greater detail that I need not repeat here, the corps' jurisdiction under the CWA did not require either actual or potential navigability.

Because of the way I construed the statute, unlike the majority, I also

---

143. See *United States* v. *Riverside Bayview Homes, Inc.,* 474 U.S. 121 (1985).
144. 531 U.S., at 178.
145. *Id.,* at 179, quoting S. Rep. No. 92-414, p. 95 (1971).
146. *Id.,* at 175.
147. *Id.,* at 180.

had to confront whether Congress even had the power to regulate the wetlands at issue — a question that touched on the balance of power between the states and federal government. The majority in fact pointed to this background constitutional question as an implicit basis for its decision to limit the CWA's reach through statutory interpretation alone, suggesting that an alternative reading of the CWA might run afoul of more recent cases limiting Congress's power under the Commerce Clause.[148] Addressing that question, I did not find any impediment to Congress's ability to protect the nation's wetlands, be they navigable or not:

> The power to regulate commerce among the several States necessarily and properly includes the power to preserve the natural resources that generate such commerce. Cf. *Sporhase v. Nebraska ex rel. Douglas,* 458 U.S. 941, 953 (1982) (holding water to be an "article of commerce"). Migratory birds, and the waters on which they rely, are such resources. Moreover, the protection of migratory birds is a well-established federal responsibility. As Justice Holmes noted in *Missouri v. Holland,* the federal interest in protecting these birds is of "the first magnitude." 252 U.S. at 435. Because of their transitory nature, they "can be protected only by national action." *Ibid.*

> Whether it is necessary or appropriate to refuse to allow petitioner to fill those ponds is a question on which we have no voice. Whether the Federal Government has the power to require such permission, however, is a question that is easily answered. If, as it does, the Commerce Clause empowers Congress to regulate particular activities causing air or water pollution, or other environmental hazards that may have effects in more than one State, it

---

148. See *id.,* at 173, citing *United States* v. *Morrison,* 529 U.S. 598 (2000); *United States* v. *Lopez,* 514 U.S. 549 (1995).

also empowers Congress to control individual actions that, in the aggregate, would have the same effect.[149]

The same five-justice majority from *Bush* v. *Gore* also decided *Circuit City Stores, Inc.* v. *Adams*,[150] which held that the Federal Arbitration Act (FAA) encompassed arbitration agreements in employment contracts, thus preempting state laws that precluded their enforcement. As in *Solid Waste Agency*, the history of the statute in question provided a clear answer at odds with the majority's conclusion.

Congress passed the FAA in 1925 as a response to the refusal of courts to enforce commercial arbitration agreements commonly used in the maritime context. When the bill was first introduced in 1922, it did not mention employment contracts, but organized labor nevertheless opposed it because of concern that it might be construed to authorize federal judicial enforcement of arbitration clauses in collective bargaining agreements. In response to that concern, then secretary of commerce Herbert Hoover, a supporter of the bill, proposed an amendment stating "that nothing herein contained shall apply to seamen or any class of workers in interstate and foreign commerce." The amendment merely confirmed that supporters of the bill neither expected nor intended it to apply to employment contracts. Yet the majority, applying the *ejusdem generis* canon of statutory interpretation, concluded that the amendment excluded from the FAA's coverage only transportation workers. It is especially ironic that the *Circuit City Stores* majority relied on the labor-backed amendment as its sole justification for its decision: As I noted in my dissent, the majority's interpretation fulfilled the originally unfounded fears that the amendment was intended to assuage.

As in *Solid Waste Agency*, the Court refused to comment on the amendment's legislative history, explaining that the amendment would have been "pointless" if all employment contracts were beyond the FAA's

---

149. *Solid Waste Agency*, 531 U.S. 159, 196 (citation and internal quotation marks omitted).
150. 532 U.S. 105 (2001).

scope. In my dissent, I responded that "it is not 'pointless' to adopt a clarifying amendment in order to eliminate opposition to a bill."[151] Indeed, I imagine the U.S. Code is replete with such belt-and-suspenders passages responding to concerns raised by interest groups.

Solid Waste Agency and *Circuit City Stores* provide apt examples of a court misusing its authority to interpret a statute by "refus[ing] to look beyond the raw statutory text."[152] I remain of the view I expressed in *Circuit City Stores* that "[a] method of statutory interpretation that is deliberately uninformed, and hence unconstrained, may produce a result that is consistent with a court's own views of how things should be, but it may also defeat the very purpose for which a provision was enacted."[153] Such "sad result[s]"[154] can have far-reaching consequences: Given the Court's holding some sixteen years earlier that the FAA applies in state courts and preempts conflicting state laws, the decision allowing the enforcement of arbitration agreements in most employment contracts extended the FAA's reach far beyond what the enacting Congress could have imagined.

A few weeks later, in *Alexander* v. *Sandoval*,[155] the Court had to decide whether private individuals may sue to enforce federal regulations prohibiting Alabama from requiring that its driver's license examinations be administered only in English. The lower courts had held that the state's English-only policy violated a federal regulation prohibiting state recipients of federal funds from engaging in discrimination on the ground of race or national origin. The same majority that decided *Bush* v. *Gore,* in an opinion authored by Nino, without reaching the merits of the issue, held that federal law did not authorize such relief. I authored a dissenting opinion, joined by David, Ruth, and Stephen. I concluded that dissent by suggesting that it was "the subconscious product of the majority's profound

---

151. *Id.,* at 120.
152. *Id.,* at 132.
153. *Id.,* at 133.
154. *Ibid.*
155. 532 U.S. 275 (2001).

distaste for implied causes of action rather than an attempt to discern the intent of the Congress that enacted Title VI of the Civil Rights Act of 1964."[156] I further noted, "The question the Court answers today was only an open question in the most technical sense. Given the consensus in the Courts of Appeals, the Court should have declined to take this case. Having granted certiorari, the Court should have answered the question differently by simply according respect to our prior decisions. But most importantly, even if it were to ignore all of our post-1964 decisions, the Court should have answered this question differently on the merits."[157]

In *Kyllo* v. *United States*,[158] the Court decided an unusually important question of constitutional law: Whether the use of a thermal-imaging device aimed at a private home from a public street to detect relative amounts of heat within the home constitutes a "search" within the meaning of the Fourth Amendment.

Two federal agents suspected that the defendant in that case was growing marijuana in his home, and they were aware of the fact that indoor marijuana growth typically requires high-intensity lamps. So they had parked across the street from his house in the middle of the night and for a few minutes used a thermal imager to measure the amount of heat being emitted from the home. Their scan showed that the roof over the garage and a side wall of the house were much warmer than the rest of the house as well as neighboring homes. They used that information to obtain a warrant, which led to their discovery of an indoor growing operation involving over one hundred marijuana plants.

Nino wrote the Court opinion concluding that the agents' use of the thermal imager constituted a search under the Fourth Amendment, and I wrote the dissent, joined by the chief, Sandra, and Tony. We disagreed both with majority's specific conclusion that the police had violated the Fourth Amendment in that case and with its formulation of a new rule

---

156. *Id.*, at 317.
157. *Ibid.*
158. 533 U.S. 27 (2001).

for cases involving sense-enhancing technology. Under that rule, "obtaining by sense-enhancing technology any information regarding the interior of the home that could not otherwise have been obtained without physical intrusion onto a constitutionally protected area... constitutes a search — at least where (as here) the technology in question is not in general public use."[159]

In my judgment there was a distinction of constitutional magnitude between "through the wall surveillance" that gives the observer or listener direct access to information in a private area, on the one hand, and the thought processes used to draw inferences from information in the public domain, on the other. The Court crafted a rule that purported to deal with direct observations of the inside of the home, but the case before us merely involved indirect deductions from "off the wall" surveillance, that is, observations of the exterior of the home. The fact that the observations were made with a thermal imager gathering data exposed on the outside of the home did not invade any constitutionally protected interest in privacy. The district court had found that the device did not record any information except the amount of heat emitted from the building.

The principal authority supporting the Court's holding and new rule was a concurring opinion in *Katz* v. *United States*,[160] authored by the second Justice John Harlan, one of the most respected jurists ever to serve on the Supreme Court. *Katz* involved eavesdropping by means of an electronic listening device placed on the outside of a telephone booth. In his concurring opinion, Justice Harlan had stated that a search occurs when the government violates a subjective expectation of privacy that society recognizes as reasonable. But in *Katz* the device had enabled the officers to hear the content of the conversation inside the booth, making them the functional equivalent of intruders because they obtained information otherwise available only to someone inside the private area. In *Kyllo* the device disclosed the amount of heat radiating from the house, not the

---

159. *Id.,* at 34 (quotation marks omitted).
160. 389 U.S. 347 (1967).

temperature within. The device was thus comparable to one in *Katz* that could measure the volume of noise generated by the conversation without enabling the listener to understand what was being said.

October Term 2001

On June 27, 1971, the second Justice Harlan also provided the fifth vote for the decision in *Bivens* v. *Six Unknown Federal Narcotics Agents*,[161] which held that a victim of a federal agent's Fourth Amendment violation may recover damages from the agent despite the absence of any statute creating such a cause of action. Underlying that result was the long-standing principle that where there is a right there is a remedy. Several years later, by a seven-to-two vote, the Court followed the reasoning in *Bivens,* and it held that a federal prisoner could recover damages for injuries inflicted by federal prison guards who violated the Eighth Amendment.[162]

In a case argued on the first day of the 2001 term, the five justices in the *Bush* v. *Gore* majority refused to recognize a similar damages remedy in a suit brought by a federal prisoner against a corporation employed by the federal government to manage a federal correction facility.[163] That decision provided protection for corporate agents of the federal government that was not available to human employees — a result that seemed especially incongruous. Nino's brief concurrence, however, made it quite clear that the decision was really based on disagreement with *Bivens* itself.

In that concurring opinion, he wrote, "*Bivens* is a relic of the heady days in which this Court assumed common-law powers to create causes of action — decreeing them to be 'implied' by the mere existence of a statute or constitutional prohibition."[164] Referring to a time when respected jurists like Justice Harlan followed the common-law view that the law

---

161. 403 U.S. 388 (1971).
162. *Carlson* v. *Green,* 446 U.S. 14 (1980).
163. *Correctional Services Corp.* v. *Malesko,* 534 U.S. 61 (2001).
164. *Id.,* at 75.

should provide a remedy for plaintiffs injured by illegal conduct as "heady days" exposed a pro-defendant bias. As I pointed out in my dissent, the majority could reach what appeared to be the absurd result that a prisoner could recover damages from an individual prison guard employed by the federal bureau of prisons, but not from an employee of a corporation managing a prison facility, only if it really disagreed with the holding in *Bivens*. I therefore ended my opinion by identifying two reasons why it was improper for the Court to allow its decision to be influenced by its disagreement with the *Bivens* case. First, Congress had effectively ratified the decision, never having expressed any disagreement with it. "Second, a rule that has been such a well-recognized part of our law for over 30 years should be accorded full respect by the Members of this Court, whether or not they would have endorsed that rule when it was first announced. For our primary duty is to apply and enforce settled law, not to revise that law to accord with our own notions of sound policy."[165]

In later years some of the Court's most egregious mistakes have involved refusals to heed that admonition.

One of the duties of every Supreme Court justice is to supervise the relations between our Court and one or more of the federal courts of appeal. During my entire tenure I served as the circuit justice for the Seventh Circuit, which includes Wisconsin, Illinois, and Indiana, and from 1990 until my retirement in 2010, I was also the circuit justice for the Sixth Circuit, which includes Michigan, Ohio, Kentucky, and Tennessee. In that capacity I ruled on motions filed by litigants in cases arising in my circuit — most of which were routine requests for extensions of time to file briefs or for permission to participate in an oral argument, but occasionally they involved emergency matters such as a request to stay the execution of a convicted capital offender — and I also attended annual conferences of all of the judges in the circuit. Those conferences combined business sessions, at which legal issues were discussed, social gatherings

---

165. *Id.,* at 83.

attended by members of the bar, and athletic events on the golf course or the tennis court. I made many close friendships in that capacity.

Among those good friends was Gilbert Merritt, who had been a respected prosecutor in Nashville before becoming a federal judge. On the golf course he typically hit his drives about three hundred yards. The fact that he also occasionally piloted his own plane buttressed our friendship. Merritt was a member of the panel of the Court of Appeals for the Sixth Circuit that vacated the death sentence that a Tennessee court imposed on Gary Cone after his conviction for an extraordinarily brutal murder of an elderly couple in Memphis.

The killings were the culmination of a two-day crime rampage that began when Cone robbed a Memphis jewelry store, eluded one officer in a high-speed chase through the city, shot another officer who tried to apprehend him, shot a citizen who confronted him, and at gunpoint demanded that another hand over his car keys. As a police helicopter hovered overhead, Cone tried to shoot the fleeing car owner, but could not fire because his gun was out of ammunition. He eluded police until early Sunday morning, when he drew a gun on an elderly resident who refused to let him in her house to use her telephone. In that afternoon Cone broke into the home of Shipley and Cleopatra Todd, aged ninety-three and seventy-nine years old, and killed them by brutally beating them with a blunt instrument. After shaving his beard, he traveled to Florida, where he was arrested for robbing a drugstore in Pompano Beach.

At his trial the defense conceded that he had committed the criminal acts, but argued that he was not guilty by reason of insanity. Experts testified that illicit drug use that began after Cone joined the army had caused hallucinations and paranoia that affected his mental capacity and his ability to obey the law. His mother testified that when he returned from Vietnam in 1969 he was a changed person, that he was honorably discharged from service, and that he had graduated from college with honors. Thereafter he was convicted of robbery; his father and his fiancée both died while he was in prison. Presumably his lawyer, John Dice, adequately represented him in the guilt phase of his trial. The Sixth Circuit concluded, however, that Cone did not receive effective assistance of counsel at his sentencing hearing, primarily because Dice failed to make any argument asking the jury to spare his client's life.

Chief Justice Rehnquist authored an opinion reversing the Sixth Circuit; I was the lone dissenter. The chief explained that the lawyer's decision not to make any argument pleading for mercy was a permissible tactical decision. The prosecution had used a junior lawyer to present its principal argument asking the jurors to impose the death penalty and saved its star advocate for rebuttal. Dice decided to waive his argument in the penalty hearing to prevent the state from using its admittedly extremely persuasive star from making any argument at all. In my judgment that decision provided stronger evidence of Dice's lack of confidence in himself than a correct estimate of the probable impact of his adversary, as I explained at some length in my dissent.

Omitting my comments on the fact that a theme of fear of possible counterthrusts by his adversary permeated Dice's loquacious explanation of his tactical decisions, as well as any comment on the fact that Dice later suffered from a severe mental impairment and committed suicide, an extended excerpt from my dissent explains some of the reasoning that led to my solo vote:

> Dice conceded that he did not interview various people from Cone's past, such as his high school teachers and classmates, who could have testified that Cone was a good person who did not engage in criminal behavior pre-Vietnam. Dice agreed that such witnesses would likely have been available if Dice had, in his words, "been stupid enough to put them on." Apparently, Dice did not interview these individuals in preparation for the penalty phase, because he assumed that the State's cross-examination of those witnesses would emphasize the seriousness of Cone's post-Vietnam criminal behavior. Dice's reasoning is doubtful to say the least because, regardless of the state of Tennessee law, these post-Vietnam crimes were already known to the jury through the State's

penalty phase evidence of respondent's prior convictions. Further, it is hard to imagine how evidence of Cone's post-Vietnam behavior would change their assessments — indeed, Dice's whole case was that Cone had changed.

Dice also failed to present to the jury mitigation evidence that he did have on hand. He admitted that other witnesses — including those whose testimony he promised to the jury in the guilt phase opening, such as Cone's mother, sister, and aunts — had been interviewed and were available to testify at the penalty phase. Dice had ready access to other mitigation evidence as well: testimony from Cone himself (in which he could have, among other things, expressed remorse and discussed his brother's drowning and his fiancée's murder), the letter of forgiveness from the victim's sister, the Bronze Star, and the medical experts. Dice's *post hoc* reasons for not putting on these additional witnesses and evidence are puzzling, but appear to rest largely on his incorrect assumption that the guilt phase record already included "what little mitigating circumstances we had," and his fear of the prosecutor, "who by all accounts was an extremely effective advocate."…

Dice did not put Cone on the stand during the penalty phase, forfeiting the opportunity for him to express the remorse he apparently felt. Dice testified that he discussed with Cone the possibility of testifying, but opted not to call him at the penalty phase because of fear that respondent might "lash out if pressed on cross-examination." He also claimed that Cone made the decision not to testify at the penalty phase because Cone feared the prosecutor. In Dice's words, Cone "realized that [the prosecutor] was a very intelligent and skilled cross-examiner and [Cone] felt that he would go off if he took the stand." However, this explanation conspicuously echoes Dice's *own* fears about the prosecutor's prowess. Furthermore, respondent testified that Dice never "urged [him] as to the importance of testifying at the penalty stage," and Dice testified that his duties did not include urging Cone to testify. Given the undisputed evidence of Cone's intelligence and no indication that his behavior in the courtroom was anything but exemplary, it is difficult to imagine why any competent lawyer would so readily abandon any effort to persuade his client to take the stand when his life was at stake. Dice's claim that he did no more than permit Cone to reach his own decision about testifying in the penalty phase is simply not credible. Rather, it appears that Dice, fearful of the prosecutor, did not specifically discuss testifying in the penalty phase with Cone, but rather discussed with him the possibility of taking the stand on only one occasion — during the guilt phase of the trial....

In addition to performing no penalty phase investigation and failing to introduce available mitigation, Dice made no closing statement after the State's affirmative case for death. Rather, Dice's "strategy" was to rely on his brief penalty phase opening statement. This opening statement did refer to the evidence of drug addiction and the expert testimony already in the record, though it is unclear to what end, as Dice believed that the jury had "completely rejected" this testimony. Dice's statement also explained that respondent's drug abuse began under the "stress and strain of combat service," even though the jurors knew that Cone had not been in combat. Otherwise, Dice failed to describe the substantial mitigating evidence of which he was aware: Cone's Bronze Star; his good character before entering the military; the deaths in his family; the rape and murder of his fiancée; and his loving relationship with his mother, his sisters, and his aunt. At best, Dice's opening statement and plea for Cone's life was perfunctory; indeed, it occupies only 4½ of the total 2,158 trial transcript pages.

Dice's decision not to make a closing argument was most strongly motivated by his fear that his adversary would make a persuasive argument depicting Cone as a heartless killer. At all costs, Dice wanted to avoid the prosecutor "slash[ing] me to pieces on rebuttal," as "[h]e's done…a hundred times." Dice hoped that by not making a closing statement, the prosecutor would "kind of follo[w] me right down the primrose path." Of course, at the time Dice waived closing argument, the aggravating circumstances had already been proved, and Dice knew that the judge would instruct the jury to return a verdict of death unless the jurors were persuaded that the aggravating circumstances were outweighed by mitigating evidence. Perhaps that burden was insurmountable, but the jury must have viewed the absence of any argument in response to the State's case for death as Dice's concession that no case for life could be made. A closing argument provided the only chance to avoid the inevitable outcome of the "primrose path" — a death sentence.[166]

Although my dissent failed to persuade any of my colleagues to change their votes in *Cone*, I have always thought that it might have influenced the decision in *Wiggins* v. *Smith*,[167] a somewhat similar case decided on the last day of the 2002 term. In that case, Sandra wrote an opinion joined by all of her colleagues except Nino and Clarence, holding that the lawyers for a defendant who had been found guilty of the brutal murder of a seventy-eight-year-old woman had failed to present available mitigating evidence and therefore had not provided him with the effective assistance of counsel.

In both of those cases the vicious crimes committed by the defendants justified the most severe retribution that a state can impose. My reflection about such cases has convinced me that a sentence of imprisonment for life without the possibility of parole should suffice.

In his opinion for the Court in *Barnhart* v. *Sigmon Coal Co.*, Clarence Thomas stated that "in all statutory construction cases, we begin with

---

166. *Bell* v. *Cone*, 535 U.S. 685, 708–15 (2002) (internal citations omitted).
167. 539 U.S. 510 (2003).

the language of the statute" and our "inquiry ceases" if the statutory language is coherent and consistent.[168] While his description of the starting point is correct, his identification of the conclusion fails to recognize, among other things, the existence of scrivener's errors in which statutory provisions that may be coherent and consistent do not reflect the intent of the enacting legislature. The three dissenters in *Sigmon Coal*— Sandra O'Connor, Steve Breyer, and myself—thought there are cases in which an analysis of the legislative history will sometimes reveal such an error.

In *Sigmon Coal*, the Court was required to decide whether the commissioner of Social Security had correctly interpreted the Coal Industry Retiree Health Benefit Act of 1992 when he assigned responsibility for paying benefits of eighty-six former employees of a coal company to the successor in interest of their former employer. The statute contains a detailed description of the order in which related companies should be made responsible for payments to former employees of formerly active employers. But the statute omits any mention of successors in interest of the former employer itself, though it does refer to successors in interest of related persons—that is, persons related to the former employer. That omission, according to the majority of the Court, prohibited the commissioner from imposing liability on the most logical entity to succeed to that liability.

The commissioner's reading of the statute was the same as that of two of the senators sponsoring the measure. Senator Rockefeller, who spoke as "the original author of this legislation," unambiguously stated that the term "signatory operator" includes "a successor in interest of such operator."[169] And in a written explanation of the measure, Senator Wallop stated that the definition of the term "related person" encompassed "successors to the collective bargaining agreement obligations of a signatory operator."[170] The majority included a footnote explaining that the

---

168. 534 U.S. 438, 450 (2002).
169. *Id.*, at 457, quoting 138 Cong. Rec. 34002, 34033 (1992).
170. *Id.*, at 456, quoting 138 Cong. Rec. at 34002.

House had passed the bill before those two senators made those statements and that there was no evidence that any other legislator agreed with their reading.[171] But the point that should be controlling is that the statutory language itself was so convoluted that it must have misled the ordinary reader. The relevant text provided:

> For purposes of this chapter, the Commissioner of Social Security shall, before October 1, 1993, assign each coal industry retiree who is an eligible beneficiary to a signatory operator which (or any related person with respect to which) remains in business in the following order
>
> (1) First, to the signatory operator which—
>
> (A) was a signatory to the 1978 coal wage agreement or any subsequent coal wage agreement, and
> (B) was the most recent signatory operator to employ the coal industry retiree in the coal industry for at least 2 years.
>
> (2) Second, if the retiree is not assigned under paragraph (1), to the signatory operator which—
>
> (A) was a signatory to the 1978 wage agreement or any subsequent coal wage agreement, and
> (B) was the most recent signatory operator to employ the coal industry retiree in the coal industry.
>
> (3) Third, if the retiree is not assigned under paragraph (1) or (2), to the signatory operator which employed the coal industry retiree in the coal industry for a longer period of time than any

---

171. *Id.*, at 457n15.

other signatory operator prior to the effective date of the 1978 coal wage agreement.[172]

When parsed carefully, neither that text nor the text of the provision defining "related persons,"[173] actually mentions successors in interest to signatory operators. But it is surely possible — I would contend likely — that most readers would not realize that the statute simply omitted any mention of that category of operators, especially if they read the language in the hurried rush of the legislative process. (Clarence Thomas himself described how "[t]he Coal Act was passed amidst a maelstrom of contract negotiations, litigation, strike threats, a presidential veto of the first version of the bill and threats of a second veto, and high pressure lobbying, not to mention wide disagreements among members of Congress."[174]) If the statute had been ambiguous, *Chevron* would have required deference to the views of the commissioner, who had interpreted the act consistent with the most logical reading of what Congress was attempting to accomplish. It is somewhat ironic that in finding no ambiguity yet reaching an absurd result, Clarence's interpretation of the act merely supported the dissenters' view that the unambiguous text was the product of a scrivener's error. An unambiguous scrivener's error is still an error, yet under Clarence's approach it became law.

Clarence also wrote the Court opinion in *Federal Maritime Commission* v. *South Carolina Ports Authority,*[175] a case extending the doctrine of sovereign immunity to preclude the Federal Maritime Commission from adjudicating a complaint filed by a private shipping company alleging that the port authority was administering its "anti-gambling policy" in a discriminatory way. The primary justification for the Court's holding rested on the premise that the "preeminent purpose of state sovereign immunity is to accord states the dignity that is consistent with their status as

---

172. 26 U.S.C. § 9706(a) (1994 ed.).
173. 26 U.S.C. § 9701(c)(2) (1994 ed.).
174. *Sigmon Coal,* 534 U.S., at 446.
175. 535 U.S. 743 (2002).

sovereign entities."[176] In his thorough dissent Steve Breyer (joined by David Souter, Ruth Ginsburg, and me) noted that nothing in the text of the Constitution mentioned the principle of law announced by the Court, and he further explained why it was unwise. I added a brief statement repeating the comment in my dissent in *Seminole Tribe* that the "dignity" rationale is "embarrassingly insufficient," in part because "Chief Justice Marshall early on laid to rest the view that the purpose of the Eleventh Amendment was to protect a State's dignity."[177] It was, rather, to protect a state from its undignified interest in avoiding its creditors.

Justice Oliver Wendell Holmes's opinion for the Court in *Pennsylvania Coal Co. v. Mahon*,[178] which invalidated a Pennsylvania statute forbidding the mining of coal in such a way as to cause damage to any building used as a home, is the source of our regulatory takings jurisprudence. His statement of the governing rule requires a careful examination of the facts of each case. "The general rule at least," stated Justice Holmes, "is that while property may be regulated to a certain extent, if regulation goes too far it will be recognized as a taking."[179] That is a fine statement of the rule as a general matter, but application of that rule to any given set of facts is another thing. One of the most respected members of the Supreme Court bar, John W. Davis, who incidentally was the unsuccessful Democratic candidate for president two years after *Mahon*, convinced Justice Holmes and his colleagues in the majority that the statute in that case had in fact gone "too far." Justice Louis Brandeis's dissenting opinion demonstrates that equally competent judges, without quarreling with the statement of the governing rule, may nonetheless disagree in its application. That these two giants of the Court could reach contrary conclusions when applying the same rule foreshadowed the disputes to come in this

---

176. *Id.*, at 760.
177. *Id.*, at 770.
178. 260 U.S. 393 (1922).
179. *Id.*, at 415.

area of the law, some of the more memorable of which occurred during my tenure on the Court.

In my first case involving an alleged regulatory taking as a member of the Court, Bill Brennan wrote the majority opinion rejecting a challenge to the application of New York City's Landmarks Preservation Law to the land occupied by the Grand Central Terminal.[180] I joined Bill Rehnquist's dissent, which concluded by quoting Justice Holmes's warning in *Mahon* that the courts were "in danger of forgetting that a strong public desire to improve the public condition is not enough to warrant achieving the desire by a shorter cut than the constitutional way of paying for the change."[181]

Though I agreed with Bill in *Penn Central,* as chief justice, he and I were on opposite sides when the Court confronted the question whether a moratorium on development imposed by the Tahoe Regional Planning Agency constituted a taking of property requiring compensation under the Constitution.[182] In his dissent, the chief explained why he believed that our cases had established that a ban on development lasting almost six years constituted a taking. He ended his dissent by acknowledging that Lake Tahoe is a "national treasure" and that he did not doubt that the agency had acted in furtherance of the public interest, but then he quoted the same statement by Justice Holmes that he had quoted in *Penn Central.*

Just as Justice Holmes had no doubt been convinced by John W. Davis in *Mahon,* as the author of the majority opinion in the Tahoe Regional Planning case, I am sure that I was influenced by the excellent argument made by the agency's lawyer, John Roberts, who was later to become our chief justice. Instead of viewing the case as a total ban lasting six years, I came to the view that we were required to examine each of the agency's decisions and to recognize that thoughtful responses to complicated development questions require a time-consuming deliberative process.

---

180. *Penn Cent. Transp. Co.* v. *New York City,* 438 U.S. 104 (1978).
181. *Id.,* at 152, quoting *Mahon,* 260 U.S., at 416.
182. *Tahoe-Sierra Preservation Council, Inc.* v. *Tahoe Regional Planning Agency,* 535 U.S. 302 (2002).

Those of us in the majority were surely influenced by the descriptions of Lake Tahoe as "uniquely beautiful," a "national treasure that must be protected and preserved," and by Mark Twain's description of the clarity of its waters as "not *merely* transparent, but dazzlingly, brilliantly so."[183] But the critical point for us was the importance of moratoria, which are widely used among land-use planners while formulating a more permanent development strategy: "In fact, the consensus in the planning community appears to be that moratoria, or 'interim development controls' as they are often called, are an essential tool of successful development. Yet even the weak version of petitioners' categorical rule would treat these interim measures as takings regardless of the good faith of the planners, the reasonable expectations of the landowners, or the actual impact of the moratorium on property values."[184] Though I was convinced by the man who would become our chief justice, the man who then held that seat was not, demonstrating, as in *Mahon,* that reasonable minds often differ when it comes to application of Justice Holmes's general rule for regulatory takings.

In 1989, in *Penry* v. *Lynaugh,*[185] the Court considered, and rejected, an argument that the execution of a murderer with the mental capacity of a seven-year-old is cruel and unusual punishment prohibited by the Eighth Amendment. In her opinion for the Court, Sandra O'Connor first acknowledged that the prohibitions of that amendment are not limited to practices that were condemned in 1789 but also included those that violate our evolving standards of decency. She then concluded, however, that the fact that Georgia and Maryland had enacted statutes prohibiting the execution of intellectually disabled people provided insufficient evidence of a national consensus to justify the adoption of a categorical rule. "In sum," she stated, intellectual disability "is a factor that may well lessen

---

183. *Id.,* at 307, quoting *Tahoe-Sierra Preservation Council, Inc.* v. *Tahoe Reg'l Planning Agency,* 34 F. Supp. 2d 1226, 1230 (D. Nev. 1999).
184. *Id.,* at 339.
185. 492 U.S. 302.

a defendant's culpability for a capital offense. But we cannot conclude today that the Eighth Amendment precludes the execution of any [intellectually disabled] person of Penry's ability convicted of a capital offense simply by virtue of his or her [intellectual disability] alone."[186]

In the ensuing thirteen years, "the American public, legislators, scholars, and judges...deliberated over the question" and, as we held in *Atkins* v. *Virginia*,[187] concluded that such a consensus had developed. Based on that consensus, as well as our conclusion that neither purpose served by the death penalty — retribution or deterrence — was furthered by executing those with intellectual disability, we recognized "a categorical rule making such offenders ineligible for the death penalty."[188]

My opinion for the Court in *Atkins*, which was joined by all of my colleagues except Chief Justice Rehnquist, Nino Scalia, and Clarence Thomas, is significant not merely because of its negative impact on popular support for the death penalty but, more importantly, for its decisive rejection of the "original intent" approach to constitutional interpretation.

When the Court struck down the death penalty in 1972 in *Furman* v. *Georgia*, even Chief Justice Burger's dissent recognized that "the Eighth Amendment cannot fairly be limited to those punishments thought excessively cruel and barbarous at the time of the adoption of the Eighth Amendment."[189] As he explained, "[A] punishment is inordinately cruel, in the sense we must deal with it in these cases, chiefly as perceived by the society so characterizing it. The standard of extreme cruelty is not merely descriptive, but necessarily embodies a moral judgment. The standard itself remains the same, but its applicability must change as the basic mores of society change."[190] Yet that view remained subject to considerable debate and uncertainty in the many death penalty cases the Court decided after

---

186. *Id.*, at 340.
187. 536 U.S. 304, 307 (2002).
188. *Id.*, at 320.
189. 408 U.S. 238, 382.
190. *Ibid.*

the Court effectively reinstated the death penalty in *Gregg* v. *Georgia*,[191] an opinion I authored along with Potter Stewart and Lewis Powell.

After *Atkins,* however, a majority of the Court has consistently looked to evolving standards of decency — rather than original intent — to prohibit the death penalty for those under the age of eighteen,[192] and for those convicted of the rape of a child where the victim did not die and death was not intended,[193] and to restrict the punishment of life without possibility of parole for juveniles convicted of non-homicide offenses,[194] and later for any juvenile offenders.[195]

The Court's Eighth Amendment jurisprudence provides perhaps the best retort to those who strictly adhere to an original-intent approach to constitutional interpretation. As I would later explain in my concurrence in *Roper,* the next major death penalty case the Court decided after *Atkins,* "that our understanding of the Constitution does change from time to time has been settled since John Marshall breathed life into its text."[196] At least in the context of the Eighth Amendment that view appears to have taken firm hold.

October Term 2002

After a seven-week trial, a Chicago jury awarded substantial damages to the National Organization for Women, Inc. (NOW), and two owners of abortion clinics against a coalition of antiabortion groups that had engaged in a nationwide conspiracy to shut down abortion clinics. The jury found that the defendants had obstructed access to the clinics, trespassed on clinic property, and used violence and threats of violence against the clinics, their employees, and their patients. The Court of Appeals for the Seventh Circuit affirmed, rejecting defendants' argument

---

191. 428 U.S. 153 (1976).
192. *Roper* v. *Simmons,* 543 U.S. 551 (2005).
193. *Kennedy* v. *Louisiana,* 554 U.S. 407 (2008).
194. *Graham* v. *Florida,* 560 U.S. 48 (2010).
195. *Miller* v. *Alabama,* 567 U.S. 460 (2012).
196. 543 U.S., at 587.

that their conduct did not violate the Hobbs Act, the federal statute prohibiting extortion, because the things that they "obtained" — the women's right to receive medical services, the clinic doctors' right to perform their jobs, and the clinics' right to conduct their businesses — were not "property" for purposes of the Hobbs Act and were not "obtained" from the plaintiffs. In his opinion for the Court in *Scheidler* v. *NOW, Inc.,*[197] Chief Justice Rehnquist accepted that argument and so did Ruth Ginsburg, though she wrote a separate concurrence, which Stephen Breyer joined, to note that Congress had recently enacted a statute specifically designed to respond to the concerns that gave rise to this litigation. I was the sole dissenter.

The majority's opinion focused largely on whether Congress had intended "extortion" in the Hobbs Act to have the same meaning it had under the common law. The Hobbs Act defines extortion as "the obtaining of property from another, with his consent, induced by wrongful use of actual or threatened force, violence, or fear, or under color of official right."[198] Citing the "general presumption that a statutory term has its common-law meaning," the majority discussed the historical definition of extortion and particularly two sources on which Congress had modeled the Hobbs Act — the Penal Code of New York and the Field Code, a nineteenth-century model penal code.[199] Looking to New York case law and limited Supreme Court precedent, the majority concluded that extortion as used in the Hobbs Act required "that a person must 'obtain' property from another party."[200] Up to this point, there was little with which I disagreed.

The majority also noted there was no dispute that the defendants in *Scheidler* had "interfered with, disrupted, and in some instances completely deprived respondents of their ability to exercise their property

197. 537 U.S. 393 (2002).
198. *Id.,* at 400, quoting 18 U.S.C. § 1951(b)(2).
199. *Id.,* at 402–3.
200. *Id.,* at 404.

rights."[201] Indeed, defendants' "counsel readily acknowledged at oral argument that aspects of his clients' conduct were criminal."[202] But the majority nonetheless concluded that "even when their acts of interference and disruption achieved their ultimate goal of 'shutting down' a clinic that performed abortions, such acts did not constitute extortion because petitioners did not 'obtain' respondents' property."[203] Although the defendants "may have deprived or sought to deprive respondents of their alleged property right of exclusive control of their business assets,... they did not acquire any such property."[204] Based on this absence of an acquisition of tangible property, the majority concluded that no "property" had been "obtain[ed]" within the meaning of the Hobbs Act's definition of extortion. I of course did not agree with this crabbed interpretation.

I began my dissent by noting that no other federal court had ever construed the Hobbs Act so narrowly. "For decades federal judges have uniformly given the term 'property' an expansive construction that encompasses the intangible right to exercise exclusive control over the lawful use of business assets. The right to serve customers or to solicit new business is thus a protected property right. The use of violence or threats of violence to persuade the owner of a business to surrender control of such an intangible right is an appropriation of control embraced by the term 'obtaining.' "[205] Then, after quoting at length from an especially well written opinion by Judge Amalya Kearse of the Court of Appeals for the Second Circuit, I added that even if the issue were close, three additional considerations strongly supported her conclusion.

First, the uniform construction of the statute that has prevailed throughout the country for decades should remain the law unless and

---

201. *Ibid.*
202. *Ibid.*
203. *Id.,* at 404–5.
204. *Id.,* at 405.
205. *Id.,* at 412.

until Congress decides to amend the statute."[206] To buttress this point, I cited Congress's correction of the earlier narrow reading of the mail fraud statute that the Court had adopted over my dissent in *McNally* v. *United States*.[207] Second, I noted that our Court, as well as other federal courts, had consistently identified the Hobbs Act as a statute the Congress had intended to be given a broad construction. And third, given the fact that Congress had recently enacted legislation specifically responsive to the conduct that had given rise to this case, "[T]he principal beneficiaries of the Court's dramatic retreat from the position that federal courts and federal prosecutors have maintained throughout the history of this important statute will certainly be the class of professional criminals whose conduct persuaded Congress that the public needed federal protection from extortion."[208]

In *Grutter* v. *Bollinger*,[209] as the senior justice in the majority of five voting to uphold the University of Michigan Law School's affirmative action program, I wisely assigned the majority opinion to Sandra O'Connor. In that opinion, she squarely held that the law school had a compelling interest in attaining a diverse student body. In explaining that holding, she relied on an amicus brief filed by Carter Philips and Virginia Seitz on behalf of high-ranking retired officers and civilian leaders of the U.S. armed forces. In that brief, they had argued that a highly qualified, racially diverse officer corps was essential to the military's mission and could not be obtained unless the service academies used race-conscious recruiting and admissions policies.

After my retirement from the Court, I wrote to Carter Philips asking if there was any truth in the rumor that Gerald Ford had played a role in the decision to file that brief. Taking pains to make sure that he did not breach any attorney-client privilege, Carter's response acknowledged not only that Ford was the "but-for" cause of the brief's preparation and

---

206. *Id.,* at 416–17.
207. 483 U.S. 350, 376 (1987).
208. 537 U.S., at 417.
209. 539 U.S. 306 (2003).

filing, but also that President Ford had been the first person to suggest that former military officers as a group had a very important message to present to the Court.

Three aspects of that message merit special comment — its legal reasoning, its historical context, and the prestige of its authors. As Sandra acknowledged in her opinion for the Court, there was a good deal of language in the Court's earlier opinions that had suggested that remedying past discrimination was the only permissible justification for race-based governmental action. (I had expressed my disagreement with that view some fifteen years earlier in my dissent in *Wygant* v. *Jackson Bd. of Ed.*[210]) Rather than discussing any need for — or indeed any interest in — providing a remedy for past sins, the military brief concentrated on describing future benefits that could be obtained from a diverse student body. The authors of the brief did not make the rhetorical blunder of relying on a dissenting opinion to support their legal approach, but they effectively endorsed the views that I had unsuccessfully espoused in *Wygant.*

The brief recounted the transition from a segregated to an integrated military. Within a few years after President Truman's 1948 executive order abolishing segregation in the armed forces, the enlisted ranks were fully integrated. Yet, during the 1960s and 1970s they were commanded by an overwhelmingly white officer corps. The chasm between the racial composition of the officer corps and the enlisted personnel undermined military effectiveness in a number of ways set forth in the brief. For instance, the brief recounted how, during the Vietnam War, racial tension in the military was exacerbated by an officer corps that was only 3 percent African American. In time, the leaders of the military recognized the critical link between minority officers and military readiness, eventually concluding that "success with the challenge of diversity is critical to national security." They met that challenge by adopting race-conscious recruiting, preparatory, and admissions policies at the service

---

210. 476 U.S. 267 (1986).

academies and in ROTC programs. The historical discussion did not merely imply that a ruling that would outlaw such programs would jeopardize national security, but also that an approval of Michigan's programs would provide significant educational benefits for civilian leaders.

The identity of the twenty-nine leaders who joined the brief added impressive force to their argument. Fourteen of them — including Wesley Clark and Norman Schwarzkopf — had achieved four-star rank. They were all thoroughly familiar with the dramatic differences between the pre-1948 segregated forces and the modern integrated military. President Ford, who also rendered heroic service during World War II, played the key role in selecting them.

Writing for the Court, Sandra quoted from and embraced this argument from the brief:

> "[T]he military cannot achieve an officer corps that is *both* highly qualified *and* racially diverse unless the service academies and the ROTC use[] limited race-conscious recruiting and admissions policies." To fulfill its mission, the military "must be selective in admissions for training and education for the officer corps, *and* it must train and educate a highly qualified, racially diverse officer corps in a racially diverse educational setting." We agree that "it requires only a small step from this analysis to conclude that our country's other most selective institutions must remain both diverse and selective."[211]

Sandra went on to conclude that "[e]ffective participation by members of all racial and ethnic groups in the civic life of our Nation is essential if the dream of one Nation, indivisible, is to be realized."[212]

---

211. *Grutter,* 539 U.S., at 331 (citations omitted).
212. *Id.,* at 332.

Given the fact that Gerald Ford played a central role in the military brief's filing, it is certainly reasonable to conclude that he shared the views that the Court adopted in that case.

After concluding that the law school had permissibly used race as a factor contributing to diversity, Sandra acknowledged that a core purpose of the Fourteenth Amendment was to do away with all discrimination based on race, and therefore that "race-conscious admissions policies must be limited in time."[213] To support the proposition that "all race-conscious programs have a termination point,"[214] she quoted this passage from a rather obscure article in the *Chicago Bar Record:* "It would be a sad day indeed, were America to become a quota-ridden society, with each identifiable minority assigned proportional representation in every desirable walk of life. But that is not the rationale for programs of preferential treatment; the acid test of their justification will be their efficacy in eliminating the need for any racial or ethnic preference at all."[215] One of the authors of the article was my former law professor Nathaniel Nathanson. I had called Sandra's attention to the article because of my especially high regard for its author. I think it prompted her to conclude her discussion of the merits with this comment: "We expect that 25 years from now, the use of racial preferences will no longer be necessary to further the interest approved today."[216] Much as I wish that were true, writing now roughly halfway to that mark, I am not sure we as a country will reach that aspirational goal.

Over the dissents of Tony Kennedy, Nino Scalia, and Clarence Thomas, in *Nevada Department of Human Resources* v. *Hibbs,*[217] the Court upheld

---

213. *Id.,* at 342.
214. *Ibid.*
215. Nathanson and Bartnik, "The Constitutionality of Preferential Treatment for Minority Applicants to Professional Schools," *Chicago Bar Rec.* 58 (May–June 1977): 282, 293.
216. 539 U.S., at 343.
217. 538 U.S. 721 (2003).

the provision in the Family and Medical Leave Act of 1993 that authorizes state employees to recover damages from the state for violations of the act. Chief Justice Rehnquist wrote an opinion for the Court that might well have been authored by Ruth Ginsburg. While he began by noting that the Commerce Clause did not authorize Congress to abrogate a state's sovereign immunity — a proposition that none of the justices who joined his opinion endorsed — he convincingly demonstrated that Section 5 of the Fourteenth Amendment granted Congress the authority to remedy and deter violations of the Equal Protection Clause "by prohibiting a somewhat broader swath of conduct, including that which is not itself forbidden by the Amendment's text.... In other words, Congress may enact so-called prophylactic legislation that proscribes facially constitutional conduct, in order to prevent and deter unconstitutional conduct."[218]

He then described at some length the evidence Congress had considered showing that a much higher percentage of employees were covered by maternity leave policies than those covered by paternity leave policies, which in turn supported the proposition that the differential leave policies were not attributable to any differential physical needs of men and women but rather "to the pervasive sex-role stereotype that caring for family members is women's work."[219] Thus the statute was upheld as a permissible method of preventing gender-based discrimination rather than an obviously permissible exercise of Congress's power to regulate the terms and conditions of state employment. Many observers familiar with Chief Justice Rehnquist's views of federalism and states' rights in particular were no doubt surprised by his vote and opinion in that case.

David Souter wrote the opinion for the Court in *Federal Election Comm'n* v. *Beaumont*.[220] Only Nino Scalia, Tony Kennedy, and Clarence

---

218. *Id.*, at 727–28.
219. *Id.*, at 731.
220. 539 U.S. 146 (2003).

Thomas refused to join its holding, which David succinctly summarized in these two opening sentences:

> Since 1907, federal law has barred corporations from contributing directly to candidates for federal office. We hold that applying the prohibition to nonprofit advocacy corporations is consistent with the First Amendment."[221]

Despite the lucidity and forcefulness of that opening, which was premised on almost a century's worth of case law, we now know of course that the Court would later greatly restrict the government's ability to limit the power of corporate speech in our electoral processes — a point I revisit in a later chapter discussing the famous (or perhaps infamous) decision in *Citizens United* v. *FEC*.[222]

John Lawrence was convicted of violating a Texas statute making it a crime for two persons of the same sex to engage in certain intimate sexual conduct and fined $200 plus court costs. After the Texas Court of Appeals upheld the conviction, we granted Lawrence's petition for certiorari to address three questions: (1) whether the conviction violated the Equal Protection Clause; (2) whether it deprived him of "liberty" protected by the Due Process Clause; and (3) whether the Court's 1986 decision in *Bowers* v. *Hardwick*[223] should be overruled.

I of course had dissented in *Bowers*, noting, among other things, that "[a]lthough the meaning of the principle that 'all men are created equal' is not always clear, it surely must mean that every free citizen has the same interest in 'liberty' that the members of the majority share. From the standpoint of the individual, the homosexual and heterosexual have the same interest in deciding how he will live his own life, and, more narrowly, how he will conduct himself in his personal and voluntary associations with his companions. State intrusion into the private conduct

---

221. *Id.*, at 149.
222. 558 U.S. 310 (2010).
223. 478 U.S. 186 (1986).

of either is equally burdensome."[224] A dissenting opinion is often a lonely perch, but one of the great benefits of our permitting the dissenting justice to share his or her views with the world is the possibility that in time others will come to agree. My dissent in *Bowers* was one such instance, and though it was unfortunate that *Bowers* remained on the books so long, I took great satisfaction when it was finally overruled.

In his opinion for the Court, Tony Kennedy began by explaining that both Byron White and Chief Justice Burger in their opinions in *Bowers* had failed to appreciate the importance of the interest in liberty that the case implicated. While the challenged statutes purported to do no more than prohibit a narrowly defined species of conduct, they actually sought to control a personal relationship that, whether or not entitled to formal recognition in the law, is within the liberty of persons to choose without being punished as criminals. Earlier decisions protecting a woman's right to use contraceptives and the right to have an abortion, while articulating a constitutional "right to privacy," actually recognized a right "to make certain fundamental decisions affecting her destiny and confirmed once more that the protection of liberty under the Due Process Clause has a substantive dimension of fundamental significance in defining the rights of the person."[225]

He also noted that prosecutions for sodomy had typically involved relations between men and unwilling minors involving the use of force, that in the last decades states with same-sex prohibitions had moved toward abolishing them, that the Model Penal Code promulgated by the American Law Institute did not recommend "criminal penalties for sexual relations conducted in private," and that a committee advising the British Parliament in 1957 had recommended a repeal of laws punishing homosexual conduct, and that Parliament had accepted that recommendation ten years later.[226] "The right the petitioners seek in this case has been accepted as an integral part of human freedom in many other

---

224. *Id.,* at 218–19.
225. *Lawrence* v. *Texas,* 539 U.S. 558, 565 (2003).
226. *Id.,* at 572–73.

countries," Tony noted, and "[t]here has been no showing that in this case the governmental interest in circumscribing personal choice is somehow more legitimate or urgent."[227]

Tony then referred to the importance of the doctrine of stare decisis but noted that there had been no individual or societal reliance on its holding that could counsel against overturning *Bowers*. He then quoted this passage from my dissenting opinion in *Bowers*:

> Our prior cases make two propositions abundantly clear. First, the fact that the governing majority in a State has traditionally viewed a particular practice as immoral is not a sufficient reason for upholding a law prohibiting the practice; neither history nor tradition could save a law prohibiting miscegenation from constitutional attack. Second, individual decisions by married persons, concerning the intimacies of their physical relationship, even when not intended to produce offspring, are a form of "liberty" protected by the Due Process Clause of the Fourteenth Amendment. Moreover, this protection extends to intimate choices by unmarried as well as married persons.[228]

Tony further declared that, in the Court's view, my analysis "should have been controlling in *Bowers* and should control here."[229] I could not have agreed more.

Though vindication is always satisfying, I've taken particular satisfaction in seeing the seeds I planted in my *Bowers* dissent (and perhaps even earlier in *Doe* v. *Commonwealth's Attorney for Richmond*) grow to strike down anti-sodomy statutes in *Lawrence,* which in turn has led to an ever greater expansion of liberty and equality for our fellow citizens in the later decisions *United States* v. *Windsor,*[230] which struck down the

---

227. *Id.,* at 577.
228. *Id.,* at 577–78, quoting *Bowers,* 478 U.S., at 216.
229. *Id.,* at 578.
230. 570 U.S. 744 (2013).

Defense of Marriage Act, and *Obergefell* v. *Hodges,*[231] which recognized that the fundamental right to marry cannot be denied to same-sex couples. Tony Kennedy was of course instrumental in these groundbreaking decisions, but I like to think that, even though I had left the bench, I had a hand in them as well.

October Term 2003

Sandra O'Connor and I were coauthors of the Court opinion that upheld the constitutionality of Titles I and II of the Bipartisan Campaign Reform Act of 2002 (BCRA), also known as the McCain-Feingold Act, in *McConnell* v. *FEC.*[232] Because of the importance of the case, we heard oral argument three weeks in advance of the first Monday in October of 2003, and we issued our 110-page opinion on December 10, 2003. The BCRA was the then most recent amendment to almost a century of measures designed "to purge national politics of the pernicious influence of 'big money' campaign contributions."[233] The law was a response to three recent developments that had convinced Congress of the need for further legislation to regulate the role that corporations, unions, and wealthy contributors play in the electoral process: the increased importance of "soft money"; the proliferation of "issue ads"; and the disturbing findings of a Senate investigation into campaign practices related to the 1996 federal elections.

Since 1971, federal law had required that contributions to political campaigns made "for the purpose of influencing any election for Federal office" must be made with money that is subject to amount and disclosure requirements. Such funds are known as "hard money," whereas donations made solely for the purpose of influencing state or local elections, which are unaffected by federal amount and disclosure requirements, are called

---

231. 135 S. Ct. 2584 (2015).
232. 540 U.S. 93 (2003).
233. *Id.,* at 115, quoting *United States* v. *Automobile Workers,* 352 U.S. 567, 572 (1957).

"soft money." The Federal Election Commission had permitted the parties to use soft money to finance campaign advertising as long as it did not expressly advocate a named candidate's election or defeat. Soft-money spending increased from $21.6 million in 1984, to $80 million in 1992, to $272 million in 1996, and to $498 million in 2000. The fact that thirty-five of the fifty largest soft money donors gave to both parties indicated that many of the corporate contributions were motivated by a desire for access to candidates and a fear of being placed at a disadvantage in the legislative process, rather than by ideological support for the candidate.

Under its 1976 decision in *Buckley* v. *Valeo*,[234] the Court had construed the statutory disclosure and reporting requirements, as well as the expenditure limitations, to reach only funds used for communications that expressly advocated the election or defeat of "a clearly identified candidate." As a result of that strict reading, the use or omission of "magic words," such as "Elect John Doe," marked a bright line separating "express advocacy" from "issue advocacy." The former could be financed only with hard money, while issue ads could be financed with soft money and without disclosing any information about their sponsors. Corporations and unions spent hundreds of millions of dollars from their general funds to pay for such ads, and those expenditures, like soft money donations to the major parties, were unregulated.

In 1998 the Senate Committee on Governmental Affairs issued a six-volume report summarizing the results of its intensive investigation into the campaign practices in the 1996 federal elections. The report concluded that the "soft money loophole" had led to a "meltdown" of the campaign finance system that had been intended "to keep corporate, union and large individual contributions from influencing the electoral process." The report discussed potential reforms, including a ban on soft money at the national and state party levels and restrictions on sham issue advocacy by nonparty groups. The BCRA, as eventually enacted, adopted

---

234. 424 U.S. 1.

the recommendations of the committee, including a number of provisions designed to curtail the use of soft money and issue advertising.

In our opinion upholding the measure against a variety of challenges, Sandra and I relied heavily on past precedent and our view that the interest in limiting the flood of money in federal elections was entitled to substantial respect. Nino, Tony, and Clarence, in their dissents, emphasized their understanding "that one, and only one, interest justified the burden" on First Amendment rights imposed by the statute: "eliminating, or preventing, actual corruption or the appearance of corruption stemming from contributions to candidates."[235] After John Roberts and Sam Alito joined the Court, the dissent's view would prevail.

When Sandra and I authored our one joint opinion, we thought it appropriate to begin with the long-standing and, until recently, uncontroversial understanding that corporate expenditures posed a distinct risk to our democratic process:

> More than a century ago the "sober-minded Elihu Root" advocated legislation that would prohibit political contributions by corporations in order to prevent "the great aggregations of wealth, from using their corporate funds, directly or indirectly," to elect legislators who would "vote for their protection and the advancement of their interests as against those of the public."…In Root's opinion, such legislation would "strike at a constantly growing evil which has done more to shake the confidence of the plain people of small means of this country in our political institutions than any other practice which has ever obtained since the foundation of our Government."[236]

One of the more momentous cases of the term was one that did not end up deciding very much — *Vieth* v. *Jubelirer* [237] — but still managed to

---

235. *McConnell,* 540 U.S., at 291.
236. *Id.,* at 115, quoting *Automobile Workers,* 352 U.S., at 571.
237. 541 U.S. 267 (2004).

produce five separate opinions vigorously debating the question whether political gerrymandering claims are justiciable. The case involved a challenge to the constitutionality of Pennsylvania's 2002 congressional districting map. Nino Scalia wrote the lead opinion, joined by the chief, Sandra, and Clarence, holding that such claims are not justiciable. Tony Kennedy agreed that the plaintiffs' complaint should be dismissed but refused to join an opinion holding that standards for evaluating political gerrymandering claims are categorically unavailable. Four of us dissented in three different opinions: David Souter wrote for himself and Ruth Ginsburg, while Stephen Breyer and I each wrote for ourselves.

In 1986, Byron White had authored *Davis* v. *Bandemer,*[238] which had held that political gerrymandering claims are justiciable, but imposed a highly difficult and less than clear standard for adjudicating them. Lewis Powell, whom I had joined, had written separately, agreeing that political gerrymandering claims were justiciable; he would have held them invalid whenever bizarre district shapes could not be explained by reference to nonpartisan criteria. In *Vieth,* Nino wanted to overrule *Bandemer* but failed to persuade Tony to do so.

Nino's opinion contains an interesting account of the early history of gerrymandering, including references to North Carolina in 1732, an attempt by Patrick Henry to gerrymander James Madison out of the First Congress, and in 1812 "the notoriously outrageous political districting in Massachusetts that gave the Gerrymander its name — an amalgam of the name of Massachusetts Governor Elbridge Gerry and the creature ('salamander') which the outline of an election district he was credited with forming was thought to resemble."[239] He quoted a scholar who had described the gerrymander as a recognized force in party politics that "was generally attempted in all legislation enacted for the formation of election districts."[240] He then pointed out that the framers had provided

---

238. 478 U.S. 109.
239. 541 U.S., at 274.
240. *Id.,* at 275.

a remedy for gerrymandering of congressional districts (though not for state legislative districts) in the Constitution itself by permitting Congress to "make or alter" the districts initially drawn by state legislatures. That power was exercised in 1842 when Congress required that representatives must be elected from single-member districts composed of contiguous territory and in 1872 when it required that districts contain "as nearly as practicable an equal number of inhabitants."[241] Requirements of contiguity, compactness, and equality of population were repeated in 1911 but not thereafter. "Today, only the single-member-district requirement remains,"[242] but occasionally bills to regulate gerrymandering of congressional maps have been introduced in Congress.

Nino then explained why, in his opinion, various proposed standards for adjudicating political gerrymandering claims were neither discernible nor manageable. In that discussion he correctly noted that much of my dissent was "addressed to the incompatibility of severe partisan gerrymanders with democratic principles" and that he did not disagree with that judgment.[243] This acknowledgment was significant: It signaled, at the least, a majority of the Court concluding that partisan gerrymanders, regardless of their historical pedigree, were inconsistent with our democratic form of government. The issue before the Court, however, was "not whether severe party gerrymanders violate the Constitution, but whether it is for the courts to say when a violation has occurred, and to design a remedy."[244] "On that point," however, Nino found my dissent "less helpful" and described it as merely saying "if we can do it in the racially gerrymandering context we can do it here."[245] That's exactly right, and it was precisely my point. But Justice Scalia was unpersuaded:

---

241. *Id.*, at 276.
242. *Ibid.*
243. *Id.*, at 292.
244. *Ibid.*
245. *Ibid.*

What we have said is impermissible is "the purpose of segregating voters on the basis of race"...that is to say, racial gerrymandering for race's sake, which would be the equivalent of political gerrymandering for politics' sake. Justice Stevens says we "err in assuming that politics is 'an ordinary and lawful motive'" in districting—but all he brings forward to contest that is the argument that an *excessive* injection of politics is *un*lawful. So it is, and so does our opinion assume. That does not alter the reality that setting out to segregate voters by race is unlawful and hence rare, and setting out to segregate them by political affiliation is (so long as one doesn't go too far) lawful and ordinary.[246]

The notion that segregating voters on the basis of political affiliation is both lawful and ordinary overlooks what I regard as the central purpose of the Equal Protection Clause of the Fourteenth Amendment—that clause imposes a duty to act impartially on all government agents, including all members of a legislature. Just as they may not use public funds to pay one party's campaign expenses, so may they not draw district lines to give one party an electoral advantage. That proposition was so obvious years earlier when the Court decided *Karcher* v. *Daggett*[247] and *Davis* v. *Bandemer*,[248] that the arguments made by the parties defending those gerrymanders consisted entirely of denials of intent to engage in the practice rather than any claim that the practice was legitimate. In those cases, as in the challenge to Pennsylvania's Sixth District in *Vieth*, the absence of any neutral explanation for the bizarre shape of certain districts provided unrefuted evidence of partisan gerrymandering. Moreover, that evidence was every bit as probative as the evidence of racial gerrymandering that was held sufficient in *Gomillion* v. *Lightfoot*[249] in 1960, and in *Shaw* v. *Reno*[250] in 1993.

---

246. *Id.*, at 293.
247. 455 U.S. 1303 (1982).
248. 478 U.S. 109 (1986).
249. 364 U.S. 339.
250. 509 U.S. 630.

Although Nino condemned racial gerrymandering as more obnoxious than political gerrymandering, his opinion in *Vieth* is particularly noteworthy for its failure to even attempt to explain why proving racial gerrymandering is any easier than proving political gerrymandering. After all, registered voters regularly disclose their political affiliation but need not identify their race. According to Nino Scalia, even assuming "that there exist standards which this Court could apply[, that] does not mean that those standards are discernible in the Constitution. This Court may not willy-nilly apply standards — even manageable standards — having no relation to constitutional harms."[251] But a standard, such as the one I proposed, that required a state to identify a non-partisan explanation for a district's bizarre shape would provide the first step in providing a remedy for an obvious and severe constitutional harm. I concluded my dissent with these two paragraphs:

> The plurality candidly acknowledges that legislatures can fashion standards to remedy political gerrymandering that are perfectly manageable and, indeed, that the legislatures in Iowa and elsewhere have done so. If a violation of the Constitution is found, a court could impose a remedy patterned after such a statute. Thus, the problem, in the plurality's view, is not that there is no judicially manageable standard to fix an unconstitutional partisan gerrymander, but rather that the Judiciary lacks the ability to determine when a state legislature has violated its duty to govern impartially.
>
> Quite obviously, however, several standards for identifying impermissible partisan influence are available to judges who have the will to enforce them. We could hold that every district boundary must have a neutral justification; we could apply Justice Powell's three-factor approach in *Bandemer;* we could apply the predominant motivation standard fashioned by the Court in its racial

---

251. *Vieth*, 541 U.S., at 294–95.

gerrymandering cases; or we could endorse either of the approaches advocated today by Justice SOUTER and Justice BREYER. What is clear is that it is not the unavailability of judicially manageable standards that drives today's decision. It is, instead, a failure of judicial will to condemn even the most blatant violations of a state legislature's fundamental duty to govern impartially.[252]

Although I remain convinced that the standard for evaluating the constitutionality of allegedly gerrymandered districts that I advocated as far back as my dissent as a Seventh Circuit judge in *Cousins* v. *City Council of the City of Chicago*[253] is correct, and that political gerrymanders and racial gerrymanders should be judged by the same standard, I have been singularly unsuccessful in persuading any of my former colleagues (except Lewis Powell) to agree with my views. I remain puzzled by my failure because the Court has had no difficulty prohibiting racial gerrymanders, and simply applying the rules that apply to those cases to political gerrymanders would readily solve the problem.

Gustav Klimt, the famous Austrian artist, was born in 1862 and died at the age of fifty-five in 1918. His custom of wearing nothing but a smock while painting may tell us something about his relations with his models, with whom he had eighteen illegitimate children, but seems unrelated to the quality or value of his artwork. One of his two portraits of Adele Bloch-Bauer was sold in New York for $135 million in 2006. That was one of six of his works that had hung in the Vienna home of Adele's husband, Ferdinand Bloch-Bauer, a wealthy sugar magnate. Adele died in 1925, leaving a will in which she asked her husband to bequeath the six Klimt paintings to the Austrian Art Gallery in Vienna. Though apparently intending to do so, he never did; he remained their owner until his death in 1945. In his will, he left his estate to three relatives, including his

---

252. *Id.,* at 340–341 (citation omitted).
253. 466 F. 2d 830 (CA7 1972).

niece, Maria V. Altmann, who had fled the country after the German Anschluss in 1938 and eventually became an American citizen.

Ferdinand, who was Jewish, had supported resistance to the German annexation of Austria. He fled the country and moved to Switzerland before the Nazis actually took over. They "Aryanized" his sugar company and his Vienna home, including the six Klimt paintings. A Nazi lawyer — aptly named "Erich Fuhrer" — took possession of the Klimt paintings, selling three to the Austrian Art Gallery and one to the Museum of Vienna while keeping one for himself. The fate of the sixth is unknown.

In 1946 Austria enacted a law declaring all transactions motivated by Nazi ideology null and void. That law did not result in the immediate return of looted artworks to exiled Austrians, however, because another Austrian law proscribed the export of artworks deemed important to the country's cultural heritage, and required anyone wishing to export art to obtain the permission of the Federal Monument Agency. Relying on that requirement, the gallery and the agency adopted a practice of forcing Jews to donate valuable artworks to the gallery in exchange for export permits for other works. Thereafter, Maria's brother and fellow heir, Robert Bentley, retained a Viennese lawyer to locate and recover property stolen from Ferdinand Bloch-Bauer during the war. When the lawyer requested the gallery to return the three Klimts that it had purchased from Fuhrer, the gallery falsely responded that Adele had bequeathed them to the gallery.

In 1998 an Austrian journalist examining the gallery's files discovered documents revealing that at all relevant times gallery officials knew that neither Adele nor Ferdinand had, in fact, donated any of the six Klimts to the gallery. The journalist published a series of articles in which he specifically noted that Klimt's first portrait of Adele, which the gallery's official publications had described as having been donated to the museum in 1936, had actually been received in 1941 accompanied by a letter from Fuhrer signed "Heil Hitler."

Prior to those revelations, Maria Altmann had believed that Adele and Ferdinand had freely donated the Klimt paintings to the gallery before the war. When she learned the true facts, she immediately sought recovery of the Klimts and other artworks. After what she characterized as a "sham" proceeding, a committee of Austrian government officials and art historians rejected her request, relying on a deliberate misreading of Adele's will as a precatory request creating a binding legal obligation requiring her husband to donate the paintings to the gallery on his death.

Maria then announced that she would file a lawsuit in Austria to recover the paintings. Because Austrian court costs are proportional to the value of the recovery sought, they would have amounted to several million dollars. In response to her request, the Austrian court entered an order reducing that amount to $350,000, but requiring payment before being allowed to proceed. The Austrian government filed an appeal from that order and while that appeal was pending, Maria dismissed her Austrian suit and filed a new action in a federal district court in California.

The defendants — the Republic of Austria and the Austrian Art Gallery, an instrumentality of the republic — filed a motion to dismiss the complaint, claiming that they were entitled to sovereign immunity. The district court and the Court of Appeals for the Ninth Circuit both rejected that defense. We granted certiorari because Austria's argument raised a novel question of interpretation of the Foreign Sovereign Immunities Act of 1976. That question was whether an exemption from the grant of immunity for cases in which property had been taken in violation of international law applied to conduct that occurred before the statute's enactment in 1976.

Because the solicitor general filed an amicus brief supporting Austria, as did the lawyers for several other sovereigns, the lawyer for Maria Altmann was extremely pessimistic about his chances of winning and later stated that he was surprised by the result. My twenty-two-page opinion for the Court rejecting Austria's argument over the dissent of Tony Kennedy, joined by Bill Rehnquist and Clarence Thomas, is far less interesting than the facts of the case.[254] It is nevertheless worth noting that in addition to the $135 million paid for the most famous painting of Adele

---

254. *Republic of Aus.* v. *Altmann,* 541 U.S. 677 (2004).

Bloch-Bauer, her second portrait sold for $88 million, Klimt's *Birch Forest,* painted in 1903, sold for $40.3 million, *Apple Tree* for $33 million, and *Houses in Unterach on Lake Atter* for $40.4 million.

After the case was remanded for trial, and after many months of debates over discovery issues, Maria ultimately agreed to have the case resolved in Austria by a panel of Austrian arbitrators who ruled in her favor. I'm sure Maria would have preferred an easier route to recovering her family's heritage. But her travails were so inspiring they caught the attention of Hollywood, which translated her plight into the 2015 film *Woman in Gold,* starring Helen Mirren in the lead role of Maria Altmann. Incidentally, the portrait of Adele Bloch-Bauer that inspired the title for the movie is now on display to the public at the Neue Galerie in New York.

Michael Newdow, an atheist who acted as his own lawyer, brought suit in a federal district court in California to challenge the constitutionality of the daily repetition in his daughter's classroom of the words "under God" that Congress in 1954 added to the previous version of the Pledge of Allegiance. As required by a California statute, his daughter's public school teacher leads her class in a recitation of the pledge every morning. Newdow did not allege that his daughter was required to participate in the ceremony, but he did claim that she was injured when she was compelled to watch and listen as her state-employed teacher led classmates in a ritual proclaiming that there is a God and that ours is "one nation under God." A divided panel of the Ninth Circuit ruled in favor of Newdow and our Court granted review.

After the Ninth Circuit announced its opinion, Sandra Banning, the mother of Newdow's daughter, intervened in the case and filed a motion to dismiss, correctly representing that she had the exclusive legal custody of their child, which included the right to make decisions about her education and welfare. Banning stated that her daughter believes in God, had no objection to reciting or hearing others recite the pledge, and might be harmed if the litigation were permitted to proceed because her classmates might incorrectly infer that she shared her father's views. In my opinion for the Court, I explained why Banning's filing had convinced six of us that Newdow did not have the right to dictate to others what they might say to his daughter about religion.[255] His lack of standing persuaded us to dismiss the case. The chief justice, Sandra, and Clarence each wrote an opinion disagreeing with that conclusion and explaining why he or she concluded that there was no valid objection to including the words "under God" in the pledge.

After completing his clerkship with me in the spring of 1999, Jeffrey Fisher accepted a teaching position at the Stanford Law School where he formed an appellate clinic and began an unusually successful career as an oral advocate in our Court. One of his particularly important victories was *Blakely* v. *Washington,*[256] which set aside a defendant's ninety-month sentence for kidnapping his wife. His guilty plea had admitted to facts that would have supported a maximum sentence of fifty-three months, but the trial judge had imposed a longer sentence after finding that he had acted with deliberate cruelty. Jeff had successfully argued that the sentence had deprived the defendant of his federal constitutional right to have a jury determine beyond a reasonable doubt all facts legally essential to his sentence.

The case represented the final chapter in a debate between Nino, David, Ruth, Clarence, and me against the chief and Sandra, Tony, and Steve that began with our decision in *Apprendi* v. *New Jersey.*[257] Because of its importance and my confidence that Nino would write a typically persuasive opinion, I assigned the opinion to him, and he correctly wrote that the facts required us to apply the rule we had announced in *Apprendi:* "Other than the fact of a prior conviction, any fact that increases the penalty for a crime beyond the prescribed statutory maximum must be

---

255. *Elk Grove Unified Sch. Dist.* v. *Newdow,* 542 U.S. 1 (2004).
256. 542 U.S. 296 (2004).
257. 530 U.S. 466 (2000).

submitted to a jury, and proved beyond a reasonable doubt."[258] That rule remains the law today.

On June 28, 2004, the Court decided the first few of several cases arising out of detentions related to the U.S. government's response to the September 11, 2001, attacks on the World Trade Center in New York City and the Pentagon in Arlington, Virginia: *Rumsfeld* v. *Padilla;*[259] *Rasul* v. *Bush;*[260] and *Hamdi* v. *Rumsfeld.*[261] The chief justice wrote the Court opinion in *Padilla,* Sandra wrote in *Hamdi,* and I wrote in *Rasul.* These cases tested the boundaries of the federal government's, and particularly the president's, power to detain individuals based on national security. They forced us to grapple with the proper balance to be struck between the nation's weighty national security concerns against the individual's equally important liberty interest.

On May 8, 2002, José Padilla, a U.S. citizen, was arrested at Chicago's O'Hare International Airport as he stepped off a plane that had just arrived from Pakistan. He was served with a material witness warrant issued by the federal district court in New York that was conducting a grand jury investigation into the September 11 terrorist attacks. He was transferred to New York where he was held in federal criminal custody. A week later the court appointed Donna Newman to represent him. She conferred with him and filed motions seeking his release on the ground that his incarceration was unconstitutional and violated a federal statute prohibiting the incarceration of citizens who have not violated any statute. The district court scheduled a hearing on the motions for Tuesday, June 11.

On Sunday, June 9, without providing any notice to Padilla or his lawyer, the president issued a written command to Donald Rumsfeld, the secretary of defense, designating Padilla an "enemy combatant" closely associated with "al Quaeda, an international terrorist organization with

---

258. 542 U.S., at 301, quoting *Apprendi,* 530 U.S., at 490.
259. 542 U.S. 426 (2004).
260. 542 U.S. 466 (2004).
261. 542 U.S. 507 (2004).

which the United States is at war," and stating that he possesses intelligence that "if communicated to the U.S., would aid U.S. efforts to prevent attacks by al Quaeda" on U.S. targets.[262] The command concluded with a direction "to receive Mr. Padilla from the Department of Justice and to detain him as an enemy combatant."[263]

In an ex parte proceeding on that same Sunday, the government notified the district court that it was withdrawing the grand jury subpoena that it had served on Padilla at the O'Hare Airport and it requested the court to enter an order vacating the material witness warrant. The district court did so, and on the following day the government announced Padilla's transfer to the custody of the Defense Department. The president's designation of Padilla as an enemy combatant provided the only basis for his detention thereafter.

On Tuesday, acting as his next friend, Donna Newman filed a habeas corpus petition in the New York district court. The district judge certified a series of questions to the Court of Appeals for the Second Circuit, which held that Padilla should be released in thirty days. We granted cert to consider two questions: whether Padilla had properly filed his petition in New York and second whether the president had the authority to detain Padilla militarily. In his opinion for the five-justice majority, the chief concluded that the petition should have been filed in South Carolina, where Padilla was actually imprisoned on Tuesday, June 11, and should have named his immediate custodian (the commander of the Consolidated Naval Brig) rather than Donald Rumsfeld, as respondent.

Tony Kennedy, joined by Sandra O'Connor, wrote separately, acknowledging that the Court has recognized exceptions to both the rule requiring the respondent to be the immediate custodian of a habeas petitioner and the rule requiring him to sue in the district where he is confined, but he nevertheless joined the chief. David, Ruth, and Stephen joined my dissenting opinion, in which I argued that it was especially appropriate to

---

262. 542 U.S., at 456.
263. *Id.,* at 457.

have the secretary of defense participating as a party because the change in Padilla's location represented a change in the rationale for his detention, and that change raised a profoundly important question about the president's power over civilians during hostilities.

It seemed obvious to me that if the government had given notice of its intent to transfer custody of Padilla to the military, Newman would have filed her petition immediately rather than waiting two days, and that the "difference between that scenario and what actually occurred should not affect our decision, for we should not permit the government to obtain a tactical advantage as a consequence of an *ex parte* proceeding. The departure from the time-honored practice of giving one's adversary notice of an intent to present an important motion to the court justifies treating the habeas application as the functional equivalent of one filed two days earlier."[264]

I found the government's tactics in the case particularly offensive because in the lower court they had candidly explained their motive for detaining Padilla: "[O]ur interest really in his case is not law enforcement, it is not punishment because he was a terrorist or working with terrorists. Our interest at the moment is to try and find out everything he knows so that hopefully we can stop other terrorist acts."[265] I closed my dissent with these two paragraphs:

At stake in this case is nothing less than the essence of a free society. Even more important than the method of selecting the people's rulers and their successors is the character of the constraints imposed on the Executive by the rule of law. Unconstrained executive detention for the purpose of investigating and preventing subversive activity is the hallmark of the Star Chamber. Access to counsel for the purpose of protecting the citizen from official mistakes and mistreatment is the hallmark of due process.

264. *Id.*, at 459.
265. *Id.*, at 464n9.

Executive detention of subversive citizens, like detention of enemy soldiers to keep them off the battlefield, may sometimes be justified to prevent persons from launching or becoming missiles of destruction. It may not, however, be justified by the naked interest in using unlawful procedures to extract information. Incommunicado detention for months on end is such a procedure. Whether the information so procured is more or less reliable than that acquired by more extreme forms of torture is of no consequence. For if this Nation is to remain true to the ideals symbolized by its flag, it must not wield the tools of tyrants even to resist an assault by the forces of tyranny.[266]

Subsequent events confirmed my understanding that the purpose of Padilla's designation as an enemy combatant was to subject him to enhanced (and patently unlawful) interrogation techniques. We don't know whether those techniques produced any useful intelligence, but we do know that he was held in incommunicado detention for months on end.

Yasir Hamdi was an American citizen born in Louisiana in 1980 who moved with his family to Saudi Arabia as a child. In 2001 he resided in Afghanistan. At some time that year he was seized by members of the Northern Alliance, a coalition of military groups opposed to the Taliban government, and later turned over to the United States military. The government initially detained and interrogated him in Afghanistan. But in January 2002, it transferred him to the United States naval base in Guantánamo Bay, Cuba, whence, in April 2002, upon learning that he was an American citizen, the navy moved him, first to a brig in Norfolk, Virginia, and then to another brig in South Carolina.

In June 2002, Hamdi's father filed a petition for a writ of habeas corpus in Virginia, naming himself and his son as petitioners, alleging

---

266. *Id.*, at 465.

that since Hamdi had been seized, the government had held his son "without access to legal counsel or notice of any charges pending against him."[267] They asked for Hamdi's release and, among other things, to order respondents to cease interrogating him.

In response, the government filed a declaration by an adviser who stated that he was familiar with the facts related to the capture and detention of Hamdi, that Hamdi had "traveled to Afghanistan" in July or August 2001, that he thereafter "affiliated with a Taliban military unit and received weapons training," and that he remained with his Taliban unit following the attacks on New York on September 11, and that a series of "U.S. military screening teams" had determined that Hamdi met the criteria for enemy combatants.[268] The district court found that the declaration was not sufficient to justify Hamdi's continued detention and ordered the government to turn over numerous materials, including a list of all interrogators who had questioned him, and the names and titles of the agents who had determined that he was an enemy combatant.

When the government stated that it would appeal the production order, the district court certified the question whether the government's declaration was sufficient to allow meaningful review of Hamdi's classification as an enemy combatant. The Court of Appeals for the Fourth Circuit agreed with the government that the district court's proposed inquiry was excessive. On the broader question whether there is legal authorization for the detention of citizens who are enemy combatants, the court expressed doubt as to whether 18 U.S.C. § 4001(a), which provides that "[n]o citizen shall be imprisoned or otherwise detained by the United States except pursuant to an Act of Congress" applied, but held that, in any event, Congress had authorized such detention in the resolution that it had adopted a week after the September 11 attacks. That resolution (the Authorization for the Use of Military Force, or AUMF) provides that "the President is authorized to use all necessary and

---

267. *Hamdi,* 542 U.S., at 511.
268. *Id.,* at 512–13.

appropriate force against those nations, organizations or persons he determines planned, authorized, committed, or aided the terrorist attacks that occurred on September 11, 2001, or harbored such organizations or persons, in order to prevent any future acts of international terrorism against the United States by such nations, organizations or persons."

We granted Hamdi's petition for certiorari to consider whether Section 4001(a) protected him from being designated an "enemy combatant" and whether the congressional resolution authorized the executive to so designate him. After hearing argument, we responded in five different opinions: Sandra, joined by the chief, Tony, and Stephen, concluded that the AUMF provided the necessary authority but that Hamdi was entitled to more procedural safeguards than he had received. David, joined by Ruth, concluded that the AUMF did not authorize Hamdi's detention and did not qualify Section 4001(a)'s prohibition of the detention of citizens without statutory authorization but joined the Court's judgment because he agreed that due process entitled Hamdi to more procedural safeguards than he had received. Although I had originally intended to join Sandra's opinion, Nino convinced me that Hamdi was entitled to a 100 percent victory—that he was entitled to have his petition for habeas corpus granted unless Congress exercised its power to suspend the writ, which it had not done. Clarence also dissented, but he would have upheld the government's position not only on the basic issue but also on the sufficiency of its procedures.

After our remand, the government agreed to a settlement with Hamdi that allowed him to return to Saudi Arabia. I do not know whether intelligence of any value was ever obtained as a result of his months of incommunicado interrogation. My principal memory of the case is based on my admiration for Nino's characteristically persuasive opinion. In that opinion he reminded us that the "very core of liberty secured by our Anglo-Saxon system of separated powers has been freedom from indefinite imprisonment at the will of the Executive."[269]

---

269. *Id.,* at 554–55.

*   *   *

Acting in response to the congressional resolution authorizing him to use force against the perpetrators of the September 11, 2001 attacks, President Bush sent U.S. armed forces into Afghanistan to wage a military campaign against Al Qaeda and the Taliban regime that supported it. In 2002 some 650 non-Americans were captured abroad and detained at the naval base at Guantánamo Bay, Cuba. The United States occupies the base, which comprises forty-five square miles of land and water along the southeastern coast of Cuba, pursuant to a 1903 lease agreement executed with the newly independent Republic of Cuba in the aftermath of the Spanish-American War. Under that agreement, "the United States recognizes the continuance of the ultimate sovereignty of the Republic of Cuba over the [leased area]," while "the Republic of Cuba consents that during the period of the occupation by the United States...the United States shall exercise complete jurisdiction and control over and within said areas."[270] A supplemental lease agreement executed in July of 1903 obligates the United States to maintain permanent fences around the base and to pay an annual rent of $2,000 in gold coin. In 1934, the parties entered into a treaty providing that, absent an agreement to modify or abrogate the lease, it would remain in effect so long as the United States shall not abandon the naval station at Guantánamo.

In 2002, the U.S. government was detaining two Australian citizens and twelve Kuwaiti citizens, who had all been captured abroad during hostilities between the United States and the Taliban, at Guantánamo. Acting through relatives, they filed petitions for writs of habeas corpus in the federal district court in Washington, D.C. All of them alleged that they had never engaged in combat against the United States and had not engaged in any terrorist activities. (They alleged that they were captured by local villagers who received bounties in exchange for their surrender to U.S. forces.) The district court and the Court of Appeals for

---

270. *Rasul*, 542 U.S., at 471, quoting Lease of Lands for Coaling and Naval Stations, Feb. 23, 1903, U.S.–Cuba, Art. III, T. S. No. 418.

the D.C. Circuit dismissed the petitions, holding that "'the privilege of litigation' does not extend to aliens in military custody who have no presence in 'any territory over which the United States is sovereign.'"[271]

The principal authority on which the courts relied was Justice Robert Jackson's 1950 opinion in *Johnson* v. *Eisentrager*. In that case, the Court had held that a federal district court lacked authority to issue a writ of habeas corpus to twenty-one German citizens who had been captured in China and convicted of war crimes by an American military commission in Nanking (now Nanjing) and incarcerated in an American prison in Germany. That case, in turn, had relied on a case decided just months after the twenty-one German citizens had filed their petition, *Ahrens* v. *Clark*,[272] which held that 120 Germans being detained at Ellis Island, New York, could not proceed against the attorney general in district court in Washington, D.C., because they were not being detained within the jurisdiction where he was located. By 2002, however, *Ahrens* had been overruled.

Putting *Eisentrager* and *Ahrens* aside, the government further argued that habeas was unavailable to the Guantánamo detainees because of the presumption against the extraterritorial application of federal statutes. Writing for the Court, I found this argument unpersuasive, because under the lease agreement with Cuba the United States exercises "complete jurisdiction and control" over the Guantánamo Bay Naval Base and may continue to do so permanently.

Five justices joined my opinion for the Court, agreeing with my view that the intervening overruling of *Ahrens* provided a sufficient basis for distinguishing *Eisentrager*. Tony Kennedy joined our judgment upholding the petitioners' right to proceed but by distinguishing *Eisentrager* on the grounds, first, that Guantánamo Bay was in every practical sense a U.S. territory, and second, unlike the petitioners in that case who had been tried and convicted by a military tribunal, the detainees at

---

271. *Al Odah* v. *United States,* 321 F. 3d 1134, 1144 (D.C. Cir. 2003), quoting *Johnson* v. *Eisentrager,* 339 U.S. 763, 777–78 (1950).
272. 335 U.S. 188 (1948).

Guantánamo Bay were being held indefinitely without the benefit of any legal proceeding to determine their status. Nino Scalia, who was joined by the chief and Clarence Thomas, dissented, arguing that *Eisentrager* was correctly decided and should be followed. Though none of us commented on Justice Black's dissent in that case, which Justices Douglas and Burton joined, the view he espoused there — particularly the view that our nation's great ideals of liberty and justice do not cease at the water's edge — was endorsed by the majority's decision in *Rasul:*

> Conquest by the United States, unlike conquest by many other nations, does not mean tyranny. For our people choose to maintain their greatness by justice rather than violence. Our constitutional principles are such that their mandate of equal justice under law should be applied as well when we occupy lands across the sea as when our flag flew only over thirteen colonies. Our nation proclaims a belief in the dignity of human beings as such, no matter what their nationality or where they happen to live. Habeas corpus, as an instrument to protect against illegal imprisonment, is written into the Constitution. Its use by courts cannot in my judgment be constitutionally abridged by Executive or by Congress. I would hold that our courts can exercise it whenever any United States official illegally imprisons any person in any land we govern. Courts should not for any reason abdicate this, the loftiest power with which the Constitution has endowed them.[273]

October Term 2004

Chief Justice Rehnquist suffered from thyroid cancer during the 2004 term of the Court. Despite his illness, which forced him to miss presiding at well over half of the oral arguments during the term, his study of the briefs, transcripts, and recordings of oral arguments; pertinent reported

---

273. *Eisentrager,* 339 U.S., at 797–98 (footnote and quotation marks omitted).

cases; and memos from his law clerks, supplemented by telephone conversations with colleagues, enabled him to perform a full share of the Court's workload. When he was absent, as the senior associate justice, I presided over oral arguments and made the assignments of Court opinions when I was in the majority. Neither was a difficult task.

Bill was ill during the week preceding President George Bush's second inauguration on January 20, 2004. His extremely competent administrative assistant, Sally Rider, provided me with a copy of the presidential oath and advised me to be prepared to pinch hit if the chief was not able to swear in the president himself. I had the draft oath with me when, with the other members of the Court, I marched onto the Capitol platform to witness the ceremony. Until only about five or six minutes before noon, we did not know whether or not the chief would show up, but he did arrive on time and performed flawlessly. He did not stay for lunch but at that occasion he was suitably thanked by the president.

After our decision in *Blakely,* I had assumed that our reliance on *Apprendi*'s essential holding to invalidate mandatory applications of the federal sentencing guidelines that produced sentences longer than could be supported by facts either found by a jury or admitted by the defendant would be relatively painless. I could not have been more wrong.

In *United States* v. *Booker,*[274] we granted the government's cert petition to review two court of appeals decisions refusing to impose such improper sentences. Nino, Clarence, David, and Ruth joined my opinion ruling against the government in both cases. Ruth, however, parted company with the rest of us and joined Steve's opinion for the Court deciding on the proper remedy for the violation. Instead of simply invalidating those excessive sentences that the guidelines mandated, they concluded that it would be wiser to invalidate all of the provisions in the guidelines that made them mandatory.

Steve thus wrote the dissent on the merits but the majority opinion

---

274. 543 U.S. 220 (2005).

prescribing the remedy, while I wrote the majority opinion on the merits and the principal dissent on the remedy. Ruth was the only member of the Court to join both majority opinions, and Steve was the only justice writing for the other side. Nino and Clarence each filed dissents discussing the remedy issue. As far as I can recall, *Booker* is the only case in which only one of the authors identifying a constitutional violation had anything to say about the remedy for that violation.

As of this writing, a little more than a decade after it was decided, *Booker* appears to have been cited almost 30,000 times in federal court decisions, including in as many as eight hundred Supreme Court decisions alone. But *Booker* was in many respects more consequential in principle than in practice. *Booker* was important in principle because it made clear that the U.S. Sentencing Guidelines were "effectively advisory."[275] It was of limited import in practice, though, because the sentencing guidelines continued to be, as the Court recently explained, " 'the starting point and the initial benchmark' for sentencing."[276] "The Guidelines thus continue to guide district courts in exercising their discretion by serving as the framework for sentencing, but they do not constrain that discretion."[277] That discretion nonetheless remains important. As Sonia Sotomayor noted the term after I left the Court, even if a district court "must still give 'respectful consideration' to the now-advisory Guidelines (and their accompanying policy statements),"[278] "a district court may in appropriate cases impose a non-Guidelines sentence based on," for example, "disagreement with the Commission's views."[279] "That is particularly true," she noted, when "the Commission's views rest on wholly

---

275. *Id.,* at 245.
276. *Beckles* v. *United States,* 137 S. Ct. 886, 894 (2017), quoting *Gall* v. *United States,* 552 U.S. 38, 49, 50 (2007).
277. *Id.,* at 894 (citations, quotation marks, and brackets omitted).
278. *Pepper* v. *United States,* 562 U.S. 476, 501 (2011), quoting *Kimbrough* v. *United States,* 552 U.S. 85, 101 (2007).
279. *Id.,* at 501.

unconvincing policy rationales not reflected in the sentencing statutes Congress enacted."[280]

The case of *Tenet* v. *Doe*[281] is memorable only because it was decided on the basis of a precedent set by Abraham Lincoln. The plaintiffs were a couple who alleged that the husband was a former Cold War spy who had been promised more continued compensation than he had received. The relevant precedent was *Totten* v. *United States*,[282] a case in which the administrator of the estate of a Union spy sought compensation for services rendered during the Civil War. Allegedly Lincoln had promised to pay him two hundred dollars per month to spy on troop placement and fort plans behind Confederate lines. Without questioning the authority of the president to make binding agreements with such secret agents, we relied on the more than century-old precedent to observe:

> Both employer and agent must have understood that the lips of the other were to be forever sealed respecting the relation of either to the matter. This condition was implied from the nature of the employment, and is to be implied in all secret employments of the government in time of war, or upon matters affecting our foreign relations where a disclosure of the service might compromise or embarrass our government in its public duties, or endanger the person or injure the agent.[283]

Although Congress could no doubt change the *Totten* rule, as the law now stands "lawsuits premised on alleged espionage agreements are altogether forbidden."[284]

---

280. *Ibid.*
281. 544 U.S. 1 (2005).
282. 92 U.S. 105 (1876).
283. 544 U.S., at 7–8, quoting *Totten,* 92 U.S., at 106–7.
284. *Id.,* at 9.

*   *   *

Thurgood Marshall frequently reminded us that there is nothing in the Constitution that prevents Congress from enacting stupid laws. In 2005, when we were required to review the validity of the act of Congress that prohibited California from authorizing the local cultivation and use of marijuana for medicinal purposes, I was firmly convinced that the federal prohibition was a tragic example of a stupid law. I was nevertheless totally convinced that the law was valid, and I authored the majority opinion upholding the federal statute. Ironically, at the end of her dissenting opinion in *Gonzales* v. *Raich*,[285] in which Sandra forcefully argued the federal statute was unconstitutional, she went out of her way to state that if she were a California citizen, she would not have voted for the medical marijuana ballot initiative, and if she were a California legislator, she would not have supported the state's Compassionate Use Act. Obviously neither of us was happy with the position that our respective views of the law required us to reach.

In 1996, California voters passed the Compassionate Use Act. Like similar laws in eight other states, it was designed to ensure that "seriously ill" residents of the state have access to marijuana for medical purposes, and to encourage federal and state governments to take steps toward ensuring the safe and affordable distribution of the drug to patients in need. The act creates an exemption from criminal prosecution for physicians, as well as for patients and primary caregivers who possess or cultivate marijuana for medicinal purposes with the approval of a physician. The two respondents in the case, Angel Raich and Diane Monson, were California women who suffered from a variety of serious medical problems, and whose doctors had concluded, after prescribing numerous other medicines, that marijuana was the only drug available that provided effective treatment. Both women relied heavily on marijuana to function on a daily basis. Monson cultivated her own while Raich relied on two caregivers who provided her with the locally grown drug at no charge.

On August 15, 2002, county sheriffs and agents from the Federal Drug

---

285. 545 U.S. 1 (2005).

Enforcement Administration came to Monson's home and, after a thorough investigation, the county officials concluded that her use of marijuana was entirely lawful as a matter of California law. Nevertheless, the federal agents seized and destroyed all six of her cannabis plants. In response, Monson and Raich brought suit against the Attorney General of the United States and the head of the DEA seeking an injunction prohibiting enforcement of the federal Controlled Substances Act to the extent that it prohibited them from possessing or obtaining marijuana for their personal medical use.

The district court denied relief, but a divided panel of the Court of Appeals for the Ninth Circuit ordered the district court to enter a preliminary injunction, reasoning that the intrastate, noncommercial cultivation and possession of cannabis for personal medical purposes as recommended by a physician pursuant to a valid state law is a separate and distinct activity different in kind from commercial drug trafficking. The dissenting judge, however, found it impossible to distinguish the relevant conduct in this case from the 1942 case of *Wickard* v. *Filburn*,[286] which upheld Congress's ability to regulate the production of wheat that a farmer grew and intended to use wholly for his own consumption. We granted certiorari and I wrote the majority opinion, agreeing with the dissenter on the Ninth Circuit. Though I was extremely troubled by doing what I thought — and still think — the law required, the opinion was not difficult to write. Five of my colleagues joined me; only the chief and Clarence joined Sandra's dissent.

My opinion for the Court in *Kelo* v. *City of New London*[287] is the most unpopular opinion that I wrote during my more than thirty-four years on the Supreme Court. Indeed, I think it is the most unpopular opinion that any member of the Court wrote during that period. After it was announced, friends and acquaintances frequently told me that they could not understand how I could have authored such an opinion. In perhaps the most creative form of protest I can recall, outraged citizens sought to

---

286. 317 U.S. 11.
287. 545 U.S. 469 (2005).

retaliate against David Souter for joining my opinion by gathering petitions urging the city of Weare, New Hampshire, to condemn his home to build the "Lost Liberty Hotel" — apparently assuming that our holding would authorize such retaliatory action.

And the decision remains unpopular to this day. Just to note one example, to mark the ten-year anniversary of the decision, legal scholar Ilya Somin published an entire book on the case, suggestively titled *The Grasping Hand*. (The publisher's summary of the book describes the decision as "empower[ing] the grasping hand of the state at the expense of the invisible hand of the market" and further notes the "unpopular ruling triggered an unprecedented political reaction, with forty-five states passing new laws intended to limit the use of eminent domain.")[288] The case was also the subject of a symposium issue of the *Connecticut Law Review,* which also marked the ten-year anniversary of the case, and I am pleased to say the entries were not uniformly negative. Though it remains telling that one of the essays in defense of the case was entitled "Kelo *Is Not* Dred Scott.[289] The title is an apparent reference to an interview that Nino Scalia gave in which he compared *Kelo* to that most infamous of decisions. Though I appreciate the authors' defense, that they felt compelled to use that particular title says something about the case. Before delving into why it was so unpopular, and why I think its infamy is ill-deserved, it is important to set the stage for the decision.

In 1990, following decades of economic decline, a Connecticut state agency designated the city of New London as a "distressed municipality."[290] Years of planning activities by state and local agencies led to the approval in the year 2000 of an integrated redevelopment plan covering ninety acres of property in the Fort Trumbull area of the city. The plan included both

---

288. *The Grasping Hand: "Kelo v. City of New London" and the Limits of Eminent Domain* (Chicago: University of Chicago Press, 2015), http://www.press.uchicago.edu/ucp/books/book/chicago/G/bo20145315.html.

289. See Wesley W. Horton and Brendon P. Levesque, "Kelo *Is Not* Dred Scott," *Conn. L. Rev.* 48 (2016) (arguing *Kelo* is "part of the legal mainstream because it gives a reasonable and long-accepted reading of the Fifth Amendment").

290. 545 U.S., at 473.

commercial uses—such as office space, a hotel, and a new residential community—and noncommercial uses—a museum, a state park, and marinas. The city's development agency was able to acquire most of the land in the targeted area by purchase from willing sellers, but because negotiations with nine owners of fifteen parcels were unsuccessful, the city initiated condemnation proceedings to acquire those parcels. Susette Kelo and the other eight owners responded by bringing an action in the New London Superior Court, claiming that even if they received just compensation, the taking of their properties would violate both state law and the U.S. Constitution.

After a seven-day trial, the court granted relief to some but not all of the plaintiffs. Both sides then appealed to the Connecticut Supreme Court, and we later granted cert to decide whether the city's proposed disposition of the petitioners' property qualified as a "public use" within the meaning of the Fifth Amendment.[291] For the purposes of our decision, the members of the Court did not dispute whether the objectives of the plan would be achieved. My majority opinion for the Court held that the city's decision to take property for the purpose of economic development was constitutional.

As anticipated, the public reaction to our decision was extremely unfavorable. The response to *Kelo* was so negative and widespread that it even attracted the attention of Congress. Senate and House committees held hearings to consider possible remedies for the injustices thought to be authorized by our holding, culminating in an amendment to a federal funding act that restricted use of the act's funds on state or local projects that would employ the eminent domain power for projects of "economic development that primarily benefit[] private entities."[292] As noted, many states also passed laws directly restricting their power to use eminent domain for economic development as well.[293]

---

291. *Id.,* at 489–90.
292. Transportation, Treasury, Housing and Urban Development, the Judiciary, the District of Columbia, and Independent Agencies Appropriations Act, Pub. L. No. 109–115, § 726, 119 Stat. 2396, 2494–95 (2005).
293. See Ilya Somin, "The Limits of Backlash: Assessing the Political Response to Kelo," *Minn. L. Rev.* 93 (2009): 2100, 2101.

Perhaps the biggest reason for the public outcry was that it appeared to be a modern tale of David versus Goliath: A large pharmaceutical corporation teamed up with the powerful state government to seize an individual's home. I fully recognize that, despite the fact that the law guarantees just compensation to every person whose property is taken by the government, condemnations of private homes, like the foreclosure of mortgages, inevitably generate emotional concerns about the impartial administration of the law. The character of the litigants in the *Kelo* case cried out for exceptional protection. One of them, Wilhemina Dery, had lived in her house since her birth in 1918; another, Susette Kelo, who had moved into the area in 1997, had made extensive improvements to her home and prized her view of the water. None of the properties was blighted or otherwise in poor condition. They were condemned solely because they happened to be located in the development area. Despite the guarantee of just compensation, the taking of such property was certainly emotional for the homeowners involved and, based on their compelling stories, unpopular with the public as well.

Those facts might have been relevant to the measure of just compensation to which the property owners were constitutionally entitled.[294] But they were not relevant to the question whether urban redevelopment is a constitutionally permissible basis for the condemnation of private property. The harsh consequences of the decision for the original property owners would have been the same if the condemnation had been made to construct a public highway or a bridge. Moreover, the constitutional merits of the petitioners' challenge would have been the same if the improvements on the condemned property had been gas stations or pool halls instead of residences.

A second reason that the decision was unpopular was that public commentary misdescribed the motivation for the city's plan. As an example, in his criticism of the case, Damon Root described the city's motivation

---

294. See Akhil Reed Amar, "America's Lived Constitution," *Yale L. J.* 120 (2011): 1734, 1776–77.

as follows: "At issue was the Pfizer corporation's 1998 plan to build a giant research and development center in New London, Connecticut. As part of the deal, city officials agreed to clear out neighboring property owners via eminent domain, giving a private developer space to complement the Pfizer facility with a new hotel, office towers, and apartments."[295] In fact, the interests of Pfizer, as well as other private entities, were the subject of significant testimony during the trial of the case. Tony Kennedy's description of that evidence in his separate concurring opinion merits quotation:

Here, the trial court conducted a careful and extensive inquiry into "whether, in fact, the development plan is of primary benefit to…the developer…and private businesses which may eventually locate in the plan area [e.g., Pfizer], and in that regard, only of incidental benefit to the city." The trial court considered testimony from government officials and corporate officers; documentary evidence of communications between these parties; respondents' awareness of New London's depressed economic condition and evidence corroborating the validity of this concern; the substantial commitment of public funds by the State to the development project before most of the private beneficiaries were known; evidence that respondents reviewed a variety of development plans and chose a private developer from a group of applicants rather than picking out a particular transferee beforehand; and the fact that the other private beneficiaries of the project are still unknown because the office space proposed to be built has not yet been rented.

The trial court concluded, based on these findings, that benefiting Pfizer was not "the primary motivation or effect of this development plan"; instead, "the primary motivation for [respondents]

---

295. Damon W. Root, "John Paul Stevens' Faint-Hearted Liberalism," *Reason*, Oct. 26, 2011, http://reason.com/archives/2011/10/26/john-paul-stevens-faint-hearte.

was to take advantage of Pfizer's presence." Likewise, the trial court concluded that "[t]here is nothing in the record to indicate that... [respondents] were motivated by a desire to aid [other] particular private entities." Even the dissenting justices on the Connecticut Supreme Court agreed that respondents' development plan was intended to revitalize the local economy, not to serve the interests of Pfizer, [the private developer], or any other private party. This case, then, survives the meaningful rational-basis review that in my view is required under the Public Use Clause.[296]

A third reason why the decision continues to be unpopular is that the project was never completed. In 2009, well after the litigation had been concluded, Pfizer decided to close down its New London facility and move out of the city.[297] While that post-decision development may suggest that there were significant deficiencies in the proposed plan, fair criticism of the Court's *Kelo* holding must be based on the assumption — not disputed by either the dissenting justices or the majority — that the projected benefits of the plan would be fully achieved.

I don't deny that the facts of the case presented in a vacuum might convince the casual observer that a different outcome was warranted. But I thought then, and I continue to think now, that the unpopularity of the decision tells us nothing about either its wisdom or its fidelity to the rule of law.

Another interesting aspect of the case that is often overlooked is the constitutional basis for the plaintiffs' claim. My majority opinion incorrectly assumed — as Tony and each of the dissenting opinions also did — that the case required us to construe the "Takings," or "Public Use," Clause of the Fifth Amendment to the Constitution.[298] That clause,

---

296. *Kelo,* 545 U.S., at 491–92 (citations omitted).
297. Patrick McGeehan, "Pfizer to Leave City That Won Land Use Case," *New York Times,* Nov. 13, 2009, A1.
298. 545 U.S., at 472; *id.,* at 490 (Kennedy, J., concurring); *id.,* at 494, 496 (O'Connor, J., dissenting); *id.,* at 506 (Thomas, J., dissenting).

however, says nothing about what sorts of property may be taken by state governments or what sorts of reasons may justify the taking. It merely requires the federal government to obey an ancient common law rule requiring the payment of compensation when the government does take private property for public use.

It is the Fourteenth Amendment that provides the limits to the states' power to deprive persons of their property. The relevant portion of that Amendment provides, "[N]or shall any State deprive any person of life, liberty, or property, without due process of law." In footnote 1 of the *Kelo* majority opinion, I quoted the Fifth Amendment Takings Clause and then stated, "That Clause is made applicable to the States by the Fourteenth Amendment."[299] It is somewhat embarrassing to acknowledge that the *Chicago* case did not even cite the Fifth Amendment. In fact, neither that case nor any later Supreme Court case with which I am familiar explained how or why the Takings Clause might have been made applicable to the states. At least one scholarly commentator — the same one who later published a book on the case — caught this issue shortly after we decided *Kelo,* though even he remarked that my mistake was "perhaps understandable in light of the fact that Justice Thomas commit[ted] the same mistake in his dissenting opinion."[300] It is never fun to make a mistake, particularly in a Supreme Court opinion, but there is some consolation in not being alone in having made it.

What the Court actually held in that 1897 case was that the Due Process Clause of the Fourteenth Amendment contains substantive as well as procedural requirements, and that an element of every permissible taking of private property is the obligation to pay compensation to the former owner.[301] Similarly, the Fifth Amendment was not cited in Justice Holmes's 1906 opinion for the Court, which upheld the taking of property needed for a private mining company to operate a two-mile

---

299. *Id.,* at 472n1, citing *Chicago, B. & Q. R. Co.* v. *Chicago,* 166 U.S. 226 (1897).
300. Ilya Somin, "Controlling the Grasping Hand: Economic Development Takings After Kelo," *S. Ct. Econ. Rev.* 15 (2007), 183, 242.
301. *Chicago,* 166 U.S., at 234–35.

aerial bucket line that delivered ore to a railway station.[302] Nor was the Fifth Amendment cited in the Court's 1905 opinion upholding a state statute that authorized the private owner of arid land to widen an irrigation ditch on his neighbor's property so that the owner alone could obtain water.[303] Those cases, like the *Kelo* case that followed them, were actually Fourteenth Amendment substantive due process cases. As the second Justice Harlan later explained in his concurring opinion in *Griswold*, while the due process inquiry "may be aided by resort to one or more of the provisions of the Bill of Rights, it is not dependent on them or any of their radiations. The Due Process Clause of the Fourteenth Amendment stands... on its own bottom."[304]

Thus, neither the text of the Fifth Amendment Takings Clause nor the common law rule that it codified placed any limit on the states' power to take private property, other than the obligation to pay just compensation to the former owner. An entirely different common law rule, however, did significantly limit the scope of the taking power. That is the rule that both Sandra O'Connor and I identified at the beginning of our respective discussions of the law in our *Kelo* opinions. As I wrote, "[I]t has long been accepted that the sovereign may not take the property of *A* for the sole purpose of transferring it to another private party *B*, even though *A* is paid just compensation."[305] And Sandra used, as the opening salvo in her opinion, the famous quotation from Justice Salmon Chase's opinion in *Calder* v. *Bull*, which states, "[A] law that takes property from A and gives it to B: It is against all reason and justice."[306] While the justices in *Kelo* agreed that this common law rule is an element of the due process that the Fourteenth Amendment mandates, the precise dimensions of that rule are not defined in the Constitution's text. The rule is rather an

---

302. *Strickley* v. *Highland Boy Gold Mining Co.,* 200 U.S. 527 (1906).
303. *Clark* v. *Nash,* 198 U.S. 361 (1905).
304. *Griswold* v. *Connecticut,* 381 U.S. 479, 500 (1965).
305. 545 U.S., at 477.
306. *Id.,* at 494 (O'Connor, J., dissenting), quoting *Calder* v. *Bull,* 3 U.S. 386 (1798).

aspect of substantive due process that had been explicated through a process of common law case-by-case adjudication, rather than a straightforward takings claim under the Fifth Amendment.

Critics of the majority's holding in *Kelo* may legitimately argue that earlier cases should not have been applied to New London's ambitious redevelopment, or that it would be wiser instead to overrule those prior cases and to hold that any taking for the purpose of economic redevelopment is impermissible. Clarence Thomas, dissenting in *Kelo,* argued exactly that.[307] It is abundantly clear, however, that nothing in the text or the relevant history of the Constitution supports such a dramatic result.

Kelo, of course, did not come out of thin air; it instead relied on two unanimous precedents. In *Berman* v. *Parker,* decided in 1954, the owners of a department store located in Washington, D.C., contended that the condemnation of their property pursuant to the District of Columbia Redevelopment Act of 1945 violated the Fifth Amendment.[308] Reasoning that the power of condemnation for a public purpose was as broad as the police power, the Court upheld the constitutionality of the statute, the slum clearance redevelopment plan that it authorized, and the taking of the appellants' store. Despite the fact that the appellants' store was itself in acceptable condition, the mere fact that it was located in the area targeted for redevelopment provided a sufficient justification for the taking. The Court explained:

> If owner after owner were permitted to resist these redevelopment programs on the ground that his particular property was not being used against the public interest, integrated plans for redevelopment would suffer greatly. The argument pressed on us is, indeed, a plea to substitute the landowner's standard of the public need for

307. *Id.,* at 514–15.
308. 348 U.S. 26, 31 (1954).

the standard prescribed by Congress. But as we have already stated, community redevelopment programs need not, by force of the Constitution, be on a piecemeal basis — lot by lot, building by building.

It is not for the courts to oversee the choice of the boundary line nor to sit in review of the size of a particular project area. Once the question of the public purpose has been decided, the amount and character of land to be taken for the project and the need for a particular tract to complete the integrated plan rests in the discretion of the legislative branch.[309]

Berman, of course, involved deference to an act of Congress, and the purpose of the plan was the elimination of a blighted area, whereas *Kelo* involved deference to state officials and state courts and a plan designed to replace a distressed area with an economically healthier community.

But our unanimous decision in *Hawaii Housing Authority* v. *Midkiff* made abundantly clear that those differences should not affect the legal analysis.[310] In *Midkiff,* the Court upheld the constitutionality of a statute that authorized the taking of title to real property from lessors and transferring it to lessees in order to reduce the concentration of property ownership in the state of Hawaii. Relying on the reasoning in *Berman,* the Court first held that the "public use" requirement is "coterminous with the scope of the sovereign's police powers."[311] Then, assuming that the standard for reviewing federal takings applied as well to Hawaii's takings, the Court stated that "deference to the legislature's 'public use' determination is required 'until it is shown to involve an impossibility.' "[312] The opinion summed up, "In short, the Court has made clear that it will

---

309. *Id.,* at 35–36.
310. 467 U.S. 229 (1984).
311. *Id.,* at 240.
312. *Ibid.*

not substitute its judgment for a legislature's judgment as to what constitutes a public use 'unless the use be palpably without reasonable foundation.' "[313] Finally, as though it were anticipating the position endorsed by the dissenting justices in the Connecticut Supreme Court's decision in *Kelo,* the *Midkiff* opinion added, "Of course, this act, like any other, may not be successful in achieving its intended goals. But 'whether *in fact* the provision will accomplish its objectives is not the question: the [constitutional requirement] is satisfied if…the [state] Legislature *rationally could have believed* that the [act] would promote its objective.' "[314]

Given these earlier cases, the majority in the *Kelo* case concluded that the Court had a duty to give deference to the decisions of the Connecticut legislature, the state agencies interpreting the state statute, and the state courts' evaluation of the particular development plan that gave rise to the litigation. The two dissenting opinions disagreed for different reasons. Sandra would permit takings for economic development only to remedy more serious harms such as the blight in *Berman* and the oligopolistic condition of Hawaii's real estate market in *Midkiff.* Clarence would overrule our earlier cases and entirely prohibit use of the government's eminent domain power for the purpose of economic development.

The three different positions represented by the opinions in *Kelo* remind me of another important substantive due process case in which the justices took three different positions: *Lochner* v. *New York.*[315] In *Lochner,* of course, the majority held that the substantive component of the Fourteenth Amendment's Due Process Clause — the same provision that limits state authority to condemn private property — was violated by a New York statute regulating the hours of work for bakery employees. For the *Lochner* majority, the interest in freedom of contract outweighed the interest in protecting the health of overworked employees. For the first Justice Harlan, writing for three dissenters, the

---

313. *Id.,* at 240–41.
314. *Id.,* at 242, quoting *W. & S. Life Ins. Co.* v. *State Bd. of Equalization,* 451 U.S. 648, 671–72 (1981).
315. 198 U.S. 45 (1905).

public health interests were sufficient to justify the statue. But Justice Holmes, writing only for himself, did not address the policy debate. Construing the word "liberty" as used in the constitutional text more narrowly than any of his colleagues, Justice Holmes concluded that the dispute about an economic issue was one that generally should be determined by the people through their democratic participation in enacting state laws, not by federal judges.[316]

Of the three different positions advanced in *Kelo,* the majority's was unquestionably the closest to Holmes's dissent. Sandra's dissent resembled the intermediate position advanced in the Harlan dissent, but Clarence's solo dissent was even more extreme than the majority's holding in *Lochner.* For Clarence's dissent would categorically invalidate economic development takings if any of the property is given to a private developer, whereas the *Lochner* majority left open the question of the permissibility of maximum hour legislation in other industries, even though not for bakery employees.

Like Justice Holmes, the *Kelo* majority reasoned that the "necessity and wisdom" of the government policy at hand was a "matter[] of legitimate public debate," but that it was for legislatures, not the courts, to resolve those disputes.[317] I am not at all sure that the plan that we approved was wise policy, but I remain firmly convinced that the Fourteenth Amendment did not deprive the state of the power to adopt it.

Kelo and the dispute it engendered provide an interesting comment on the possible connection between popularity and the doctrine of substantive due process. On more than one occasion, I have repeated this paragraph from a talk that I gave to the Chicago Bar Association in 1974, explaining why I am opposed to the popular election of judges:

---

316. *Id.,* at 74–77 (Holmes, J., dissenting).
317. *Kelo,* 545 U.S., at 489–90.

[T]here is a critical difference between the work of the judge and the work of other public officials. In a democracy, issues of policy are properly decided by majority vote; it is the business of legislators and executives to be popular. But in litigation, issues of law or fact should not be determined by majority vote; it is the business of judges to be indifferent to unpopularity. [Sir Matthew Hale] described an essential attribute of judicial office in words which have retained their integrity for centuries: "That popular or court applause, or distaste, have no influence upon any thing I do in point of distribution of justice. That I not be solicitous what men will say or think, so long as I keep myself exactly according to the rules of justice."[318]

As I suggested at the outset of this discussion, an important explanation for the unpopularity of the *Kelo* decision was the fact that it upheld the taking of a private home, rather than a commercial property. That fact may also explain why justices who normally profess strong opposition to substantive due process were willing to take action to expand that doctrine to protect Susette Kelo and Wilhelmina Dery from the loss of their residences. In my view, the *Kelo* majority opinion was rightly consistent with the Supreme Court's precedent and the Constitution's text and structure. Whether the decision was popular or represented sound policy is another matter.

In 1963, in *School Dist. of Abington Township* v. *Schempp*,[319] Justice Tom Clark wrote the Court opinion holding that the religion clauses of the First Amendment, as applied to the states through the Fourteenth Amendment, were violated by state laws that required that public schools begin each day with readings from the Bible. In so holding, he relied on an unpublished opinion by Judge Alphonso Taft, the father of the former

---

318. John Paul Stevens, "The Office of an Office," *Ann. Surv. Am. L.* (1992–1993): xiv–xv.
319. 374 U.S. 203.

president and chief justice, describing the "absolute equality before the law, of all religious opinions and sects."[320] Clark's opinion was the principal authority on which the Court relied when it first confronted the question whether governmental displays of the text of the Ten Commandments are constitutional, in *Stone* v. *Graham*.[321]

In *Stone*, in an unsigned per curiam opinion decided without oral argument, the Court summarily reversed a Kentucky Supreme Court decision upholding a state statute that required the posting of a copy of the Ten Commandments on the wall of each public classroom in the state. Chief Justice Burger and Harry Blackmun dissented from the summary disposition, arguing that the case should have received plenary consideration, while Potter Stewart and Bill Rehnquist also dissented, but they would have affirmed.

The constitutionality of government displays of the text of the Ten Commandments came before the Court again in two cases decided the same day in the 2004 term: *Van Orden* v. *Perry*[322] and *McCreary County* v. *American Civil Liberties Union of Kentucky*.[323] *Van Orden* involved a monument on the grounds of the state capitol in Austin, Texas, and *McCreary* involved posted versions of the Ten Commandments on the walls of two county courthouses in Kentucky.

McCreary was in many respects the more straightforward of the two. There, executives in two counties posted versions of the Ten Commandments on the counties' courthouses and, after suits were filed challenging the displays, issued resolutions calling for modifications of the displays to demonstrate that the Ten Commandments were the state's "precedent legal code."[324] Relying in part on *Stone*, the Court concluded that "the counties' manifest objective may be dispositive of the constitutional enquiry" and that the manifest objective here was predominantly

---

320. *Id.*, at 215.
321. 449 U.S. 39 (1980).
322. 545 U.S. 677 (2005).
323. 545 U.S. 844 (2005).
324. *Id.*, at 850.

religious — despite the counties' subsequent efforts to modify the exhibit to tone down some of its more overt religious aspects.[325] David Souter had no difficulty affirming the district court's injunction ordering that the religious display be removed from each courthouse "IMMEDI-ATELY." He wrote the Court opinion, joined by Sandra, Ruth, Steve, and me, while Sandra also filed a concurring opinion, and Nino, the chief, Clarence, and Tony filed or joined dissenting opinions.

In contrast, a majority of the Court found no constitutional violation with the display of the Ten Commandments on the Texas state capitol grounds in *Van Orden*. Writing for the Court, Chief Justice Rehnquist, joined by Nino, Tony, and Clarence, concluded that, based on the nature of the display and our Nation's history, "[t]he placement of the Ten Commandments monument on the Texas state capitol grounds [was] a far more passive use of those texts than was the case in *Stone,* where the text confronted elementary school students every day."[326] Steve concurred, while Sandra, Ruth, David, and I filed or joined dissenting opinions.

The result in *McCreary* was consistent with the argument I articulated in *Van Orden* and in previous cases that "at the very least, the Establishment Clause has created a strong presumption against the display of religious symbols on public property."[327] The reasons for this presumption are clear. As I explained in my dissent, the sole function of the monument in *Van Orden* was to display an overtly religious message: "The monument [was] not a work of art and [did] not refer to any event in the history of the State.... The message transmitted by Texas' chosen display is quite plain: This State endorses the divine code of the 'Judeo-Christian' God."[328] And "it seems beyond peradventure that allowing the seat of government to serve as a stage for the propagation of an unmistakably Judeo-Christian message of piety would have the tendency to make non-monotheists and nonbelievers 'feel like [outsiders] in matters of faith, and

---

325. *Id.,* at 850–51.
326. 545 U.S., at 691.
327. *Id.,* at 708.
328. *Id.,* at 707.

[strangers] in the political community.'"[329] Sandra had long articulated a similar point with respect to the Establishment Clause, noting as early as 1984 that government endorsement of religion "sends a message to non-adherents that they are outsiders, not full members of the political community, and an accompanying message to adherents that they are insiders, favored members of the political community."[330] This point applies with equal force to displays of the Ten Commandments at a public school, county courthouse, or state capitol grounds, and for that reason such displays should be presumptively impermissible on public property.

Although Stephen joined David's opinion in *McCreary*, he surprised us by writing a separate opinion in *Van Orden*, concluding that the state intended the secular message conveyed by the monument to outweigh its religious message. Stephen began his concurring opinion by quoting *Schempp*, authored by Stephen's former boss Justice Arthur Goldberg, and noting "in respect to the First Amendment's Religion Clauses... there is 'no simple and clear measure by which precise application can readily and invariably demark the permissible from the impermissible.'"[331] And for him, the Ten Commandments on the Texas state capitol grounds was a "borderline case," because, "[o]n the one hand, the Commandments' text undeniably has a religious message," while "[o]n the other hand, focusing on the text of the Commandments alone cannot conclusively resolve this case."[332] To decide this case, Stephen looked to the context of how the text is used and concluded that the secular message predominated. That Stephen and I could reach such opposing conclusions in one case, while agreeing in another case raising a very similar question and decided the same day, is a reminder of how often it is difficult to predict the outcome of cases raising questions about the meaning of the religion clauses of the Constitution. As Stephen put it, "If the

---

329. *Van Orden*, 545 U.S., at 720 (Stevens, J., dissenting), quoting *Capitol Square Review and Advisory Bd.* v. *Pinette*, 515 U.S. 753, 799 (1995) (Stevens, J., dissenting).
330. *Lynch* v. *Donnelly*, 465 U.S. 668, 688 (1984) (O'Connor, J., concurring).
331. *Van Orden*, 545 U.S., at 698, quoting *Schempp*, 374 U.S., at 306.
332. *Id.*, at 700–701.

relation between government and religion is one of separation, but not of mutual hostility and suspicion, one will inevitably find difficult border-line cases."[333] I, of course, did not think either *McCreary* or *Van Orden* was a borderline case. That Stephen, a colleague I've long admired, could disagree, however, is confirmation that the question was indeed a difficult one.

---

333. *Id.,* at 700.

30

The Roberts and Alito Courts

October Term 2005

On July 1, 2005, Sandra O'Connor announced that she would retire from the Court as soon as her successor was confirmed. She explained that her husband, John, was convalescing in New Mexico and that she planned to spend more time with him. The president then publicized his intent to name John Roberts, an experienced litigator and much admired lawyer, as her replacement. Before he could do so, however, on September 4, Chief Justice Rehnquist died and the president promptly decided to name Roberts as the new chief. During his confirmation hearings, he famously described the task of a federal judge as comparable to that of an umpire calling balls and strikes. He was confirmed by a vote of 78–22.

On October 3, 2005, the president nominated Harriet Miers, who was then the White House counsel, to replace John Roberts as the nominee to succeed Sandra O'Connor. Miers had been a successful lawyer in Dallas before joining President Bush's staff. She had clerked for the chief judge of the Northern District of Texas after her graduation from Southern Methodist University Law School and went on to become the senior partner in a respected Dallas law firm and president of the state bar association. Despite the fact that she was not a graduate of Harvard, Yale, or

Columbia, and had no experience in litigating or writing about constitutional issues, I thought her well qualified to fill the vacancy. I verified my impression of her qualifications in a long telephone conversation with a judge on the Court of Appeals for the Fifth Circuit who strongly supported her nomination. Nevertheless, in prehearing meetings with conservative senators, she obviously failed to convince them that she would be a predictable judge (unlike my friend David Souter, for whom I had profound admiration) and was persuaded to withdraw her nomination. She did so on October 27, 2005.

A few days later, the president nominated Sam Alito, a judge on the Third Circuit Court of Appeals. He was well known by opponents for his vote to uphold the constitutionality of a Pennsylvania statute requiring (with certain exceptions) a wife to obtain her husband's consent before obtaining an abortion. At his confirmation hearings, however, he was strongly supported by all of his colleagues on the Third Circuit. He was confirmed on January 31, 2006, by a vote of 58–42.

A week after my eighty-fifth birthday, Georgetown Law School held its annual reception to thank the lawyers who had participated as mock judges in its Supreme Court Institute's Moot Court program. The event was planned also to honor the completion of my thirtieth term on the Court, and included a gift of a Chicago Cubs baseball jacket that had been arranged by my former clerk, Dave Freeman, counsel for the Boston Red Sox, and Michael Lufrano, the general counsel of the Chicago Cubs. Correspondence with Lufrano thereafter led to an invitation from the Cubs to become the first Supreme Court justice to throw out the first pitch in a major league game at Wrigley Field. Given my childhood memories of attending Cubs games with my father, including the first World Series played at Wrigley Field, you can imagine the awe I felt at the Cubs' invitation.

Although I had had brief experience as a second baseman for the Texaco Oilers in Delavan, Wisconsin, in 1939, and as a substitute on the

Supreme Court police team as a new justice, it was a good many years since I had thrown a ball. When I first tried, I bounced my first pitch into Maryan's shin, but then gradually improved during practice sessions with Sue and my two law clerks, Jean Galbraith and Dan Lenerz. I learned that if I imagined that I was an outfielder who had just caught a long fly against the bleacher wall and was trying to nail a base runner at the plate, I could throw a strike. On the evening of the game against the Cincinnati Reds — with thirty members of our families in the stands — that's exactly what I did. My pitch was a little high and outside, but it made it to the plate. That was unquestionably the high point of my career.

(I attended another Cubs game at Wrigley Field in 2016, cheering on my team yet again in the World Series. I didn't bring them much luck, as they lost the game I attended, but I was more than pleased to see them go on to win their first championship in over a century.)

Shortly thereafter, Maryan and I traveled to San Antonio, Texas, to participate in the dedication of a high school named after me. The school district followed a practice of naming schools after Supreme Court justices, and I was the second living member of the Court (Sandra was the first) who had been chosen on the basis of a student competition. The school had been constructed on the site where Pope John Paul had said mass in 1987 before the largest crowd in the history of Texas. When we were driven onto the school grounds, I received an unusually warm welcome that was the work product of educationally handicapped students at the school — they had prepared an array of dozens of large bow ties mounted on stakes that lined the sides of the driveway. That was an unusually thoughtful welcome that I shall never forget. (A few years later, to celebrate my ninetieth birthday, the high school sent me a photograph of its marching band in the formation of a bow tie, which is prominently featured in my chambers.)

During the dedication ceremony I gave a talk to the students that summarized thoughts that I had frequently expressed and still think worthy of repetition. I said,

For over two years I have looked forward to this occasion because it gives me the opportunity to thank you for naming your high school after me and also because it gives me the opportunity to express my high regard for two Texans who had a profound influence on my career. I shall first identify those heroes, then explain why I am particularly grateful for your decision to name your school after me, and finally I shall ask you for a commitment.

Leon Green was a Texas lawyer and scholar who spent several years of his career as the Dean of the Northwestern Law School when I studied there after the end of World War II. He was brilliant, inspiring and ruthless. In class, he made us stand up to describe the reasoning in an assigned case, and then subjected us to rigorous cross-examination about the case. Most of the students, who were recently discharged veterans, regarded the experience as more frightening than enemy fire in combat. The lessons Dean Green taught us included far more than knowledge of the law; he taught us the importance of thorough and careful preparation for stressful situations.

After he retired from Northwestern, Dean Green returned to Texas and spent several years on the faculty of the University of Texas Law School. His status as a scholar and teacher is reflected in the fact that the school gives an annual award in his name to an outstanding alumnus. I am especially pleased that the recipient of the Leon Green award for 2001, the Honorable Royal Furgeson, United States District Judge sitting in the Western District of Texas, is with us tonight. Judge Furgeson and I not only share an admiration for Leon Green, but other characteristics as well: we were both captains of high school basketball teams, we both majored in English literature in college, we both received the same decoration as a result of our service in the armed forces of our country, and we are both firmly committed to the preservation of an independent judiciary.

My second Texas hero was Justice Tom C. Clark, whose name was selected by one of your rival schools in this District. He and I also shared something in common: we both favored bow ties. I found this out while appearing before him as a lawyer when he was an active Member of the Supreme Court. After retiring from active service on that court, he generously volunteered his services as a trial judge and as a judge on intermediate courts of appeals. When he was acting as a district judge, I tried a long case before him, and when I was serving as a circuit judge on the Court of Appeals in Chicago in the early 1970's he frequently sat with us because we had great difficulty keeping up with our workload. He was not only a fine judge, and delightful companion, but he always insisted on writing the most difficult and uninteresting opinions because he knew that that was how he could be most helpful to us. He taught his colleagues by his diligent example that true acts of charity can be motivated by the simple interest in helping others despite the total absence of public recognition or acclaim. Tom Clark was a great American and a great Texan.

It is my understanding that the Northside Independent School District has adopted a policy of naming high schools after Justices of the United States Supreme Court. The policy is somewhat unusual because public buildings are more frequently named after elected officials — in many cases after legislators who were active in procuring the funding necessary to complete the project. Elected officials represent the views of the majority of voters; if they perform their jobs effectively, they will be popular leaders in the community, and if they are popular, they can usually count on re-election. The job of the judge is fundamentally different. The judge's decisions must uphold the rule of law no matter how unpopular the result may be. Just as an umpire has a duty to call close plays as he sees them regardless of the impact on the outcome of the game, so must we put the popularity or unpopularity of the outcome entirely to one side when we are deciding difficult questions of law. A person motivated by an interest in popularity should not seek to become an umpire or a judge. By choosing to honor judges instead of popularly elected officials, your school district celebrates the principle that an independent judiciary administering neutral rules of law, rather than catering to popular opinion, is a matter of fundamental importance in a free society.

The fact that you have honored me by selecting my name for your newest high school is particularly gratifying because I believe so deeply in the importance of an independent judiciary. I was surprised and pleased to learn that your school is located on the site that the late Pope John Paul the Second used to say mass before the largest gathering of parishioners in the history of Texas. I had the good fortune to meet the Pope on the occasion of his visit to the White House during President Carter's administration and intend to present the school with a picture that was taken on that occasion. The persons in the picture include President Carter and one of my beautiful daughters who was then a high school student.

As a parent I insisted that my daughters obey certain arbitrary rules. I shall not describe them all, but there are three that I would ask the students of the John Paul Stevens High School to observe:

First, be healthy! You should always — and by that I mean at least three times a week — engage in physical exercise. Whether you play competitive sports, do pushups, run-in-place, or just flex your muscles if you are unable to do anything more vigorous, please exercise regularly. I have followed this rule all my life — I still manage to hold my own on the tennis court — and I have never regretted it.

Second, be serious about your studies! Few things in life produce as much joy as learning something new, and your years in school will provide countless opportunities for the acquisition of fascinating and useful ideas and information. Moreover, talk to your fellow students about what you are learning, share your reactions to your lessons and your teachers, help those who may not grasp new concepts as easily as you do, and you will find extra rewards in the learning process.

Third, play by the rules. Listen to your parents, to your teachers and to your spiritual advisers. A disciplined falcon is a powerful bird capable of performing valuable important missions. An untrained falcon is like a ship without a rudder — where it will go nobody knows. A cheater harms himself far more than those that he tries to fool. Polonius was dead right when he told his son: "To thine own self be true and thou cans't not be false to any man."

If you follow my simple advice, I assure you that you will achieve the joy of learning, the power to help your friends and neighbors, and success in securing the blessings of liberty for yourselves and for posterity. It is this kind of "joy, power, and success" (JPS) that should characterize the graduates of the John Paul Stevens High School.

The day after our return from San Antonio, John Roberts was sworn in as chief justice of the United States in a ceremony at the White House. Because of my firm conviction that such ceremonies should be held at the Court, I had not attended one since Tony Kennedy's appointment. I had nevertheless decided to do the honors at John's ceremony because I had thoroughly approved of his selection as our chief and did not want to create the public impression that I opposed his selection. That was a correct decision that I have never regretted.

John's first term as our presiding officer also saw the end of Sandra's service as an active justice and the arrival of Sam Alito, following his swearing in on January 31, 2006. As I noted earlier, any time a new justice joins the Court, the whole institution itself changes, and it is a rare occurrence to have two new justices in such close succession. During the first four months of the October 2005 term, John demonstrated his ability to preside fairly and effectively, with occasional examples of his ready wit, while Sandra continued to set an example of thorough preparation and astute questioning from the bench. She authored a unanimous opinion in an abortion case,[1] and provided me with the necessary fifth vote in an important bankruptcy case that upheld Congress's authority to abrogate the states' sovereign immunity from certain private suits initiated by bankruptcy trustees against state agencies.[2]

Three other cases decided that term by five-to-four votes were first argued before Sandra retired and set for reargument thereafter. Given the fact that Sam was a member of the majority in all three of those cases, astute observers of the Court correctly inferred that Sandra had provided the decisive vote for the opposite result in all three before she retired. Otherwise there would have been no need to reargue any of them.

After the first arguments in *Garcetti* v. *Ceballos* on October 12, 2005, and in *Kansas* v. *Marsh* on December 7, 2005, I assigned the majority opinions to David Souter. But after the cases were reargued following Sandra's retirement, I could only assign the dissents to David. Likewise, in *Hudson* v. *Michigan,* which was first argued on January 9, 2006, I had originally assigned the majority opinion to Stephen Breyer, but, after the reargument on May 18, 2006, his opinion turned out to be a dissent.

In *Garcetti,* the Court held that speech by public employees pursuant to their official duties was not protected by the First Amendment,

---

1. *Ayotte* v. *Planned Parenthood of Northern New England,* 546 U.S. 320 (2006).
2. *Central Virginia Community College* v. *Katz,* 546 U.S. 356 (2006).

explaining that public "employees are not speaking as citizens for First Amendment purposes" in such circumstances.[3] I found that rationale illogical because "it is senseless to let constitutional protection for exactly the same words hinge on whether they fall within a job description" and "it seems perverse to fashion a new rule that provides employees with an incentive to voice their concerns publicly before talking frankly to their supervisors."[4]

In *Hudson,* the Court refused to suppress evidence obtained by officers who had violated the rule requiring them to knock on the front door and announce their identity before entering to serve a search warrant.[5] The knock-and-announce rule had long been understood to protect individual privacy rights, to avoid needless destruction of property, and to lessen the chance of violence between citizens and law enforcement. The majority reasoned that "[s]ince the interests that *were* violated in this case have nothing to do with the seizure of the evidence, the exclusionary rule is inapplicable," and, moreover, any deterrence to be gained from suppression did not outweigh its social costs.[6] Recourse for such violations, the majority concluded, was to be found instead in civil suits brought under 42 U.S.C. § 1983 or *Bivens* v. *Six Unknown Fed. Narcotics Agents.*[7] As in *Garcetti,* I found the majority's analysis unpersuasive, and I agreed with Stephen's dissent, which correctly observed that the majority's holding "destroys the strongest legal incentive to comply with the Constitution's knock-and-announce requirement."[8] In later cases, a majority of the Court would rely, in part, on the *Hudson* majority's balancing approach to the suppression question, weighing deterrence against social costs, to further dilute the exclusionary rule in other contexts.[9]

---

3. 547 U.S. 410, 421 (2006).
4. *Id.,* at 427.
5. 547 U.S. 586, 594 (2006).
6. *Ibid.*
7. 403 U.S. 388 (1971).
8. 547 U.S., at 605.
9. See *Davis* v. *United States,* 564 U.S. 229, 237 (2011) (noting, in general, "[f]or exclusion to be appropriate, the deterrence benefits of suppression must outweigh its heavy costs").

In *Marsh,* the Court reversed a Kansas Supreme Court decision invalidating a state statute mandating juries to impose the death penalty whenever they concluded that mitigating and aggravating circumstance had equal weight.[10] I was (and still am) particularly disturbed by the majority's decision in this case, because it enhances the danger of making an uncorrectable mistake in the kind of case in which experience has shown that the risk of error is particularly high. As David pointed out, "[T]he period since 1989 ha[d] seen repeated exonerations of convicts under death sentences, in numbers never imagined before the developments of DNA tests.... [O]ne recent study report[ed] that between 1989 and 2003, 74 American prisoners condemned to death were exonerated,... many of them cleared by DNA evidence."[11] Based on this new factual understanding, David soundly explained, "We are...in a period of new empirical argument about how 'death is different.'"[12] As I noted in my discussion of *Gregg* in an earlier chapter, when the Court reviewed the constitutionality of the death penalty at length in 1976, none of us seriously considered the magnitude of the risk of error in capital cases. It is now perfectly clear that it is a risk that no civilized society should tolerate.

In *Randall* v. *Sorrell,*[13] the Court reversed a decision of the Court of Appeals for the Second Circuit upholding the validity of a Vermont statute that limited the amount that candidates for state office may spend on their political campaigns and also the amounts that their supporters may contribute to their campaigns. The reason for the statute was that campaign finance limits are needed to ensure that candidates do not spend too much time fund-raising. The majority rejected the validity of that objective, concluding that *Buckley* had already decided in 1976 that any expenditure limits violate the First Amendment. For the first time, the Court also struck down a contribution limit, reasoning that Vermont's

---

10. *Kansas* v. *Marsh,* 548 U.S. 163, 165 (2006).
11. *Id.,* at 207–8, 209.
12. *Id.,* at 210, quoting *Gregg* v. *Georgia,* 428 U.S. 153, 188 (1976).
13. 548 U.S. 230 (2006).

contribution limits were so low that they excessively burden an individual's freedom of speech and the parties' freedom of association. Ruth Ginsburg and I joined David Souter's dissent, which is significant because it recognizes and emphasizes the governmental interest in saving public officials the vast amount of time that they necessarily spend raising money during political campaigns. His opinion further demonstrates that the doctrine of stare decisis should not foreclose a reexamination of this issue.

The six opinions occupying some 113 pages in the U.S. Reports in *League of United Latin American Citizens* v. *Perry*[14] are primarily of interest because of their description of the change of the Texas legislature from an unconstitutionally elected Democratic body to an unconstitutionally elected Republican body — that is, from one egregious gerrymander to another. In the 1990s, Texas Democrats, on the wane as the dominant party in Texas, gerrymandered the state legislative and congressional districting maps to give them an advantage through the next decennial redistricting. In 2003, Republicans finally managed to gain control of the state legislature and could not resist turning the tables on their adversary. They undertook the highly unusual step of redistricting in the middle of the decade, which could have served no other purpose than a partisan gerrymander. Those opinions will convince many readers that identifying the purpose of legislators engaged in gerrymandering is not a difficult task, and that the effects of their efforts are also quite obvious. As I have long stated, a legislator's overriding duty to act impartially whenever he or she is exercising governmental power should provide a sufficient basis for condemning drawing district lines in a way that enhances the likelihood that members of the party drawing those lines will win the election.

In the 2005 term, we confronted yet another case in the series of detainee cases stemming from the United States' post-9/11 engagements in the Middle East. This case involved Salim Ahmed Hamdan, who had served

---

14. 548 U.S. 399 (2006).

as a bodyguard and driver for Osama bin Laden and was captured in November of 2001 in Afghanistan and turned over to the U.S. military. In June of 2002, he was transferred to Guantánamo Bay, Cuba, where some two years later he was charged with the crime of conspiracy to commit "offenses triable by military commission." In 2004, the District Court for the District of Columbia granted his request for a writ of habeas corpus in which he argued, first, that conspiracy is not a crime that violates the common law of war, and, second, that the procedures of the military commission violate international law, including the principle that the defendant must be permitted to see and hear the evidence against him. The Court of Appeals for the D.C. Circuit reversed and we decided to review the case. I wrote the opinion for the Court sustaining his challenge to the court-martial procedures, but only three of my colleagues agreed with my analysis of the conspiracy issue.[15] That was particularly disappointing because, having spent so much time both in private practice and on the bench studying conspiracy, I thought I was especially well qualified to discuss the issue.

Congress responded to our decision with the Military Commissions Act (MCA), which would be the subject of the next case in the detainee saga before the Court, *Boumediene* v. *Bush*. After Congress passed the MCA, Hamdan was tried and found guilty of "providing material support" to Al Qaeda, but was acquitted of terrorism conspiracy charges. He was sentenced to five and a half years in prison but was given time served credit for the roughly five years he had already spent in jail. In November 2008, the U.S. government transferred him to Yemen to serve the remainder of his sentence. And in October 2012, the D.C. Circuit overturned his entire conviction and acquitted him of all charges, concluding the MCA did not retroactively punish new crimes and "providing material support for terrorism" was not a crime when Hamdan worked as a driver for bin Laden.[16] The D.C. Circuit, sitting en banc, later overturned

---

15. *Hamdan* v. *Rumsfeld,* 548 U.S. 557, 566 (2006).
16. *Hamdan* v. *United States,* 696 F. 3d 1238, 1241 (CADC 2012).

that decision's statutory holding, but it still held that MCA prosecutions for providing material support for terrorism violate the Ex Post Facto Clause if based on conduct predating the statute's enactment.[17]

October Term 2006

When carbon dioxide is released into the atmosphere, it acts like the ceiling of a greenhouse, trapping solar energy and restricting the escape of reflected heat. It is therefore a species — the most important species — of a "greenhouse gas."

The debate about global warming caused by greenhouse gases arrived at the Supreme Court in the 2006 October term.

In 1959, when the U.S. Weather Bureau began monitoring atmospheric carbon dioxide levels, an observatory in Mauna Loa, Hawaii, recorded a mean level of 316 parts per million. In 1970, when Congress drafted the Clean Air Act, those levels had reached 325 parts per million. In the late 1970s, the federal government began devoting serious attention to the possibility that carbon dioxide emissions associated with human activity could provoke climate change. In 1978, Congress enacted the National Climate Program Act, which required the president to establish a program to "assist the Nation and the world to understand and respond to natural and man-induced climate processes and their implications."[18] President Carter then asked the working arm of the National Academy of Sciences to investigate the subject. They responded unequivocally: "If carbon dioxide continues to increase, the study group finds no reason to doubt that climate changes will result and no reason to believe these changes will be negligible....A wait and see policy may mean waiting until it is too late."[19] The carbon dioxide level was then 337 parts per million.

---

17. *Bahlul* v. *United States,* 767 F. 3d 1, 29–30 (CADC 2014).
18. Pub. L. 95-367, 92 Stat. 601, § 3.
19. Climate Research Board, *Carbon Dioxide and Climate: A Scientific Assessment* (1979), viii.

Congress next addressed the issue by enacting the Global Climate Protection Act in 1987,[20] when the carbon dioxide level had risen to 351. Finding that "manmade pollution — the releases of carbon dioxide, chlorofluorocarbons, methane, and other trace gases into the atmosphere — may be producing a long-term substantial increase in the average temperature on Earth,"[21] Congress directed the Environmental Protection Agency to propose a "coordinated national policy on global climate change,"[22] and ordered the secretary of state to coordinate diplomatic efforts to combat global warming.[23]

In 1990, the Intergovernmental Panel on Climate Change (IPCC), a multinational scientific body organized by the United Nations, published its first comprehensive report, which concluded that emissions resulting from human activities were substantially increasing the atmospheric concentrations of greenhouse gases, which in turn were producing additional warming of the earth's surface. In 1992, President Bush attended the Earth Summit convened by the United Nations in Rio de Janeiro and signed the United Nations Framework Convention on Climate Change; the Senate unanimously ratified the treaty. Five years later, after the IPCC issued another report, the treaty signatories met in Kyoto, Japan, and adopted a protocol that assigned mandatory targets for industrialized nations to reduce greenhouse gas emissions. Because those targets did not include China and India, the United States did not enter into the Kyoto Protocol. In 1997 the carbon dioxide level had risen to 367 parts per million.

In 1999 a group of nineteen private organizations filed a rulemaking petition asking the EPA to regulate "greenhouse gas emissions from new motor vehicles under § 202 of the Clean Water Act."[24] They "maintained that 1998 was the 'warmest year on record'; that carbon dioxide,

---

20. Pub. L. 100-204, 101 Stat. 1407.
21. § 1102(a), 101 Stat. 1408.
22. § 1103(b).
23. § 1103(c).
24. *Massachusetts* v. *EPA (Massachusetts II)*, 549 U.S. 497, 510 (2007), quoting App. 5.

methane, nitrous oxide, and hydrofluorocarbons are 'heat trapping greenhouse gases'; that greenhouse gas emissions have significantly accelerated climate change; and that the IPCC's 1995 report [had] warned that 'carbon dioxide remains the most important contributor to [man-made] forcing of climate change' "[25] and that climate change will have serious adverse effects on human health and the environment.[26] The petition further alleged, with respect to the EPA's statutory authority, that in 1998 the EPA's general counsel and again in 1999 his successor had confirmed that the agency had statutory power to regulate carbon dioxide. Fifteen months later the agency requested public comment on the petition and received over 50,000 responses.

On September 8, 2003, the EPA denied the rulemaking petition, giving two reasons for its decision: (1) that contrary to the two opinions issued by its former general counsels, the EPA does not have statutory authority to issue mandatory regulations to respond to global climate change; and (2) even if it had such authority, it would be unwise to set mandatory emission standards at this time.[27]

The original petitioners, joined by several intervening states and local governments, including Massachusetts, sought review in the Court of Appeals for the D.C. Circuit, which, over the dissent of Judge David Tatel, upheld the EPA's decision.[28] Judge Tatel explained at length why he believed the text of the statute supported the petitioners and why the policy concerns expressed by the agency did not.[29] We granted the petitioners' request for review and, like the D.C. Circuit panel, decided the case by a one-judge margin.[30] I wrote the opinion for the Court, joined by Tony Kennedy, David Souter, Ruth Ginsburg, and Steve Breyer, with Chief Justice Roberts and Nino Scalia, joined by Clarence Thomas and

---

25. *Ibid.*, quoting App. 13.
26. *Ibid.*
27. *Id.*, at 511.
28. *Massachusetts* v. *EPA (Massachusetts I),* 415 F. 3d 50 (CADC 2005).
29. *Id.*, at 61–82.
30. See *Massachusetts II,* 549 U.S. 497 (2007).

Sam Alito, writing dissents. My opinion for the majority agreed with Judge Tatel.

The principal issue that divided us was whether the petitioners had alleged a sufficiently definite redressable injury to give them standing. Arguably my opinion for the Court made new law by relying on the state of Massachusetts's sovereign interest in protecting its citizens from the potential harm to its coastline.[31] But petitioners' unchallenged affidavits described a concrete injury to the state's own interests as well. According to those affidavits, sea levels rose somewhere between ten and twenty centimeters over the twentieth century as a result of global warming. Thus rising seas had already begun to swallow Massachusetts's coastal land, a substantial portion of which is owned by the state itself. It thus had alleged a particularized injury to itself as a landowner.

"In sum — at least according to petitioners' uncontested affidavits — the rise in sea levels associated with global warming has already harmed and will continue to harm Massachusetts. The risk of catastrophic harm, though remote, is nevertheless real. That risk would be reduced to some extent if petitioners received the relief they seek."[32] We therefore held that petitioners had standing to challenge the EPA's denial of their rulemaking petition. At the time of our ruling, the carbon dioxide level had risen to about 385 parts per million. As of this writing, it has reached 410.

In *Philip Morris USA* v. *Williams*,[33] a jury decided that the plaintiff was entitled to recover punitive damages from a cigarette company because the company had deliberately and falsely led her deceased husband to believe that it was safe to smoke cigarettes. The jury's award of $821,000 in actual damages was not at issue, but the amount of the punitive damages award ($79.5 million) was. The Supreme Court of Oregon had permitted the jury to treat punishment of parties not before the court as the

---

31. *Id.*, at 518–21.
32. *Id.*, at 526.
33. 549 U.S. 346 (2007).

basis for its award. The question we had to decide was whether that award deprived the cigarette company of property without due process of law. By an unusual five-to-four vote, we held for the cigarette company.

Steve, joined by the chief, Tony, David, and Sam, wrote the opinion for the majority. They believed that it was unconstitutional to permit a jury to punish a defendant for an injury that it inflicted on persons who are not before the court because the defendant had no opportunity to show, for example, that the third party had not relied on the defendant's deception in deciding to smoke cigarettes. It was permissible to rely on the harm to third parties to prove the reprehensibility of the defendant's conduct but not to punish the defendant directly for the harm visited on nonparties. They therefore reversed the judgment of the state court and ordered it to recalculate the punitive damages award.

Ruth, Nino, Clarence, and I dissented. In her dissent, Ruth demonstrated that the Court's opinion permitted the jury to consider the extent of the harm suffered by third parties as a measure of the reprehensibility of the defendant's conduct but not to mete out punishment for the injuries in fact sustained by those parties, and that the Oregon Supreme Court did not rule otherwise. While Clarence and Nino joined her dissent, they also wrote separately to repeat their position that the Constitution does not place any limit on the amount of punitive damages that a state may impose. I also expressed my agreement with Ruth's explanation of why the state court had not made any procedural error but repeated my agreement with earlier cases holding that the Due Process Clause does impose both procedural and substantive constraints on a state's power to collect punitive damages from a tortfeasor. Of greater importance to me, however, was the Court's imposition of a novel limit on the state's power to impose punishment in civil litigation, particularly in a state like Oregon where a part of the punitive damages award is payable to the state. I saw "no reason why the measure of punishment for engaging in a campaign of deceit in distributing a poisonous and addictive substance to thousands of cigarette smokers statewide should not include consideration of the harm to those 'bystanders' as well as the harm to the individual plaintiff."[34]

In *Stenberg* v. *Carhart*,[35] Stephen, writing for a five-justice majority that included Sandra, explained why a Nebraska law prohibiting "partial birth abortion" unless the procedure is necessary to save the life of the mother was unconstitutional. Tony Kennedy wrote one of the dissents from that holding. Congress reacted to the decision by enacting the Partial-Birth Abortion Ban Act of 2003.[36] In 2007, Tony wrote the Court opinion in *Gonzales* v. *Carhart*,[37] upholding the constitutionality of that statute. Ruth's comprehensive dissent from that holding is probably the most persuasive opinion dealing with abortion issues that any member of the Court has written. She noted that for the first time since *Roe* v. *Wade*[38] the Court had blessed a prohibition with no exception safeguarding a woman's health. She supported her statement that many of the act's recitations are incorrect by noting that Congress's determination that "no medical schools provide instruction on intact D&E" overlooked the fact that "among the schools that now teach the intact variant are Columbia, Cornell, Yale, New York University, Northwestern University, University of Pennsylvania, University of Rochester and University of Chicago."[39] The Court did not seriously try to justify its decision by relying on some significant distinction between the statute invalidated in *Stenberg* and the statute upheld in *Gonzales;* rather, as Ruth noted, the only apparent explanation was that the Court was now "differently composed,"[40] in that Sam had replaced Sandra. Partial birth abortions are unquestionably gruesome procedures, but they are sometimes necessary to protect the life of the mother.

Ruth also wrote an important and especially persuasive dissent in

---

34. *Id.,* at 360 (Stevens, J., dissenting).
35. 530 U.S. 914 (2000).
36. Pub. L. 108–105, 117 Stat. 1201.
37. 550 U.S. 124.
38. 410 U.S. 113 (1973).
39. 550 U.S., at 175–76, quoting Brief for ACOG as *Amicus Curiae* 18.
40. *Id.,* at 191.

Ledbetter v. *Goodyear Tire & Rubber Co.*[41] Lilly Ledbetter was a supervisor at a Goodyear plant in Alabama from 1970 until her retirement in 1998, working in a position mostly occupied by men. While originally her salary was in line with the pay received by her male counterparts, by the end of 1997 the pay discrepancy had become stark: Ledbetter was paid $3,727 per month while the salaries of male area managers ranged from $4,286 to $5,236. In her lawsuit alleging that she was paid a discriminatorily low salary because of her sex, the jury found Goodyear liable and the district court entered judgment in her favor. The Court of Appeals for the Eleventh Circuit reversed, holding that each pay adjustment over the years was a separate act of discrimination that had to be challenged within 180 days. We granted Ledbetter's petition for certiorari, which contended that she had a right to challenge the company's continuing practice of paying her a discriminatorily low salary, rather than just each decision setting her salary at an unlawfully low level. Four of us (David, Ruth, Stephen, and I) voted to reverse, but Sam Alito wrote a strikingly unpersuasive majority opinion affirming. I assigned the dissent to Ruth, who not only wrote an unanswerable dissent but also stated her views in an oral announcement from the bench when the decision was announced. That oral statement played an important part in Congress's later decision to amend the statute, an amendment that expressly endorsed Ruth's and the other dissenters' reading of the statute and was aptly titled the Lilly Ledbetter Fair Pay Act.[42]

Ruth was also the only member of the Court to join my dissent from the majority's decision in *Bell Atlantic Corp.* v. *Twombly*, which dismissed a complaint alleging a violation of Section 1 of the Sherman Act because the plaintiffs had "not nudged their claims across the line from conceivable to plausible."[43] Although I had (and still have) profound respect for David Souter's judgment, my lengthy dissent explains why I thought his decision in this case was profoundly misguided. As a matter of pleading,

---

41. 550 U.S. 618 (2007).
42. Pub. L. 111-2, 123 Stat. 5.
43. 550 U.S. 544, 570 (2007).

his opinion crafted a novel test of plausibility, instead of asking the simple question whether the plaintiff's complaint gave the defendants adequate notice of the legal basis for the claim, which had long been the rule as stated in *Conley* v. *Gibson*.[44] This major departure from long and well-settled practice in interpreting our basic rules of pleading was supposedly justified by the interest in protecting defendants in antitrust litigation from the high cost of pretrial discovery. But the opinion was actually misguided from an antitrust perspective, because it unrealistically assumed that the defendants' self-interest would not have been served by participating in the alleged agreement not to compete with one another.

The 1984 divestiture of the American Telephone & Telegraph Company's local telephone business had produced several incumbent local exchange carriers (ILECs) and a separate competitive market for long-distance service from which the ILECs were excluded. Over a decade later, Congress had enacted the Telecommunications Act of 1996 which restructured local telephone markets by subjecting ILECs to duties that facilitated market entry by new carriers; in exchange, the act authorized ILECs to enter the long-distance market. Under the new scheme, each ILEC had to share its network with new competitors that became known as competitive local exchange carriers (CLECs).

In a class action brought against four ILECs (Bell South, Qwest, SBC, and Verizon), a class consisting of subscribers of local telephone and high-speed internet services sought treble damages from the ILECs for agreeing to refrain from competing with one another; they allegedly failed to pursue attractive business opportunities in contiguous markets, thereby preventing effective competition by CLECs. While the majority assumed that such parallel decisions by competitors were not probative of conspiracy, I made this comment in my dissent: "Many years ago a truly great economist perceptively observed that '[p]eople of the same trade seldom meet together, even for merriment and diversion, but the conversation ends in a conspiracy against the public, or in some contrivance to

---

44. 355 U.S. 41, 47 (1957).

raise prices.'"[45] While I was not so "cynical as to accept that statement at face value,"[46] I did point to the complaint's reference to a comment by one of the defendants' executives implying that their simultaneous decisions not to compete with one another were the product of an agreement.

It is safe to say that both *Twombly* and the later case *Ashcroft* v. *Iqbal*[47] have had a profound impact on the law — so much so that the cases, which are now taught together to first-year law students, are often referred to as *Twiqbal*. As Professor Arthur Miller, perhaps the country's preeminent scholar on procedure, explained, both cases "should be seen as the latest steps in a long-term trend that has favored increasingly early case disposition in the name of efficiency, economy, and avoidance of abusive and meritless lawsuits. It also marks a continued retreat from the principles of citizen access, private enforcement of public policies, and equality of litigant treatment in favor of corporate interests and concentrated wealth."[48] To the average citizen attempting to have his or her day in court, "the liberal-procedure ethos of 1938," when the federal rules swept aside the archaic system of code pleading, "has given way to a restrictive one."[49] Professor Miller persuasively demonstrates how the two cases are emblematic of other procedural changes, such as the ever expanding application of arbitration clauses and their enforcement in federal court under the Federal Arbitration Act in contexts far afield from those envisioned by the drafters of that act. "The cumulative effect of these procedural developments," he notes, "may well have come at the expense of access to the federal courts and the ability of citizens to obtain an adjudication of their claims' merits."[50] As I discussed in my dissent, the Court's departure from the simple notice pleading required under the federal

---

45. *Twombly,* 550 U.S., at 591, quoting A. Smith, "An Inquiry into the Nature and Causes of the Wealth of Nations," in *Great Books of the Western World,* vol. 39, ed. R. Hutchins and M. Adler (Chicago: Encyclopaedia Britannica, 1952), 5.
46. *Ibid.*
47. 556 U.S. 662 (2009).
48. Arthur R. Miller, "From *Conley* to *Twombly* to *Iqbal:* A Double Play on the Federal Rules of Civil Procedure," *Duke L. J.* 60, no. 1 (2010): 10.
49. *Ibid.*
50. *Id.,* at 14.

rules, as explained in the long-standing *Conley* decision, was thus a profound change in the law and one that will continue to affect access to the courts for years to come.

In the last week of June 2007, the chief justice announced the judgment of the Court in two highly consequential First Amendment cases, the first approving the discipline of a high school student for engaging in expressive activity and the second protecting a corporation from discipline for engaging in campaign speech prohibited by an act of Congress.

In *Morse* v. *Frederick*,[51] the Court held that high schools may take steps to safeguard students entrusted to their care from speech that can reasonably be regarded as encouraging illegal drug use. On January 24, 2002, the Olympic Torch Relay passed through Juneau, Alaska, on its way to the winter games in Salt Lake City. The principal of a local high school allowed teachers and students to leave class to watch the relay from either side of the street. After Joseph Frederick, a senior, joined his fellow students across the street from the school, and as torchbearers and television camera crews were passing by, he and his friends unfurled a fourteen-foot banner bearing the words "BONG HITS 4 JESUS."

The principal then crossed the street and demanded that Frederick take down the banner, which she confiscated. She suspended Frederick for ten days, later explaining that she thought the banner encouraged illegal drug use. On appeal, the school superintendent upheld the discipline but reduced the suspension to eight days. Frederick sued the school board and the principal claiming that they had violated his First Amendment rights. The district court denied relief but the Court of Appeals for the Ninth Circuit reversed because the school had punished Frederick without finding that his display of the banner had created a "risk of substantial disruption."[52] Our Court reversed the Ninth Circuit, concluding that

---

51. 551 U.S. 393 (2007).
52. *Morse* v. *Frederick,* 439 F. 3d 1114, 1121 (CA9 2006).

even though the message on the banner was unclear, it was reasonable for the principal to believe that students would interpret it as advocating the use of marijuana. Frederick denied any such motive, explaining that he had just wanted to get on television.

While I agreed that it was permissible for the principal to take down the banner during a student event, I dissented from the decision approving the imposition of punishment on a student for arguably advocating a message with which the school authorities disagreed. David, Ruth, and Steve joined my characterization of the school's position as viewpoint discrimination, tending to preclude healthy debate about such controversial issues as the Vietnam War, Prohibition, and the sale and use of marijuana. Ironically, the chief justice announced his opinion in the case involving "BONG HITS 4 JESUS" on the same day as his opinion in *Federal Election Commission* v. *Wisconsin Right to Life, Inc.*[53]

An important issue decided in that case involved the interpretation of Section 203 of the Bipartisan Campaign Reform Act of 2002, a provision that we had held to be constitutional in an opinion that Sandra and I had coauthored just three years earlier — *McConnell* v. *Federal Election Commission.*[54] That section enlarged the previous provision prohibiting corporations and labor unions from using funds in their treasuries to finance "express advocacy" — ads expressly advocating the election or defeat of a named candidate — to encompass "electioneering communications" as well. In his opinion in *Wisconsin Right to Life,* the chief justice stated that "a court should find that an ad is the functional equivalent of express advocacy only if the ad is susceptible of no reasonable interpretation other than as an appeal to vote for or against a specific candidate."[55] That construction of Section 203 effectively narrowed its coverage so completely as to be tantamount to a repeal. Writing for four of us in his dissent, David correctly pointed out that the demand for campaign money in huge amounts from large contributors had produced a cynical electorate; that

53. 551 U.S. 449 (2007).
54. 540 U.S. 93 (2003).
55. 551 U.S., at 469–70.

the congressional recognition of the ensuing threat to democratic integrity had been reflected in a century of legislation; and that the decision that the Court made that day effectively overruled *McConnell.* His dissent further recognized the dramatic change in the rules relating to campaign financing that the Court was inaugurating.

The judgment that the chief justice announced three days later was equally distressing to the four dissenters. The question in that case, *Parents Involved in Community Schools* v. *Seattle School District No. 1,*[56] was whether school districts in Jefferson County, Kentucky, and Seattle, Washington, could allocate children to different public schools based on their race. In both cases the courts of appeals had affirmed district court findings that the school district had a compelling state interest in maintaining racially diverse schools and the plans were narrowly tailored to serve that interest. Despite the absence of any conflict among the lower courts on the issue, the Court granted certiorari and reversed in both cases. The chief wrote the principal opinion in the two cases, and Tony and Clarence wrote concurring opinions arguing that racial classification designed to benefit a minority race violated the Equal Protection Clause. Stephen wrote a full and accurate dissent and I added a brief comment in which I said,

> There is a cruel irony in The Chief Justice's reliance on our decision in *Brown* v. *Board of Education,* 349 U.S. 294 (1955). The first sentence in the concluding paragraph of his opinion states: "Before *Brown,* schoolchildren were told where they could and could not go to school based on the color of their skin." *Ante,* at 747. This sentence reminds me of Anatole France's observation: "[T]he majestic equality of the law ... forbids rich and poor alike to sleep under the bridges, to beg in the streets, and to steal their bread." The Chief Justice fails to note that it was only black schoolchildren who were so ordered; indeed, the history books do not tell stories

---

56. 551 U.S. 701 (2007).

of white children struggling to attend black schools. In this and other ways, the Chief Justice rewrites the history of one of this Court's most important decisions.... The Court has changed significantly since... [*Brown's* progeny decided in the 1960s and 1970s]. It was then more faithful to *Brown* and more respectful of our precedent than it is today. It is my firm conviction that no Member of the Court that I joined in 1975 would have agreed with today's decision.[57]

October Term 2007

In *Stoneridge Investment Partners, LLC* v. *Scientific-Atlanta, Inc.*,[58] David Souter and Ruth Ginsburg joined my dissent from the Court's holding that a plaintiff may not recover damages from a company that aids and abets a violation of Rule 10(b)(5) of the Securities Exchange Commission. That rule makes it unlawful to "engage in any act, practice, or course of business which operates or would operate as a fraud or deceit upon any person, in connection with the purchase or sale of any security."[59]

Plaintiffs, investors in Charter Communications, Inc., brought a class action alleging that Charter had disseminated fraudulent financial statements. In late 2000, after realizing that the company's receipts would fall short of predictions by $15–20 million, Charter agreed to overpay Motorola and Scientific-Atlanta $20 for each set-top box that it purchased until the end of the year on the understanding that those companies would return the overpayments by purchasing advertising from Charter. The net result of the transactions was the dissemination of misleading financial statements but neither Motorola nor Scientific-Atlanta had made any misstatements to the public. They had only aided and abetted the violations. As the Court concluded, "Unconventional as the

---

57. *Id.,* at 799, 803 (footnote omitted).
58. 552 U.S. 148 (2008).
59. 17 CFR § 240.10b-5.

arrangement was, it took place in the marketplace for goods and services, not in the investment sphere."[60]

I began my dissent by pointing out that Charter had inflated its revenues by $17 million to cover up the $15–20 million expected cash-flow shortfall and could not have done so without the knowingly fraudulent actions of Scientific-Atlanta and Motorola, and then pointed out that the case fit into a campaign to render the Section 10(b) private cause of action toothless. "The Court's current view of implied causes of action," I noted, "is that they are merely a 'relic' of our prior 'heady days.' . . . Those 'heady days' persisted for two hundred years."[61]

I felt the Court's current view was wrong as a general matter but also in the specific context then before the Court. First, the Court dismissed out of hand our nation's long history of judges developing law in a common law tradition. The animating principle behind this tradition was the idea, which is taught to every law school student, that "every wrong shall have a remedy." "Fashioning appropriate remedies for the violation of rules of law designed to protect a class of citizens was the routine business of judges,"[62] as reflected in this long tradition. Second, the Court failed to appreciate that Congress itself legislated against the backdrop of this tradition, and surely "enacted § 10(b) with the understanding that federal courts respected the principle that every wrong would have a remedy."[63] Whatever one might think of the "heady days" of yore, they were certainly relevant to understanding Congress's intent and whether it would have legislated with the understanding that courts would do what they had long done before.

In a claim Mexico brought against the United States in 2004, the International Court of Justice in The Hague held that fifty-one Mexican citizens were entitled to review of their Texas convictions for capital murder.

---

60. 552 U.S., at 166.
61. *Id.,* at 176 (citation omitted).
62. *Id.,* at 177 (footnote omitted).
63. *Id.,* at 180.

One of them, José Ernesto Medellin, who had lived in the United States since preschool, was convicted of raping and murdering two high school teenagers. In violation of the Vienna Convention, the Texas authorities had failed to inform the Mexican consul of Medellin's arrest or to inform Medellin of his right to obtain assistance from the Mexican consul. When he raised his Vienna Convention claim in state post-conviction proceedings, the trial court held that he had waived it by failing to raise it earlier. He then unsuccessfully sought review in a federal habeas corpus proceeding. While his unsuccessful appeal was pending in the court of appeals, the International Court of Justice entered its judgment and President George W. Bush issued a memorandum stating that the United States would discharge its treaty obligations by giving effect to the ICJ judgment. In Texas's view, neither the ICJ judgment nor the president's memorandum was binding federal law that overrode the state's rule prohibiting post-conviction review of Medellin's conviction.

The Texas courts accordingly denied relief and we granted certiorari.

Writing for a majority of five justices, Chief Justice Roberts explained that the Geneva Convention did not create any obligations binding on the United States in the absence of implementing legislation.[64] The requirement that Congress take action to implement a non-self-executing treaty meant that the president's memorandum had no legal effect. I agreed with the majority's result because I thought Article 94(1) of the United Nations Charter, which provides that each member "undertakes to comply" with the decision of the ICJ in any case to which it is a party, was most naturally read as a promise to take additional steps to comply with ICJ judgments. Writing for David Souter and Ruth Ginsburg in a dissent, Steve Breyer argued that ICJ decisions were enforceable against parties. While I did not agree with Steve's legal analysis, I thought he was definitely correct in arguing that Texas should have voluntarily agreed to comply with the president's request to determine whether the breach of the treaty had prejudiced Medellin.

---

64. *Medellin* v. *Texas,* 552 U.S. 491 (2008).

*   *   *

When the Court granted cert in *Baze* v. *Rees*,[65] I had assumed that our decision would bring the debate about lethal injection as a method of execution to a close. Instead of ending that controversy, however, I became convinced that the case would generate debate about the death penalty itself.

At issue in *Baze* was the use of a paralytic agent, pancuronium bromide, as part of a lethal-injection protocol. The use of this particular paralytic agent highlighted much that was wrong with the way the death penalty is practiced in this country. Pancuronium bromide serves no therapeutic purpose: Its primary use is instead to prevent involuntary muscle movements. Yet, in preventing such muscle movements, it creates the very real risk that an inmate will suffer excruciating pain before death occurs because it masks any outward sign of distress. This risk of pain is sufficiently serious that there is a general understanding among veterinarians that it should not be used when ending the life of an animal. As a result of that consensus, several states, including Kentucky, had enacted legislation prohibiting the use of the drug in animal euthanasia. Yet Kentucky was planning to use that very drug to kill the two petitioners in *Baze;* Kentucky's justification was preservation of the execution's dignity.

The opinions written by the chief justice and Ruth Ginsburg, the former upholding Kentucky's method of execution and the latter dissenting, convinced me that the decisions by state legislatures, by Congress, and by our Court to retain the death penalty were the product of habit and inattention rather than an acceptable deliberative process that weighed the costs and risks of administering the penalty against the benefits. This inertia rested in part on a faulty assumption about the retributive force of the death penalty.

Each of the three societal purposes for the death penalty — incapacitation, deterrence, and retribution — had recently been called into question. Incapacitation may have been a legitimate rationale for the death penalty when we upheld it in 1976, but the recent rise in statutes

---

65. 553 U.S. 35 (2008).

providing for life imprisonment without the possibility of parole demonstrated that incapacitation is neither a necessary nor sufficient justification for the death penalty now. The legitimacy of deterrence as an acceptable justification is also questionable at best. Despite thirty years of empirical research in the area, there remains no reliable statistical evidence that capital punishment in fact deters potential offenders. Retribution, then, remains the only viable rationale for imposing the death penalty.

The cruel treatment of victims provides the most persuasive arguments for prosecutors seeking the death penalty; such treatment naturally stirs a jury or judge to want to impose punishment as vengeance for the wrongful act. At the same time — as the chief justice's and Ruth's opinions demonstrated — our society has moved away from public and painful retribution toward ever more humane forms of punishment. But by requiring that an execution be relatively painless, we necessarily protect the inmate from enduring any punishment that is comparable to the suffering that he inflicted on his victim. This trend thus actually undermines the very premise on which public approval of the retribution rationale is based. The use of pancuronium bromide to mask any indication of distress exemplified this trend, though it in many ways suggested a greater interest in the appearance of humaneness because its masking of distress perversely increased the risk of excruciating pain.

Debates over the manner in which executions are carried out come long after other systemic errors may have contributed to imposition of a death sentence in the first place. Of special concern to me are rules that deprive capital defendants of a trial by jurors representing a fair cross section of the community. Litigation involving both challenges for cause and peremptory challenges has convinced me that the process of obtaining a "death qualified jury" is really a procedure that has the purpose and effect of obtaining a jury that is biased in favor of the prosecution. Another serious concern is that the risk of error in capital cases may be greater than in other cases because the facts are often so disturbing that the interest in making sure that the crime does not go unpunished may overcome residual doubt concerning the identity of the offender. Another significant concern is the risk of discriminatory application of the death penalty. And finally, given the real risk of error in this class of cases, the irrevocable character of the penalty, combined with the unacceptable number of convicted defendants who were later exonerated, means that the risk of executing an innocent defendant is simply unacceptable. Putting aside the lack of a rationale for the death penalty, these systemic problems only further counsel against having the death penalty at all.

In 2005, Indiana enacted a statute requiring citizens voting in person on election day or casting a ballot at the office of the circuit clerk prior to election day to present government-issued photo identification. The measure was supported by all of the Republican members of the legislature and opposed by all of the Democrats. Promptly after its enactment, the Indiana Democratic Party filed suit in federal court seeking a judgment declaring the statute unconstitutional. The complaint alleged that the law would unfairly burden the right to vote, that it was neither a necessary nor appropriate method of avoiding election fraud, and that it would arbitrarily disenfranchise qualified voters.

After discovery, Judge Sarah Barker, an excellent judge, granted the defendants' motion for summary judgment. She found that the plaintiffs had not introduced evidence of a single Indiana voter who would be unable to vote as a result of the new law, and rejected as "utterly incredible" an expert's report that up to 989,000 registered voters in Indiana did not possess either a driver's license or other acceptable photo identification; she estimated that the correct number was closer to 43,000. By a two-to-one vote, the Court of Appeals for the Seventh Circuit affirmed. We granted certiorari, and, by a six-to-three vote, affirmed.[66]

The chief assigned me the opinion, which he and Tony Kennedy joined. Nino Scalia, in an opinion joined by Clarence Thomas and Sam Alito, expressed the view that there was even less merit to the plaintiffs'

---

66. *Crawford* v. *Marion County Election Bd.,* 553 U.S. 181, 189 (2008).

attack on the statute than I acknowledged. David Souter, joined by Ruth Ginsburg, wrote a dissent, and Stephen Breyer also dissented. Although I was convinced that Judge Barker had correctly concluded that the plaintiffs had failed to prove their case, the opinion was difficult to write because I thought the statute was an example of particularly unwise partisan legislation that did not really serve the public interest.

In 2005 Congress passed the Detainee Treatment Act providing certain procedures for the review of the status of detainees being held at Guantánamo Bay, Cuba. In *Boumediene* v. *Bush*,[67] the last of the cases in the detainee saga discussed in earlier chapters, we confronted the question whether those procedures were an adequate substitute for the common law writ of habeas corpus that would avoid violating the Suspension Clause of the Constitution, which provides, "The Privilege of the Writ of Habeas Corpus shall not be suspended, unless when in Cases of Rebellion or Invasion the public Safety may require it."[68]

Following the September 11, 2001, terrorist attacks, Congress had passed the Authorization for Use of Military Force (AUMF), granting the president the authority to use all necessary and appropriate force against those nations, organizations, or persons he determines planned, authorized, committed, or aided the terrorist attacks that occurred on September 11, 2001, or harbored such organizations or persons, in order to prevent any future acts of international terrorism against the United States by such persons. In *Hamdi* v. *Rumsfeld*,[69] we recognized that the AUMF authorized the detention of individuals who fought against the United States in Afghanistan for the duration of that particular conflict. The deputy secretary of defense then established Combatant Status Review Tribunals (CSRTs) to determine whether individuals being detained at Guantánamo were "enemy combatants" and also issued a memorandum defining the procedures to be used in making those determinations.

---

67. 553 U.S. 723 (2008).
68. Art. I, § 9, cl. 2.
69. 542 U.S. 507 (2004).

Most of the individuals detained at Guantánamo had been apprehended on the battlefield in Afghanistan, but many others had been apprehended from as far away as Bosnia and Gambia. Though all the petitioners in *Boumediene* were foreign nationals, not one was a citizen of a country then at war with the United States. And each had denied he was a member of Al Qaeda. Yet, interpreting the AUMF, the Department of Defense had ordered them detained as enemy combatants and transferred them from wherever they had been apprehended to Guantánamo.

By the time the *Boumediene* case reached the Court, each petitioner had appeared before a CSRT, had been determined to be an enemy combatant, and had sought a writ of habeas corpus in the federal district court in Washington, D.C. That court dismissed the cases for want of jurisdiction because the Guantánamo naval base is outside the sovereign territory of the United States. The Court of Appeals for the D.C. Circuit affirmed, we granted certiorari, and then reversed, holding in *Rasul* v. *Bush*[70] that statutory habeas corpus jurisdiction had been extended to Guantánamo. Petitioners' claims were then consolidated in two separate proceedings before two separate judges. One set was dismissed; in the other, the judge held that the detainees had rights under the Due Process Clause.

While appeals were pending, Congress passed the Detainee Treatment Act of 2005, which provides that "no court, justice, or judge shall have jurisdiction to hear or consider…an application for a writ of habeas corpus filed by or on behalf of an alien detained by the Department of Defense at Guantánamo Bay, Cuba." We had held, in *Hamdan* v. *Rumsfeld*,[71] that this provision did not apply to cases then pending when the DTA was enacted. Congress followed up with yet another statute, the Military Commissions Act of 2006, which amended the statute at issue in *Hamdan* to make clear that the above-quoted provision "shall apply to all cases, without exception, pending on or after the date of" enactment.

In *Boumediene,* we were finally confronted with the question whether

---

70. 542 U.S. 466, 473 (2004).
71. 548 U.S. 557, 576–77 (2006).

aliens detained at Guantánamo had the constitutional privilege of habeas corpus. This question really encompassed two questions, requiring us to "determine whether petitioners [were] barred from seeking the writ or invoking the protections of the Suspension Clause either because of their status, *i.e.*, petitioners' designation by the Executive Branch as enemy combatants, or their physical location, *i.e.*, their presence at Guantánamo Bay."[72] In an opinion that I assigned to Tony Kennedy, over the dissents of the chief justice and Nino Scalia, joined by Clarence Thomas and Sam Alito, we held that they were not. Technical sovereignty was less significant than the actual control over Guantánamo in judging the courts' ability to hold appropriate hearings, which effectively resolved both subsidiary questions. Tony Kennedy concluded his opinion for the Court with this eloquent defense of the great writ and rule of law: "The laws and Constitution are designed to survive, and remain in force, in extraordinary times. Liberty and security can be reconciled; and in our system they are reconciled within the framework of the law. The Framers decided that habeas corpus, a right of first importance, must be a part of that framework, a part of that law."[73] I could not have agreed more and thought this a fitting conclusion to this series of cases and dialogue with Congress.

Throughout most of our history there was no federal objection to laws regulating the civilian use of firearms. When I joined the Court in 1975, both state and federal judges accepted the Court's unanimous decision in *United States* v. *Miller*[74] as having established that the Second Amendment's protection of the right to bear arms was possessed only by members of the militia and applied only to weapons used by the militia. In that case, the Court upheld the indictment of a man who possessed a short-barreled shotgun, writing, "In the absence of any evidence that the possession or use of a 'shotgun having a barrel of less than eighteen inches in length' has some reasonable relationship to the preservation or

---

72. *Boumediene,* 553 U.S., at 739.
73. *Id.,* at 798.
74. 307 U.S. 174 (1939).

efficiency of a well regulated militia, we cannot say that the Second Amendment guarantees the right to keep and bear such an instrument. Certainly it is not within judicial notice that this weapon is any part of the ordinary military equipment or that its use could contribute to the common defense."[75] Moreover, the Court might well have added, its use by civilians unconnected with the militia would not contribute to the "well regulated" character of the militia.

As Steve Breyer pointed out in his dissent in *District of Columbia* v. *Heller,*[76] colonial history contains many examples of firearm regulations in urban areas that imposed obstacles to their use for protection of the home. Boston, Philadelphia, and New York — the three largest cities in America at that time — all imposed restrictions on the firing of guns in the city limits. Boston enacted a law in 1746 prohibiting the "discharge" of any gun or pistol that was later revived in 1778, Philadelphia prohibited firing a gun or setting off fireworks without a governor's special license, and New York banned the firing of guns for three days surrounding New Year's Day. Moreover, those and other cities regulated the storage of gunpowder. Boston's gunpowder law imposed a ten-pound fine on any person who took any loaded firearm into any dwelling house or barn within the town. Most, if not all, of those regulations would violate the Second Amendment as it was construed in the five-to-four decision Nino Scalia announced in *Heller* on June 26, 2008.

Heller is unquestionably the most clearly incorrect decision that the Court announced during my tenure on the bench. The text of the Second Amendment unambiguously explains its purpose: "A well regulated Militia being necessary to the security of a free State, the right of the people to keep and bear Arms, shall not be infringed." When it was adopted, the country was concerned that the power of Congress to disarm the state militias and create a national standing army posed an intolerable threat to the sovereignty of the several states. The interest in protecting citizens

75. *Id.,* at 177.
76. 554 U.S. 570, 681 (2008).

from the type of firearm regulation Steve identified in his dissent was proposed by a minority of Pennsylvania delegates who voted against ratification, but it was not thereafter considered. Despite the fact that Madison had before him proposals that would have protected such nonmilitary uses, it is striking that his draft omitted any mention of such a purpose. Had that been a concern, it surely would have been discussed when the amendment was proposed and debated.

For most of our history, the invalidity of Second Amendment–based objections to firearms regulations had been well settled and uncontroversial. The first two federal laws directly restricting the civilian use and possession of firearms — the 1927 act prohibiting mail delivery of handguns and the 1934 act prohibiting the possession of sawed-off shotguns and machine guns — were enacted over minor Second Amendment objections that were dismissed by the vast majority of legislators participating in the debates. After reviewing many of the same sources that are discussed at greater length by Nino Scalia in his majority opinion in *Heller,* the *Miller* Court unanimously concluded that the Second Amendment did not apply to the possession of a firearm that did not have "some relationship to the preservation or efficiency of a well regulated militia."[77] And in 1980, in a footnote to an opinion upholding a conviction for receipt of a firearm, the Court effectively affirmed *Miller,* writing: "[T]he Second Amendment guarantees no right to keep and bear a firearm that does not have 'some reasonable relationship to the preservation or efficiency of a well regulated militia.' "[78] So well settled was the issue that, speaking on the PBS *NewsHour* in 1991, the retired Chief Justice Warren Burger described the National Rifle Association's lobbying in support of an interpretation of the Second Amendment as a limitation on regulation of the civilian uses of firearms in these terms: "One of the greatest pieces of fraud, I repeat the word 'fraud,' on the American public by special interest groups that I have ever seen in my lifetime."

---

77. 307 U.S., at 178.
78. *Lewis* v. *United States,* 445 U.S. 55, 65n8 (1980), quoting *Miller,* 307 U.S., at 178.

Even if the lobbyists who oppose gun control regulation actually do endorse the dubious proposition that the Second Amendment was intended to limit the federal power to regulate the civilian use of handguns — that Warren Burger incorrectly accused them of "fraud" — I find it incredible that policymakers in a democratic society have failed to impose more effective regulations on the ownership and use of firearms than they have. I have written in other contexts that an amendment to the Constitution to overrule *Heller* is desperately needed to prevent tragedies such as the massacre of twenty grammar schoolchildren at Sandy Hook Elementary School on December 14, 2012, from ever happening again. Yet, in the course of my writing this chapter, on October 1, 2017, a gunman fired from the thirty-second floor of a hotel in Las Vegas, killing at least fifty-eight people and injuring over five hundred more who were attending an outdoor concert. In the aftermath of this tragedy, the NRA initially came out in support of prohibitions on so-called bump stocks, which the Las Vegas shooter used to turn his semiautomatic weapons into fully automatic ones. Many applauded the normally intransigent NRA for at least supporting some form of gun regulation, but it struck me as a cynical ploy to appear reasonable when their position on gun regulation is anything but. Devices that make such deadly weapons even deadlier should be banned. But prohibiting bump stocks alone will do little to curtail the scourge of gun violence plaguing this country. (Indeed, I could not even finish writing this chapter before another mass shooting occurred, this one involving the death of twenty-six people — including three generations of a single family — at a church on November 5, 2017, in Sutherland Springs, Texas.)

Even if there were some merit to the legal arguments advanced in the *Heller* case, all could foresee the negative consequences of the decision, which should have provided my colleagues with the justification needed to apply stare decisis to *Miller*. At a minimum, it should have given them greater pause before announcing such a radical change in the law that would greatly tie the hands of state and national lawmakers endeavoring to find solutions to the gun problem in America. Their twin failure in that case — first, the misreading of the intended meaning of the Second Amendment, and second, the failure to respect settled precedent — represent the worst self-inflicted wound in the Court's history.

They also represent the most disappointing task on which I worked as a member of the Court. After the oral argument and despite the narrow vote at our conference about the case, I continued to think it possible to persuade either Tony Kennedy or Clarence Thomas to change his vote. During the drafting process, I had frequent conversations with Tony, as well as occasional discussions with Clarence Thomas about historical issues, because I thought each of them had an open mind about the case. In those discussions — particularly those with Tony — I now realize that I failed to emphasize sufficiently the human aspects of the issue as providing unanswerable support for the stare decisis argument for affirmance. After all, Tony had been one of the three decisive votes that had saved *Roe v. Wade* from being overruled in *Planned Parenthood* v. *Casey*.[79]

But an unusual development that occurred while the case was under advisement made excessive reliance on *Miller* seem unwise: Legal scholarship published while *Heller* was under consideration called *Miller* into question.[80] The criticism of *Miller* did not raise any new question about the reasoning in the opinion, but pointed out that the defendant had not been represented in the argument in our Court. Of course, that had been true of the losing litigant in *Marbury* v. *Madison* as well, but it persuaded me to place more emphasis on the merits and less on the strength of precedent in my talks with Tony.

Before the argument, I had decided that stare decisis provided a correct and sufficient basis for upholding the challenged gun regulation, but I nonetheless asked my especially competent law clerk, Kate Shaw, to make a thorough study of the merits of the argument that an independent review of the historical materials would lead to the same result. I wanted that specific study to help me decide which argument to feature

---

79. 505 U.S. 833 (1992).
80. See, e.g., Brian L. Frye, "The Peculiar History of *United States* v. *Miller*," *N.Y.U.J.L. & Liberty* 3, no. 48 (2008): 65–68.

in my dissent, which I planned to complete and circulate before Nino Scalia completed his opinion for the majority. Kate convinced me that *Miller* had been correctly decided; accordingly, I decided to feature both arguments in my dissent, which we were able to circulate on April 28, 2008, five weeks before Nino Scalia circulated the majority opinion on June 2, 2008. In the cover memorandum for my probable dissent, I wrote,

> The enclosed memorandum explains the basis for my firm belief that the Second Amendment does not impose any limit whatsoever on the power of the federal government to regulate the nonmilitary use or possession of firearms. I have decided to take the unusual step of circulating the initial draft of a probable dissent before Nino circulates his majority because I fear the members of the majority have not yet adequately considered the unusual importance of their decision.

> While I think a fair reading of history provides overwhelming support for Warren Burger's view of the merits, even if we assume that the present majority is correct, I submit that they have not given adequate consideration to the certain impact of their proposed decision on this Court's role in preserving the rule of law. We have profound differences over our role in areas of the law such as the Eighth Amendment and substantive due process, but I believe we all agree that there are areas of policy-making in which judges have a special obligation to let the democratic process run the show. With the unique exceptions of the court of appeals decisions in *Emerson* and in this case, that has been the governing view of gun control issues throughout the federal judiciary for decades.

> What has happened that could possibly justify such a massive change in the law? The text of the amendment has not changed. The history leading up to the adoption of the amendment has not changed. The commentary by Story and the other nineteenth

century commentators has not changed. There has been a change in the views of some law professors, but I assume there are also some professors out there who think Congress does not have the authority to authorize a national bank, or to regulate small firms engaged in the production of goods for sale in other states, or to enact a graduated income tax. In my judgment, none of the arguments advanced by respondents or their numerous amici justify judicial entry into a quintessential area of policy-making in which there is no special need or justification for judicial supervision.

This is not a case in which either side of the policy debate can be characterized as an "insular minority" in need of special protection from the judiciary. On the contrary, there is a special risk that the action of the judiciary will be perceived as the product of policy arguments advanced by an unusually powerful political force. Because there is still time to avoid a serious and totally unnecessary self-inflicted wound, I urge each of the Members of the majority to give careful consideration to the impact of this decision on the future of this institution when weighing the strength of the arguments I have set forth in what I hope will not be a dissent.

In the end of course, beating Nino to the punch did not change the result, but I do think it forced him to significantly revise his opinion to respond to the points I raised in my dissent. And although I failed to persuade Tony to change his vote, I think our talks may have contributed to his insisting on some important changes before signing on to the Court's opinion.

October Term 2008

In 1978, Chief Justice Warren Burger and Bill Rehnquist joined all of my opinion announcing the judgment of the Court in *FCC* v. *Pacifica*

Foundation,[81] and Harry Blackmun and Lewis Powell joined most of it. In that case we held that the Federal Communications Commission had correctly concluded that an afternoon radio broadcast of George Carlin's satiric monologue entitled "Filthy Words" used indecent language prohibited by a federal statute. In its opinion, the FCC had defined "indecent" speech as "language that describes, in terms patently offensive as measured by contemporary community standards for the broadcast medium, sexual or excretory activities and organs, at times of the day when there is a reasonable risk that children may be in the audience."[82]

In my opinion for the Court, I noted that "[s]ome uses of even the most offensive words are unquestionably protected," but "the constitutional protection accorded to a communication containing such patently offensive sexual and excretory language need not be the same in every context."[83] As Justice George Sutherland noted years before, "a 'nuisance may be merely a right thing in the wrong place, — like a pig in the parlor instead of the barnyard.'"[84] The FCC, we concluded, was within its regulatory power to determine that an obscenity-laced monologue was out of place in an early afternoon radio broadcast that might be heard by young children — as indeed it was, which had led to the complaint that resulted in the case then before us.

Lewis wrote separately because he thought my opinion failed to recognize the strength of the First Amendment's protection of the language in the monologue. Later in 1978 the FCC noted that my opinion had relied on the repetitive use of the indecent words, and a few years later it explained that it would not prohibit the fleeting use of isolated indecent words. Tolerance of the fleeting use of isolated indecent words remained its policy, which reflected the need to avoid getting too close to the constitutional line as set forth in Lewis's separate opinion in *Pacifica*.

In 2004, however, the FCC for the first time declared that the use of

---

81. 438 U.S. 726.
82. 56 F. C. C. 94, 98.
83. 438 U.S., at 746–47.
84. *Id.*, at 750, quoting *Euclid* v. *Ambler Realty Co.*, 272 U.S. 365, 388 (1926).

the f-word or the s-word could be actionably indecent even if used only once in a broadcast. It reversed a staff ruling that the performer Bono's comment on a network broadcast of the Golden Globe Awards — "This is really, really, f***ing brilliant" — was not indecent because any use of that word "invariably invokes a coarse sexual image."[85] In its ruling, the FCC acknowledged that its prior rulings had indicated that isolated or fleeting uses of the f-word in broadcasts would not be characterized as indecent or penalized, but it determined that view was no longer good law. Although the FCC did not impose sanctions on the network for Bono's fleeting vulgarity, the network nevertheless sought review in the Court of Appeals for the Second Circuit, which reversed the FCC's order because it found the agency's reasoning unpersuasive. We granted the agency's petition for certiorari and, by a five-to-four vote, reversed.[86]

Nino Scalia wrote the opinion of the Court, which the chief justice and Tony Kennedy, Clarence Thomas, and Sam Alito joined and which Tony and Clarence also supported with separate concurrences. The four dissenters all joined Steve Breyer's principal dissent, and Ruth Ginsburg and I also authored separate dissents. Among the issues we debated were whether an administrative agency exercises legislative or executive power when it engages in rulemaking, whether its burden of explaining a change in a settled rule is heavier than when it promulgates a brand-new rule, and how serious the risk of unforeseeable liability is for a small station. Notably, none of the opinions answered any First Amendment question.

I thought there was a critical difference between the use of an expletive to describe a sexual or excretory function and, for example, a golfer's utterance after shanking a short approach. I also thought it was ironic for the FCC to patrol the airwaves for words that have a tenuous relationship with sex or excrement while commercials broadcast during primetime hours frequently asked participants whether they are battling erectile dysfunction or having trouble going to the bathroom. Ruth thought the

---

85. In re *Complaints Against Various Broadcast Licensees Regarding Their Airing of the "Golden Globe Awards" Program*, 19 FCC Rcd. 4975, 4978–79, pp. 8–9 (2004).
86. *FCC v. Fox TV Stations, Inc.*, 556 U.S. 502 (2009).

distinction between the solitary use of an indecent word and the repetition of multiple obscenities, so heavily stressed in the *Pacifica* opinion, should have been decisive, and Steve thought the agency had utterly failed to explain why it had changed a policy that had been so well settled for so long.

In the wake of the September 11, 2001, terrorist attacks, federal officials arrested and detained Javaid Iqbal, a Muslim and citizen of Pakistan, on charges of fraud in relation to certain immigration documents. He was one of 184 arrestees whom the federal government designated as persons of "high interest" to the investigation of the terrorist attacks and held under restrictive conditions that prevented them from communicating with the general prison population or the outside world. He was kept in lockdown for twenty-three hours a day, spending the remaining hour outside his cell in handcuffs and leg irons accompanied by a four-officer escort. He pleaded guilty to the criminal charges, served a term of imprisonment, and was removed to his native Pakistan.

After his release, he filed a lawsuit against several federal agents, including former attorney general John Ashcroft and former director of the FBI Robert Mueller, alleging that they had adopted an unconstitutional policy that subjected him to especially harsh conditions of confinement because of his race, religion, and nationality. In short, he alleged that, in the wake of the terrorist attacks, the federal government rounded up Muslims and individuals perceived to be Muslim based on their religion or ethnic origin alone and without reason to believe they had participated in the terrorist attacks.

Ashcroft and Mueller moved to dismiss the complaint, arguing that it failed to allege facts showing their personal involvement in the alleged unconstitutional treatment of Iqbal and the other detainees. The district court denied their motion and they appealed. While their appeal was pending, our Court decided *Bell Atlantic Corp.* v. *Twombly,* in which David Souter had crafted a new, more defendant-friendly standard for judging motions to dismiss complaints in antitrust cases. In his opinion for the Court in *Ashcroft* v. *Iqbal,* Tony Kennedy stated that the new "plausibility standard" announced in *Twombly* obliged the pleader "to amplify a claim with some factual allegations in those contexts where such amplification is needed to render the claim *plausible.*"[87] He concluded that all the complaint plausibly suggested was that the nation's top law enforcement officers, in the wake of a devastating terrorist attack, sought to keep suspected terrorists in the most secure conditions available until the suspects could be cleared of terrorist activity.

As the senior of the four dissenting justices, I took special pleasure in assigning the dissent to David, the author of the Court's opinion in *Twombly.* In that dissent, David clearly stated that the detention policy allegedly developed by Ashcroft and Mueller was much harsher than the majority had described: "Iqbal claims that on the day he was transferred to the special unit, prison guards, without provocation, 'picked him up and threw him against the wall, kicked him in the stomach, punched him in the face, and dragged him across the room'.... He says that after being attacked a second time he sought medical attention but was denied care for two weeks, [that] prison staff in the special unit subjected him to unjustified strip and body cavity searches,... verbally berated him as a 'terrorist' and 'Muslim killer,'... refused to give him adequate food... [,] intentionally turned on air conditioning during the winter and heating during the summer," and "interfered with his attempts to pray and engage in religious study."[88]

David said he could not understand why the majority had treated as merely conclusory Iqbal's allegations that after September 11 the FBI had designated Iqbal and other Arab Muslims as being of "high interest" because of their race, religion, and national origin and not because of their involvement in supporting terrorist activity and that Ashcroft and Mueller knew of, condoned, and maliciously agreed to that discrimination. He could not find any principled basis for the majority's disregard of

87. 556 U.S. 662, 670 (2009).
88. *Id.,* at 688–89.

the allegations linking Ashcroft and Mueller to their subordinates' discrimination. Neither could the scholars writing about the Court's new rules for judging the sufficiency of complaints against official mistreatment of alleged terrorists.[89]

As I noted in earlier chapters, a federal statute, 42 U.S.C. § 1983, creates a remedy for violations of federal rights committed by persons acting under color of state law. Haywood, an inmate in a New York prison, filed two cases in the state trial court against New York corrections officers claiming that they had violated his federal rights in prison disciplinary proceedings and an altercation; he sought damages and attorney's fees. The trial court dismissed the action on the ground that a New York statute deprived it of jurisdiction over any case in which the plaintiff sought damages against a corrections officer for actions taken in the course of his employment. The statute provided that the inmate could only recover from the state. Applying that state statute, the New York courts dismissed Haywood's action.

Our Court granted review of Haywood's petition, which argued that New York's remedy for the alleged violation of Haywood's federal rights was inferior to his federal remedy: He was not entitled to a jury trial, had no right to attorney's fees, and could not obtain punitive damages or injunctive relief. By a five-to-four vote, we held that New York's treatment of Haywood's Section 1983 claim violated the Supremacy Clause of the Constitution.[90] I wrote the majority opinion and Clarence Thomas wrote the dissent.

In its Corrections Law, New York had made a judgment that corrections officers should not be burdened with suits arising out of their employment, presumably because it regarded such suits as frivolous. But Congress in Section 1983 had made a judgment that all persons who violate federal rights when acting under color of state law shall be held liable in damages.

---

89. See Arthur R. Miller, "From *Conley* to *Twombly* to *Iqbal*: A Double Play on the Federal Rules of Civil Procedure," *Duke L. J.* 60 (2010): 1, 10.
90. *Haywood* v. *Drown*, 556 U.S. 729, 741–42 (2009).

New York admittedly would allow such a suit against a police officer to be resolved in a state court, and therefore may not deny access to its courts to litigants seeking a comparable remedy against different state agents.

In dissent, Clarence argued that New York could refuse to allow prisoners access to their courts to enforce Section 1983 in suits against corrections officers as long as it imposed the same limits on state court actions: "The sole consequence of [New York's] jurisdictional barrier is that the law cannot be enforced in one particular forum."[91] He concluded that our majority opinion had "transformed a single exception to the rule of state judicial autonomy into a virtually ironclad obligation to entertain federal business."[92]

As I noted in my majority opinion, however, the "Court has long made clear that federal law is as much the law of the several States as are the laws passed by their legislatures."[93] And "state courts as well as federal courts are entrusted with providing a forum for the vindication of federal rights violated by state or local officials acting under color of state law."[94] These suits were as much state business as federal business.

In 1986 in *Michigan* v. *Jackson*,[95] I wrote the Court opinion upholding, by a six-to-three vote, the Michigan Supreme Court's ruling that two post-arraignment confessions had been improperly obtained — and the Sixth Amendment had been violated — because the defendants had "requested counsel during their arraignments, but were not afforded an opportunity to consult with counsel before the police initiated further interrogations."[96] Our ruling relied on Byron White's opinion for the Court in *Edwards* v. *Arizona*,[97] which held that "an accused... having expressed his desire to deal with the police only through counsel, is not

---

91. *Id.*, at 769.
92. *Id.*, at 777.
93. *Id.*, at 734.
94. *Id.*, at 735.
95. 475 U.S. 625.
96. *People* v. *Bladel*, 365 N.W. 56, 69 (Mich. 1984).
97. 451 U.S. 477 (1981).

subject to further interrogation by the authorities until counsel has been made available to him, unless the accused himself initiates further communication, exchanges, or conversations with the police."[98] We specifically rejected the dissenters' objection to what they character-ized as an unjustified extension of the *Edwards* rule to the Sixth Amendment.

In *Montejo* v. *Louisiana*,[99] the defendant was informed at his arraign-ment that counsel had been appointed to represent him, but before he met his lawyer, he voluntarily responded to questioning by the police. After they obtained highly incriminating evidence from him, he met for the first time with his court-appointed attorney who was upset that the detectives had interrogated his client in his absence. His lawyer rightly contended that the evidence the police obtained was inadmissible under the reasoning in *Jackson*. The Louisiana courts disagreed, because the defendant in *Jackson* had affirmatively requested that counsel be appointed to represent him whereas Montejo had simply stood mute during his pre-liminary hearing. Under Louisiana law, however, counsel is automatically appointed, so there was no reason for Montejo to say anything. The Loui-siana courts held that *Miranda* warnings were sufficient to allow the questioning to proceed without the presence of counsel even though counsel by then had been appointed for Montejo. He was sentenced to death, and we granted certiorari.

After the oral argument, a majority of the Court voted to reverse, and I assigned the majority opinion to myself. During the argument, Monte-jo's counsel had effectively pointed to the anomalous distinctions between defendants in different states that would result if we made the availability of *Jackson*'s protection turn on whether the appointment of counsel for indigent defendants was routine or required a request from the defen-dant. In my draft opinion, I therefore took the position that the

---

98. *Id.*, at 484–85.
99. 556 U.S. 778 (2009).

protection of the *Jackson* rule stemmed from the commencement of formal criminal proceedings and did not depend on the defendant's request for counsel. After I circulated my draft majority opinion, however, only three justices joined me. The Court subsequently decided to order supplemental briefing to address whether *Jackson* should be overruled. After the supplemental briefs were received, that is exactly what it did.

Our Court decided the case by the familiar five-to-four split with Nino Scalia writing for himself, the chief, Tony, Clarence, and Sam, while David, Ruth, and Stephen joined my dissenting opinion. The majority agreed that *Jackson* controlled and required reversal of the Louisiana courts, but the majority decided to overrule *Jackson* largely on the grounds that it was not well reasoned. To reach that conclusion, however, Nino had to narrowly interpret *Jackson* as resting entirely on the anti-badgering rationale that motivated Byron White's majority in *Edwards* v. *Arizona*. In contrast, I viewed the rule announced in *Jackson* as bottomed on the Sixth Amendment right to counsel that automatically protects defendants at every critical stage of a prosecution as soon as the attorney-client relationship is created. Police interrogation of an indicted defendant is certainly (and most obviously) a critical stage of a prosecution. Moreover, the *Jackson* rule merely required adherence to professional standards that independently govern the conduct of police and prosecutors. Rules of professional conduct endorsed by the American Bar Association and by every bar association in the country prohibit prosecutors from conversing with represented defendants without counsel present in all but the most limited circumstances. I thought it clear that even if *Jackson* had never been decided, the interrogation of Montejo violated his Sixth Amendment rights.

Nino's opinion emphasized what he perceived were the excessive costs of the *Jackson* rule, the unpersuasive quality of my opinion, the assumption that *Miranda* warnings were adequate for an already represented defendant, and the relative novelty (twenty-three years) of the *Jackson* rule. Despite the weaknesses in each of these considerations, Nino persuaded four of his colleagues to overrule a case that had proven itself to be a workable and sensible bright-line rule over the previous two decades.

The practice of electing judges in many parts of this country has long been controversial. Indeed, following her retirement from the Court, Sandra O'Connor became an outspoken critic of the practice and encouraged an end to it. One of the cases we heard in the 2008 term demonstrated in stark terms the danger that the practice posed to the public's confidence in a fair and impartial judiciary.

In August 2002, a West Virginia jury found the A. T. Massey Coal Company liable for various torts and awarded the plaintiffs $50 million in compensatory and punitive damages. The state trial court later denied Massey's posttrial motions challenging the jury's verdict and damages award. Before Massey prosecuted its appeal from the trial judge's order, West Virginia held its judicial elections.

No doubt knowing that the victors in the election to the Supreme Court would decide Massey's appeal, Don Blankenship, Massey's chief executive officer, threw his support behind Brent Benjamin, a lawyer contesting the seat of one of the justices seeking reelection. In addition to contributing the $1,000 statutory maximum to Benjamin's campaign, Blankenship donated almost $2.5 million to a political organization supporting Benjamin's election and just over $500,000 on independent expenditures for his election. The $3 million that Blankenship spent exceeded by 300 percent the amount that Benjamin's campaign committee spent and exceeded by $1 million the amount both candidates' campaign committees spent. Benjamin won the election. Though the parties disputed whether Benjamin would have won the election regardless of the contributions because of some of his opponents' fumbles during the race, few would doubt that he surely appreciated Blankenship's very generous support.

Before Massey filed its appeal from the trial court order, the plaintiffs moved to disqualify the just elected Justice Benjamin under both the

West Virginia Code of Judicial Conduct and the Due Process Clause of the Constitution. Justice Benjamin denied the motion, and later provided the decisive vote in the three-to-two decision reversing the $50 million verdict against Massey. After the West Virginia Supreme Court reconsidered and adhered to the earlier decision with a newly constituted composition of justices but still including the decisive vote from Justice Benjamin, our Court granted review to consider whether his failure to recuse himself violated due process. By a five-to-four vote, we reversed.[100] Without questioning Justice Benjamin's actual impartiality, Tony Kennedy's opinion for the majority held that the probability of actual bias required Justice Benjamin to recuse himself even if he was not actually prejudiced by Blankenship's extraordinary support of his campaign.

The chief justice, joined by Nino, Clarence, and Sam, crafted an unusual dissent in which he posed forty questions the majority failed to answer about his predicted flood of disqualification motions. Those of us in the majority thought that the opinion had made it clear that only in comparably extreme cases would the Constitution require disqualification and that local rules would solve similar problems without the necessity of reaching any due process issue. I think subsequent events have demonstrated that the dissenters' fears of an avalanche of disqualification motions were grossly exaggerated. And I think few would doubt that the extraordinary facts of that case called for the result the majority reached.

On the evening of March 22, 1993, two men picked up a prostitute in Anchorage, Alaska, and one of them vaginally raped her while using a blue condom. The men then brutally beat her, shot her, and left her in the woods, thinking she was dead. She survived and made her way to the police to report the horrendous crime.

A jury later convicted William Osborne and another man of attempted murder and sexual assault, and a trial judge sentenced Osborne to prison for twenty-six years with five suspended. After serving his sentence and

---

100. *Caperton* v. *A. T. Massey Coal Co.,* 556 U.S. 868 (2009).

after a more advanced form of DNA testing had become available, Osborne asked the state to use that test on the evidence on the condom. Although both the state and Osborne agreed that the results of the test would establish either his guilt or his innocence, the state refused to perform the test.

Osborne brought a federal action and both the district court and the Court of Appeals for the Ninth Circuit held that he had a constitutional right to obtain evidence that would either establish his innocence or his guilt. We granted certiorari, and in a five-to-four decision, reversed.[101] Writing for the familiar majority favoring the prosecution in criminal matters, the chief justice held that the state should be free to fashion rules governing the accessibility of this important new category of evidence to the total exclusion of the federal courts. I wrote a dissent arguing that there was no valid reason for delaying access to the evidence.

In his opinion, the chief wrote, "The Court of Appeals below relied only on procedural due process, but Osborne seeks to defend the judgment on the basis of substantive due process as well. He asks that we recognize a freestanding right to DNA evidence untethered from the liberty interests he hopes to vindicate with it. We reject the invitation and conclude, in the circumstances of this case, that there is no such substantive due process right."[102] In support of this conclusion, he further noted, "There is no long history of such a right, and '[t]he mere novelty of such a claim is reason enough to doubt that "substantive due process" sustains it.'"[103] In an ironic twist, the chief and four of the three justices who joined his opinion would later rely on the doctrine of substantive due process as the basis for concluding that the Second Amendment is applicable to the states.

---

101. *District Attorney's Office for the Third Judicial District* v. *Osborne,* 557 U.S. 52, 56 (2009).
102. *Id.,* at 72.
103. *Ibid.,* quoting *Reno* v. *Flores,* 507 U.S. 292, 303 (1993).

31

The Sotomayor Court

October Term 2009

On May 1, 2009, David Souter informed his eight colleagues that he would be notifying the president later that day that he was retiring at the end of the current term. This announcement was especially sad news for me. Over the years, David had become Maryan's and my closest friend on the Court. I knew I would miss seeing him on a regular basis around the Court and in Washington. On many cases and issues, particularly those on which the Court seemed to be dividing more regularly, we agreed with each other far more often than we disagreed. And for several years prior to his retirement, we had also had an understanding that he would be frank and tell me when I had gone far enough downhill mentally that it was time for me to resign. On his retirement, he assured me — perhaps erroneously — that I had not yet reached that point, but the decision was all mine after he left. He has remained an especially close friend.

I first met his successor, Sonia Sotomayor, during the summer after the Senate had confirmed her by a 68–31 vote. She has the rare distinction of having been nominated to a federal bench by three different presidents: President George H. W. Bush appointed her to the Southern District of New York, President Bill Clinton appointed her to the Court of Appeals for the Second Circuit, and President Barack Obama appointed her to the Supreme Court. Shortly after her confirmation, I stopped in her office at the Court, intending to stay only a few minutes. Finding her one of the most engaging and friendliest people I had ever met, however, I stayed for a visit that lasted over two hours. I do not remember what we talked about but I do know that my warm feelings for her have not changed at all. She is a wonderful person and a superb addition to the Court. Aside from her contributions on the bench, I have also been impressed by her efforts to reach out to the public, including an appearance on *Sesame Street,* to bring the Court closer to the American people.

Sonia joined the Court at a particularly important time. A (then) relatively unknown nonprofit corporation called Citizens United had produced a documentary called *Hillary: The Movie,* which was critical of Senator Hillary Clinton, who was then a candidate for president. Citizens United then sought to enjoin the Federal Election Commission from enforcing Section 203 of the Bipartisan Campaign Reform Act of 2002 against its proposed distribution of the film. As the case came to us in November 2008, the questions it presented were largely limited to whether the BCRA's disclosure requirements for and regulations of "electioneering communications" were unconstitutional under existing doctrine as applied to the circumstances of the case. Among other things, the case presented the question whether the film, which was to be distributed in theaters, on DVDs, and through a video-on-demand platform, was to be treated as the type of "ad" subject to regulation as an electioneering commission under the Court's decision in *McConnell* v. *FEC.*[1] As many readers know, these questions were far more limited than the sweeping constitutional holding the Court would ultimately announce in *Citizens United* v. *FEC.*[2]

The case was originally argued in March 2009 while David was still on the bench. A majority opinion had circulated and David had begun a draft dissent prior to his retirement. Before the end of the term, however, the

---

1. 540 U.S. 93 (2003).
2. 558 U.S. 310 (2010).

Court decided to set the case for reargument the following term and issued an order directing the parties to address the question whether it should overrule either or both *Austin* and the part of *McConnell* that addresses the facial validity of Section 203 of the BCRA. The Court would take up that question the following term, after, of course, Sonia had replaced David.

Elena Kagan, the new solicitor general and my eventual successor, represented the United States in the reargument of *Citizens United,* and, of course, Sonia was on the bench as the successor to David by that time as well. As a result of the reargument, then, eleven justices participated in the decision of the case — a majority of six supported the constitutionality of the statute that the Court ultimately invalidated. Unfortunately the five votes to invalidate the statute and overrule the two precedents authorizing Congress and the states to regulate corporate spending in federal elections controlled the outcome of the case.

Tony Kennedy announced the opinion of the Court on January 10, 2010. His opinion was a disaster for our election law. I wrote the dissent, which relied heavily on David's draft dissent from the original draft majority that had circulated after the first argument.

One of the points that I made in my dissent was that if the majority were correct in arguing that the identity of a speaker is never relevant to the government's ability to regulate his speech, the propaganda broadcasts to our troops by Tokyo Rose during World War II were entitled to the same constitutional protection as speech by Allied commanders. That part of my opinion may have led President Obama in his State of the Union message a few days later to include in his criticism of the Court opinion a comment on the fact that it enabled foreign corporations, as well as foreign stockholders of corporate donors of campaign funds, to have a voice in American elections. Sitting in the audience during that speech, Sam Alito incorrectly mouthed the words: "Not true." Despite Sam's protest, it is perfectly clear that if the identity of a speaker cannot provide the basis for regulating his (or its) speech, the majority's rationale in *Citizens United* would protect not only the foreign shareholders of corporate donors to political campaigns but also foreign corporate donors themselves. Moreover, there is abundant evidence that nonresidents frequently contribute substantial sums to candidates for the Senate or for Congress. That practice obviously tends to undermine the ability of residents to choose their own representatives.

At the federal level, the distinction between corporate and individual political spending on elections stretches back to 1907, when Congress passed the Tillman Act, which banned all corporate contributions to candidates. The Senate report on that legislation observed that "the evils of the use of [corporate] money in connection with political elections are so generally recognized that the committee deems it unnecessary to make any argument in favor of the general purpose of this measure. It is in the interest of good government and calculated to promote purity in the selection of public officials." In his 1905 annual message to Congress, President Theodore Roosevelt declared that all contributions by corporations to any political committee for any political purpose should be forbidden by law.

In the Taft Hartley Act of 1947, Congress extended the prohibition on corporate support of candidates to cover not only direct contributions but independent expenditures as well. When Congress enacted comprehensive campaign finance reform in the Federal Election Campaign Act of 1971, it retained the prohibition on using general treasury funds for either contributions or expenditures, and even though a variety of plaintiffs challenged most of the provisions in the statute in *Buckley* v. *Valeo,* no one argued that the bar on corporate contributions and expenditures was unconstitutional.

The majority in *Citizens United* did, however, rely on *Buckley's* statement that "the concept that government may restrict the speech of some elements of our society in order to enhance the relative voice of others is wholly foreign to the First Amendment."[3] Although that statement has often been cited as authoritative, it is glaringly inaccurate: The Constitution does in fact permit numerous restrictions on speech for the purpose of preventing the voices of a few from drowning out the many—

---

3. *Id.,* at 349–50.

arguments in court and debates in Congress are obvious examples. Indeed, even though the interest in preventing corruption and the appearance of corruption provides ample justification for limiting corporate spending on elections, as explained at length in the *Citizens United* opinions, the interest in equalizing the opportunities of candidates to conduct effective campaigns provides ample justification for placing reasonable limits on the amounts of money that they may spend. Thus, as I explained in my dissent, "[T]his elegant phrase cannot bear the weight that our colleagues have placed on it."[4]

On the morning that the opinions were announced, I made an oral statement summarizing my dissent that I had finished editing at about 7:15 a.m. before leaving my apartment in Arlington for a tennis game with my friend Jim Mitchell at the Washington Golf and Country Club. As I frequently did, I arrived at the Court in time for a shower before going on the bench.

During my announcement, for the first time in my life, I had difficulty pronouncing a significant number of the words in what I had prepared to say — enough difficulty that members of the press commented on my failing in their coverage of the case. Unbeknownst to me, I apparently had suffered a mini-stroke. The experience convinced me that I should retire at the end of that term.

When I got back to my chambers after the arguments that morning, Steve Breyer was there to tell me that he thought my announcement was effective, and my law clerks conveyed a similar message to me, to which I responded by expressing my contrary opinion. In the next few days, as a result of conferences with Dr. Brian Monahan, the Capitol physician, I began taking the blood thinner Coumadin. And in due course I advised President Obama that he would have another vacancy to fill in June.

In the course of my many years on the bench, I did not give much thought to who would fill my seat when I retired. But I could not have been more pleased at President Obama's choice of Elena Kagan to fill my vacancy. Elena came to the Court with what can only be described as an

---

4. *Id.*, at 441.

impeccable resume. A graduate of Princeton, Oxford, and Harvard, she had gone on to clerk for Judge Abner Mikva of the Court of Appeals for the D.C. Circuit and then Thurgood Marshall on the Supreme Court. She distinguished herself as a well-respected legal scholar before becoming the first female dean of Harvard Law School and then the first female solicitor general of the United States. Since taking the bench she has only continued to distinguish herself as a gifted writer and pointed questioner at oral argument — I am told by my law clerks who have had the pleasure of observing her on the bench that her questions are often the most helpful in focusing on the most difficult issues, though my clerks do not envy the lawyers at the lectern who face her tough questions.

The Hague Convention on the Civil Aspects of International Child Abduction provides that a child abducted in violation of "rights of custody" must be returned to the child's country of habitual residence unless certain exceptions apply. The question in *Abbott* v. *Abbott*[5] was whether the writ of *ne exeat* — a parent's right to consent before the other parent may take their child to another country — is a "right of custody" within the meaning of the convention.

Timothy Abbott, a British citizen, and Jaquelyn Vaye Abbott, an American citizen, were married in 1992, their son was born in 1995, and they moved to Chile in 2002, where they separated. The Chilean courts awarded the mother daily care and control of their child while providing the father with visitation rights every other weekend and for the whole month of February each year. Chilean law gave the father what is commonly known as a *ne exeat* right — a right to consent before the other parent may take the child out of the country. After the father obtained a British passport for their son, the mother sought and obtained a *"ne exeat* of the minor" order from the Chilean family court prohibiting the boy from being taken out of Chile. It was the mother, however, who removed their child from Chile without the permission of the court or the other parent.

---

5. 560 U.S. 1 (2010).

After learning that mother and child were in Texas, the father filed an action in the U.S. District Court for the Western District of Texas seeking an order requiring their son's return to Chile, arguing that his *ne exeat* right constituted a right of custody entitling him to the return of his child to Chile pursuant to the convention. The district court and the Court of Appeals for the Fifth Circuit rejected this argument, concluding that the right granted by the convention belonged only to the custodial parent — in this case only to the mother. The court's reasoning agreed with the conclusion of the Second Circuit in a case from which then judge Sotomayor had dissented, and cases from two other circuits, but conflicted with a decision from the Fourth Circuit.

We granted cert to resolve the conflict, and Tony wrote the opinion for the majority of six, including Sonia, that reversed the lower court and held that a parent has a right of custody under the convention by reason of that parent's *ne exeat* right. Although I agreed with Sonia in most cases, I wrote the dissent, joined by Clarence Thomas and Steve Breyer. I was — and still am — convinced that the right of return granted by the convention belonged only to the parent with custody of the child, and that the *ne exeat* right is more accurately characterized as a mere veto over the custodial parent's right to decide where the child shall live; a violation of that right may well give rise to a remedy under Chilean law but should not have been held to violate the convention.

The National Football League is an unincorporated association that now includes thirty-two separately owned teams. Each team has its own name, colors, and logo, and owns its own intellectual property. Prior to 1963, each team made its own arrangements for marketing trademarked items such as caps and jerseys. In that year they formed National Football League Properties (NFLP) to market such items. Between 1963 and 2000 NFLP granted nonexclusive licenses to several vendors, including American Needle, Inc., permitting them to sell apparel bearing team insignia. In December 2000, however, the teams voted to authorize NFLP to grant exclusive licenses, and NFLP granted Reebok International Ltd. an exclusive license to manufacture and sell trademarked headwear for all thirty-two teams. NFLP thereafter declined to renew American Needle's nonexclusive license, and American Needle sued the teams and NFLP for treble damages, alleging violations of federal antitrust law. The district court granted summary judgment to the defendants, reasoning that, with respect to the marketing of their intellectual property, the NFL and its thirty-two teams "have so integrated their operations that they should be deemed a single entity rather than joint ventures cooperating for a single purpose."[6]

The Court of Appeals for the Seventh Circuit affirmed, agreeing with American Needle that when making a single-entity determination, the court must examine whether the conduct in question deprives the marketplace of the independent sources of economic control that competition assumes. But it discounted the significance of potential competition among the teams regarding their use of their intellectual property, because the teams "can function only as one source of economic power when collectively producing NFL football."[7] Noting that the teams have marketed their intellectual property jointly since 1963, the court held that the relevant federal antitrust law did not apply. The novelty of the issue prompted us to grant certiorari.

Though we agreed with the Seventh Circuit that the teams should be viewed as a single entity for the purpose of producing NFL football, it did not follow that their agreement to form NFLP to manage the marketing of their intellectual property was immune from antitrust scrutiny.[8] But our unanimous conclusion that they were engaged in joint action whose legality should be determined under the antitrust rule of reason left open the question whether the conduct was perfectly lawful. In the last antitrust opinion that I authored, we unanimously directed the lower courts to consider that question on remand. The case apparently settled before they could decide whether the conduct at issue was reasonable. Given my background in antitrust law before becoming a federal judge, it was satisfying to

---

6. *Am. Needle, Inc.* v. *New Orleans La. Saints,* 496 F. Supp. 2d 941, 943 (N. D. Ill. 2007).
7. *Am. Needle, Inc.* v. *NFL,* 588 F. 3d 736, 743 (CA7 2008).
8. *American Needle, Inc.* v. *National Football League,* 560 U.S. 183 (2010).

have the opportunity to write on such a novel question of antitrust law in one of my final opinions on the bench.

In my opinion for the Court in *Samantar* v. *Yousuf*,[9] we held that the former minister of defense and prime minister of Somalia, who had left that country and moved to Virginia, was not protected by the Foreign Sovereign Immunities Act of 1976 (FSIA) for alleged torture and judicial killings committed by the military regime that controlled that country during the 1980s. The plaintiffs were members of a clan of well-educated Somalians who were subjected to systematic persecution by the regime that governed the country during those years and alleged that the defendant aided and abetted the commission of abuses by his subordinates. The district court dismissed the action, relying expressly on the FSIA, which it construed as applying to individuals acting on behalf of foreign states. The Court of Appeals for the Fourth Circuit had reversed, and in my opinion for the Court we unanimously agreed that Congress had intended to leave individual official immunity outside the coverage of the statute.

My opinion for the Court was straightforward. "Reading the FSIA, as a whole," I explained, "there is nothing to suggest we should read 'foreign state' in § 1603(a) to include an official acting on behalf of the foreign state, and much to indicate that this meaning was not intended."[10] I added a rather innocuous footnote observing that nothing in the legislative history suggested a contrary result and in fact confirmed my reading of the statute.[11] This rather benign observation nonetheless precluded Nino Scalia from joining what he generously characterized as an "admirably careful textual analysis" demonstrating that the term "foreign state" did not include a foreign official. He not only refused to join the opinion but devoted a three-page concurring opinion to his by then familiar argument against the consideration of legislative history in statutory interpretation. (Both Sam Alito and Clarence Thomas also wrote short, one-sentence concurrences, stating

---

9. 560 U.S. 305 (2010).
10. *Id.*, at 319.
11. *Id.*, at 316n9.

their view that the legislative history references were extraneous to the textual analysis.)

Our disagreement over a collateral issue obviously did not enhance the quality of my opinion, but I stand by the point I made in that footnote. Quoting from Byron White, I noted, "As for the propriety of using legislative history at all, common sense suggests that inquiry benefits from reviewing additional information rather than ignoring it. As Chief Justice Marshall put it, 'Where the mind labours to discover the design of the legislature, it seizes every thing from which aid can be derived.' "[12] Or, as Chief Judge Robert Katzmann of the Court of Appeals for the Second Circuit recently explained, "Why should courts, *a priori*, exclude consideration of relevant legislative history materials that could be useful in understanding legislative meaning? We judges can use all the help we can get!"[13] It had seemed in recent years that defenders of legislative history had ceded the playing field to strict textualists who eschew any consideration of legislative history whatsoever. So I was glad to see Chief Judge Katzmann take up the fight in his book *Judging Statutes* and was more than happy to write a short blurb for its jacket. As the quotation from Byron in my *Samantar* footnote remarked, "Our precedents demonstrate that the Court's practice of utilizing legislative history reaches well into its past" and "We suspect that the practice will likewise reach well into the future."[14]

Federal immigration law has changed dramatically during the past century. Once there were only a few offenses for which conviction led to the defendant's deportation, and judges, both state and federal, possessed broad discretionary authority to prevent the deportation of convicted offenders. Changes in the law have expanded the number of offenses that required deportation to follow conviction and have limited the power of judges to

---

12. *Ibid.,* quoting *Wisconsin Public Intervenor* v. *Mortier,* 501 U.S. 597, 610n4 (1991).
13. Robert A. Katzmann, "Response to Judge Kavanaugh's Review of Judging Statutes," *Harv. L. Rev. F.* 129 (2016): 388.
14. 560 U.S., at 316n9, quoting *Mortier,* 501 U.S., at 610n4.

waive deportation for convicted offenders. Now deportation is virtually automatic for a vast number of noncitizens convicted of crimes. Lawyers for indigent defendants, including counsel appointed to represent José Padilla for the transportation of a large amount of marijuana in his tractor trailer, are not fully aware of the extent of this development of the law.

Because Padilla had been a lawful permanent resident for more than forty years and had served honorably in the U.S. armed forces during the Vietnam War, his lawyer advised him that he "did not need to worry about his immigration status since he had been in the country so long." Based on that erroneous advice, Padilla entered a guilty plea that in fact mandated his deportation. In a post-conviction proceeding, the trial judge refused to grant any relief, reasoning that deportation was a collateral consequence of his conviction that his lawyer had no duty to explain to him. In that court's view, neither the failure to advise Padilla about that collateral consequence, nor even the incorrect advice about it, provided a basis for post-conviction relief. We disagreed and remanded the case to determine whether Padilla had been prejudiced by his lawyer's incompetence.[15]

I wrote the Court opinion, which Ruth, Stephen, Tony, and Sonia joined. We began by explaining that the distinction between collateral and direct consequences was not well suited to evaluating a claim that counsel provided deficient performance when erroneously advising his client about the risk of deportation. The proper measure was simply reasonableness under prevailing professional norms as reflected in American Bar Association standards and the like, especially as those standards had been adapted to deal with the intersection of modern criminal prosecutions and immigration law. The weight of prevailing professional norms overwhelmingly supported the view that counsel must advise his or her client about the risk of deportation. In this case the text of the statute that Padilla was charged with violating was sufficient to disclose that risk. In less clear cases, we suggested that describing the risk of deportation would be sufficient.

---

15. *Padilla* v. *Kentucky,* 559 U.S. 356 (2010).

Sam Alito, joined by the chief justice, wrote a long concurrence, stressing the many difficulties in determining exactly when deportation will occur and suggesting that we were affording more protection to alien defendants than was necessary or appropriate. He agreed, however, that providing incorrect advice to Padilla did prove incompetence. Nino, joined by Clarence, however, dissented. They accepted the state court's view that deportation was just a collateral consequence of the conviction that the lawyer had no duty to discuss with his client.

In 2001, Enron Corporation, then the seventh-highest revenue-grossing company in America, crashed into bankruptcy. The prosecution of Jeffrey Skilling, a longtime executive of the company, for crimes committed before the company collapsed required us to decide whether pretrial publicity prevented Skilling from receiving a fair trial and whether the jury properly convicted him of conspiracy to commit "honest-services" wire fraud. Ruth Ginsburg wrote a persuasive opinion explaining that the district court's elaborate questioning of prospective jurors adequately protected the defendant from the substantial risk of potential prejudice and that the lower courts had correctly interpreted the congressional endorsement of my solitary dissent in *McNally* v. *United States* in 1987.[16]

In *Bilski* v. *Kappos*,[17] all the justices on our Court — and all but one of the twelve judges on the Court of Appeals for the Federal Circuit who heard the case en banc before us — agreed that a process that explains how buyers and sellers of commodities in the energy market can hedge against the risk of price changes was not eligible for patent protection. The patent examiner rejected the application because it was not implemented on a specific apparatus and merely manipulated an abstract idea; the Board of Patent Appeals and Interferences affirmed, reasoning that the application involved only mental steps that did not transform physical matter. The majority of the en

---

16. *Skilling* v. *United States,* 561 U.S. 358 (2010).
17. 561 U.S. 593 (2010).

banc Federal Circuit concluded that it did not qualify as a patentable process because it (1) was not tied to a particular machine or apparatus, and (2) did not transform a particular article into a different state or thing. We granted certiorari to decide whether the Federal Circuit had correctly decided that the "machine-or-transformation" test was the exclusive requirement for determining whether a process was eligible for a patent.

We agreed that the failure to pass that test was a sufficient basis for concluding that the claimed process was not eligible for patent protection, but we did not agree whether such processes are ever eligible. We also agreed that the application before us was not eligible because it claimed an abstract idea.

In its opposing briefs, both at the certiorari and merits stages, the government danced around the issue whether "business methods" should be categorically excluded from eligibility as process patents without taking a definitive position one way or the other, though I think much of its argument could be read as supporting such a categorical rule. At oral argument, the government's attorney did the same thing even when pressed by my colleagues to take a position, though he ultimately counseled against such a categorical rule.

The chief assigned the majority opinion to me, and because I was firmly convinced that the law would be well served by accepting the argument that business patents should be categorically excluded from patentability, I drafted a comprehensive Court opinion espousing that view. The case was argued on November 9, 2009, and I circulated my first draft on May 19, 2010. Ruth, Steve, and Sonia joined me, but Tony wrote a separate opinion that reached a similar result without going as far as my draft opinion in ruling out patent eligibility for business methods. Our four other colleagues joined his separate opinion and, because I had failed to get a majority, on June 16, 2010, the chief reassigned the opinion to Tony. The clinching vote came from Nino, who I think largely agreed with me but could not get past the textual reference to "method of doing or conducting business" in 35 U.S.C. § 273. Pointing to that reference, Tony's majority opinion noted that "[t]he argument that business methods are categorically outside of [35 U.S.C.] § 101's scope is further undermined by the fact that federal law explicitly contemplates the existence of at least some business method patents."[18] I thought that read too much into what Congress was trying to accomplish in Section 273 and that the provision was really a red herring, but a majority of my colleagues were not convinced. That was a most disappointing development for me both because I was so firmly convinced that business patents are categorically undesirable, and because I thought I had written a persuasive draft. I ended up converting my draft majority opinion into an opinion concurring in the judgment (that my opinion started out as a majority may come as no surprise to some readers based on its depth of analysis and the fact that it is roughly three times the length of the majority's opinion).

I was even more disappointed by the Court's decision in *McDonald* v. *Chicago*,[19] which held that the right to own guns for self-defense purposes was a fundamental aspect of the liberty protected from deprivation by the states by the Due Process Clause of the Fourteenth Amendment. The *Heller* decision two years earlier invalidating the District of Columbia law prohibiting the possession of handguns in the home was bad enough — both for its faulty legal analysis and for its predictable impact on the lives of so many citizens — but the extension of its holding to invalidate state regulation of firearms was unquestionably the most unwelcome event in my forty-year tenure as a federal judge.

I must admit that Sam wrote a more persuasive opinion supporting that view than I had thought possible, but the contrast between his interpretation of the doctrine of substantive due process in that case and the dissenters' criticism of that doctrine in same-sex marriage and abortion cases is still rather remarkable. Although Sam described his analysis in that case as merely an extension of the Court's "incorporation" of the Bill of Rights against the states, as I explained at length in my dissent, incorporation is just a subset of substantive due process and is really no

18. *Bilski*, 561 U.S., at 607.
19. 561 U.S. 742 (2010).

different from the application of that doctrine, which conservative members of the Court are so fond of maligning.

Reviewing Sam's opinion these many years later, I find two aspects of it stand out as especially striking. First, toward the end of his opinion, Sam dismisses out of hand the municipal respondents' contention that the Second Amendment differs in kind from every other provision of the Bill of Rights because it concerns the right to possess a deadly weapon with tremendous consequences for public safety. His brief response to this weighty concern was that "[t]he right to keep and bear arms...is not the only constitutional right that has controversial public safety implications."[20] He then compared the public safety costs of firearms with "substantial social costs" generated by protections often afforded criminal defendants, such as the exclusionary rule of the Fourth Amendment and certain trial rights guaranteed by the Constitution. Equating the public safety costs of occasionally letting a guilty man go free because the government violated his right to a fair trial or freedom from warrantless or unreasonable searches and seizures with the public safety costs of firearms is, quite simply, absurd: "A defendant's invocation of his right to remain silent, to confront a witness, or to exclude certain evidence cannot directly cause any threat. The defendant's liberty interest is constrained by (and is itself a constraint on) the adjudicatory process. The link between handgun ownership and public safety is much tighter. The handgun is itself a tool for crime; the handgun's bullets *are* the violence."[21]

In addition to the attenuated social costs of the other rights Sam identified as similar to the right to own a handgun, Sam's false equivalence failed to appreciate the more limited relationship between gun ownership and liberty. As I explained in my dissent, firearms, unlike the constitutional rights just described, "have a fundamentally ambivalent relationship to liberty."[22] "Guns may be useful for self-defense, as well as for

---

20. *Id.,* at 783.
21. *Id.,* at 895.
22. *Id.,* at 891.

hunting and sport, but they also have a unique potential to facilitate death and destruction and thereby to destabilize ordered liberty. *Your* interest in keeping and bearing a certain firearm may diminish *my* interest in being and feeling safe from armed violence. And while granting you the right to own a handgun might make you safer on any given day — assuming the handgun's marginal contribution to self-defense outweighs its marginal contribution to the risk of accident, suicide, and criminal mischief — it may make you and the community you live in less safe overall, owing to the increased number of handguns in circulation."[23] In more basic terms, "[It] does not appear that the ability to own a handgun, or any particular type of firearm, is critical to leading a life of autonomy, dignity, or political equality."[24]

A second striking aspect of his opinion is the damage it did to federalism, a value so often cherished and touted by the justices in the majority. "Even accepting the *Heller* Court's view that the Amendment protects an individual right to keep and bear arms disconnected from militia service, it remains undeniable that 'the purpose for which the right was codified' was 'to prevent elimination of the militia.' "[25] In other words, it "was the States, not private persons, on whose immediate behalf the Second Amendment was adopted. Notwithstanding the *Heller* Court's efforts to write the Second Amendment's preamble out of the Constitution, the Amendment still serves the structural function of protecting the States from encroachment by an overreaching Federal Government."[26] It follows that the Second Amendment is, at base, a federalism protection and "is directed at preserving the autonomy of the sovereign States, and its logic therefore resists incorporation by a federal court *against* the States."[27] And despite the many groans and complaints over the years about the costs imposed on state sovereignty by extending provisions of

---

23. *Id.,* at 891–92.
24. *Id.,* at 893.
25. *Id.,* at 897, quoting *Heller,* 554 U.S., at 599.
26. *Ibid.* (quotation marks omitted).
27. *Ibid.*

the Bill of Rights to the States — criticisms often leveled by those in the majority — compared to *McDonald*, "most if not all of this Court's decisions requiring the States to comply with other provisions in the Bill of Rights did not exact nearly so heavy a toll in terms of state sovereignty."[28] *McDonald* severely curtailed the prerogatives states had previously possessed to craft firearm regulations unique to the character of their own geography and population under their inherent police powers.

The federalism implications of *McDonald* also touch on the more fundamental problem with a theory often advanced in support of an individual right to bear arms — the idea that individuals need to possess firearms to fight off an oppressive government. The problem with this theory is that "it is a foundational premise of modern government that the State holds a monopoly on legitimate violence: 'A basic step in organizing a civilized society is to take [the] sword out of private hands and turn it over to an organized government, acting on behalf of all the people.'"[29] This premise is perfectly consistent with the Second Amendment when one considers that the amendment protects not the right of individuals to possess firearms for possible insurrection but the right of the state to maintain a well-regulated militia in its capacity as a dual sovereign in our federalist system of government. Of course, as I noted in my *McDonald* dissent, there may be merit to the idea that there is a substantive due process right to possess a certain type of weapon for a certain purpose in a certain location, which would not cast doubt on the state's monopoly on legitimate violence or the state's inherent police powers to decide how best to address these difficult questions. But much of the majority's opinion, as with *Heller*, suggests a more far-reaching individual right to bear arms that has troubling consequences for our democracy. I remain hopeful that future cases may yet be able to cabin those cases to an individual's right to possess a handgun in his own home, or that Americans will rally behind a constitutional amendment to limit the reach of those cases.

---

28. *Id.*, at 902.
29. *Id.*, at 892, quoting *Robertson* v. *United States ex rel. Watson,* 560 U.S. 272, 282 (2010) (Roberts, C. J., dissenting).

The Court decided *McDonald* on June 28, 2010, and it was the second-to-last opinion issued in my last term on the Court. In many ways, the dialogue I had with Nino Scalia in that opinion was a fitting end to my legal career. Largely in response to Nino's extensive discussion of my dissenting opinion, I offered a closing defense of my views of the judge's role in constitutional interpretation. Nino had touted, as he had in so many other cases and settings, his view that a historical approach to determine the meaning of the liberty protected by the Fourteenth Amendment was a more objective and restrictive method.

"That approach," I explained in response to the majority's analysis, "is unfaithful to the expansive principle Americans laid down when they ratified the Fourteenth Amendment and to the level of generality they chose when they crafted its language; it promises an objectivity it cannot deliver and masks the value judgments that pervade any analysis of what customs, defined in what manner, are sufficiently "rooted"; it countenances the most revolting injustices in the name of continuity, for we must never forget that not only slavery but also the subjugation of women and other rank forms of discrimination are part of our history; and it effaces this Court's distinctive role in saying what the law is, leaving the development and safekeeping of liberty to majoritarian political processes. It is judicial abdication in the guise of judicial modesty."[30]

I responded at greater length to Nino's more specific criticism — "that his preferred method of substantive due process analysis, a method 'that makes the traditions of our people paramount,'[31] is both more restrained and more facilitative of democracy than the method I...outlined."[32] "It is hardly a novel insight," I noted, "that history is not an objective science."[33] "Even when historical analysis is focused on a discrete proposition, such as the original public meaning of the Second Amendment, the evidence often points in different directions. The historian must choose

---

30. *Id.,* at 876.
31. *Id.,* at 792.
32. *Id.,* at 906.
33. *Id.,* at 907.

which pieces to credit and which to discount, and then must try to assemble them into a coherent whole."[34] In *Heller,* for example, Nino relied on some sources and I on others. "No mechanical yardstick can measure which of us was correct, either with respect to the materials we chose to privilege or the insights we gleaned from them."[35]

But the "malleability and elusiveness of history increases exponentially when we move from a pure question of original meaning, as in *Heller,* to Justice Scalia's theory of substantive due process. At least with the former sort of question, the judge can focus on a single legal provision; the temporal scope of the inquiry is (or should be) relatively unbounded; and there is substantial agreement on what sorts of authorities merit consideration. With Justice Scalia's approach to substantive due process, these guideposts all fall away. The judge must canvas the entire landscape of American law as it has evolved through time, and perhaps older laws as well.... In conducting this rudderless, panoramic tour of American legal history, the judge has more than ample opportunity to 'look over the heads of the crowd and pick out [his] friends.' "[36]

Because the remainder of my dissent captures much of what I viewed as the role of the judge in interpreting the Constitution, I think it is worth quoting it at length:

> My point is not to criticize judges' use of history in general or to suggest that it always generates indeterminate answers; I have already emphasized that historical study can discipline as well as enrich substantive due process analysis. My point is simply that Justice Scalia's defense of his method, which holds out objectivity and restraint as its cardinal — and, it seems, only — virtues, is unsatisfying on its own terms. For a limitless number of subjective judgments may be smuggled into his historical analysis. Worse,

---

34. *Ibid.*
35. *Ibid.*
36. *Id.,* at 907–8, quoting *Roper* v. *Simmons,* 543 U.S. 551, 617 (2005) (Scalia, J., dissenting).

they may be *buried* in the analysis. At least with my approach, the judge's cards are laid on the table for all to see, and to critique. The judge must exercise judgment, to be sure. When answering a constitutional question to which the text provides no clear answer, there is always some amount of discretion; our constitutional system has always depended on judges' filling in the document's vast open spaces. But there is also transparency.

Justice Scalia's approach is even less restrained in another sense: It would effect a major break from our case law outside of the "incorporation" area. Justice Scalia does not seem troubled by the fact that his method is largely inconsistent with the Court's canonical substantive due process decisions.... To the contrary, he seems to embrace this dissonance. My method seeks to synthesize dozens of cases on which the American people have relied for decades. Justice Scalia's method seeks to vaporize them. So I am left to wonder, which of us is more faithful to this Nation's constitutional history? And which of us is more faithful to the values and commitments of the American people, as they stand today? In 1967, when the Court held in *Loving* [v. *Virginia*], that adults have a liberty-based as well as equality-based right to wed persons of another race, interracial marriage was hardly "deeply rooted" in American tradition. Racial segregation and subordination were deeply rooted. The Court's substantive due process holding was nonetheless correct — and we should be wary of any interpretive theory that implies, emphatically, that it was not.

Which leads me to the final set of points I wish to make: Justice Scalia's method invites not only bad history, but also bad constitutional law. As I have already explained, in evaluating a claimed liberty interest (or any constitutional claim for that matter), it makes perfect sense to give history significant weight: Justice Scalia's position is closer to my own than he apparently feels comfortable acknowledging. But it makes little sense to give history dispositive weight in every case. And it makes *especially* little sense to answer questions like whether the right to bear arms is "fundamental" by focusing only on the past, given that both the practical signifi-cance and the public understandings of such a right often change as society changes. What if the evidence had shown that, whereas at one time firearm possession contributed substantially to per-sonal liberty and safety, nowadays it contributes nothing, or even tends to undermine them? Would it still have been reasonable to constitutionalize the right?

The concern runs still deeper. Not only can historical views be less than completely clear or informative, but they can also be wrong. Some notions that many Americans deeply believed to be true, at one time, turned out not to be true. Some practices that many Americans believed to be consistent with the Constitution's guar-antees of liberty and equality, at one time, turned out to be incon-sistent with them. The fact that we have a written Constitution does not consign this Nation to a static legal existence. Although we should always "pa[y] a decent regard to the opinions of former times," it is "not the glory of the people of America" to have "suf-fered a blind veneration for antiquity." The Federalist No. 14, pp. 99, 104 (C. Rossiter ed. 1961) (J. Madison). It is not the role of federal judges to be amateur historians. And it is not fidelity to the Constitution to ignore its use of deliberately capacious language, in an effort to transform foundational legal commitments into narrow rules of decision.

As for "the democratic process," a method that looks exclusively to history can easily do more harm than good. Just consider this case. The net result of Justice Scalia's supposedly objective analysis is to vest federal judges — ultimately a majority of the judges on this Court — with unprecedented lawmaking powers in an area in which they have no special qualifications, and in which the give-and-take of the political process has functioned effectively for decades. Why this "intrudes much less upon the democratic process" than an approach that would defer to the democratic process on the regulation of firearms is, to say the least, not self-evident. I cannot even tell what, under Justice Scalia's view, constitutes an "intrusion."

It is worth pondering, furthermore, the vision of democracy that underlies Justice Scalia's critique. Very few of us would welcome a system in which majorities or powerful interest groups always get their way. Under our constitutional scheme, I would have thought that a judicial approach to liberty claims such as the one I have outlined — an approach that investigates both the intrinsic nature of the claimed interest and the practical significance of its judicial enforcement, that is transparent in its reasoning and sincere in its effort to incorporate constraints, that is guided by history but not beholden to it, and that is willing to protect some rights even if they have not already received uniform protection from the elected branches — has the capacity to improve, rather than "[im]peril," our democracy. It all depends on judges' exercising careful, reasoned judgment. As it always has, and as it always will.[37]

---

37. *Id.,* at 908–11 (citations and footnote omitted).

32

The Kagan Court

October Term 2010

Sam Erman, a graduate of the University of Michigan Law School, served as my law clerk during my first year of retirement. In my years off the bench, I have had the opportunity to devote more time to personal pursuits, such as writing books and giving speeches. Sam recalls that the most memorable event of the year he spent clerking for me (and Tony Kennedy, with whom I generally shared my clerks in retirement) was a speech I delivered on the tenth anniversary of the establishment of the National Japanese American Memorial Foundation. The speech came not long after a national controversy had erupted over the proposed construction of an Islamic Center in New York City near the site of the September 11, 2001, terrorist attacks. Like many, Sam was disturbed by the strong opposition to the mosque; I shared his concern, but I also recognized the feelings underlying the opposition, feelings that I admit to having felt, at least initially, with respect to the USS *Arizona* memorial at Pearl Harbor. As Sam eloquently summarized in an email to me, my speech was aimed at "cutting through political bickering to illuminate the human experience of confronting real anger and loss, staring down the temptation to respond with fear and hate, and instead saving oneself and improving the world by choosing hope and acceptance instead."

Given Sam's appraisal of the speech, and the fact that its relevance has only increased in light of world events occurring years after I left the bench, I thought it appropriate to include the full text here:

> Today I plan to say a few words about memorials, mosques, and monuments. Like Lieutenant Ichikawa, who is being honored today, I served in the Pacific theater during World War II. The Empire of Japan was our principal enemy in that theatre. Lieutenant Ichikawa, like literally thousands of other patriotic Japanese Americans — including residents of Hawai'i as well as residents of the Mainland — made a magnificent contribution to our war effort there.
>
> During 1941, the dean of students at the University of Chicago, where I went to college, was an undercover recruiting agent for the communications intelligence branch of the Navy. He persuaded me to sign up for a confidential correspondence course in cryptography. When I had successfully completed the course, I received a letter inviting me to go to the Great Lakes Naval Station to take a physical exam and to apply for a commission in the Naval Reserve. I did so on Saturday, December 6, 1941. Whether or not that application had any impact on what happened the next day, it was the beginning of an important chapter in my life.
>
> When the commission came through, I reported for duty in Washington, D.C., and was assigned to what was known as "Op-20-GT," the traffic analysis section of Communication Intelligence. The job of a traffic analyst is, without decrypting the messages, to obtain information about enemy activities based on interceptions of their wireless transmissions. We examined the routing of the messages, the codes being used, and the identity of the naval units

or commands that sent and received them. After a few months in Washington, I was transferred to the naval base at Pearl Harbor, where I served until about a week before the atom bomb was dropped on Hiroshima. For over two and a half years Pearl Harbor was my home, as well as the place where my waking hours were devoted to the defeat of our enemy.

Although I visited Hawai'i a few times after becoming a lawyer, I did not return to the naval base itself until 1994, when I met with students at the law school at the University of Hawai'i. On that visit, Admiral Retz took me on a tour of the harbor on his barge, pointing out changes that had occurred in the past 50 years. The most memorable and moving event during that tour was our approach to the Arizona Memorial — which spans the USS Arizona and the over a thousand American sailors still entombed in that sunken battleship. As we approached the Arizona I could plainly see that the dozens of visitors on board that day were Japanese tourists. My first reaction to that sight was more emotional than you might expect from a senior citizen. Several thoughts flashed through my mind: "Those people don't really belong here. We won the war, they lost it. We shouldn't allow them to celebrate their attack on Pearl Harbor even if it was one of their greatest victories."

But then I realized that those visitors must also have been experiencing a number of mixed and conflicting emotions. Perhaps a few did remember Pearl Harbor with pride. Some of them may even have been descendants of pilots who participated in the attack. Others may have remembered relatives that died or were wounded during the war. Still others may merely have reflected about how horrible all wars are to all who participate in them and the costs that they impose on civilians as well as soldiers. Most significantly, I realized that I was drawing inferences about every member of the tourist group that did not necessarily apply to any single one of them. We should never pass judgment on barrels and barrels of apples just because one of them may be rotten.

I suspect that many New Yorkers who lost friends or relatives as a result of the terrorist attack on the World Trade Center on 9/11 may have reacted to the news that Muslims are planning to erect a mosque or a religious center in the neighborhood much as I reacted to the sight of the Japanese tourists on the Arizona. Perhaps some of them may have thought: "This is no place for a mosque; Muslims killed innocent Americans here; they should build their places of worship in Afghanistan or Iraq or anywhere else, but not here."

But then, after a period of reflection, some of those New Yorkers may have had second thoughts, just as I did at the Arizona. The Japanese tourists were not responsible for what some of their countrymen did decades ago; the Muslims planning to build the mosque are not responsible for what an entirely different group of Muslims did on 9/11. Indeed, terrorists like those who killed over 3,000 Americans — including Catholics, Jews, Protestants, atheists and some of the 600,000 Muslims who live in New York — have also killed many more Muslims who disagree with their radical views in other parts of the world. Many of the Muslims who pray in New York mosques may well have come to America to escape the intolerance of radicals like those who dominate the Taliban. Descendants of pilgrims who came to America in the 17th century to escape religious persecutions — as well as those who thereafter joined the American political experiment that those people of faith helped launch — should understand why American Muslims should enjoy the freedom to build their places of worship wherever permitted by local zoning laws.

A monument that is located a few blocks away from my office in the Supreme Court conveys the central message that visitors to the Arizona and participants in the debate about the New York Mosque should heed. That message tells us to beware of stereotypical conclusions about groups of people that we don't know very well. Because a few Protestant extremists committed atrocities on Irish Catholics in Northern Ireland some years ago, we should not conclude that all Protestants are terrorists, or let that sliver of history affect our thinking about where the millions of peace-loving Christians in the United States may worship.

There are two parts to the message conveyed by the Monument, which you have probably already recognized is the National Japanese American Memorial. The first part tends to be especially moving to those, like Lieutenant Ichikawa and me, who lived through World War II. Much like the Vietnam Veterans Memorial, it is a listing inscribed in stone of the names of the hundreds of Japanese-American soldiers who were killed in World War II fighting for the freedom of their country. Like the Arizona, it is a poignant reminder of military bravery and unselfish service: The predominantly Japanese-American 442d Infantry Combat Team, for instance, became the most decorated regiment, for its size and length of service, in the history of the United States Armed Forces. Its members earned over 9,000 Purple Hearts.

The second part of the message might well be described as a monument to stupidity. It commemorates the fact that fear of the possibility of sabotage by Japanese-Americans living on the West Coast led to the unnecessary internment of literally thousands of loyal American citizens for the duration of the War. The monument tells us that some 40 years after that tragic decision was made, President Reagan and the U.S. Congress made a formal apology on behalf of the country and authorized reparations payments of $20,000 to interned citizens. Not only was the internment grossly unfair because large groups of citizens were deprived of their liberty without due process — indeed, without any process at all and without any evidentiary basis for the decision — but it was also manifestly stupid because no similar precaution was taken in Hawai'i, where both the concentration of Japanese-Americans and the risk of sabotage were far greater than on the West Coast.

Our Constitution protects every one of us from being found guilty of wrongdoing based on the conduct of our associates. Guilt by association is unfair. The monument teaches us that it is also profoundly unwise to draw inferences based on a person's membership in any association or group without first learning something about the group. Its message is a powerful reminder of the fact that ignorance — that is to say, fear of the unknown — is the source of most invidious prejudice.

That speech reminds me of the White House ceremony at which President Obama awarded me the Presidential Medal of Honor in 2012. The president made a brief comment about each of the recipients, including these words about a former Japanese-American intern, who sadly had died a few weeks before the January ceremony: "Gordon Hirabayashi knew what it was like to stand alone. As a student at the University of Washington, Gordon was one of only three Japanese Americans to defy the executive order that forced thousands of families to leave their homes, their jobs, and their civil rights behind and move to internment camps during World War II. He took his case all the way to the Supreme Court, and he lost. And it would be another 40 years before that decision was reversed, giving Asian Americans everywhere a small sense of justice. In Gordon's words, 'It takes a crisis to tell us that unless citizens are willing to stand up for the [Constitution], it's not worth the paper it's written on.'

And this country is better off because of citizens like him who are willing to stand up."

For health-related reasons, Maryan did not accompany me to the ceremony, but my daughters Kada, Liz, and Sue — as well as her daughter Cathy Simon — did. Their picture with the president is an even more treasured memento of the occasion than the medal itself. Liz, however, also especially enjoyed the opportunity to talk with John Glenn, another recipient of the medal, because he had been the commencement speaker at her graduation ceremony at Ohio State a few years earlier.

My high regard for the president made me especially grateful for his kind remarks. They did not, however, compare with the following praise in the letter that Gerald Ford sent to then dean William Treanor of Fordham Law School on September 21, 2005:

> Historians study the significant diplomatic, legislative and economic events that occurred during a Presidential term to evaluate that Presidency. Normally, little or no consideration is given to the long term effects of a President's Supreme Court nominees. Eisenhower's Earl Warren, John Adams' John Marshall and Wilson's Louis Brandeis immediately come to mind; although references to these great jurists are usually absent in Presidential biographies.
>
> Let that not be the case with my Presidency. For I am prepared to allow history's judgment of my term in office to rest (if necessary, exclusively) on my nomination thirty years ago of Justice John Paul Stevens to the U.S. Supreme Court. I endorse his constitutional views on the secular character of the Establishment Clause and the Free Exercise Clause, on securing procedural safeguards in criminal cases and on the Constitution's broad grant of regulatory authority to Congress. I include as well my special admiration for his charming wit and sense of humor; as evidence in his dissent in the 1986 commerce clause case of *Maine* v. *Taylor and United*

States, involving the constitutionality of a Maine statute that broadly restricted any interstate trade of Maine's minnows. In words perhaps somewhat less memorable than, "Shouting fire in a crowded theater," Justice Stevens wrote, "There is something fishy about this case."

He has served his nation well, at all times carrying out his judicial duties with dignity, intellect and without partisan political concerns. Justice Stevens has made me, and our fellow citizens, proud of my three decade old decision to appoint him to the Supreme Court. I wish him long life, good health and many more years on the bench.

My Ninety-Fourth Birthday

T HE MOST SIGNIFICANT event that occurred during my retirement from the Court took place in Arlington, Virginia, on my ninety-fourth birthday. As was our custom, Maryan and I had spent the 2013–14 winter in our condominium in Fort Lauderdale, Florida.

My principal activities in Florida were much like they had been while I was an active justice, except that instead of reading briefs and writing opinions, I read what I wanted to and wrote two books — *Five Chiefs* and *Six Amendments*. My exercise routines continued to include swimming in the Atlantic Ocean when friends like my neighbors Nick Tortorella, Eileen Winkler, or John Hawkinson were available to help me get in and out of the ocean. I had played singles tennis on a regular basis since my coronary bypass operation in 1974 under medical advice to include a minute of rest when changing courts after every other game — a period that provided an opportunity for interesting conversation with my good friends Strouse Campbell, Dick Cobb, and Jim Baker in Virginia and Vern Howe in Florida. In retirement, I swapped the tennis court for the Ping-Pong table and played five or six games two or three times a week with Steve Eschen, a retired New York police officer, taking our conversation break and watching the activity on the beach after the third game. Maryan and I helped support the casinos in the Fort Lauderdale area with our close friends Jack and Maureen Nugent. (Jack was even more critical of my opinion in *Kelo* than Nino Scalia.) I played nine holes of golf once or twice a week with Shaw McCutcheon, the son of the famous cartoonist for the *Chicago Tribune,* who could boast to having once won a few dollars from Sam Snead. I enjoyed the company of Jose Gonzalez, the most respected federal judge in Florida, and his wife, Mary. I was also well fed by a beautiful dietician who happened to be my wife.

Unbeknownst to me, Maryan was a participant in a three-person plot to provide me with a surprise party on my ninety-fourth birthday, which she planned and prepared for while we were still in Florida. Since the persons that she planned to invite included residents of Canada, California, Illinois, and the Washington area, many of the arrangements as well as the invitations and replies necessarily required the use of the mails, which she needed to conceal from me. She therefore enlisted the assistance of my daughter Liz in the Chicago area and our good friend and neighbor Michele Taylor, who lived two floors above us in our Florida condominium, to help with the arrangements. I knew nothing about any pre-party conversations that Maryan had with either Liz or Michele.

On the morning of my birthday, we had returned to Virginia and, as had often happened during the preceding months, Maryan was not feeling well; she told me that she would not be able to attend our planned birthday meal at the Washington Golf and Country Club even though my daughters Kada and Liz, and their families, had come all the way from Chicago to celebrate the occasion. At the last minute, however, she changed her mind and insisted on driving to the club. I remember her parking in an unusual location. It was from there that we entered a crowded room, where I was surprised by dozens of friends and family members who greeted us with a rousing welcome. The surprise welcome — from friends like Judges Bill Bauer and Abner Mikva, who had traveled all the way from Chicago; Art Seder, my law school classmate who was also celebrating his ninety-fourth birthday and who had driven up from Charlottesville; Vern's son, Jeremy Howe, from Toronto; Ken Manaster from California; and of course many Virginia and Florida friends — was a touching display of affection for Maryan and the birthday boy. To put it mildly, the party was a smashing success. Even if I live another ninety-four years, I will never forget it. Thank you, Maryan.

This letter was read aloud at the party:

THE WHITE HOUSE
WASHINGTON

April 17, 2014

The Honorable John Paul Stevens
Arlington, Virginia

Dear Justice Stevens:

Michelle and I send our warmest wishes for your upcoming 94th birthday, and we hope the love and laughter that surround you on this special occasion bring you great joy.

As you reflect on over nine decades of memories, I would like to express my admiration for your extraordinary service to our Nation. With unwavering integrity, you have stood as an impartial guardian of the law and protected the principles enshrined in our founding documents. Your steadfast commitment to justice and your understanding of how the law affects the lives of ordinary Americans have set a proud example and built a legacy worthy of celebration.

I wish you all the best for a wonderful birthday, and for many years of happiness and low handicaps.

Sincerely,

We miss you on the Court!

Acknowledgments

In postscripts to *Five Chiefs* and *Six Amendments*—the two books I wrote after retiring from active service on the Supreme Court in June of 2010—I expressed my gratitude to the competent employees of the Court who had given me especially valuable assistance in their preparation. In doing so, I named my secretary, Janice Harley; my aide to chambers, Peter Edwards; and all of my former clerks, noting my pride in my ability to select those vitally important assistants. Because all of them contributed importantly to the opinions summarized in this book, I must repeat my message of thanks to them, as well as to Gillian Grossman, Teresa Reed, Donald Goodson, and Sarah Sloan, who have assisted me while also clerking for Justice Kennedy or Justice Kagan.

My work during my retirement years has strongly reinforced my conviction that the staff of the Supreme Court is remarkable, not merely because of its high level of competence, but even more so because of the genuine quality of respect and affection that every one of them provides to each of the members of the Court on a daily basis.

Index

Note: The abbreviation JPS in subheadings refers to John Paul Stevens.

INDEX

About the Author

John Paul Stevens served as a judge on the United States Court of Appeals for the Seventh Circuit from 1970 to 1975. President Gerald Ford nominated him as an associate justice of the Supreme Court, and he took his seat on December 19, 1975. Justice Stevens retired from the Supreme Court on June 29, 2010. He is the author of a memoir, *Five Chiefs,* and *Six Amendments: How and Why We Should Change the Constitution.*